Hot Gimmick

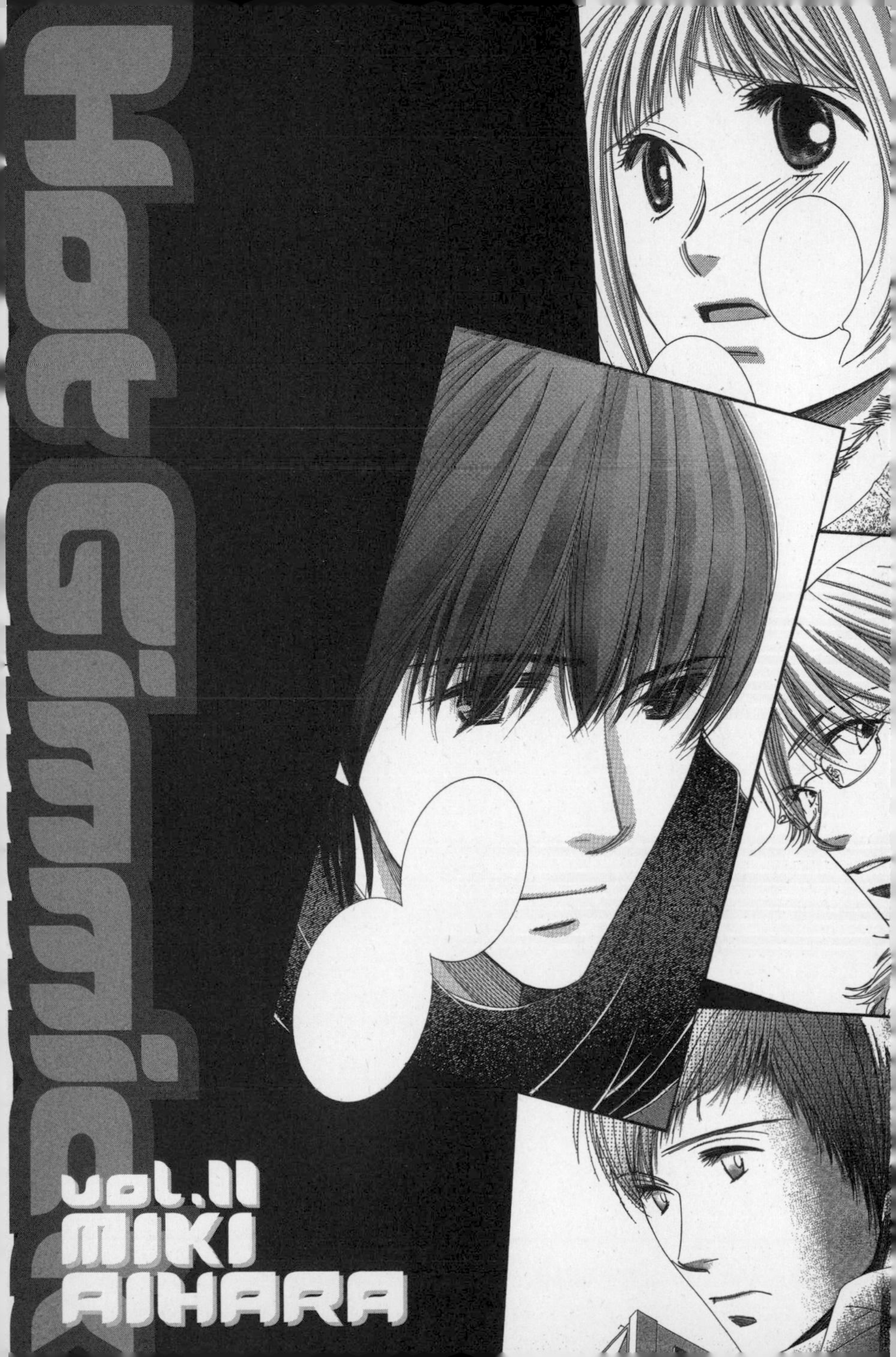

vol. 11

MIKI AIHARA

HOT GIMMICK
CONTENTS

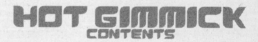

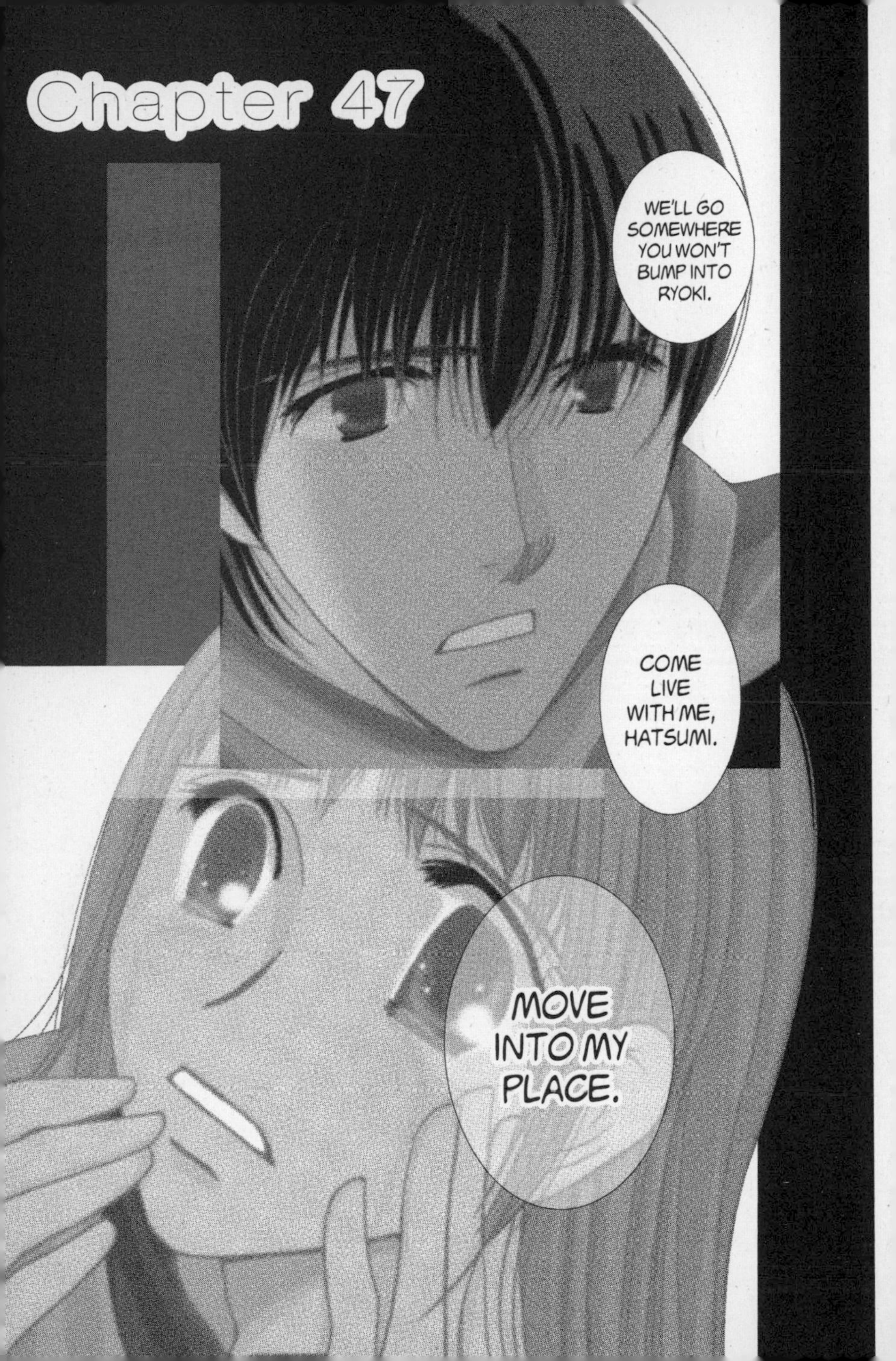
Chapter 47
WE'LL GO SOMEWHERE YOU WON'T BUMP INTO RYOKI.
COME LIVE WITH ME, HATSUMI.
MOVE INTO MY PLACE.

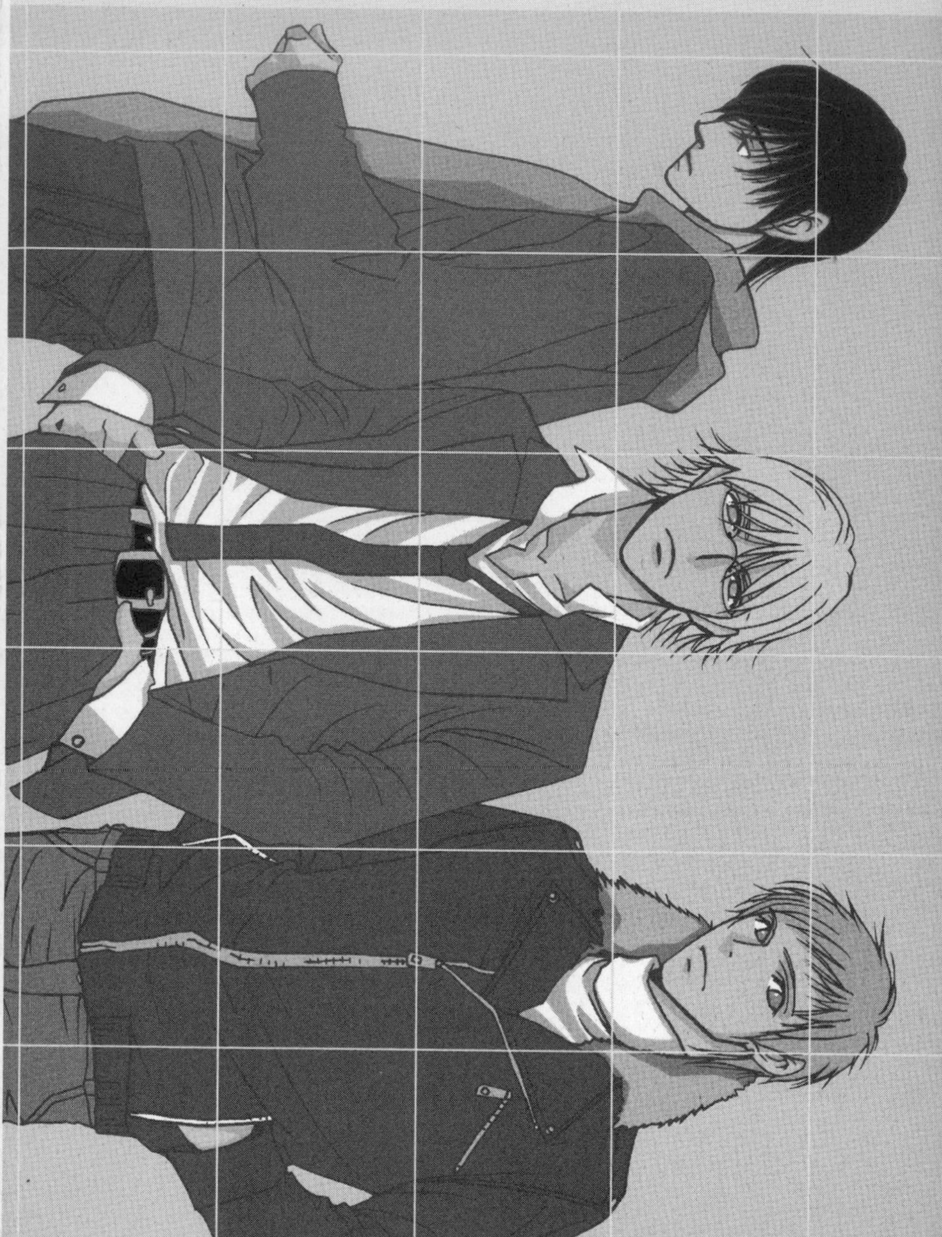

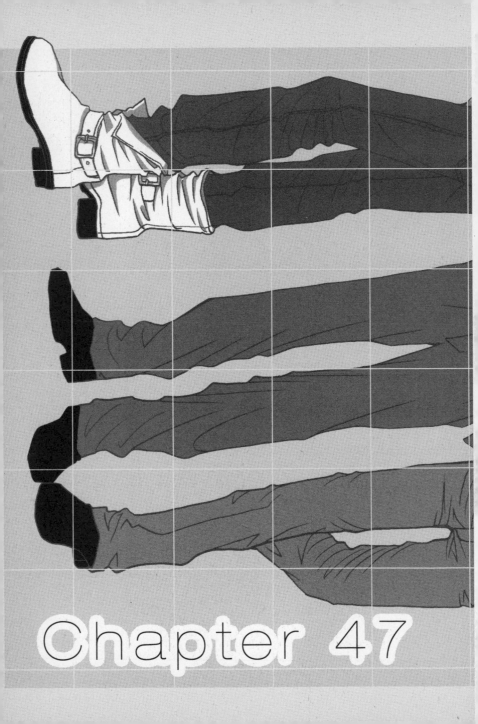

Chapter 47

hot gimmick

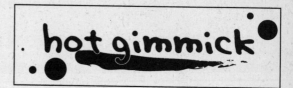

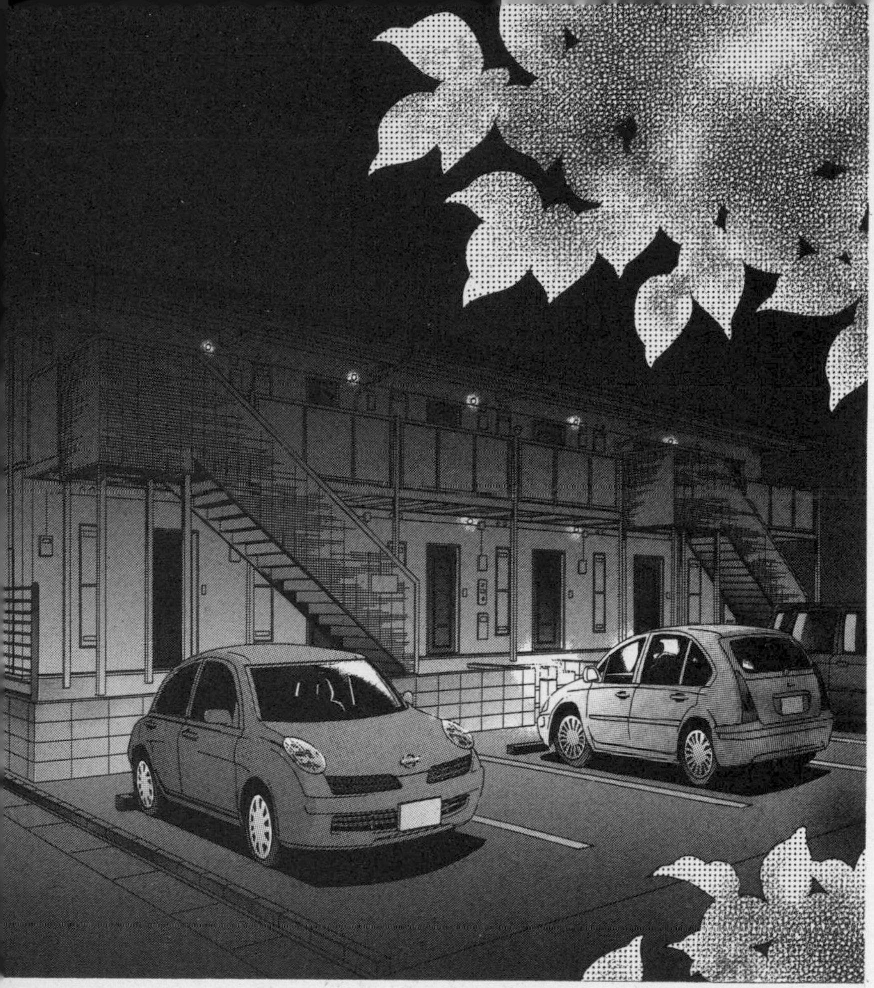

hot
gimmick

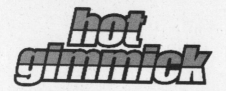

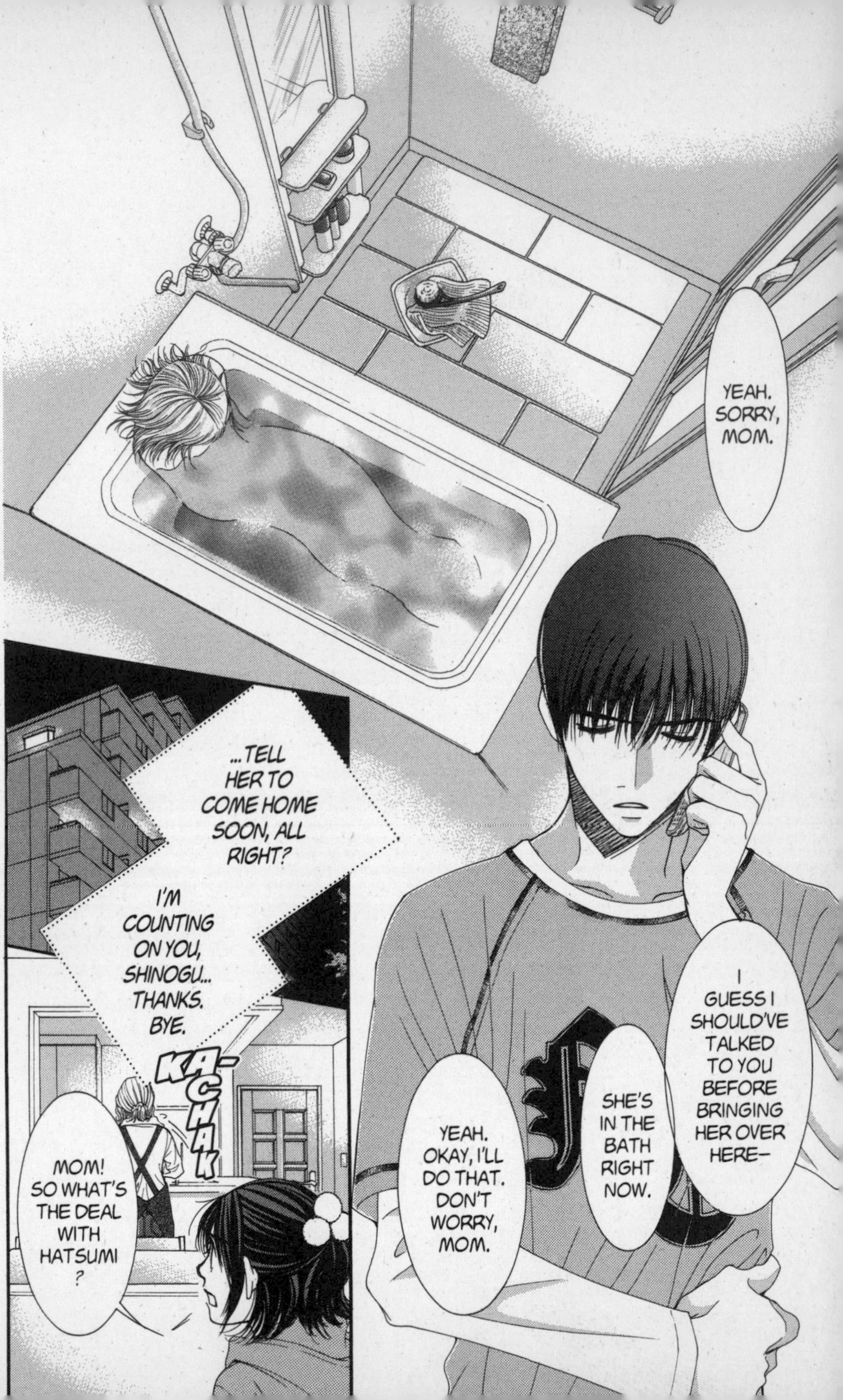
YEAH. SORRY, MOM.
I GUESS I SHOULD'VE TALKED TO YOU BEFORE BRINGING HER OVER HERE–
SHE'S IN THE BATH RIGHT NOW.
...TELL HER TO COME HOME SOON, ALL RIGHT?
YEAH. OKAY, I'LL DO THAT. DON'T WORRY, MOM.
I'M COUNTING ON YOU, SHINOGU... THANKS. BYE.
KA-CHAK
MOM! SO WHAT'S THE DEAL WITH HATSUMI ?

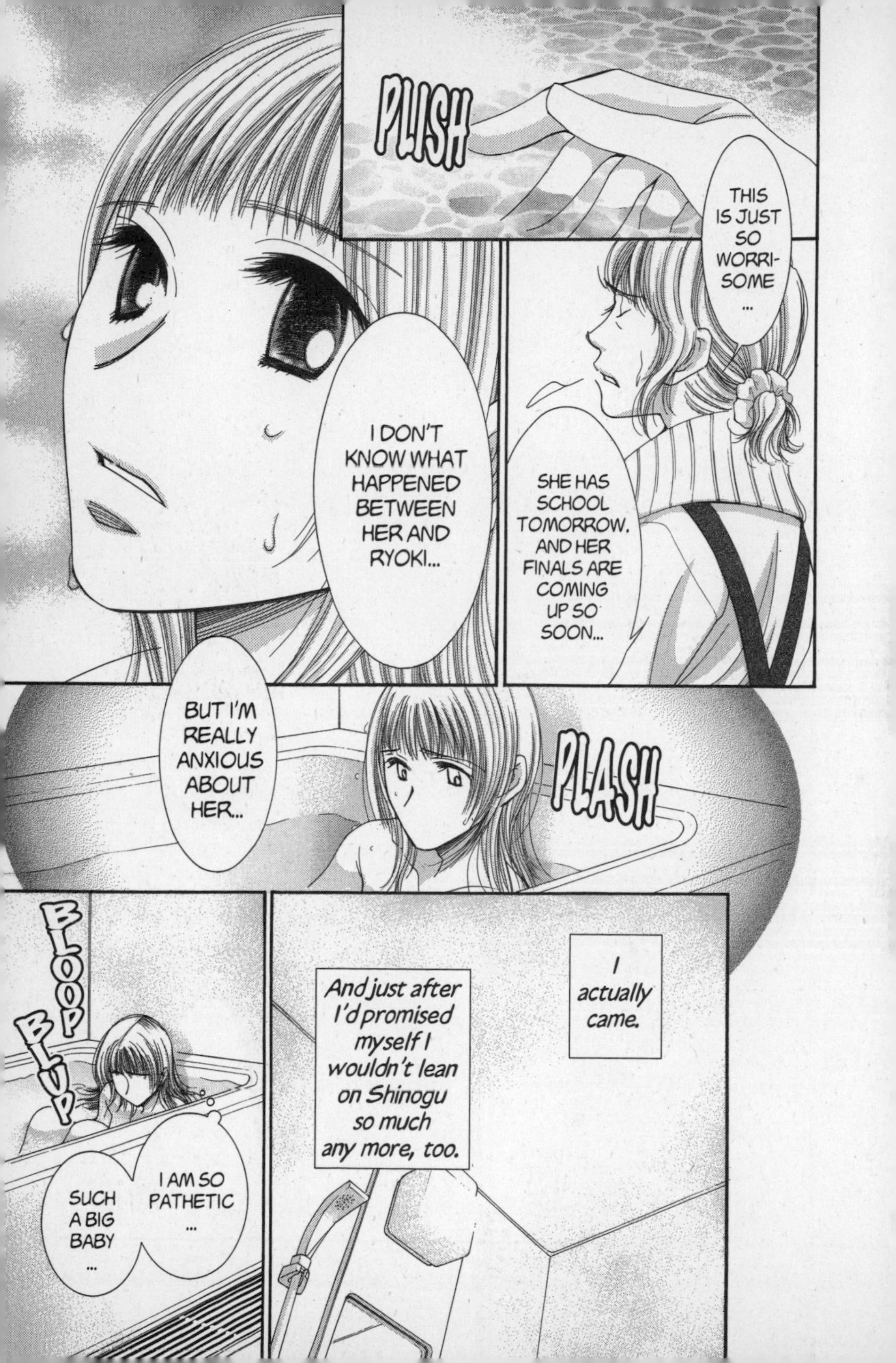

PLISH
THIS IS JUST SO WORRISOME...
SHE HAS SCHOOL TOMORROW. AND HER FINALS ARE COMING UP SO SOON...
I DON'T KNOW WHAT HAPPENED BETWEEN HER AND RYOKI...
BUT I'M REALLY ANXIOUS ABOUT HER...
PLASH
I actually came.
And just after I'd promised myself I wouldn't lean on Shinogu so much any more, too.
BLOOP
BLUP
I AM SO PATHETIC...
SUCH A BIG BABY...

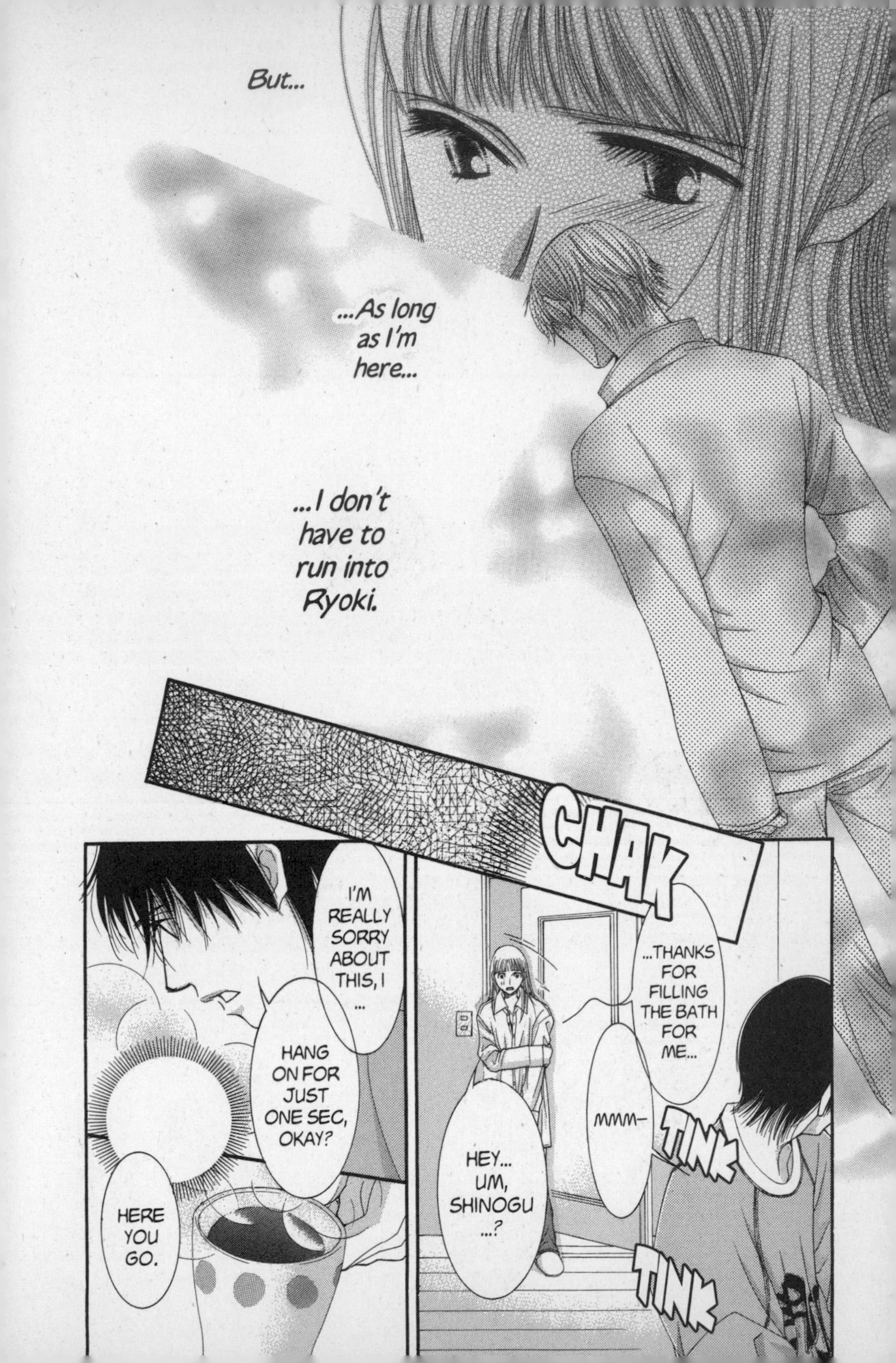
But...
...As long as I'm here...
...I don't have to run into Ryoki.
CHAK
...THANKS FOR FILLING THE BATH FOR ME...
MMM—
TINK
HEY... UM, SHINOGU ...?
TINK
I'M REALLY SORRY ABOUT THIS, I ...
HANG ON FOR JUST ONE SEC, OKAY?
HERE YOU GO.

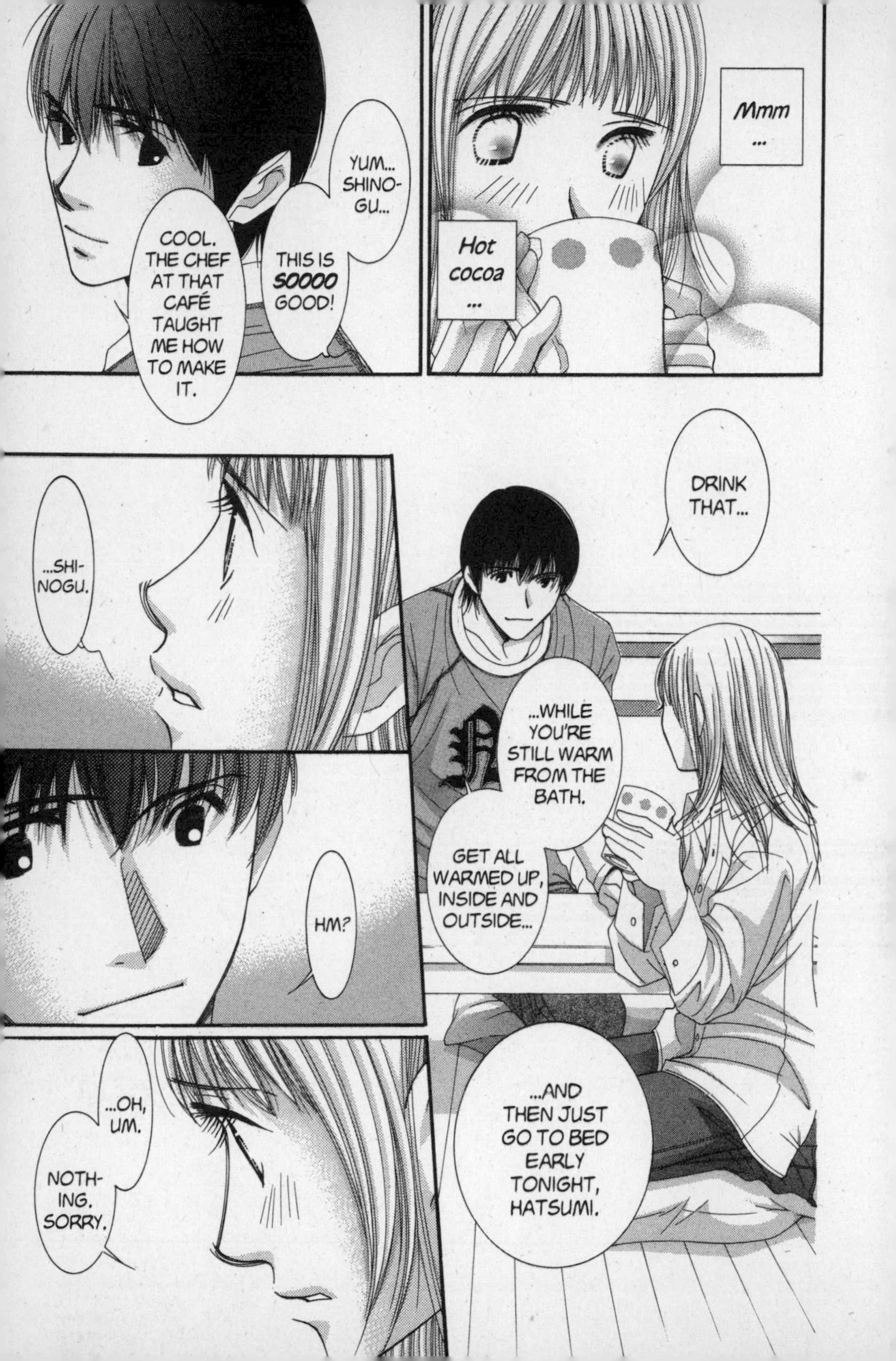

Mmm ...
Hot cocoa ...
YUM... SHINOGU...
THIS IS **SOOOO** GOOD!
COOL. THE CHEF AT THAT CAFÉ TAUGHT ME HOW TO MAKE IT.
DRINK THAT...
...WHILE YOU'RE STILL WARM FROM THE BATH.
GET ALL WARMED UP, INSIDE AND OUTSIDE...
...AND THEN JUST GO TO BED EARLY TONIGHT, HATSUMI.
...SHI-NOGU.
HM?
...OH, UM.
NOTH-ING. SORRY.

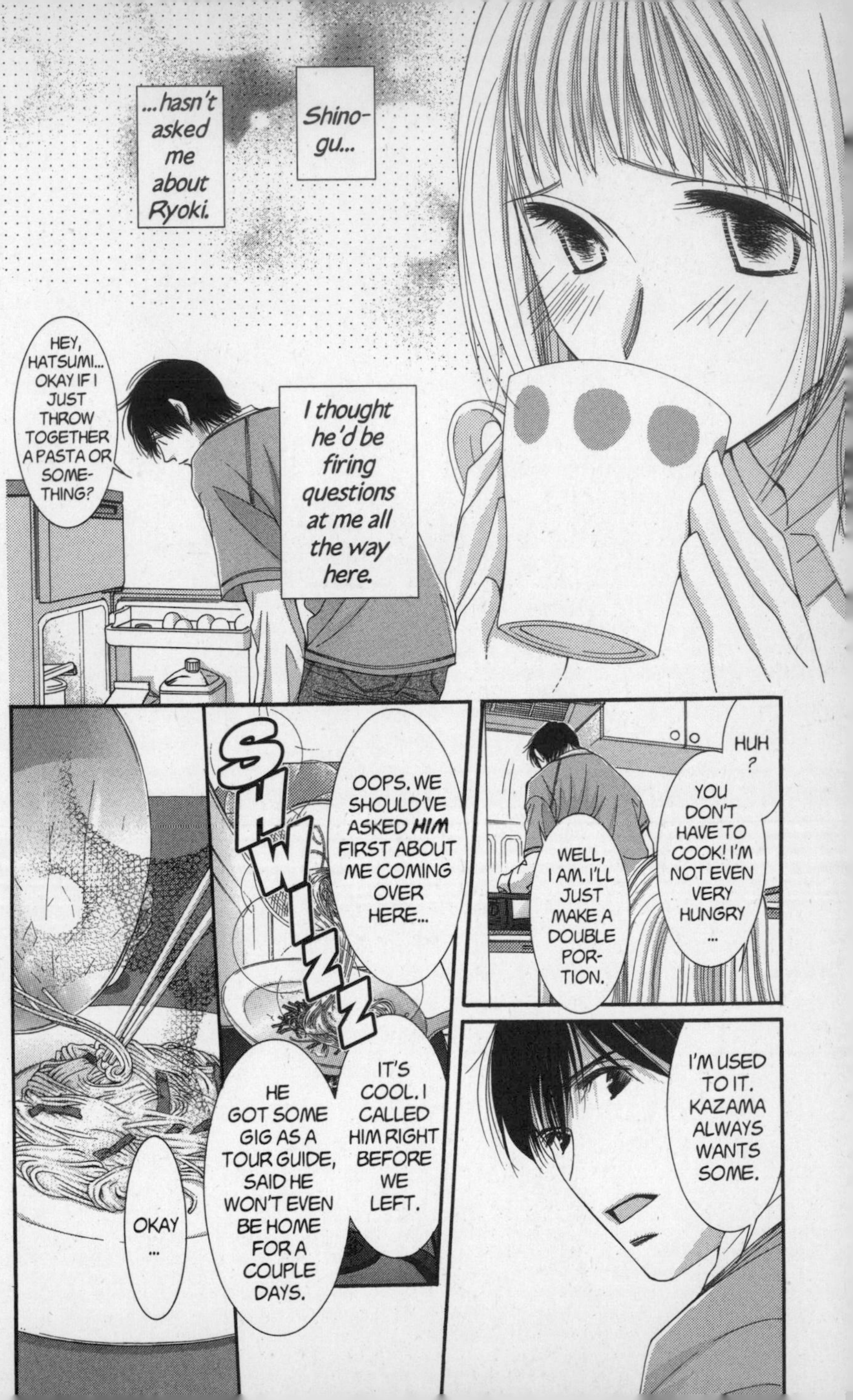
Shino-gu...
...hasn't asked me about Ryoki.
I thought he'd be firing questions at me all the way here.
HEY, HATSUMI... OKAY IF I JUST THROW TOGETHER A PASTA OR SOME-THING?
HUH ?
YOU DON'T HAVE TO COOK! I'M NOT EVEN VERY HUNGRY ...
WELL, I AM. I'LL JUST MAKE A DOUBLE POR-TION.
I'M USED TO IT. KAZAMA ALWAYS WANTS SOME.
SHWIZZ
OOPS. WE SHOULD'VE ASKED HIM FIRST ABOUT ME COMING OVER HERE...
IT'S COOL. I CALLED HIM RIGHT BEFORE WE LEFT.
HE GOT SOME GIG AS A TOUR GUIDE, SAID HE WON'T EVEN BE HOME FOR A COUPLE DAYS.
OKAY ...

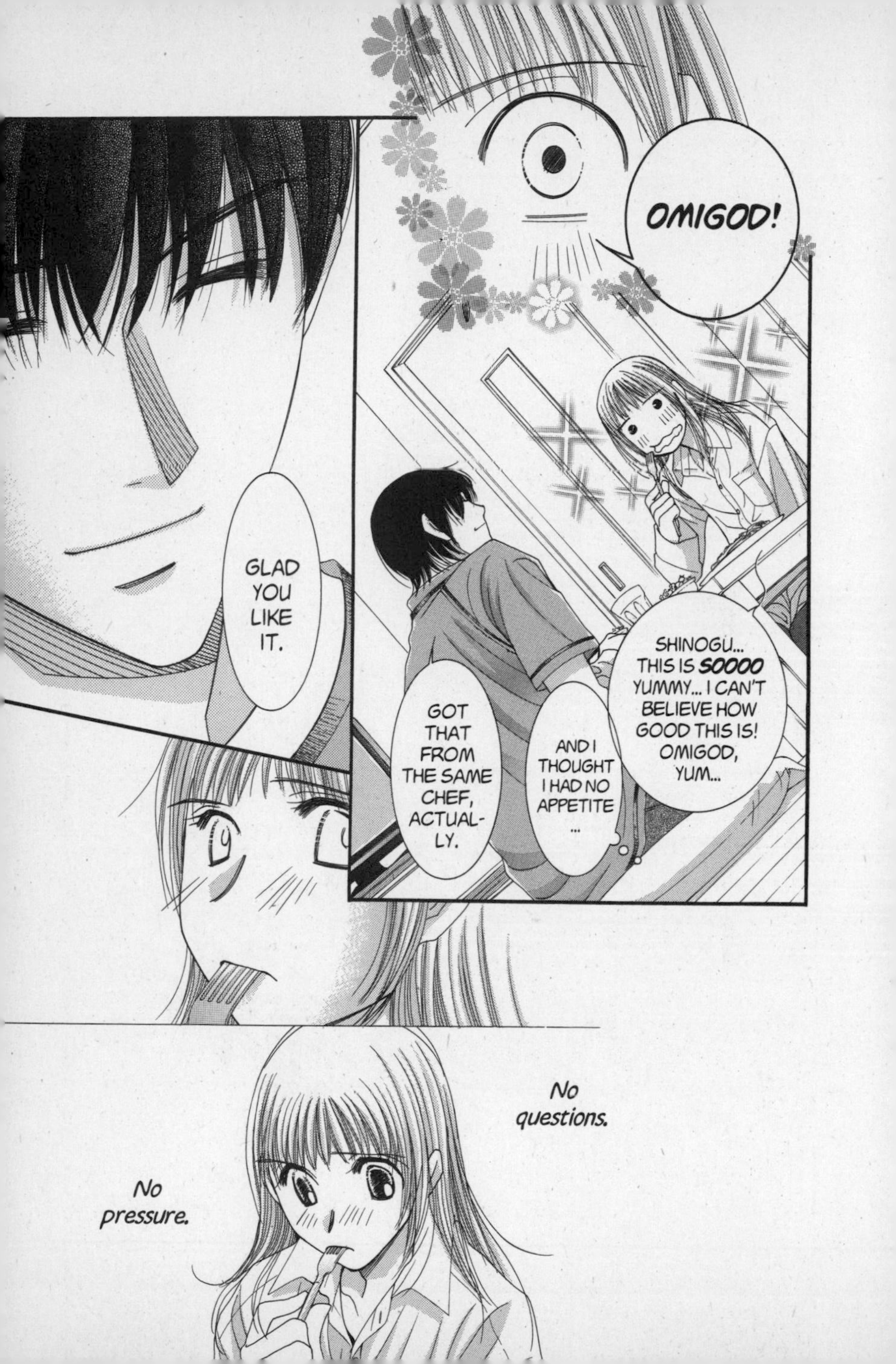
OMIGOD!
SHINOGU... THIS IS SOOOO YUMMY... I CAN'T BELIEVE HOW GOOD THIS IS! OMIGOD, YUM...
AND I THOUGHT I HAD NO APPETITE ...
GOT THAT FROM THE SAME CHEF, ACTUAL-LY.
GLAD YOU LIKE IT.
No questions.
No pressure.

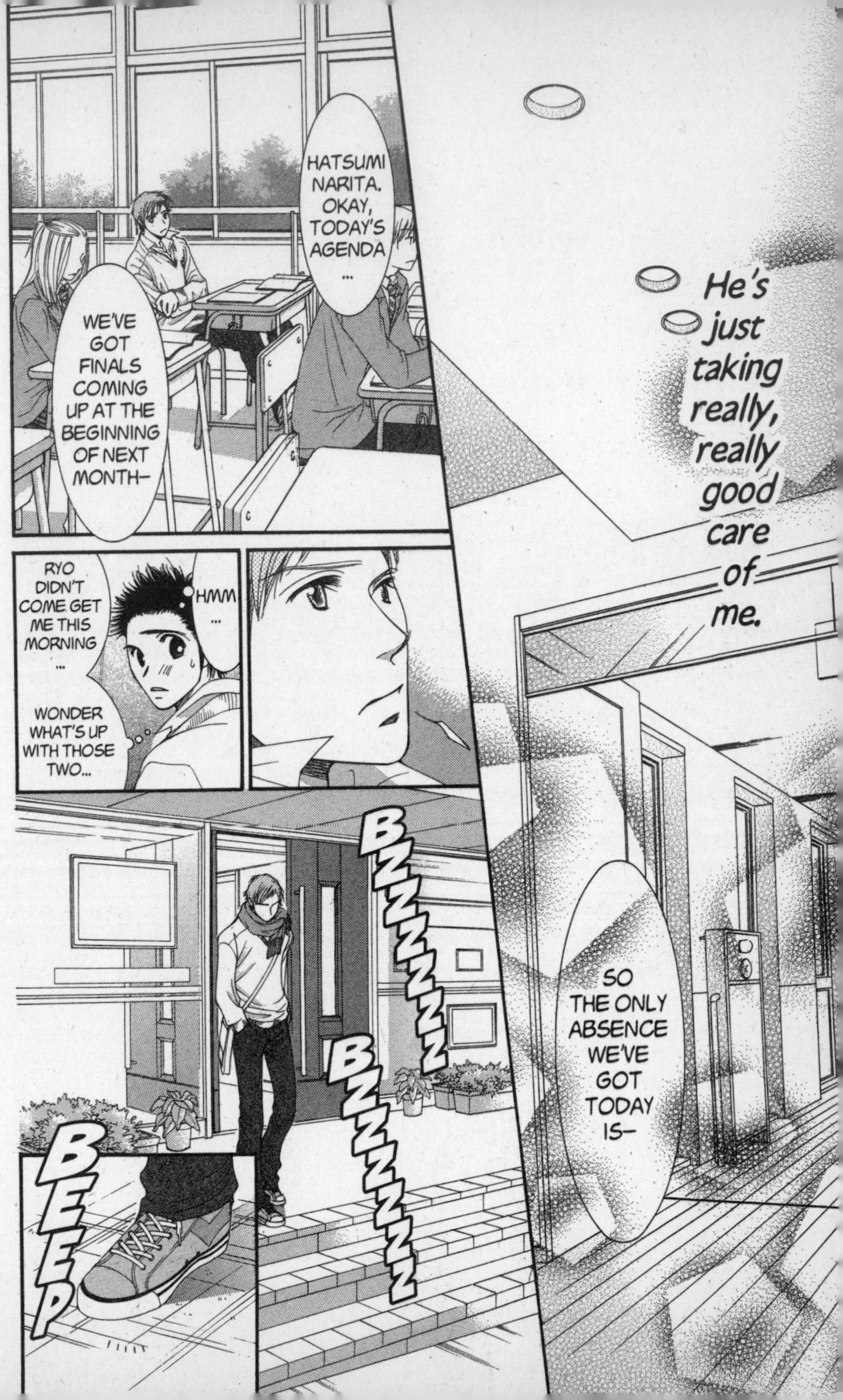
He's just taking really, really good care of me.
SO THE ONLY ABSENCE WE'VE GOT TODAY IS—
HATSUMI NARITA. OKAY, TODAY'S AGENDA...
WE'VE GOT FINALS COMING UP AT THE BEGINNING OF NEXT MONTH—
HMM...
RYO DIDN'T COME GET ME THIS MORNING...
WONDER WHAT'S UP WITH THOSE TWO...
BZZZZZZ
BZZZZZZZ
BEEP

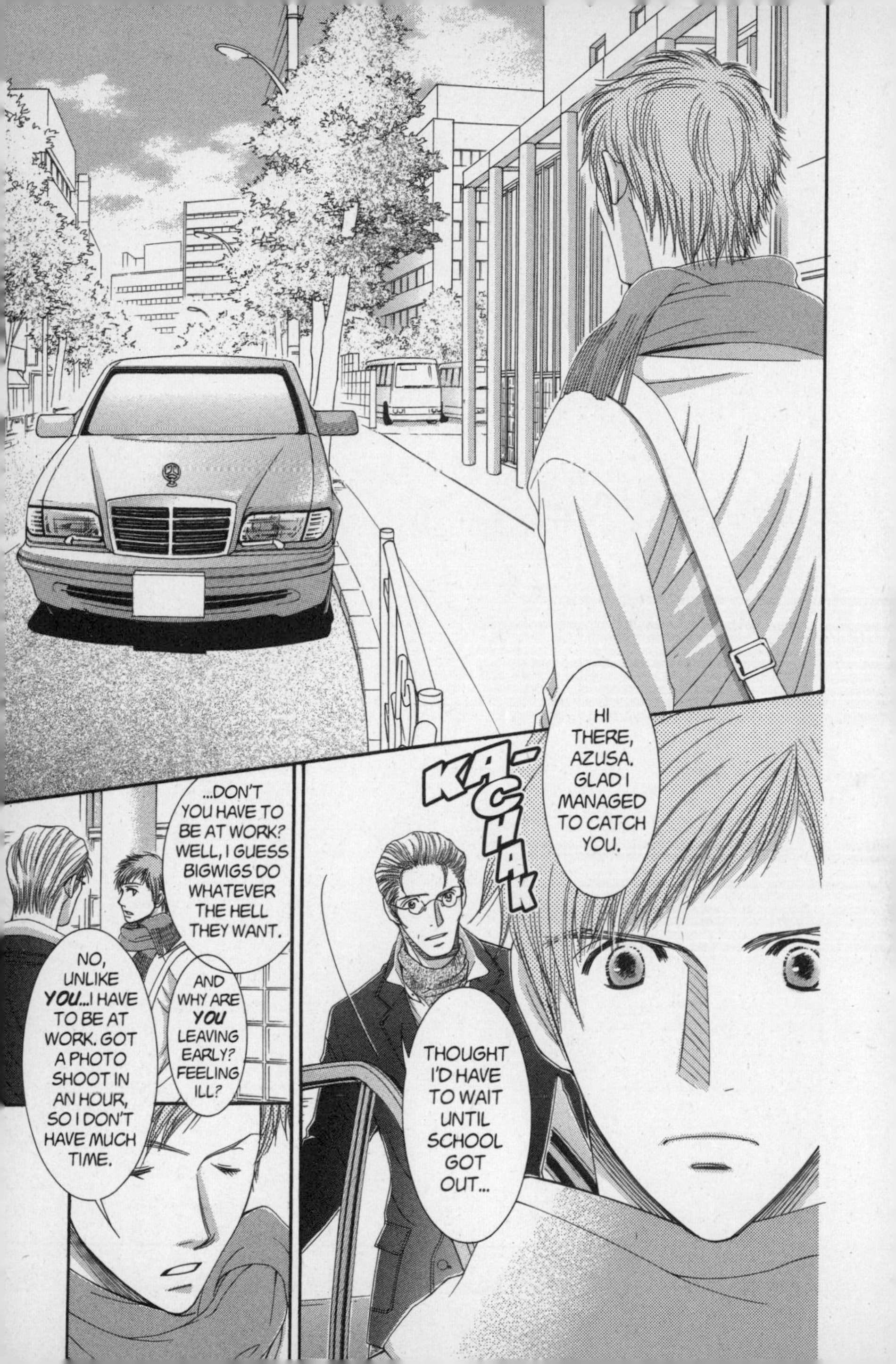
HI THERE, AZUSA. GLAD I MANAGED TO CATCH YOU.
KA-CHAK
THOUGHT I'D HAVE TO WAIT UNTIL SCHOOL GOT OUT...
...DON'T YOU HAVE TO BE AT WORK? WELL, I GUESS BIGWIGS DO WHATEVER THE HELL THEY WANT.
NO, UNLIKE *YOU*...I HAVE TO BE AT WORK. GOT A PHOTO SHOOT IN AN HOUR, SO I DON'T HAVE MUCH TIME.
AND WHY ARE *YOU* LEAVING EARLY? FEELING ILL?

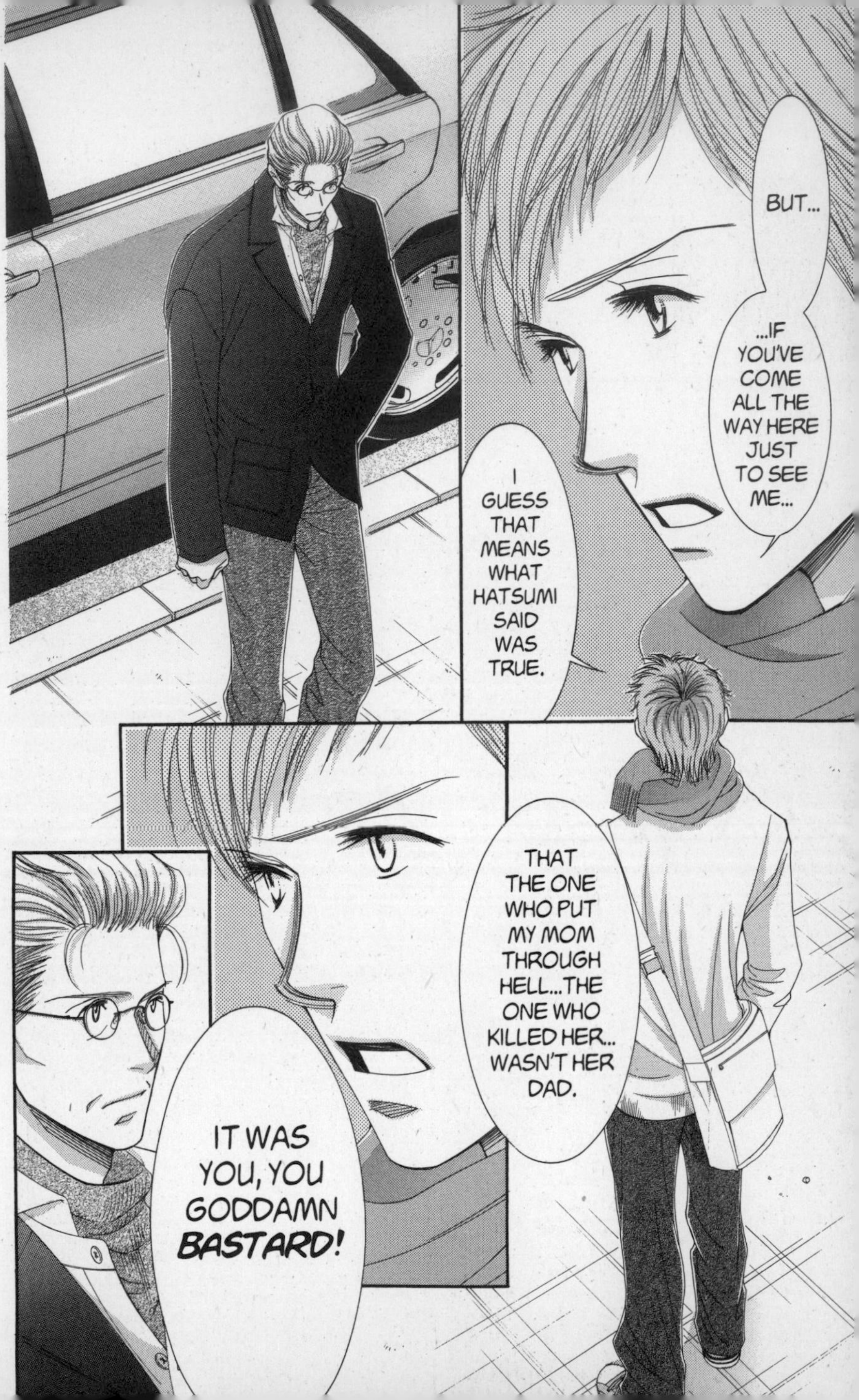
BUT...
...IF YOU'VE COME ALL THE WAY HERE JUST TO SEE ME...
I GUESS THAT MEANS WHAT HATSUMI SAID WAS TRUE.
THAT THE ONE WHO PUT MY MOM THROUGH HELL...THE ONE WHO KILLED HER... WASN'T HER DAD.
IT WAS YOU, YOU GODDAMN **BASTARD!**

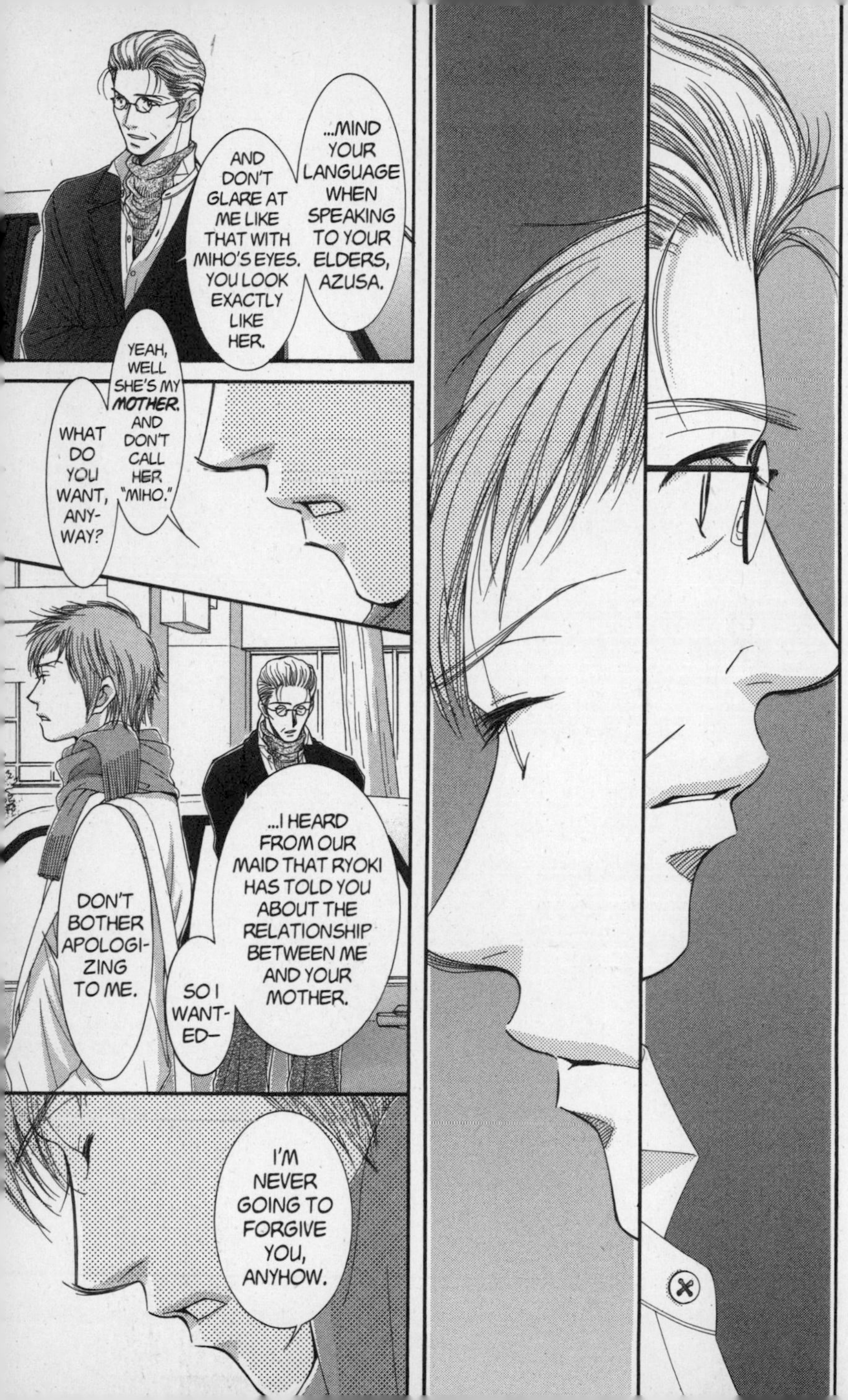
...MIND YOUR LANGUAGE WHEN SPEAKING TO YOUR ELDERS, AZUSA.
AND DON'T GLARE AT ME LIKE THAT WITH MIHO'S EYES. YOU LOOK EXACTLY LIKE HER.
YEAH, WELL SHE'S MY *MOTHER*. AND DON'T CALL HER "MIHO."
WHAT DO YOU WANT, ANY-WAY?
...I HEARD FROM OUR MAID THAT RYOKI HAS TOLD YOU ABOUT THE RELATIONSHIP BETWEEN ME AND YOUR MOTHER.
SO I WANT-ED—
DON'T BOTHER APOLOGI-ZING TO ME.
I'M NEVER GOING TO FORGIVE YOU, ANYHOW.

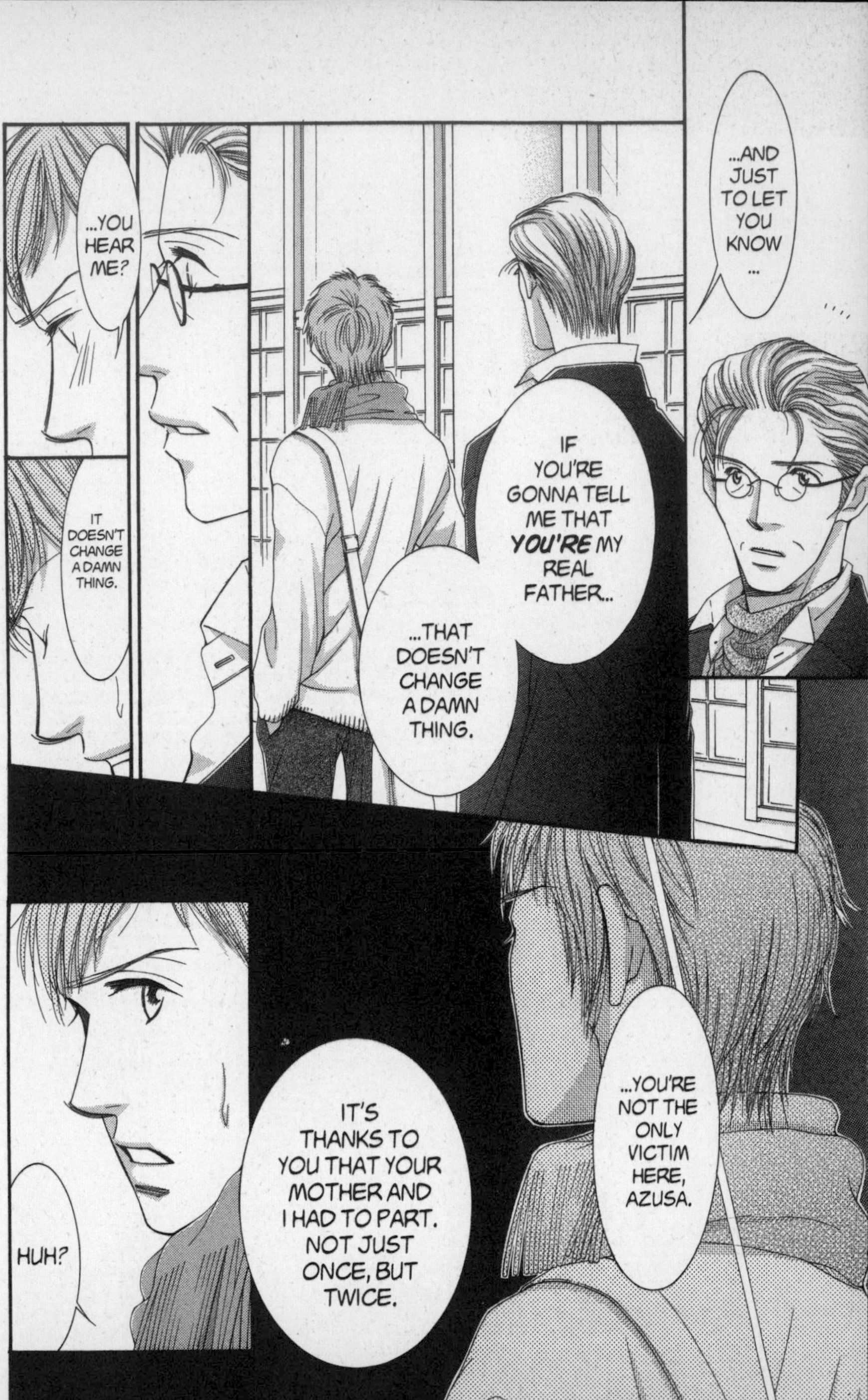
...AND JUST TO LET YOU KNOW ...
IF YOU'RE GONNA TELL ME THAT YOU'RE MY REAL FATHER...
...THAT DOESN'T CHANGE A DAMN THING.
...YOU HEAR ME?
IT DOESN'T CHANGE A DAMN THING.
...YOU'RE NOT THE ONLY VICTIM HERE, AZUSA.
IT'S THANKS TO YOU THAT YOUR MOTHER AND I HAD TO PART. NOT JUST ONCE, BUT TWICE.
HUH?

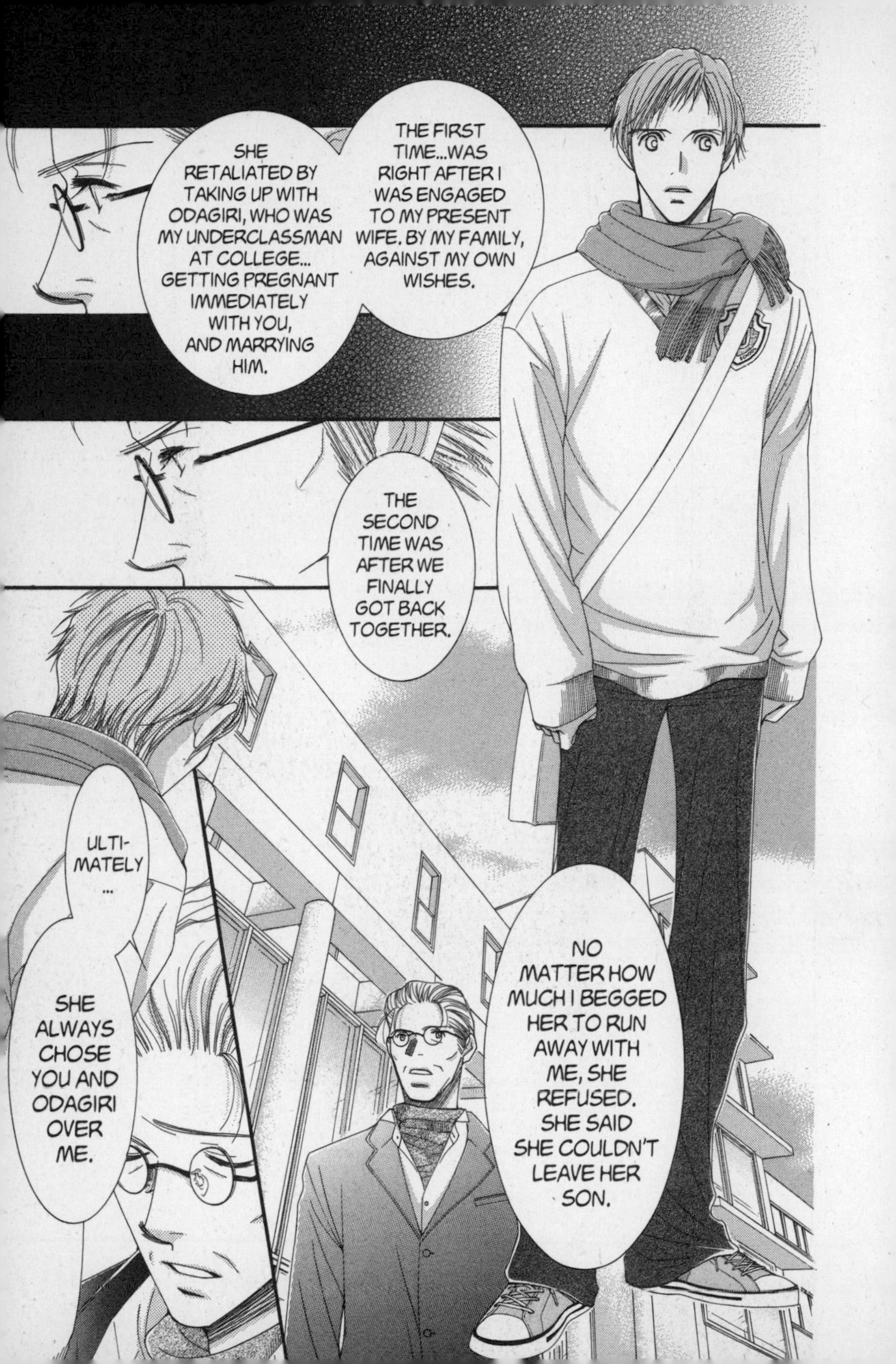
THE FIRST TIME...WAS RIGHT AFTER I WAS ENGAGED TO MY PRESENT WIFE. BY MY FAMILY, AGAINST MY OWN WISHES.
SHE RETALIATED BY TAKING UP WITH ODAGIRI, WHO WAS MY UNDERCLASSMAN AT COLLEGE... GETTING PREGNANT IMMEDIATELY WITH YOU, AND MARRYING HIM.
THE SECOND TIME WAS AFTER WE FINALLY GOT BACK TOGETHER.
NO MATTER HOW MUCH I BEGGED HER TO RUN AWAY WITH ME, SHE REFUSED. SHE SAID SHE COULDN'T LEAVE HER SON.
ULTI-MATELY...
SHE ALWAYS CHOSE YOU AND ODAGIRI OVER ME.

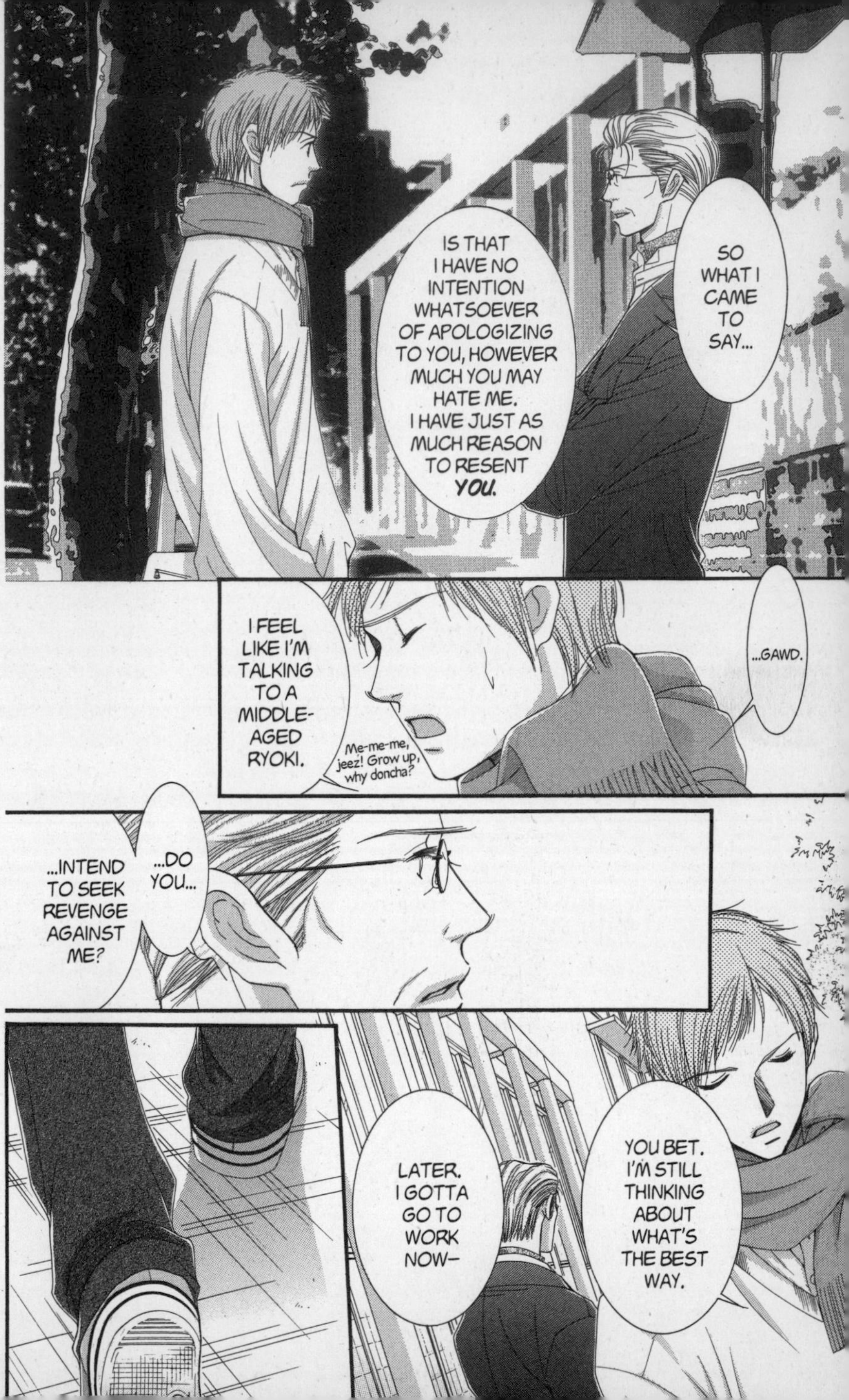
SO WHAT I CAME TO SAY...
IS THAT I HAVE NO INTENTION WHATSOEVER OF APOLOGIZING TO YOU, HOWEVER MUCH YOU MAY HATE ME. I HAVE JUST AS MUCH REASON TO RESENT **YOU.**
...GAWD.
I FEEL LIKE I'M TALKING TO A MIDDLE-AGED RYOKI.
Me-me-me, jeez! Grow up, why doncha?
...DO YOU...
...INTEND TO SEEK REVENGE AGAINST ME?
YOU BET. I'M STILL THINKING ABOUT WHAT'S THE BEST WAY.
LATER. I GOTTA GO TO WORK NOW–

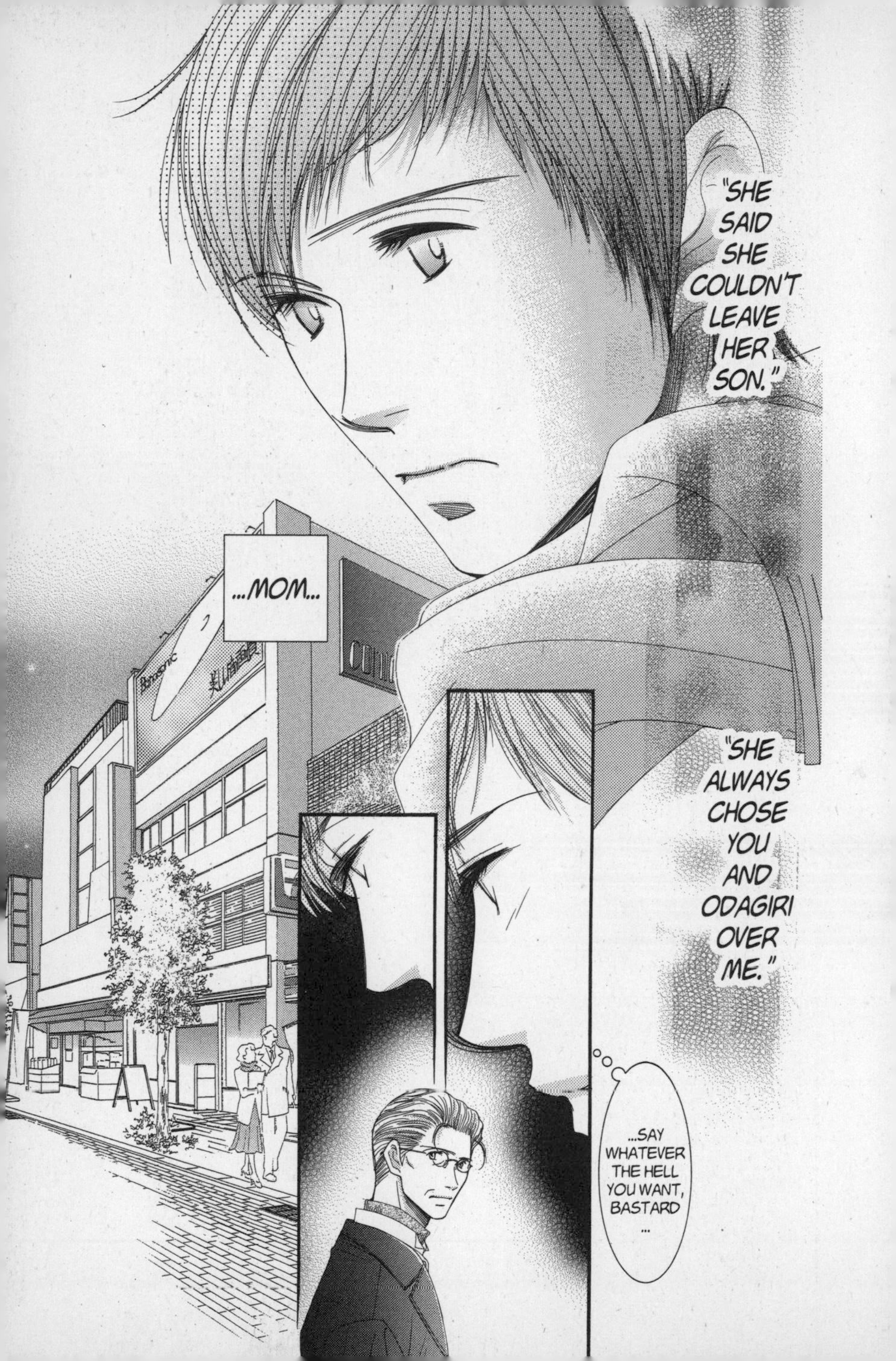
"SHE SAID SHE COULDN'T LEAVE HER SON."
...MOM...
"SHE ALWAYS CHOSE YOU AND ODAGIRI OVER ME."
...SAY WHATEVER THE HELL YOU WANT, BASTARD ...

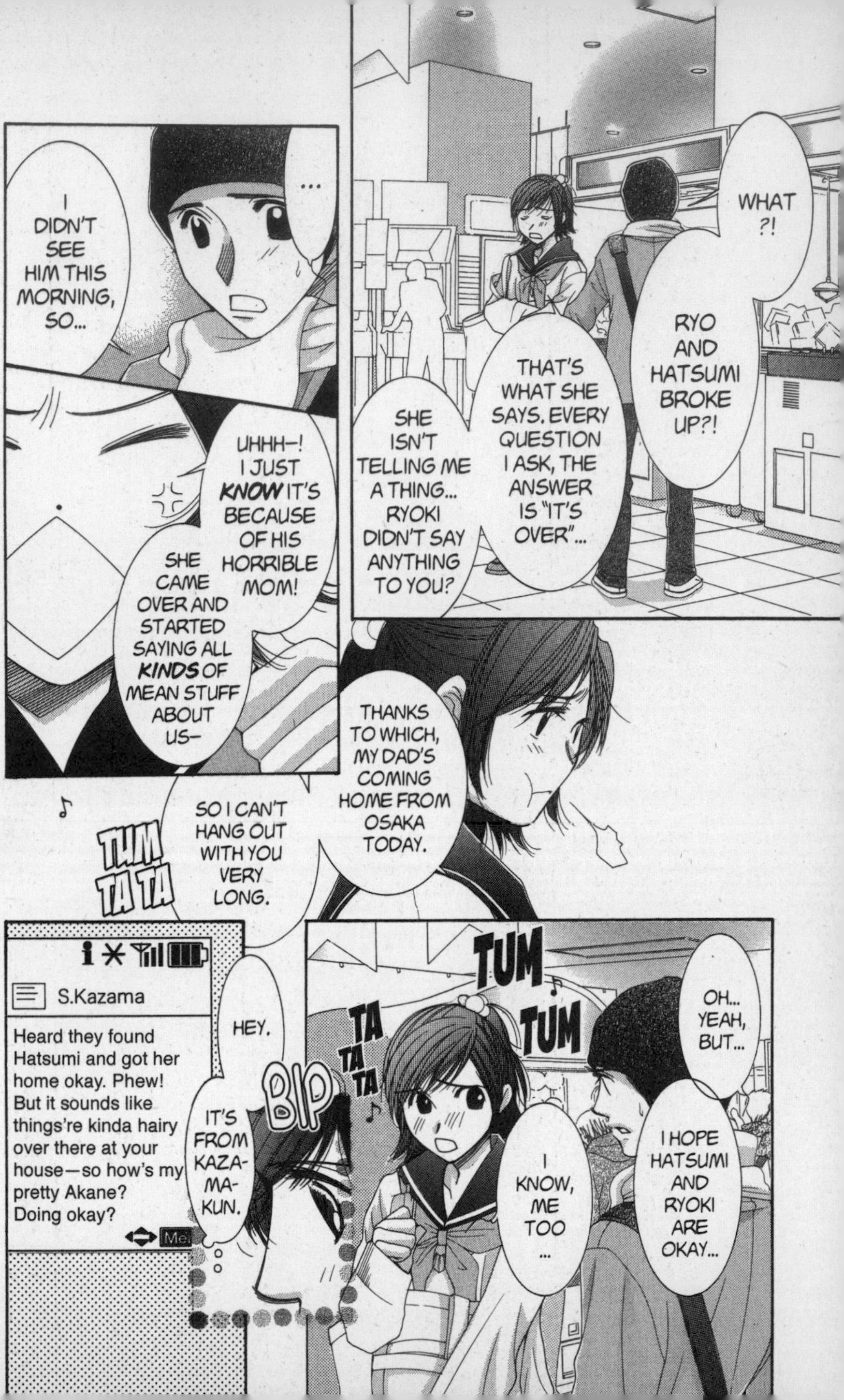
WHAT?!
RYO AND HATSUMI BROKE UP?!
THAT'S WHAT SHE SAYS. EVERY QUESTION I ASK, THE ANSWER IS "IT'S OVER"...
SHE ISN'T TELLING ME A THING... RYOKI DIDN'T SAY ANYTHING TO YOU?
...
I DIDN'T SEE HIM THIS MORNING, SO...
UHHH—! I JUST KNOW IT'S BECAUSE OF HIS HORRIBLE MOM!
SHE CAME OVER AND STARTED SAYING ALL KINDS OF MEAN STUFF ABOUT US—
THANKS TO WHICH, MY DAD'S COMING HOME FROM OSAKA TODAY.
SO I CAN'T HANG OUT WITH YOU VERY LONG.
TUM TA TA
TUM TUM
OH... YEAH, BUT...
I HOPE HATSUMI AND RYOKI ARE OKAY...
I KNOW, ME TOO ...
TA TA TA
BIP
HEY.
IT'S FROM KAZAMA-KUN.
S.Kazama
Heard they found Hatsumi and got her home okay. Phew! But it sounds like things're kinda hairy over there at your house—so how's my pretty Akane? Doing okay?

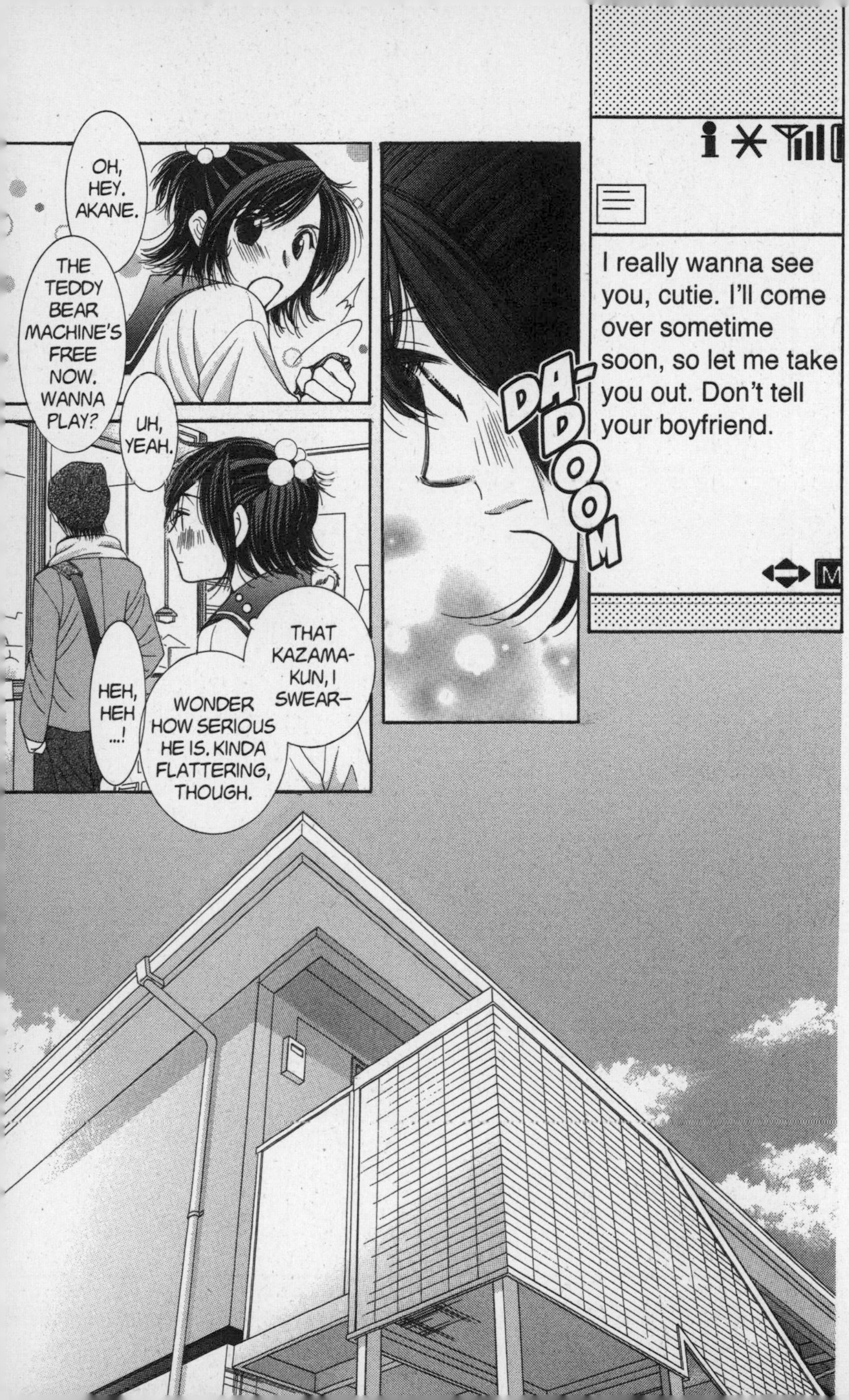
I really wanna see you, cutie. I'll come over sometime soon, so let me take you out. Don't tell your boyfriend.
M
DA-DOOM
OH, HEY. AKANE.
THE TEDDY BEAR MACHINE'S FREE NOW. WANNA PLAY?
UH, YEAH.
THAT KAZAMA-KUN, I SWEAR—
WONDER HOW SERIOUS HE IS. KINDA FLATTERING, THOUGH.
HEH, HEH ...!

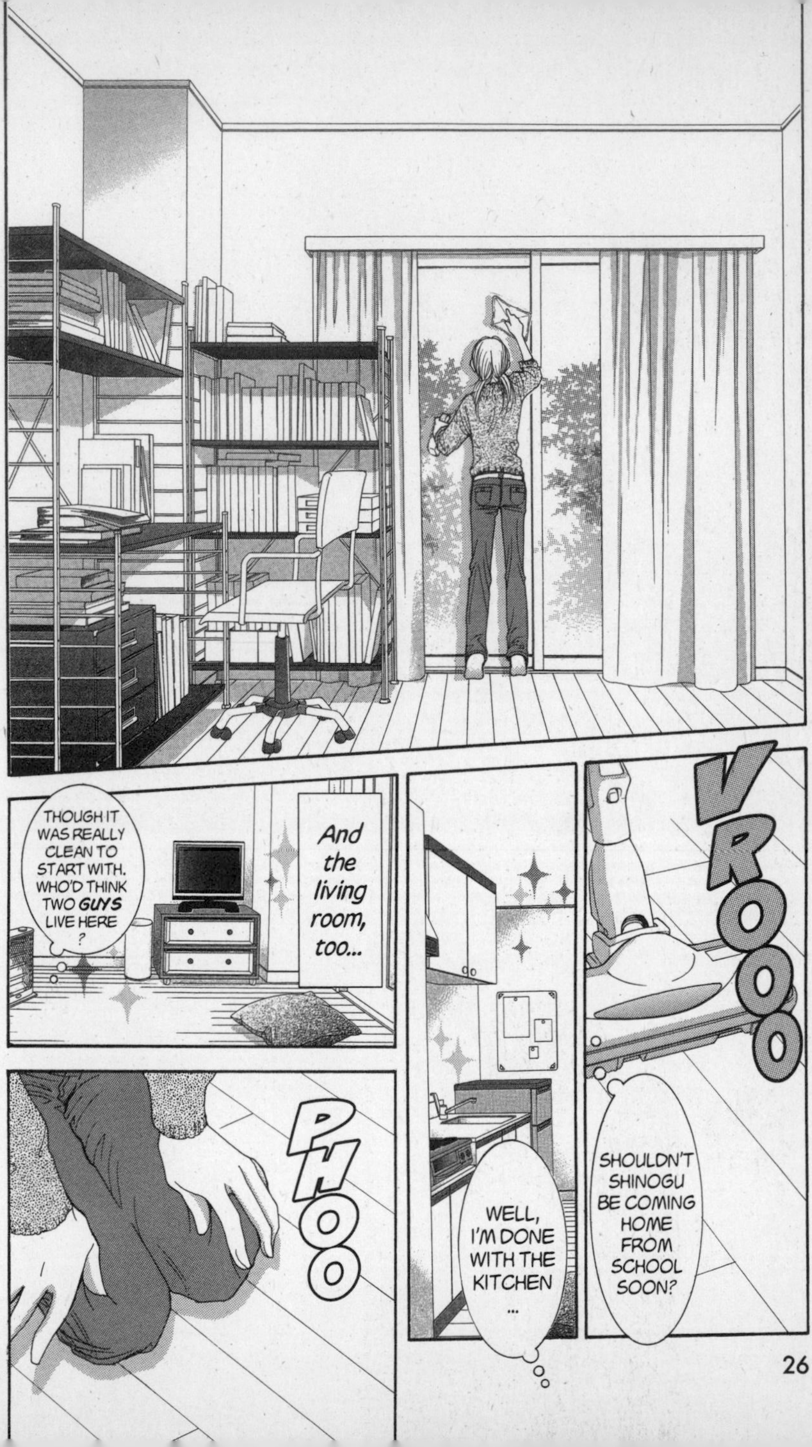
VROOO
SHOULDN'T SHINOGU BE COMING HOME FROM SCHOOL SOON?
WELL, I'M DONE WITH THE KITCHEN ...
And the living room, too...
THOUGH IT WAS REALLY CLEAN TO START WITH. WHO'D THINK TWO GUYS LIVE HERE ?
PHOO

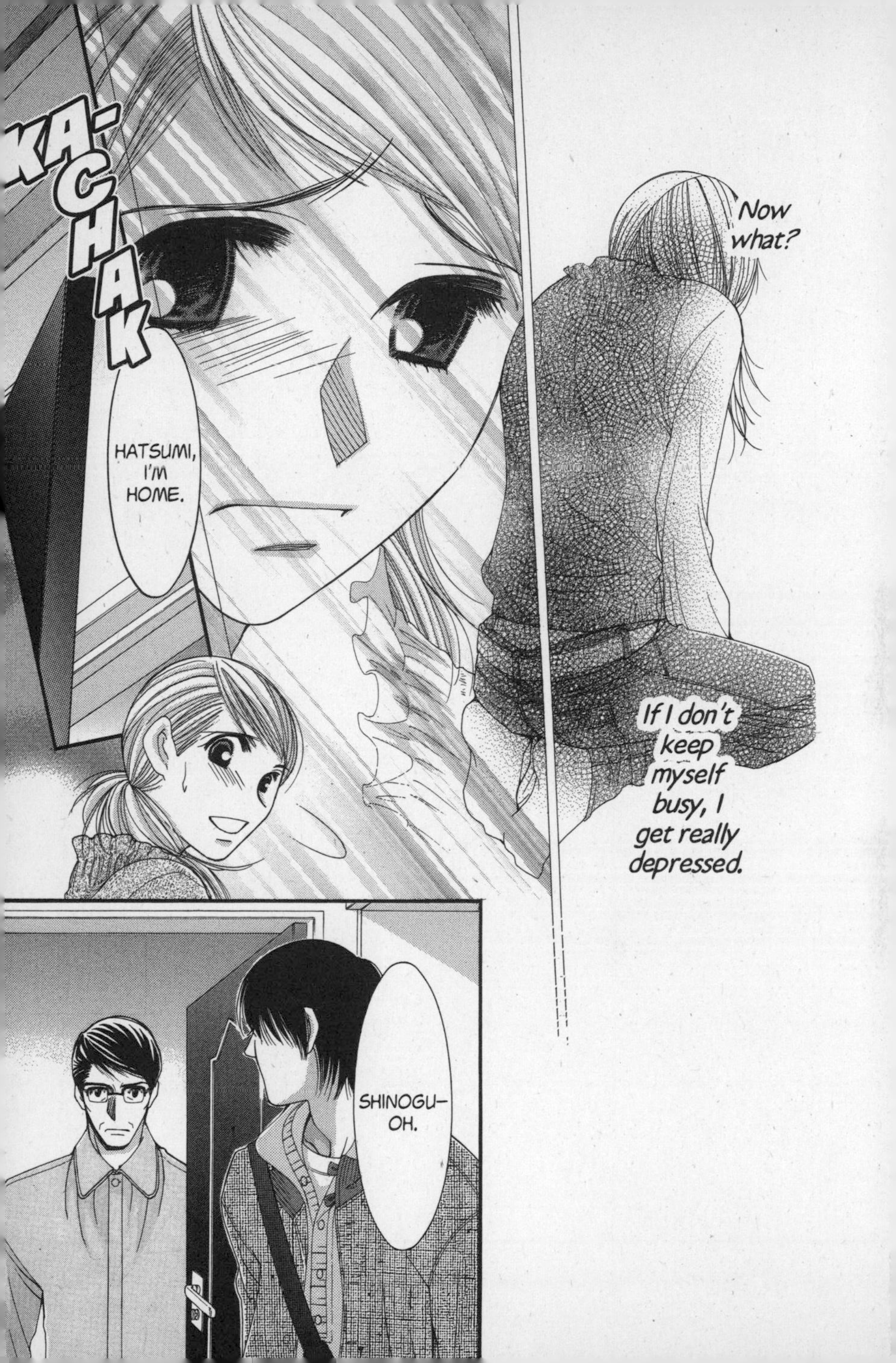
Now what?
If I don't keep myself busy, I get really depressed.
KA-CHAK
HATSUMI, I'M HOME.
SHINOGU— OH.

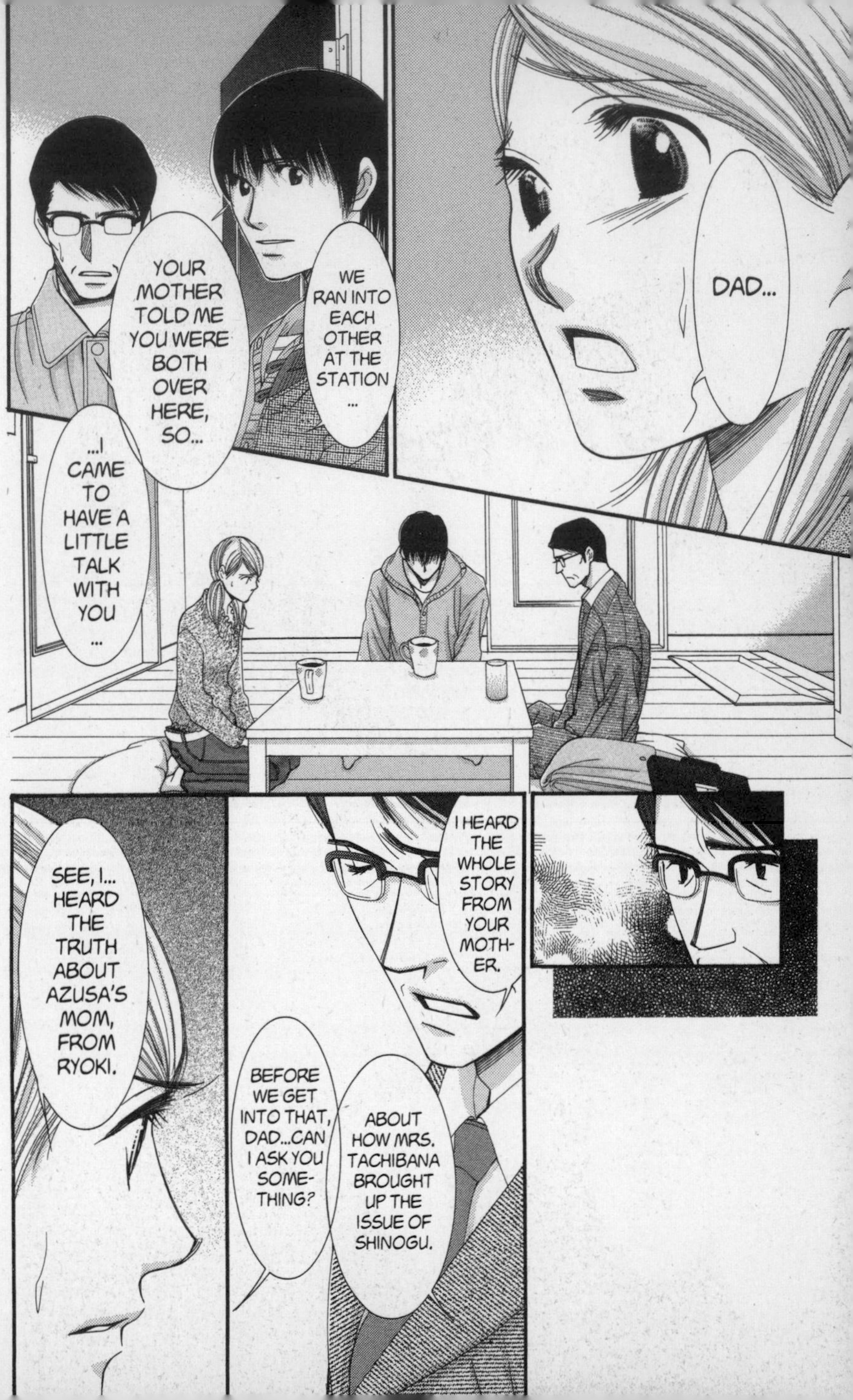
DAD...
WE RAN INTO EACH OTHER AT THE STATION ...
YOUR MOTHER TOLD ME YOU WERE BOTH OVER HERE, SO...
...I CAME TO HAVE A LITTLE TALK WITH YOU ...
I HEARD THE WHOLE STORY FROM YOUR MOTH-ER.
ABOUT HOW MRS. TACHIBANA BROUGHT UP THE ISSUE OF SHINOGU.
BEFORE WE GET INTO THAT, DAD...CAN I ASK YOU SOME-THING?
SEE, I... HEARD THE TRUTH ABOUT AZUSA'S MOM, FROM RYOKI.

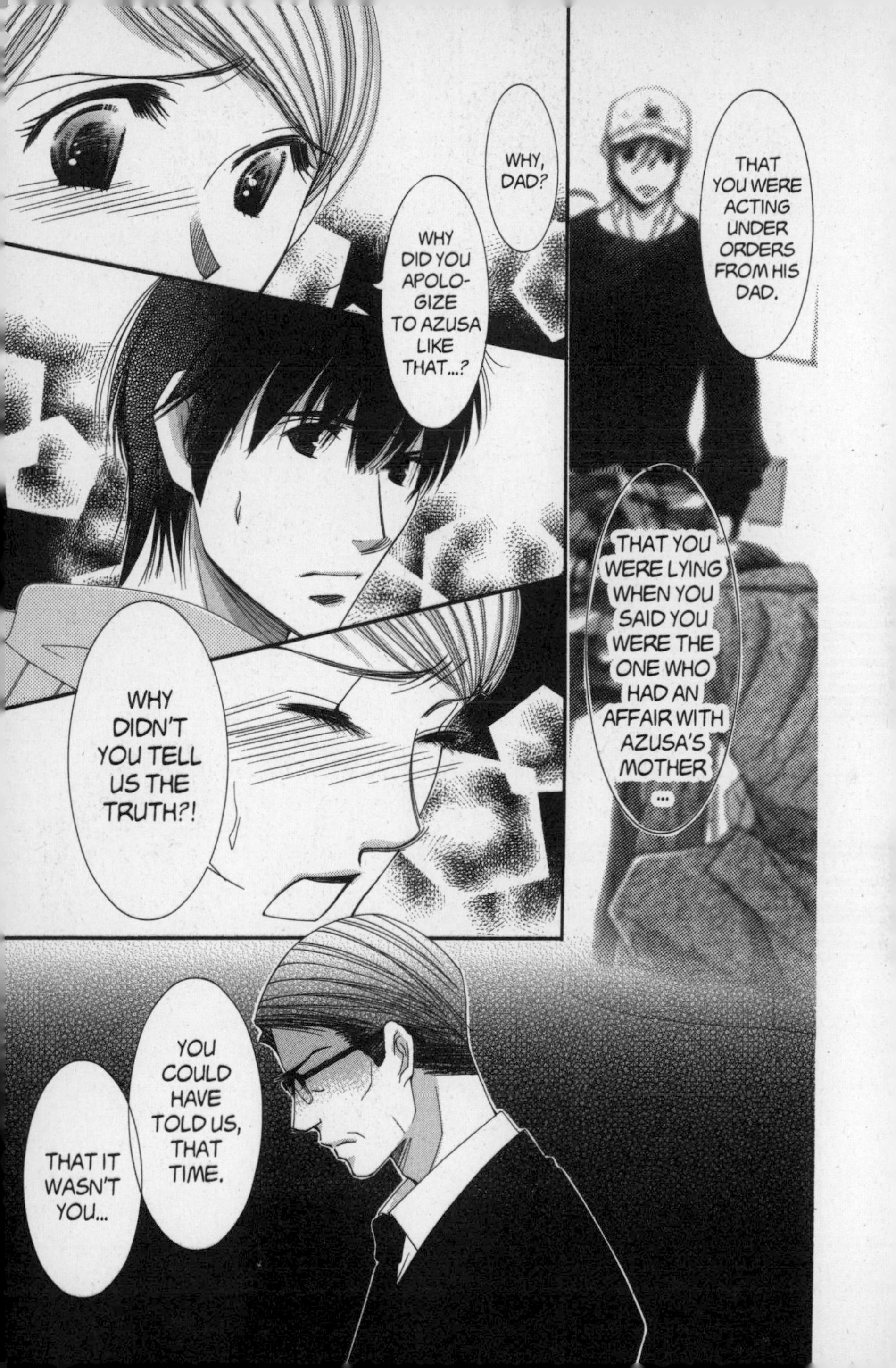
THAT YOU WERE ACTING UNDER ORDERS FROM HIS DAD.
THAT YOU WERE LYING WHEN YOU SAID YOU WERE THE ONE WHO HAD AN AFFAIR WITH AZUSA'S MOTHER ...
WHY, DAD?
WHY DID YOU APOLO-GIZE TO AZUSA LIKE THAT...?
WHY DIDN'T YOU TELL US THE TRUTH?!
YOU COULD HAVE TOLD US, THAT TIME.
THAT IT WASN'T YOU...

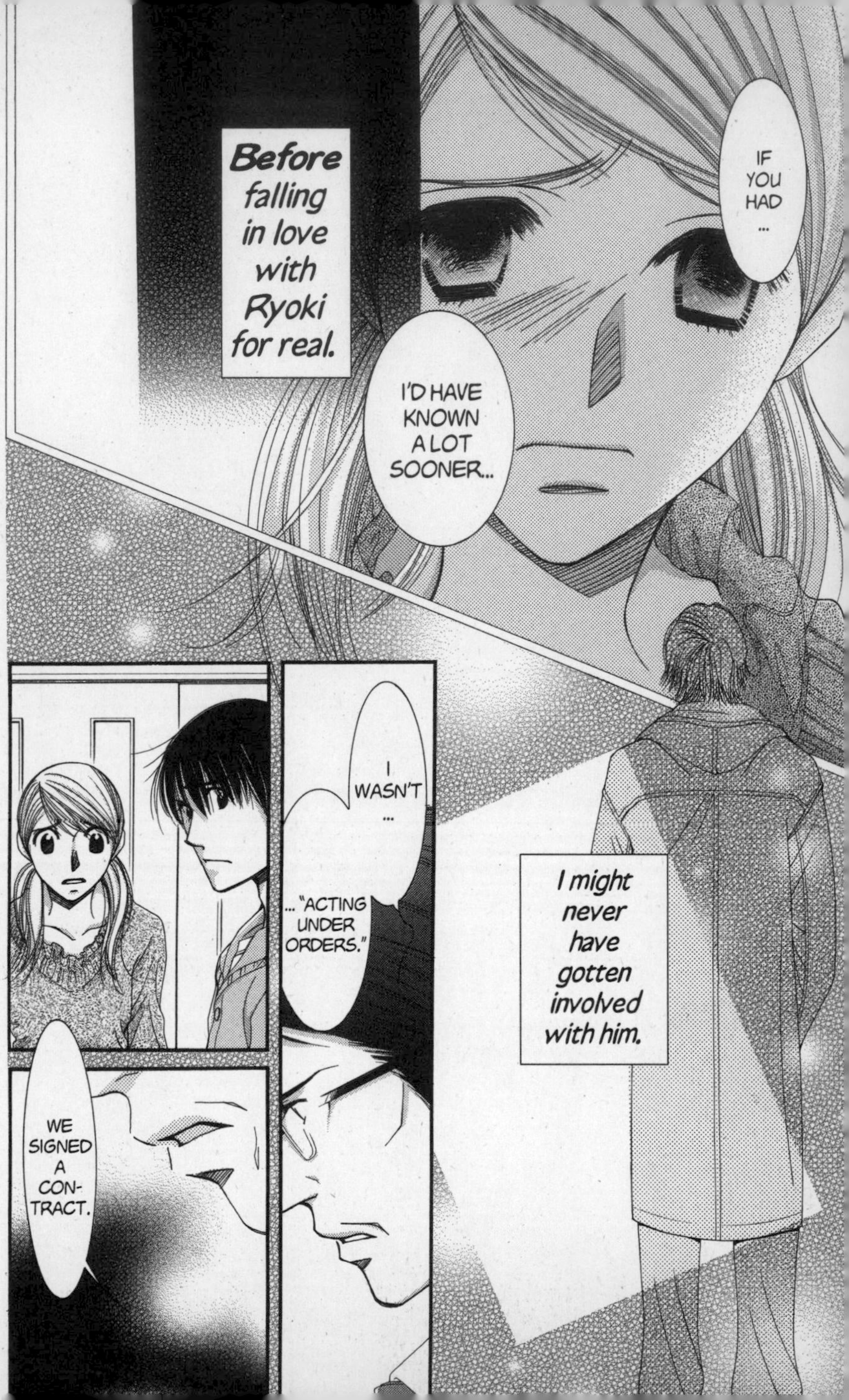
IF YOU HAD ...
I'D HAVE KNOWN A LOT SOONER...
Before falling in love with Ryoki for real.
I might never have gotten involved with him.
I WASN'T ...
..."ACTING UNDER ORDERS."
WE SIGNED A CONTRACT.

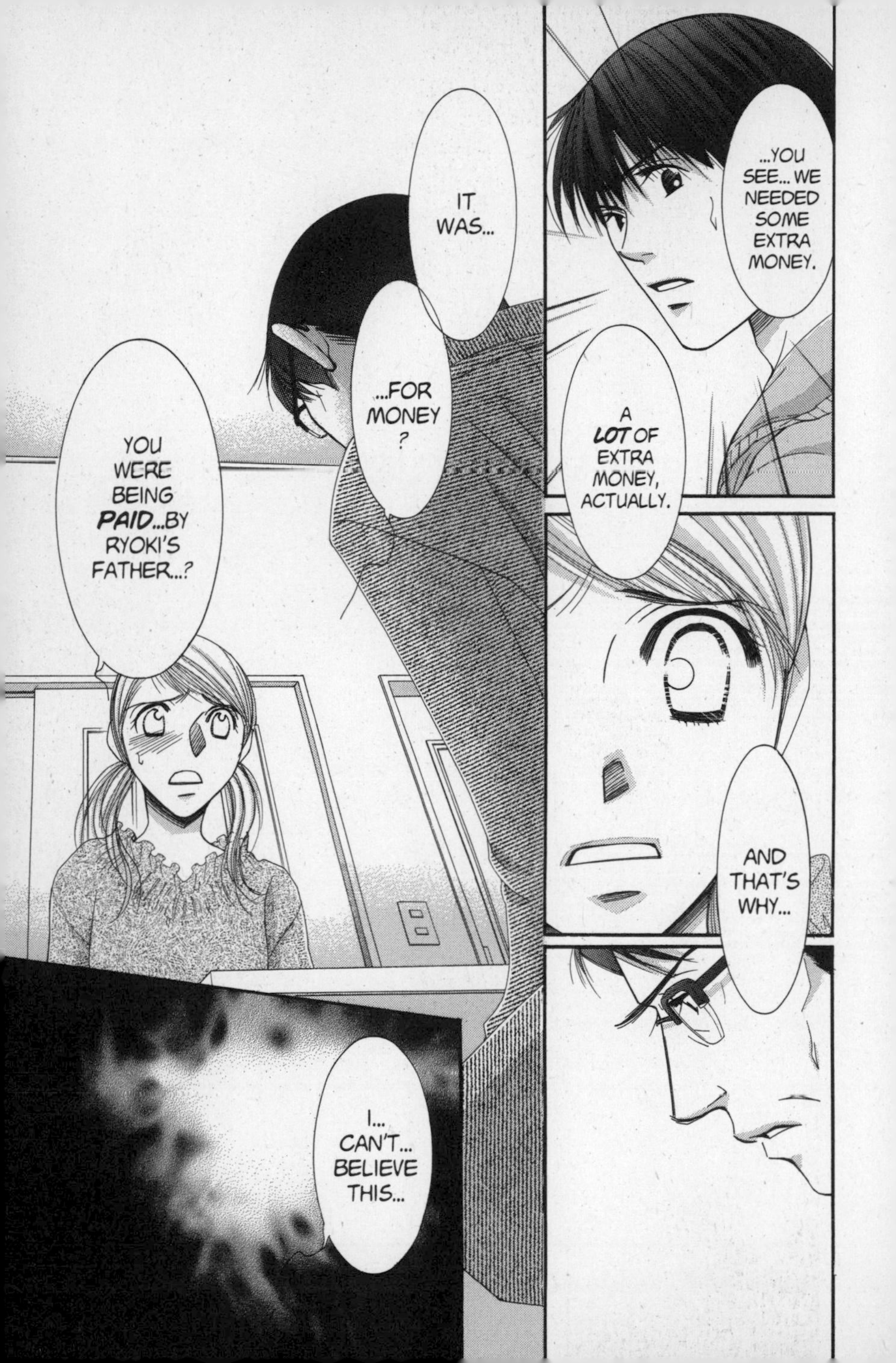
...YOU SEE... WE NEEDED SOME EXTRA MONEY.
A **LOT** OF EXTRA MONEY, ACTUALLY.
AND THAT'S WHY...
IT WAS...
...FOR MONEY?
YOU WERE BEING **PAID**...BY RYOKI'S FATHER...?
I... CAN'T... BELIEVE THIS...

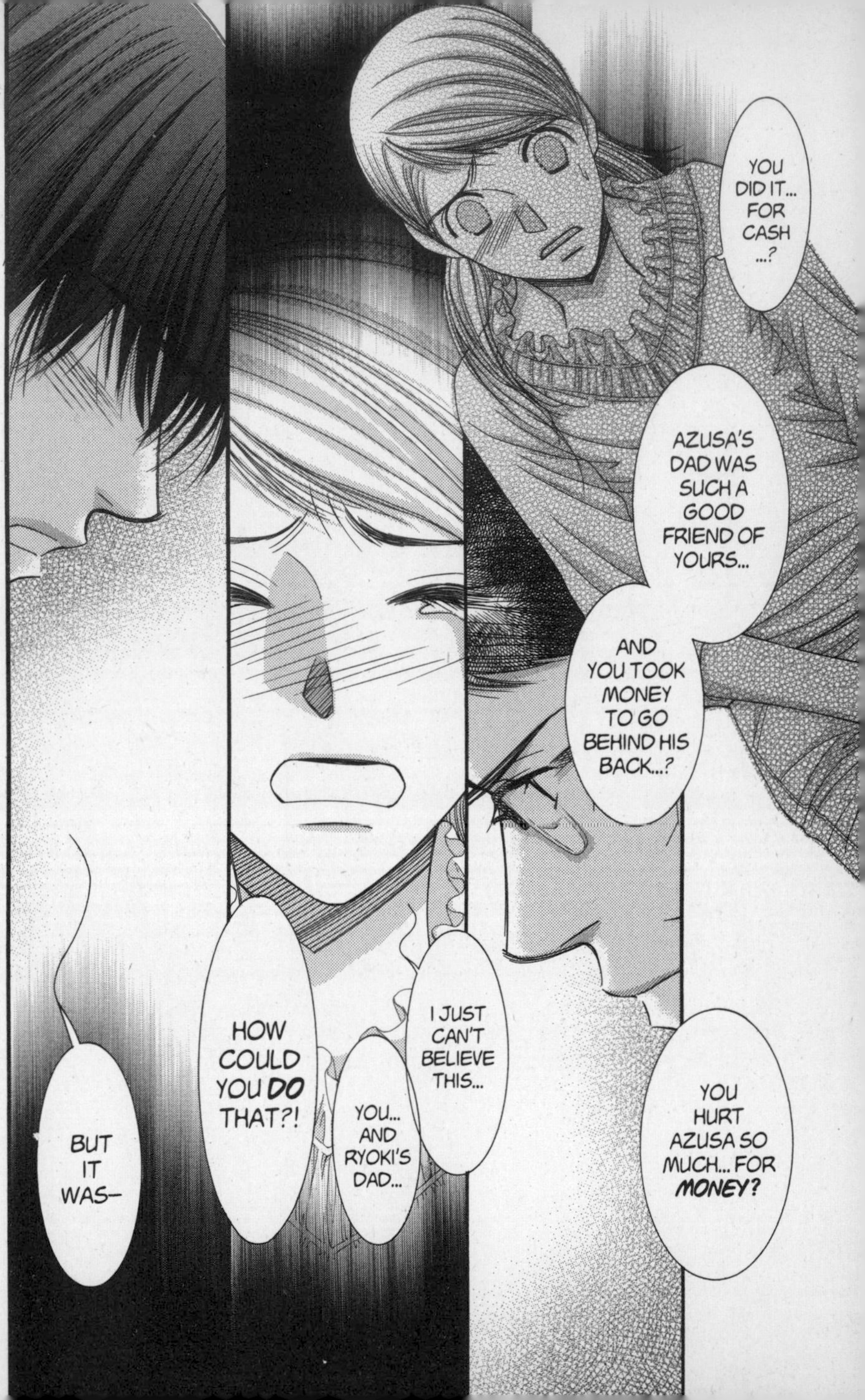
YOU DID IT... FOR CASH ...?
AZUSA'S DAD WAS SUCH A GOOD FRIEND OF YOURS...
AND YOU TOOK MONEY TO GO BEHIND HIS BACK...?
YOU HURT AZUSA SO MUCH... FOR **MONEY?**
I JUST CAN'T BELIEVE THIS...
YOU... AND RYOKI'S DAD...
HOW COULD YOU **DO** THAT?!
BUT IT WAS—

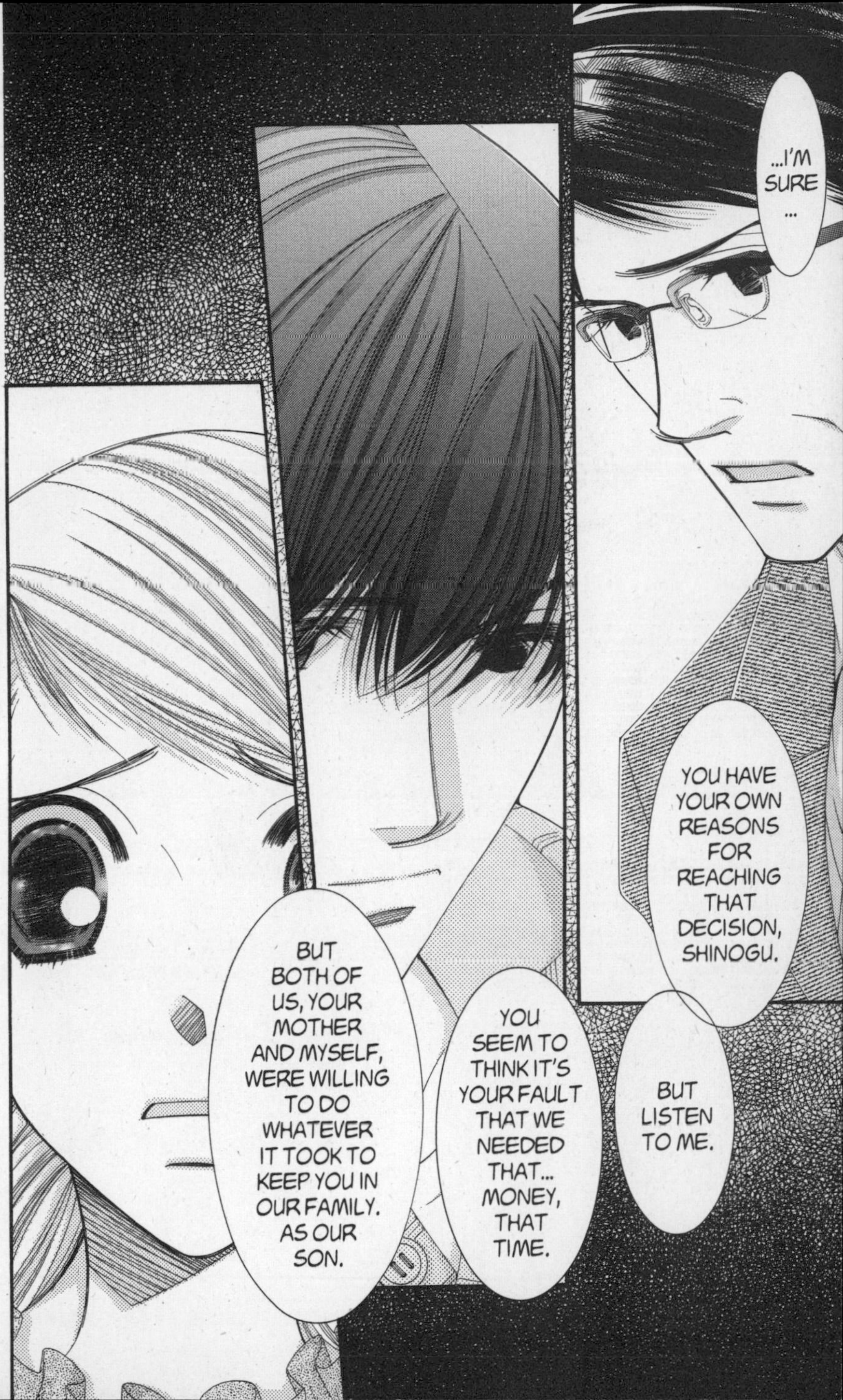
...I'M SURE ...
YOU HAVE YOUR OWN REASONS FOR REACHING THAT DECISION, SHINOGU.
BUT LISTEN TO ME.
YOU SEEM TO THINK IT'S YOUR FAULT THAT WE NEEDED THAT... MONEY, THAT TIME.
BUT BOTH OF US, YOUR MOTHER AND MYSELF, WERE WILLING TO DO WHATEVER IT TOOK TO KEEP YOU IN OUR FAMILY. AS OUR SON.

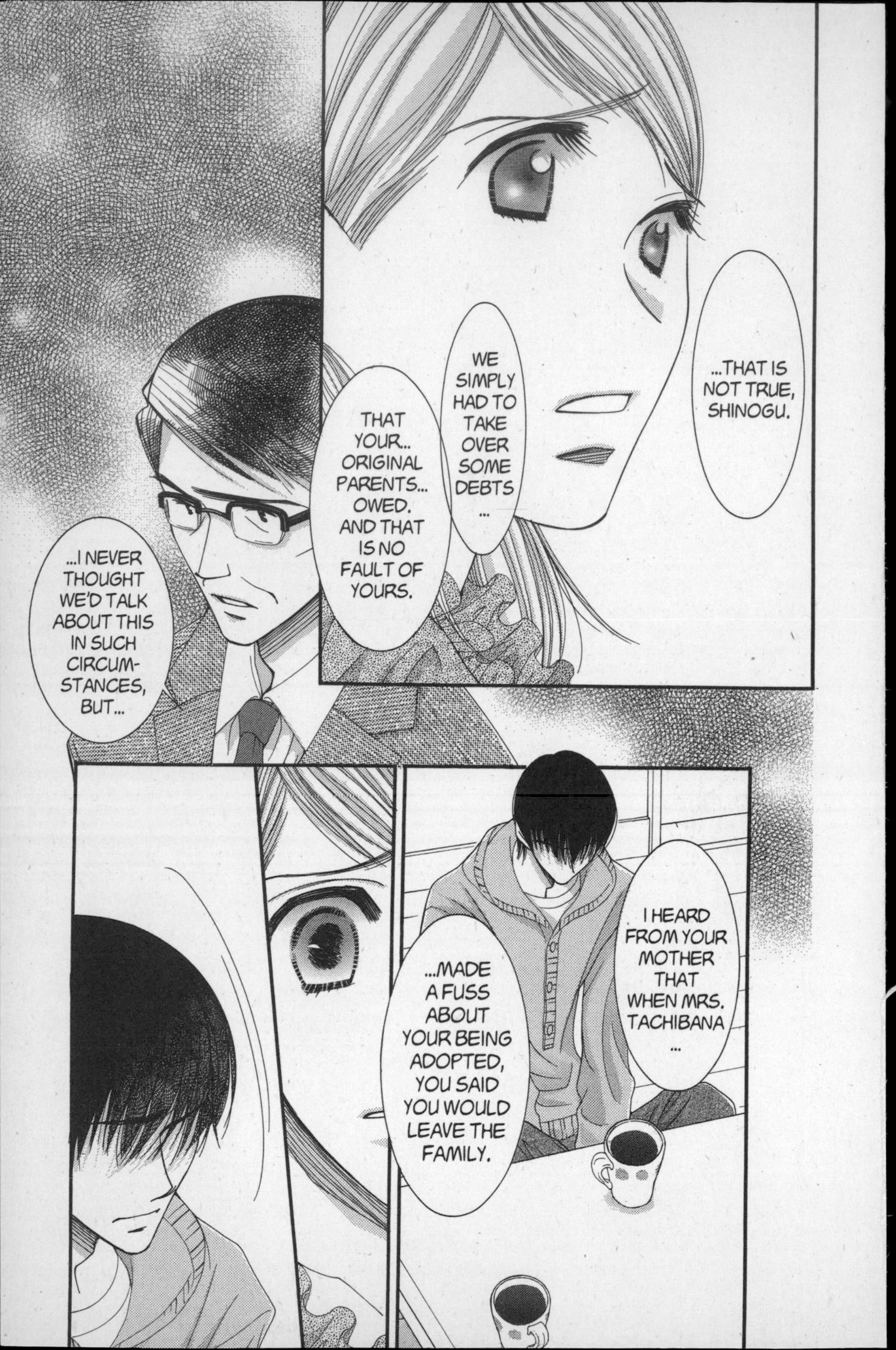
...THAT IS NOT TRUE, SHINOGU.
WE SIMPLY HAD TO TAKE OVER SOME DEBTS...
THAT YOUR... ORIGINAL PARENTS... OWED. AND THAT IS NO FAULT OF YOURS.
...I NEVER THOUGHT WE'D TALK ABOUT THIS IN SUCH CIRCUM-STANCES, BUT...
I HEARD FROM YOUR MOTHER THAT WHEN MRS. TACHIBANA...
...MADE A FUSS ABOUT YOUR BEING ADOPTED, YOU SAID YOU WOULD LEAVE THE FAMILY.

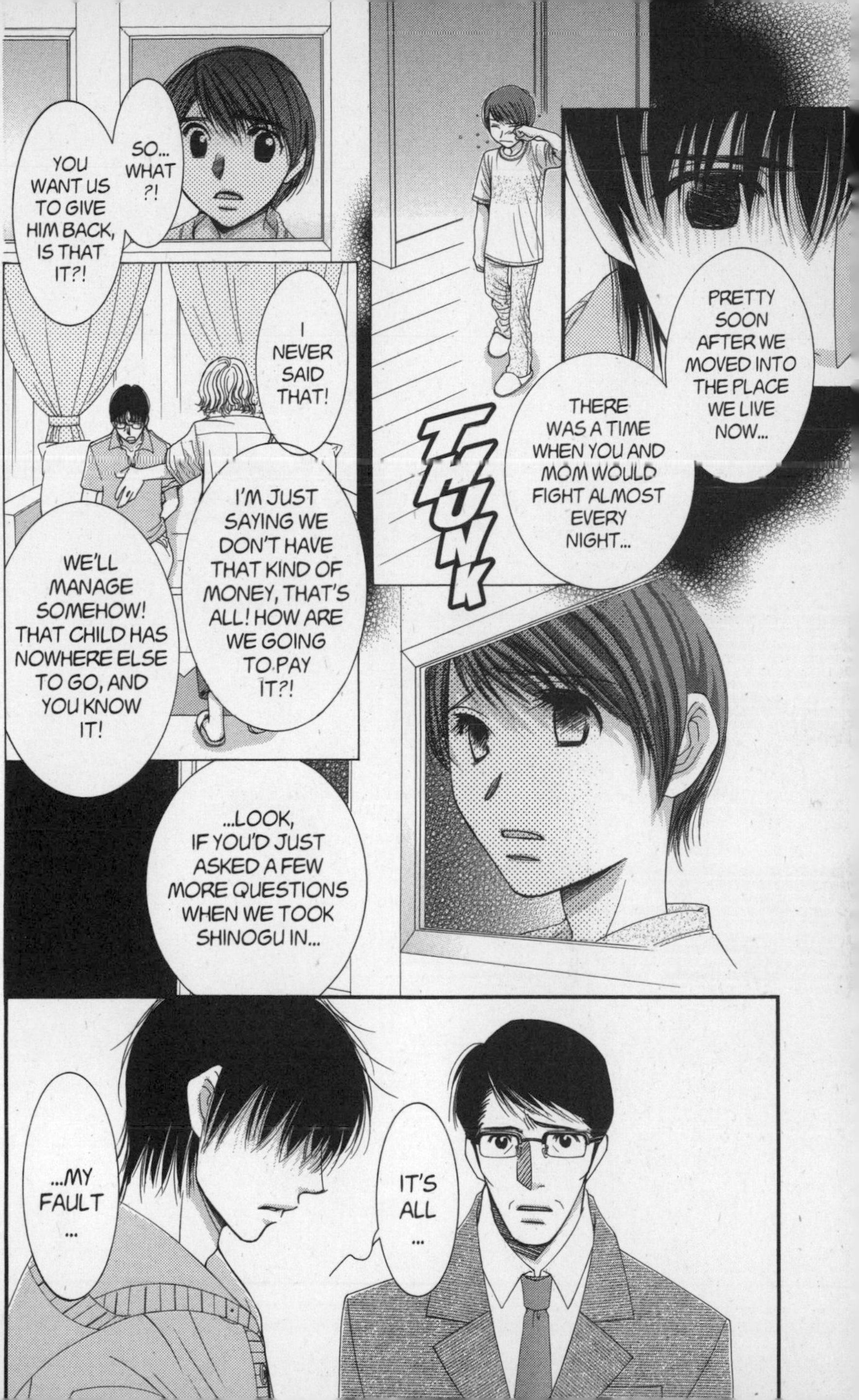
PRETTY SOON AFTER WE MOVED INTO THE PLACE WE LIVE NOW...
THERE WAS A TIME WHEN YOU AND MOM WOULD FIGHT ALMOST EVERY NIGHT...
THUNK
SO... WHAT?!
YOU WANT US TO GIVE HIM BACK, IS THAT IT?!
I NEVER SAID THAT!
I'M JUST SAYING WE DON'T HAVE THAT KIND OF MONEY, THAT'S ALL! HOW ARE WE GOING TO PAY IT?!
WE'LL MANAGE SOMEHOW! THAT CHILD HAS NOWHERE ELSE TO GO, AND YOU KNOW IT!
...LOOK, IF YOU'D JUST ASKED A FEW MORE QUESTIONS WHEN WE TOOK SHINOGU IN...
IT'S ALL ...
...MY FAULT ...

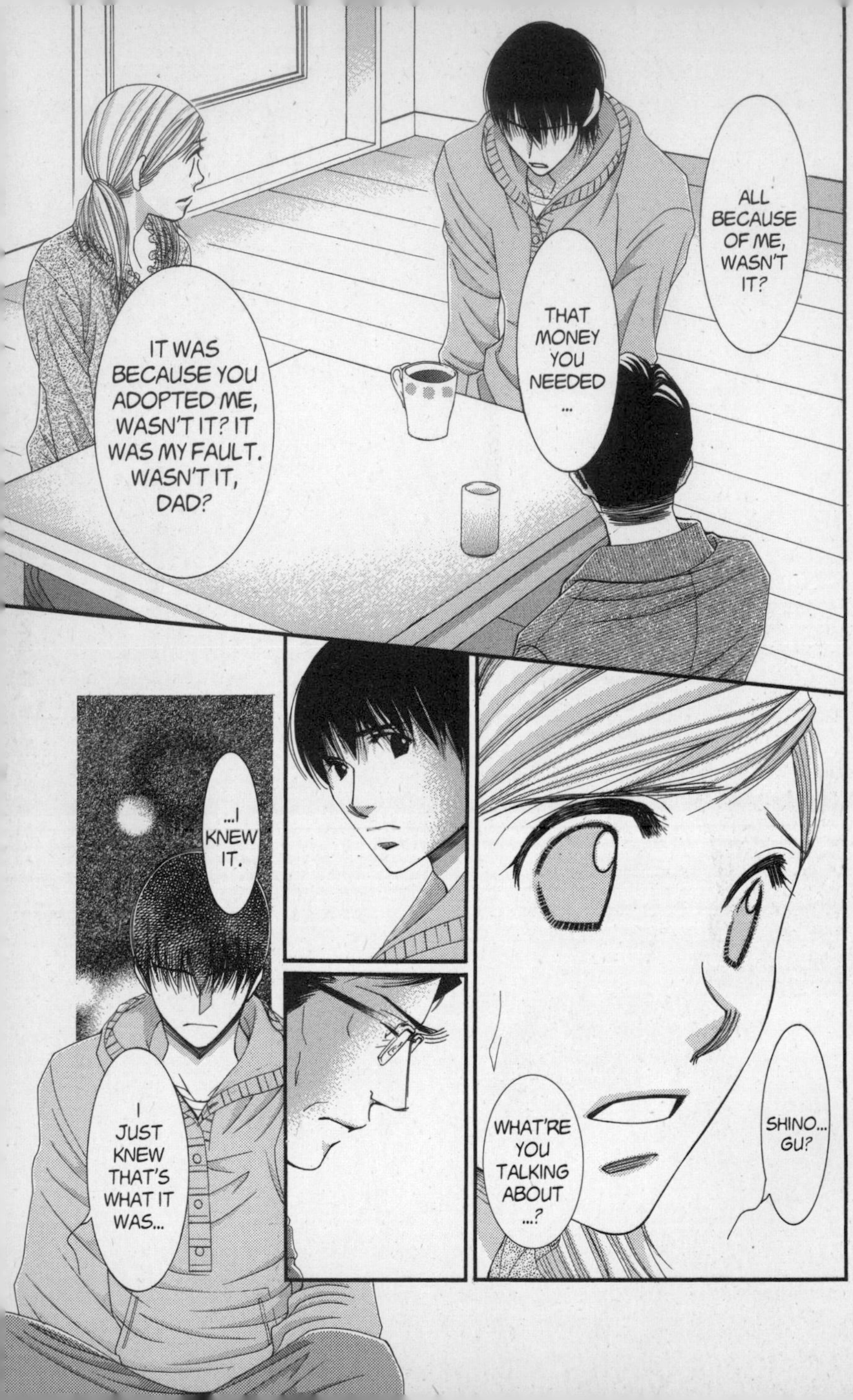
ALL BECAUSE OF ME, WASN'T IT?
THAT MONEY YOU NEEDED ...
IT WAS BECAUSE YOU ADOPTED ME, WASN'T IT? IT WAS MY FAULT. WASN'T IT, DAD?
SHINO... GU?
WHAT'RE YOU TALKING ABOUT ...?
...I KNEW IT.
I JUST KNEW THAT'S WHAT IT WAS...

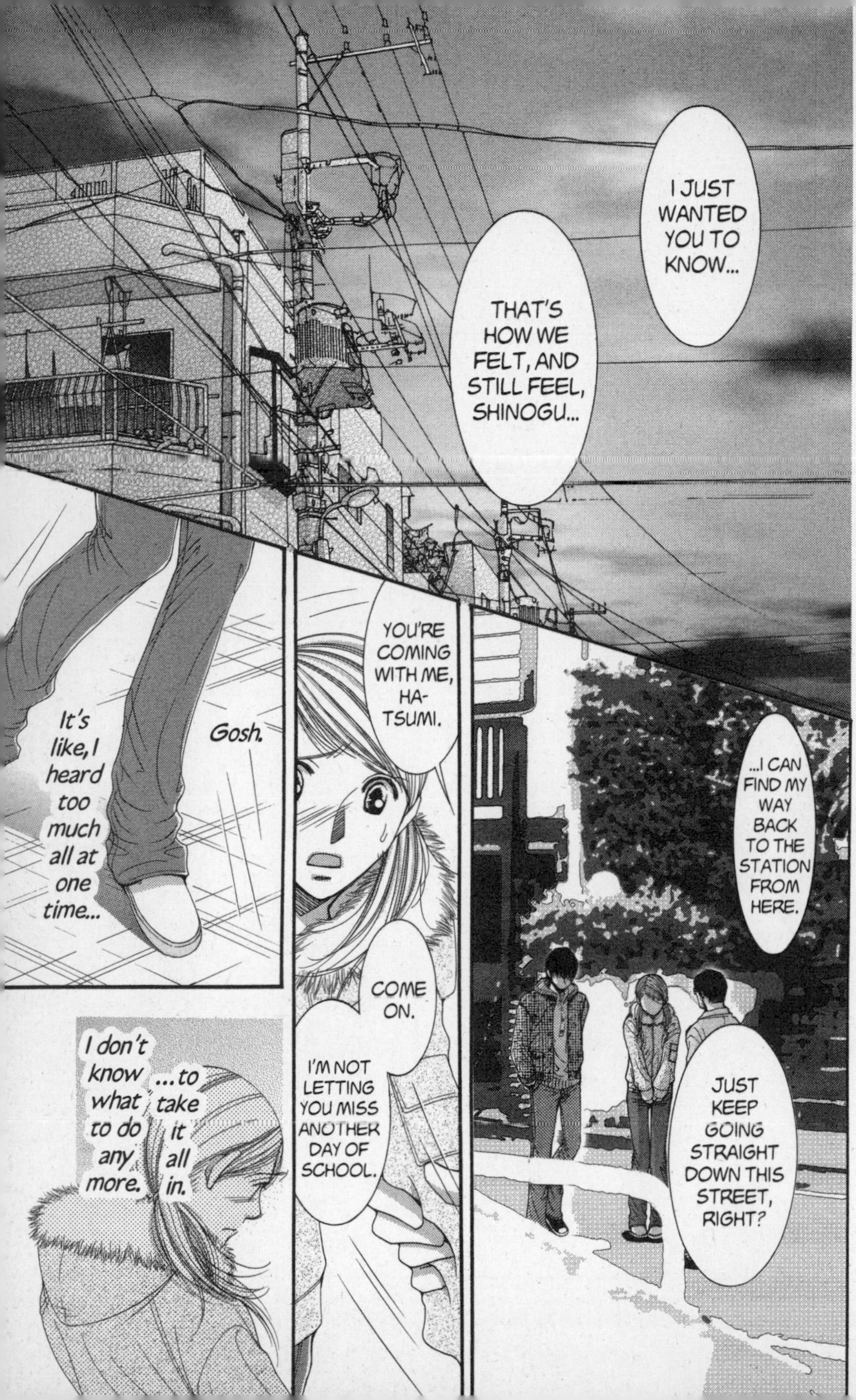
I JUST WANTED YOU TO KNOW...
THAT'S HOW WE FELT, AND STILL FEEL, SHINOGU...
...I CAN FIND MY WAY BACK TO THE STATION FROM HERE.
JUST KEEP GOING STRAIGHT DOWN THIS STREET, RIGHT?
YOU'RE COMING WITH ME, HA-TSUMI.
COME ON.
I'M NOT LETTING YOU MISS ANOTHER DAY OF SCHOOL.
Gosh.
It's like, I heard too much all at one time...
...to take it all in.
I don't know what to do any more.

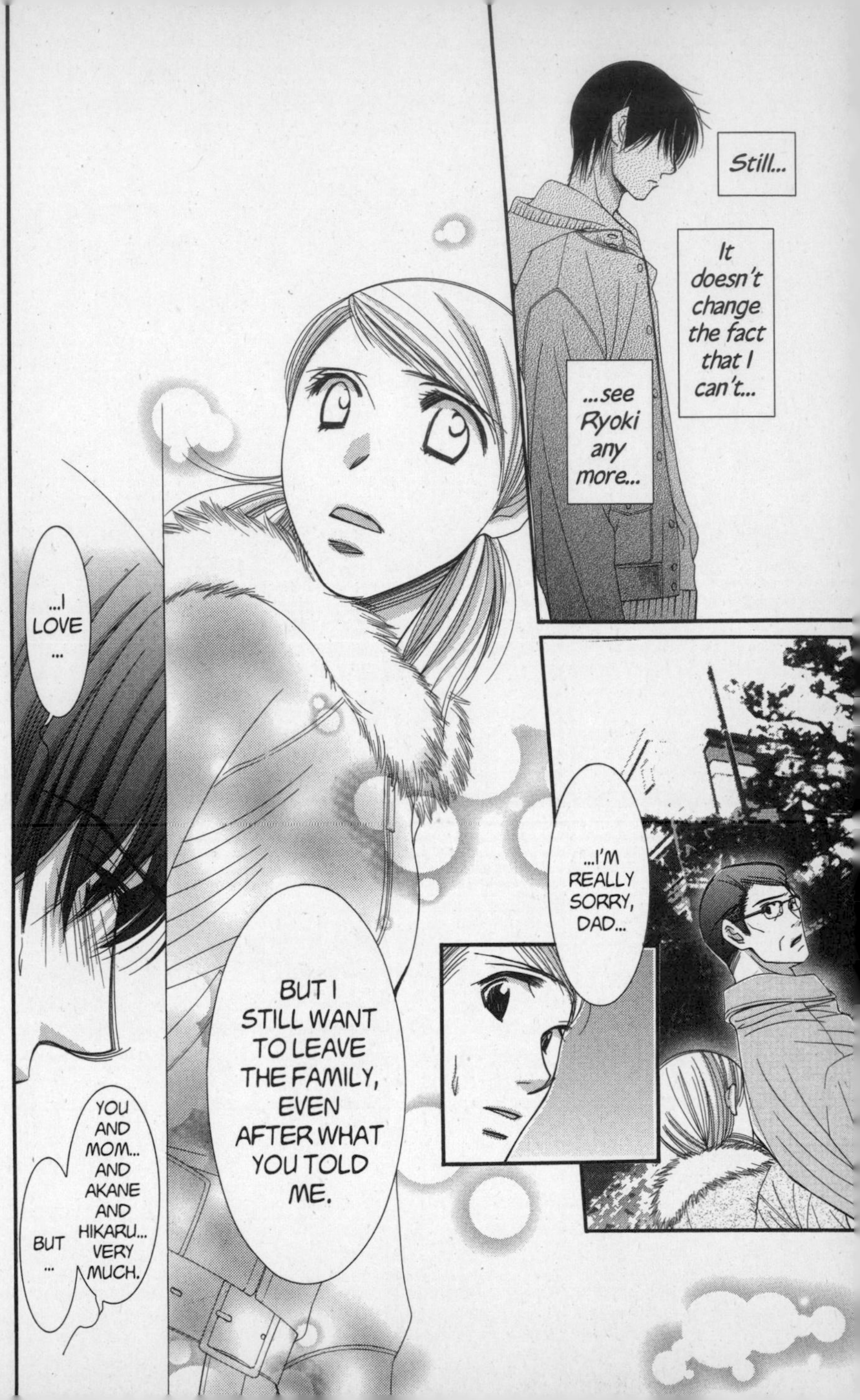
Still...
It doesn't change the fact that I can't...
...see Ryoki any more...
...I'M REALLY SORRY, DAD...
BUT I STILL WANT TO LEAVE THE FAMILY, EVEN AFTER WHAT YOU TOLD ME.
...I LOVE...
YOU AND MOM... AND AKANE AND HIKARU... VERY MUCH.
BUT...

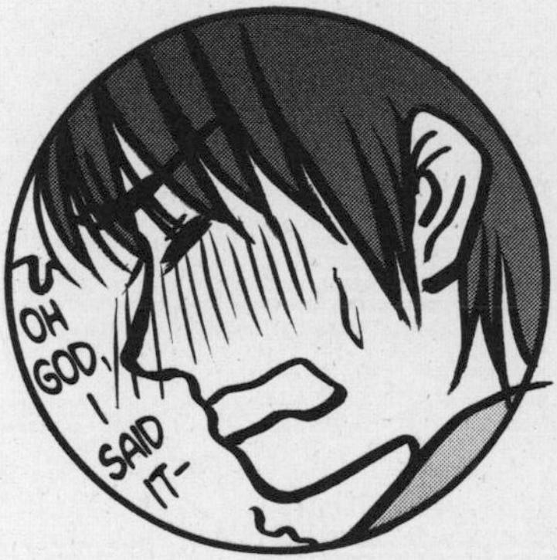
OH GOD, I SAID IT-

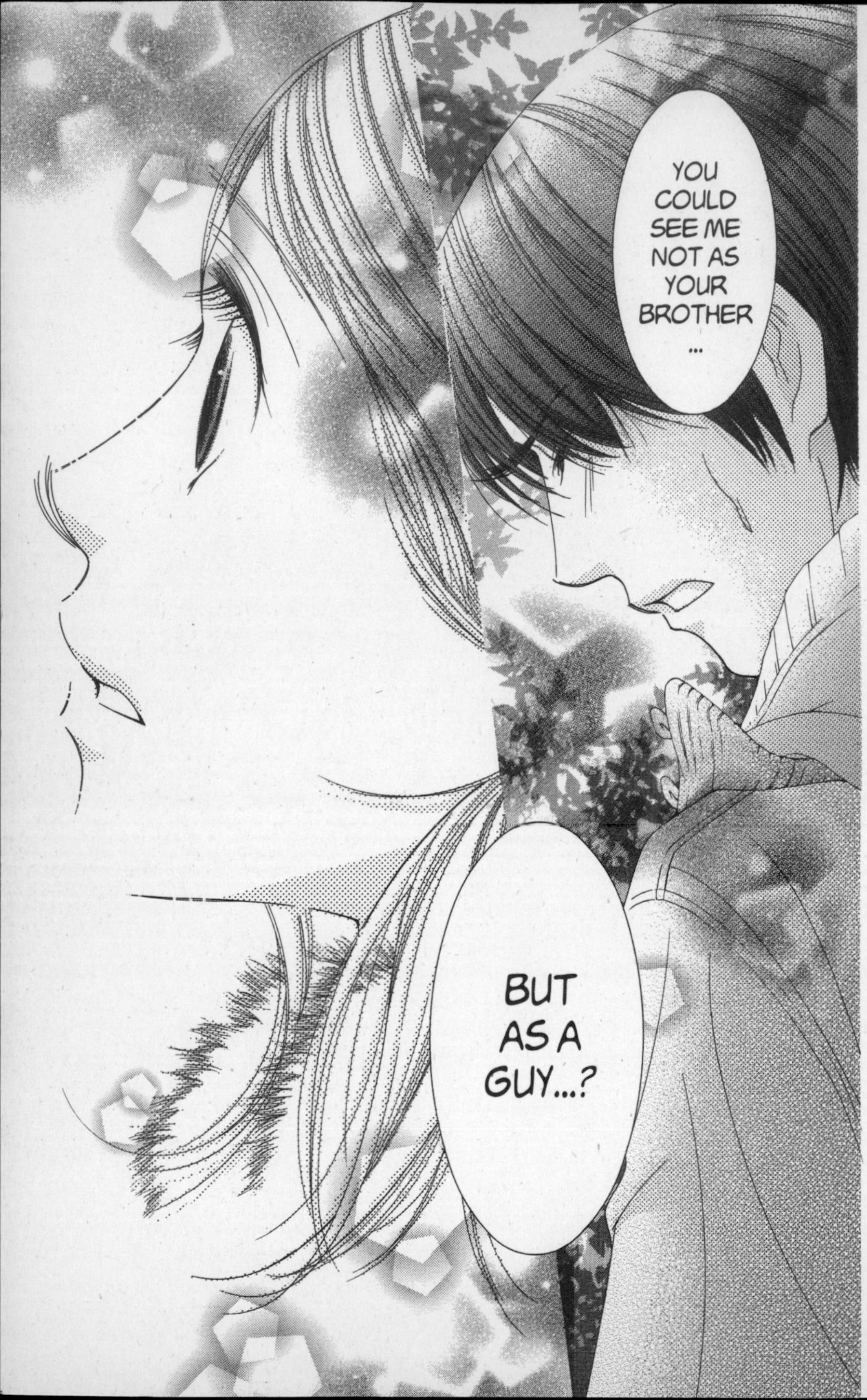
YOU COULD SEE ME NOT AS YOUR BROTHER ...
BUT AS A GUY...?

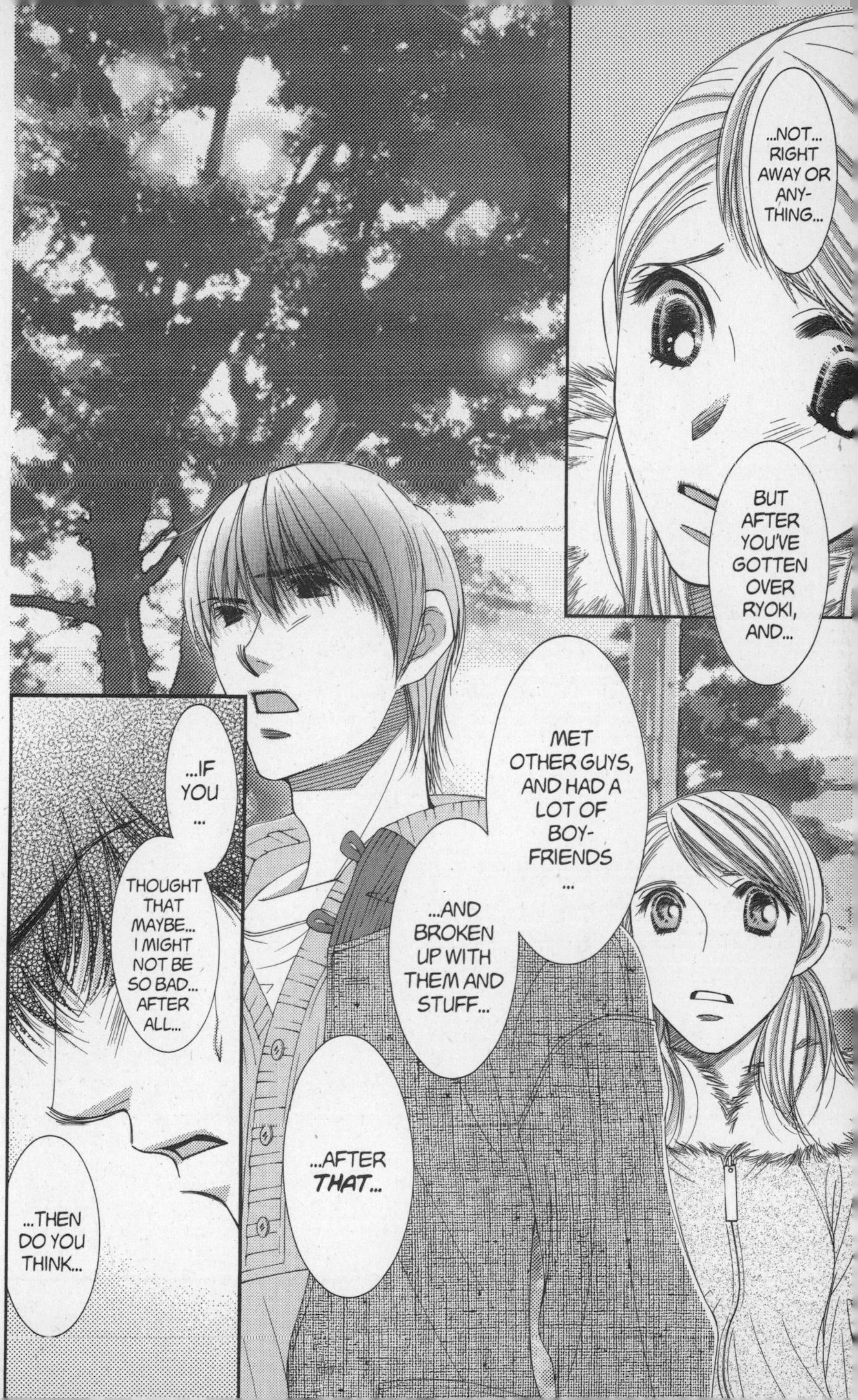
...NOT... RIGHT AWAY OR ANY-THING...
BUT AFTER YOU'VE GOTTEN OVER RYOKI, AND...
MET OTHER GUYS, AND HAD A LOT OF BOY-FRIENDS ...
...AND BROKEN UP WITH THEM AND STUFF...
...AFTER *THAT*...
...IF YOU ...
THOUGHT THAT MAYBE... I MIGHT NOT BE SO BAD... AFTER ALL...
...THEN DO YOU THINK...

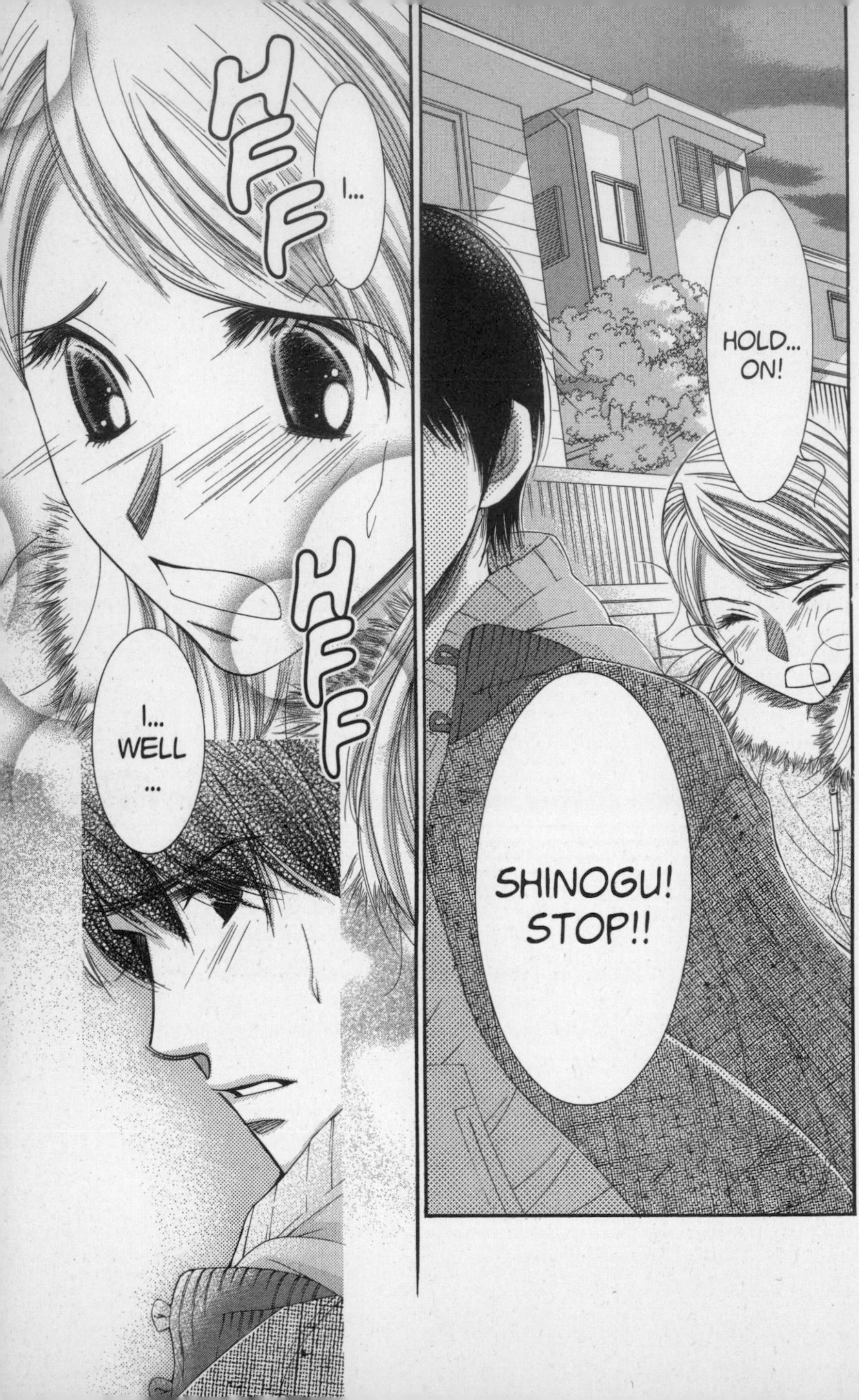
HOLD... ON!
SHINOGU! STOP!!
I...
HEFF
HEFF
I... WELL ...

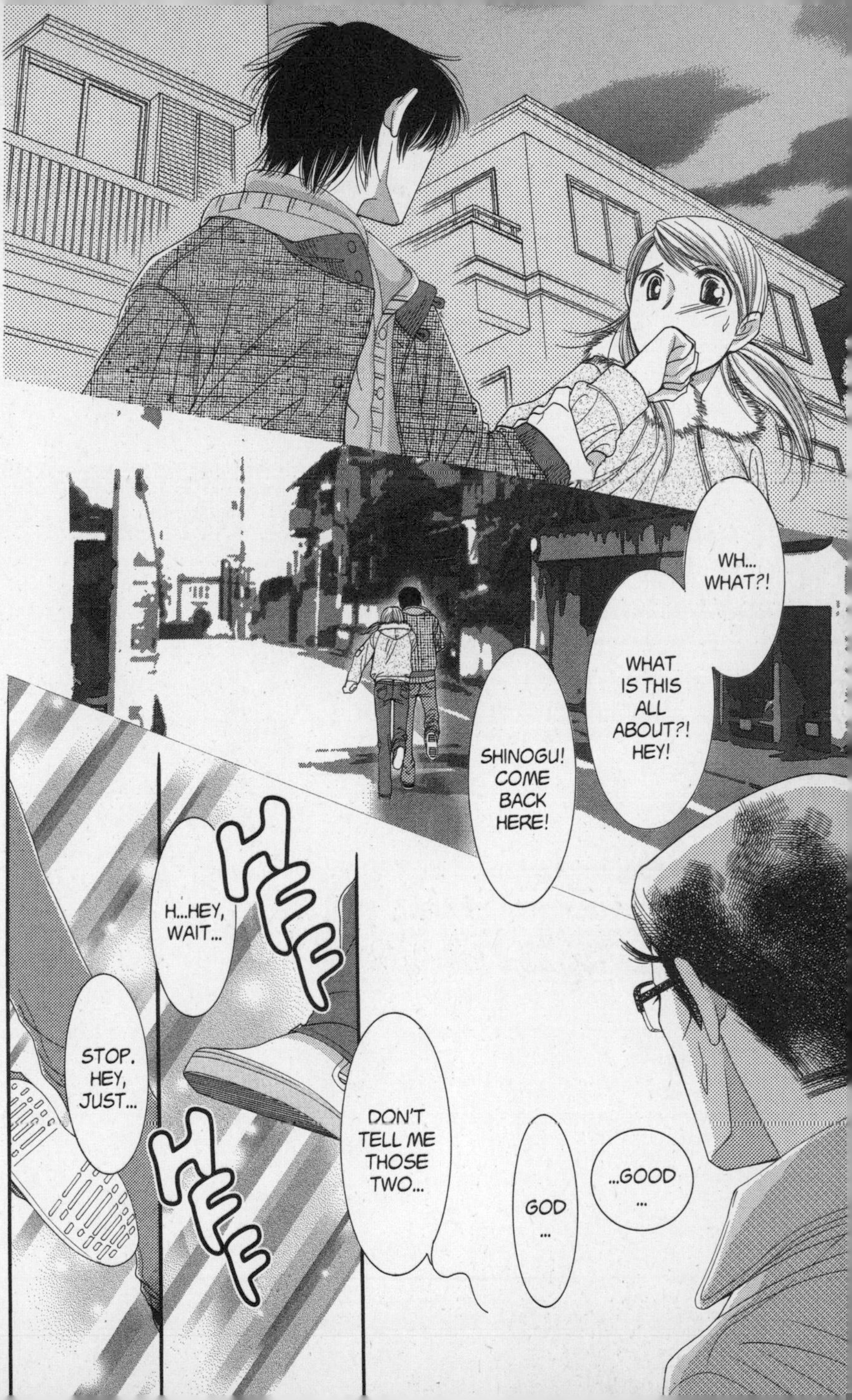
WH... WHAT?!
WHAT IS THIS ALL ABOUT?! HEY!
SHINOGU! COME BACK HERE!
...GOOD ...
GOD ...
DON'T TELL ME THOSE TWO...
H...HEY, WAIT...
HEF
STOP. HEY, JUST...
HEF

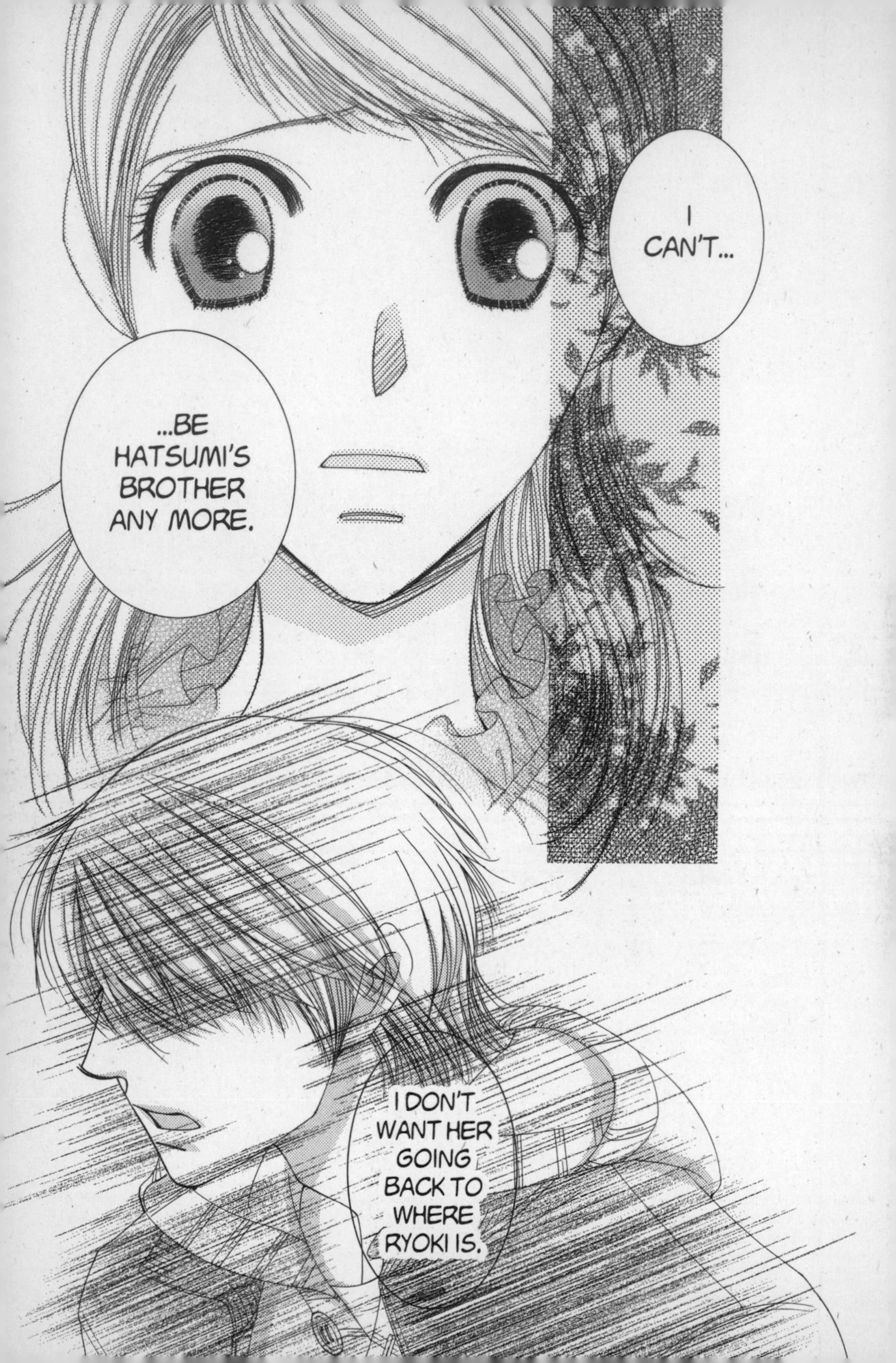
I CAN'T...
...BE HATSUMI'S BROTHER ANY MORE.
I DON'T WANT HER GOING BACK TO WHERE RYOKI IS.

Chapter 48

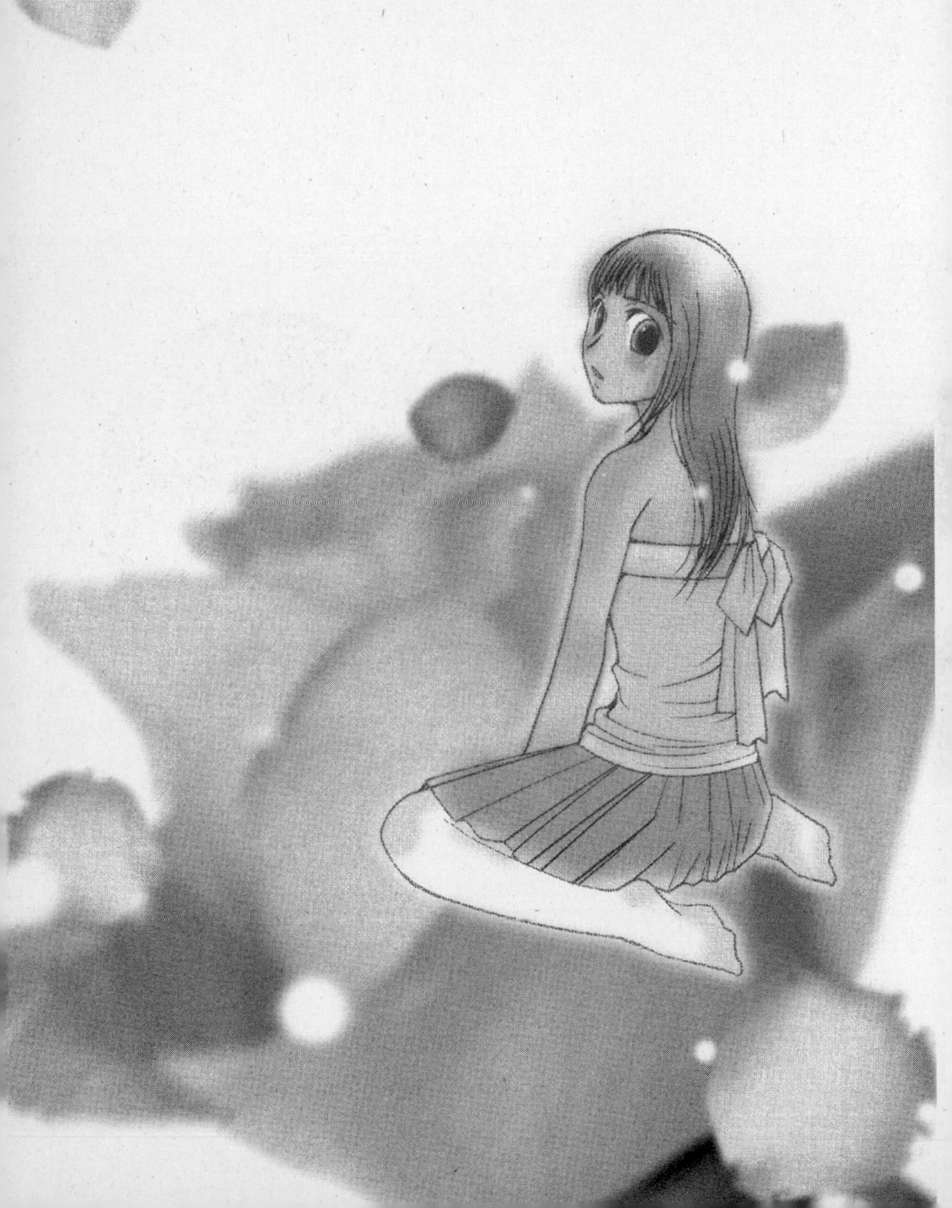

hot gimmick

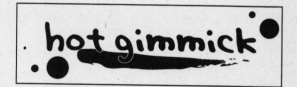

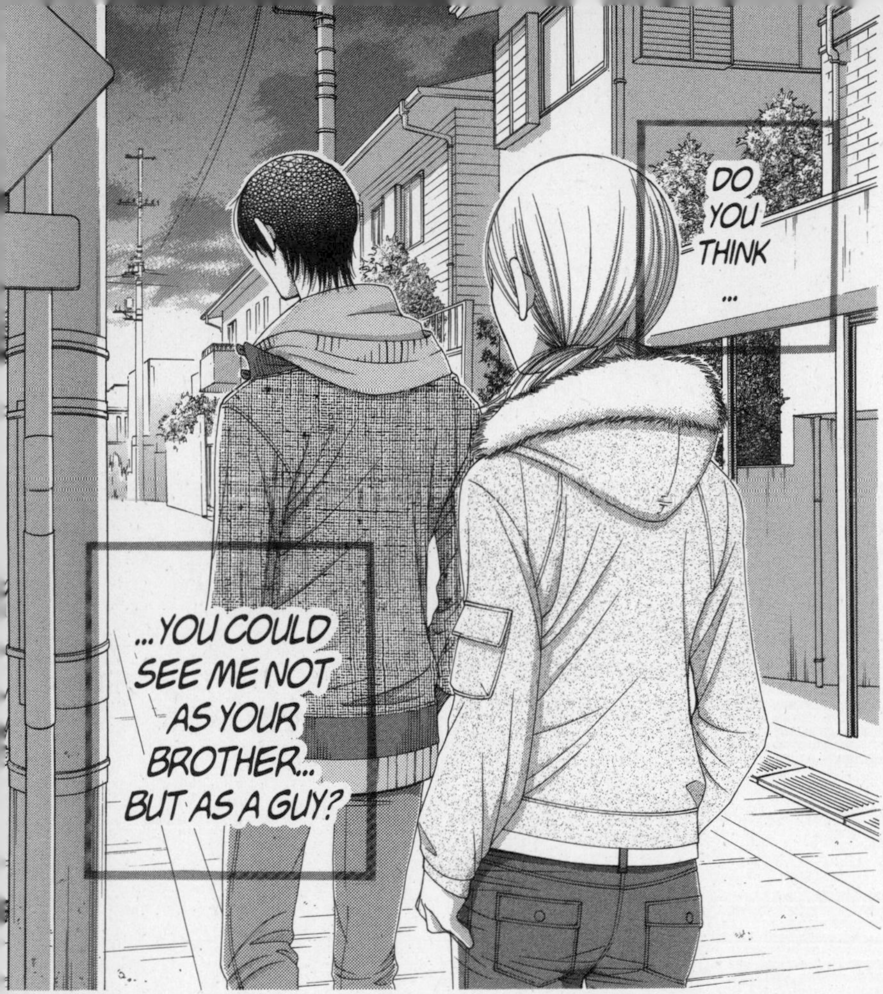
DO YOU THINK ...
...YOU COULD SEE ME NOT AS YOUR BROTHER... BUT AS A GUY?

hot gimmick

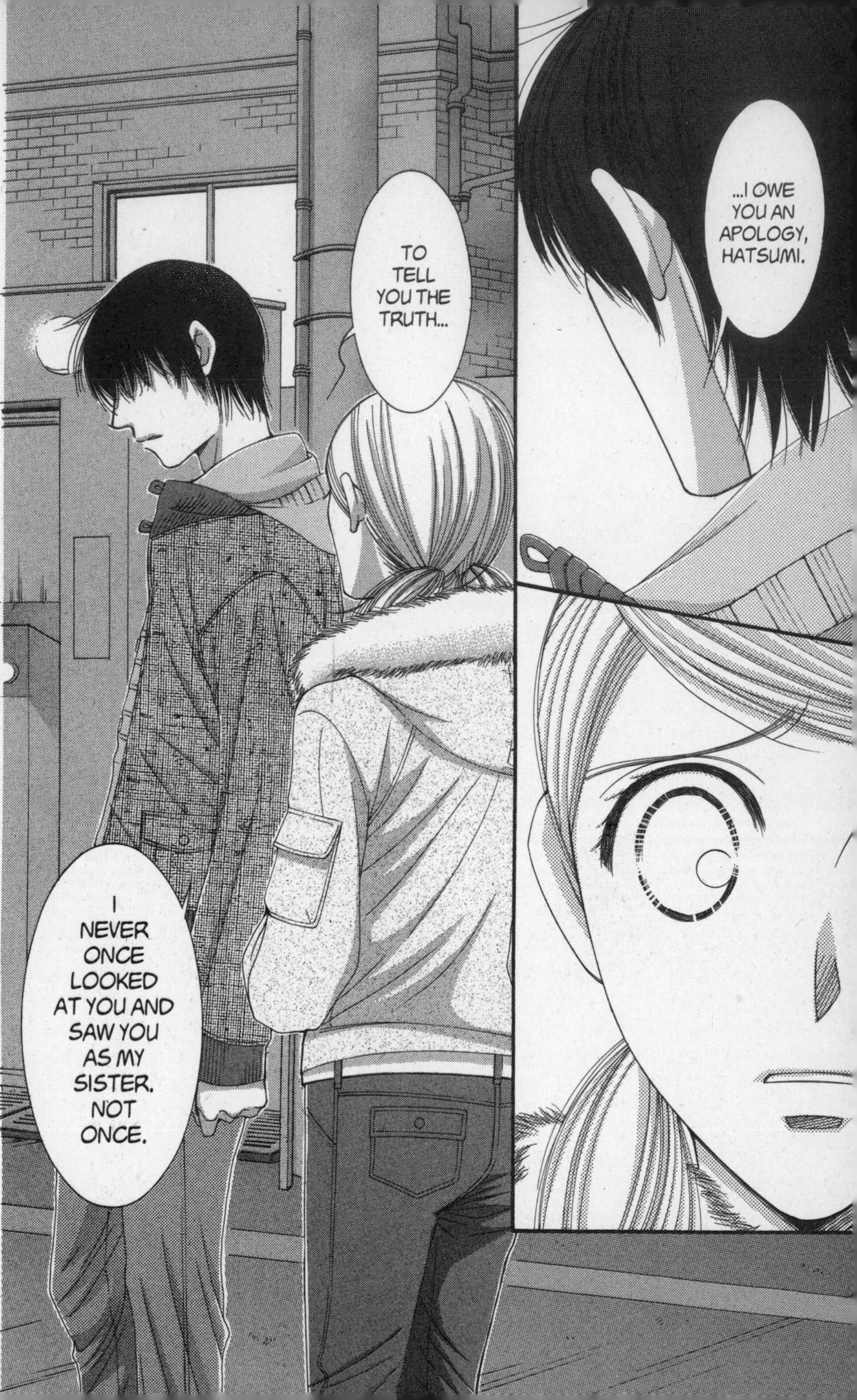
...I OWE YOU AN APOLOGY, HATSUMI.
TO TELL YOU THE TRUTH...
I NEVER ONCE LOOKED AT YOU AND SAW YOU AS MY SISTER. NOT ONCE.

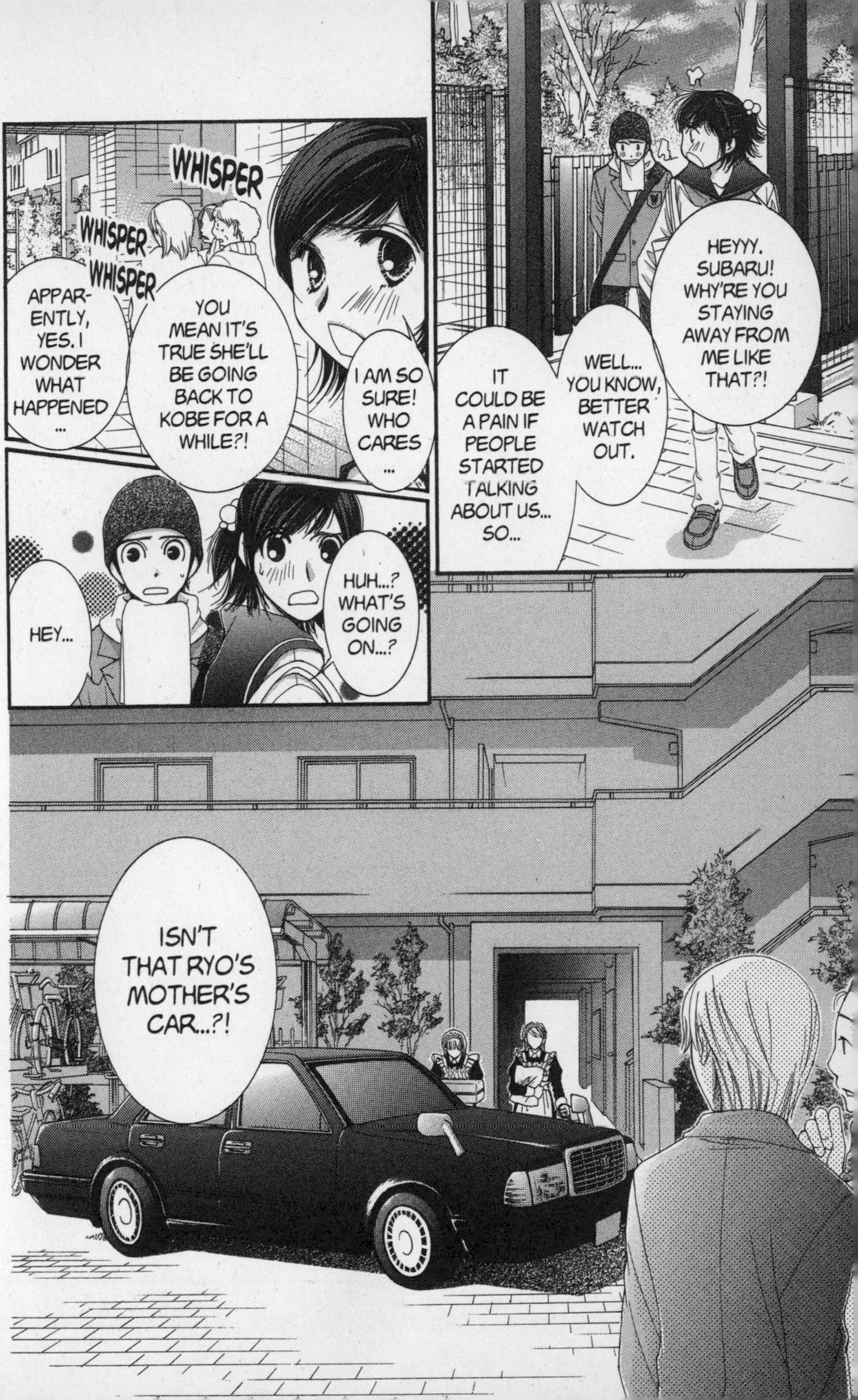
HEYYY. SUBARU! WHY'RE YOU STAYING AWAY FROM ME LIKE THAT?!
WELL... YOU KNOW, BETTER WATCH OUT.
IT COULD BE A PAIN IF PEOPLE STARTED TALKING ABOUT US... SO...
WHISPER
WHISPER
WHISPER
YOU MEAN IT'S TRUE SHE'LL BE GOING BACK TO KOBE FOR A WHILE?!
APPAR-ENTLY, YES. I WONDER WHAT HAPPENED...
I AM SO SURE! WHO CARES...
HUH...? WHAT'S GOING ON...?
HEY...
ISN'T THAT RYO'S MOTHER'S CAR...?!

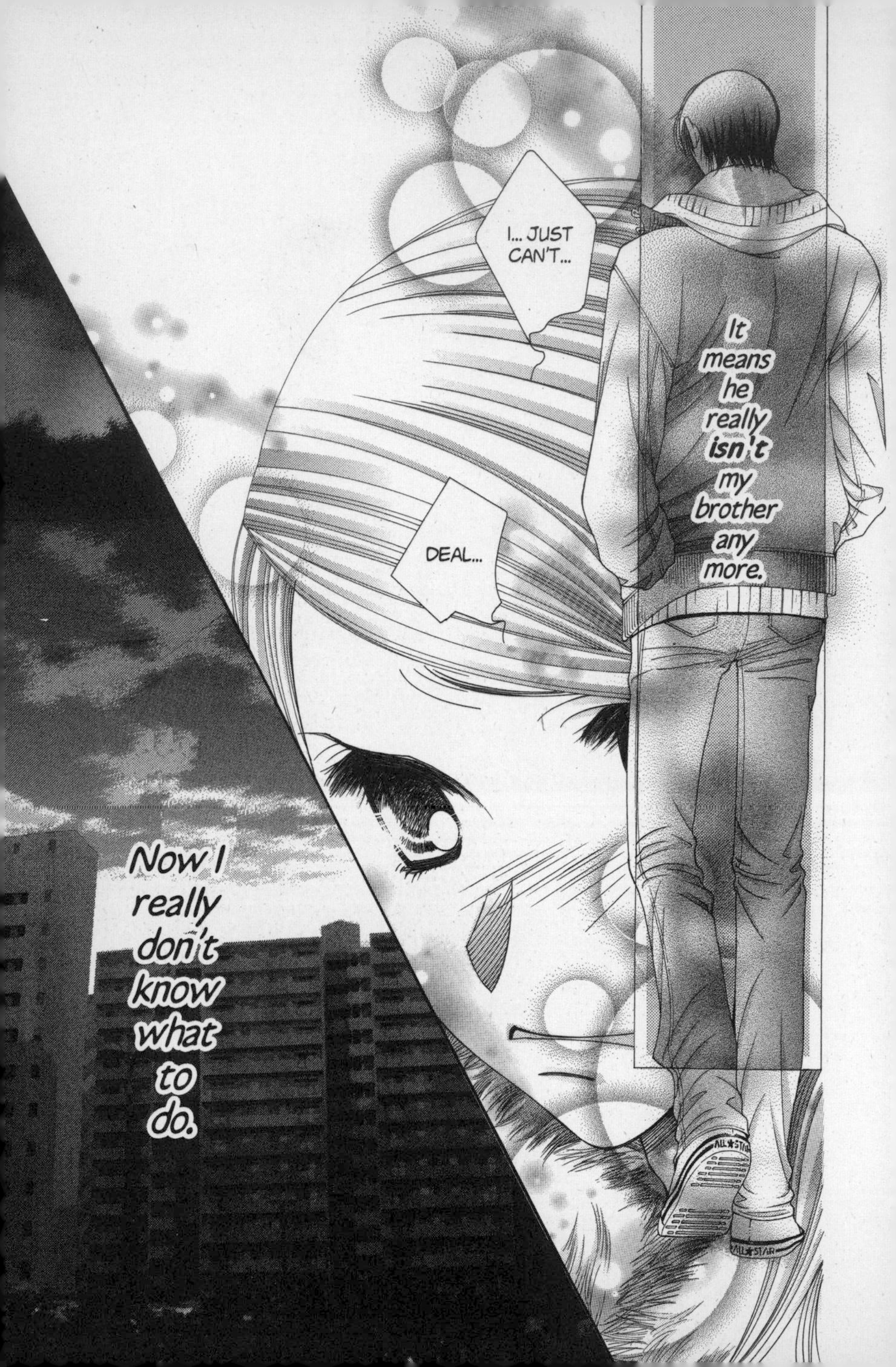
It means he really isn't my brother any more.
I... JUST CAN'T...
DEAL...
Now I really don't know what to do.

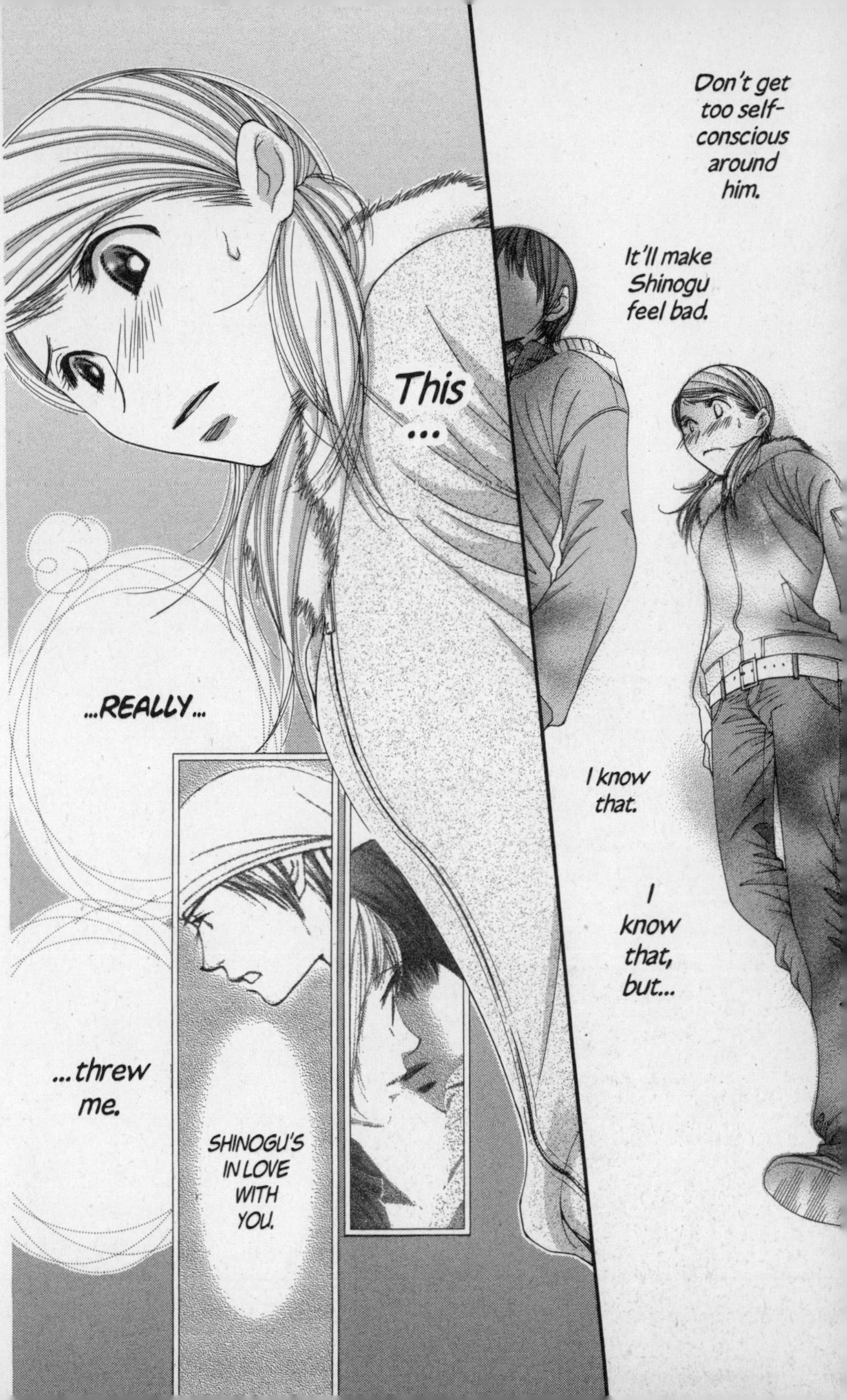

Don't get too self-conscious around him.
It'll make Shinogu feel bad.
I know that.
I know that, but...
This...
...REALLY...
...threw me.
SHINOGU'S IN LOVE WITH YOU.

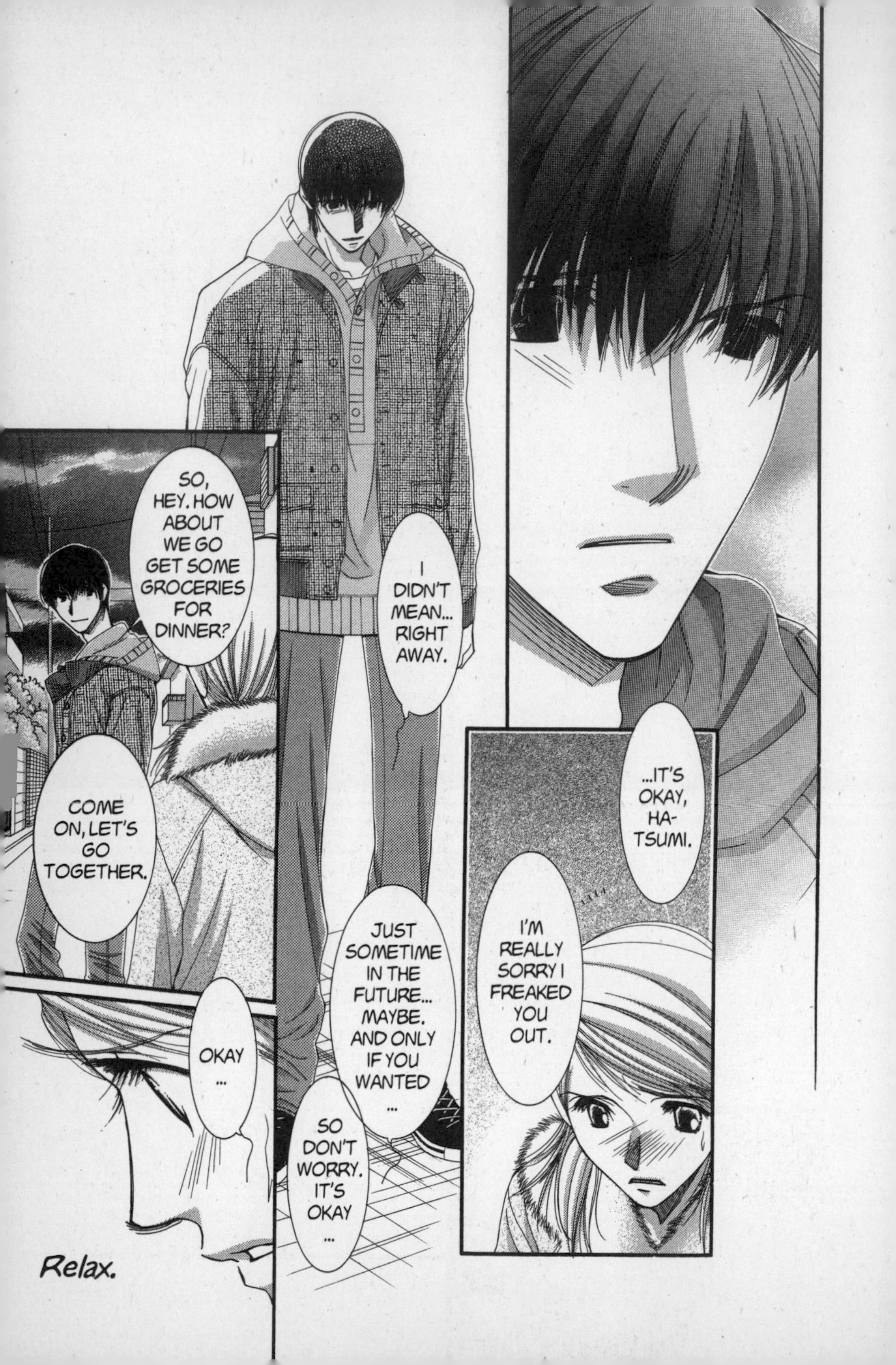
...IT'S OKAY, HA-TSUMI.
I'M REALLY SORRY I FREAKED YOU OUT.
I DIDN'T MEAN... RIGHT AWAY.
JUST SOMETIME IN THE FUTURE... MAYBE. AND ONLY IF YOU WANTED ...
SO DON'T WORRY. IT'S OKAY ...
SO, HEY. HOW ABOUT WE GO GET SOME GROCERIES FOR DINNER?
COME ON, LET'S GO TOGETHER.
OKAY ...
Relax.

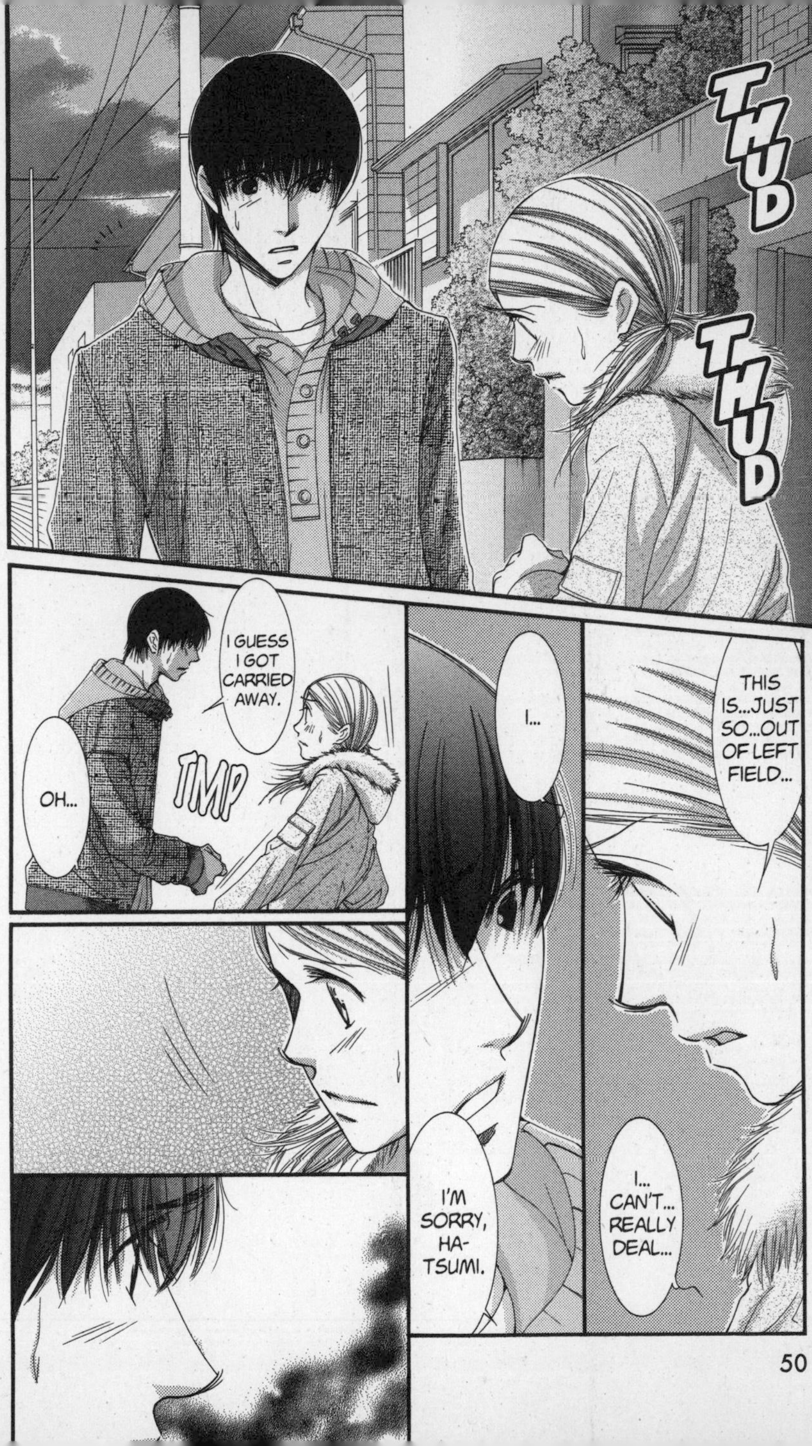
THUD
THUD
THIS IS...JUST SO...OUT OF LEFT FIELD...
I... CAN'T... REALLY DEAL...
I...
I'M SORRY, HA-TSUMI.
I GUESS I GOT CARRIED AWAY.
OH...
TMP

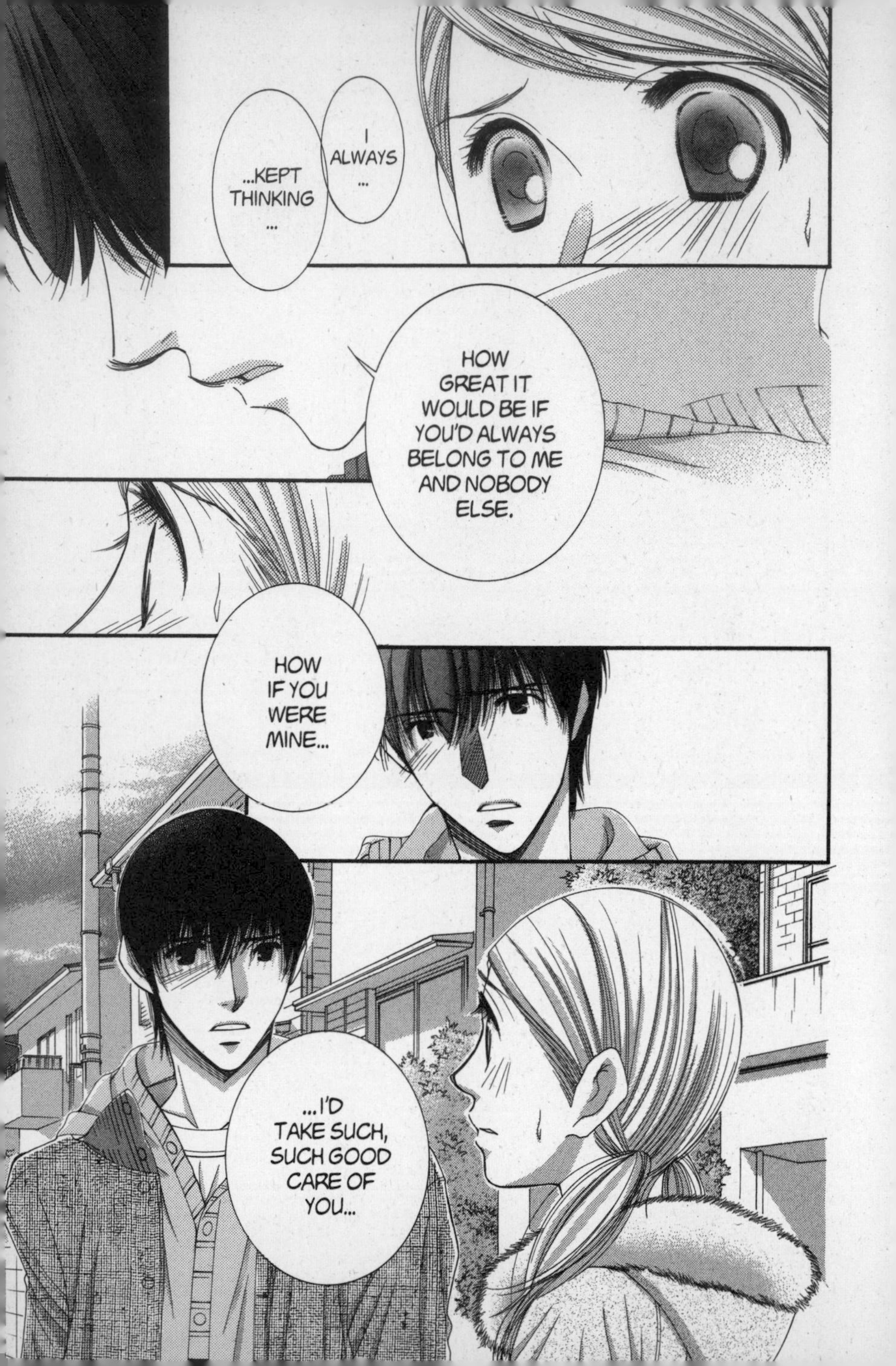
I ALWAYS...
...KEPT THINKING...
HOW GREAT IT WOULD BE IF YOU'D ALWAYS BELONG TO ME AND NOBODY ELSE.
HOW IF YOU WERE MINE...
...I'D TAKE SUCH, SUCH GOOD CARE OF YOU...

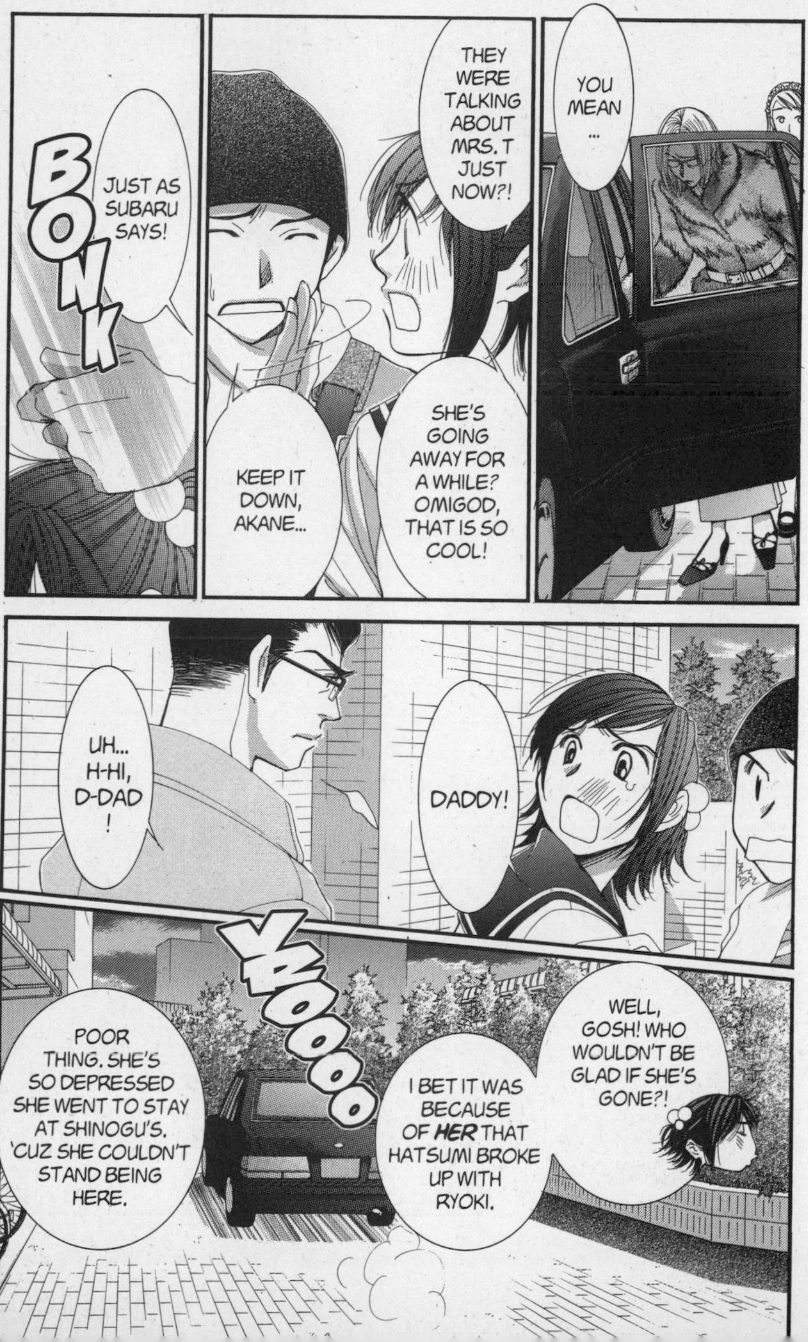
YOU MEAN ...
THEY WERE TALKING ABOUT MRS. T JUST NOW?!
SHE'S GOING AWAY FOR A WHILE? OMIGOD, THAT IS SO COOL!
KEEP IT DOWN, AKANE...
JUST AS SUBARU SAYS!
BONK
DADDY!
UH... H-HI, D-DAD!
VROOOO
WELL, GOSH! WHO WOULDN'T BE GLAD IF SHE'S GONE?!
I BET IT WAS BECAUSE OF HER THAT HATSUMI BROKE UP WITH RYOKI.
POOR THING. SHE'S SO DEPRESSED SHE WENT TO STAY AT SHINOGU'S. 'CUZ SHE COULDN'T STAND BEING HERE.

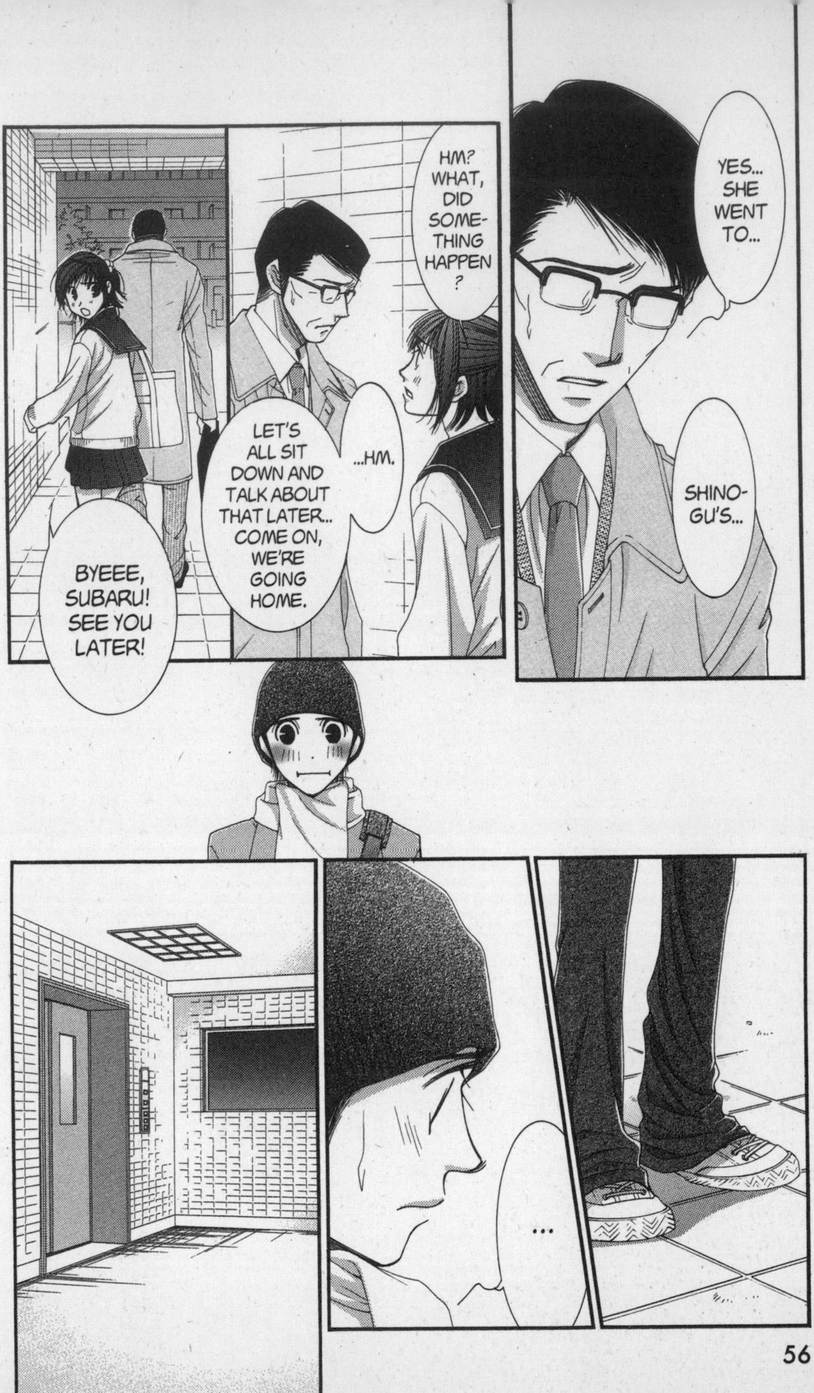
YES... SHE WENT TO...
SHINOGU'S...
HM? WHAT, DID SOMETHING HAPPEN?
...HM.
LET'S ALL SIT DOWN AND TALK ABOUT THAT LATER... COME ON, WE'RE GOING HOME.
BYEEE, SUBARU! SEE YOU LATER!
...
...

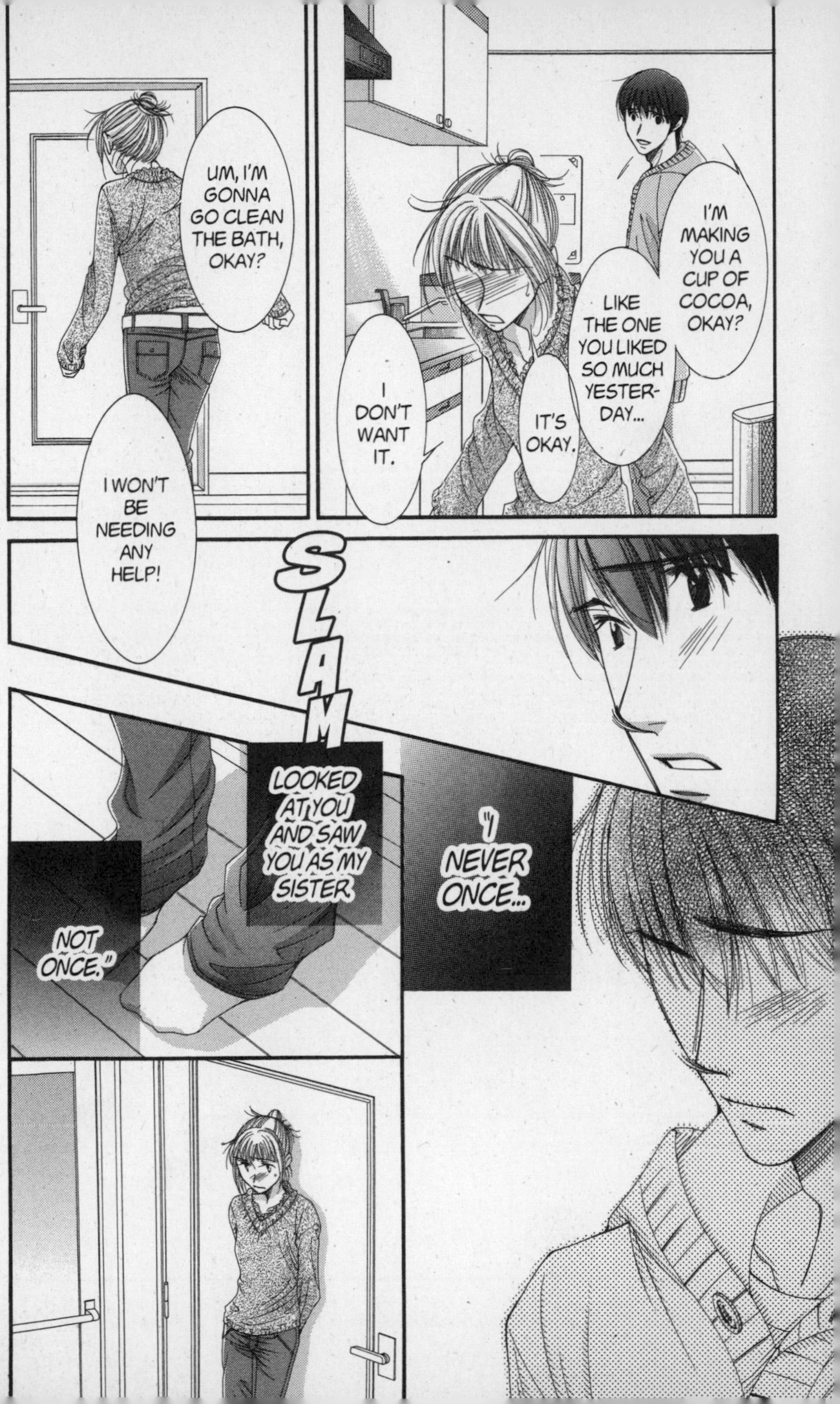
I'M MAKING YOU A CUP OF COCOA, OKAY?
LIKE THE ONE YOU LIKED SO MUCH YESTER-DAY...
IT'S OKAY.
I DON'T WANT IT.
UM, I'M GONNA GO CLEAN THE BATH, OKAY?
I WON'T BE NEEDING ANY HELP!
SLAM
"I NEVER ONCE...
LOOKED AT YOU AND SAW YOU AS MY SISTER.
NOT ONCE."

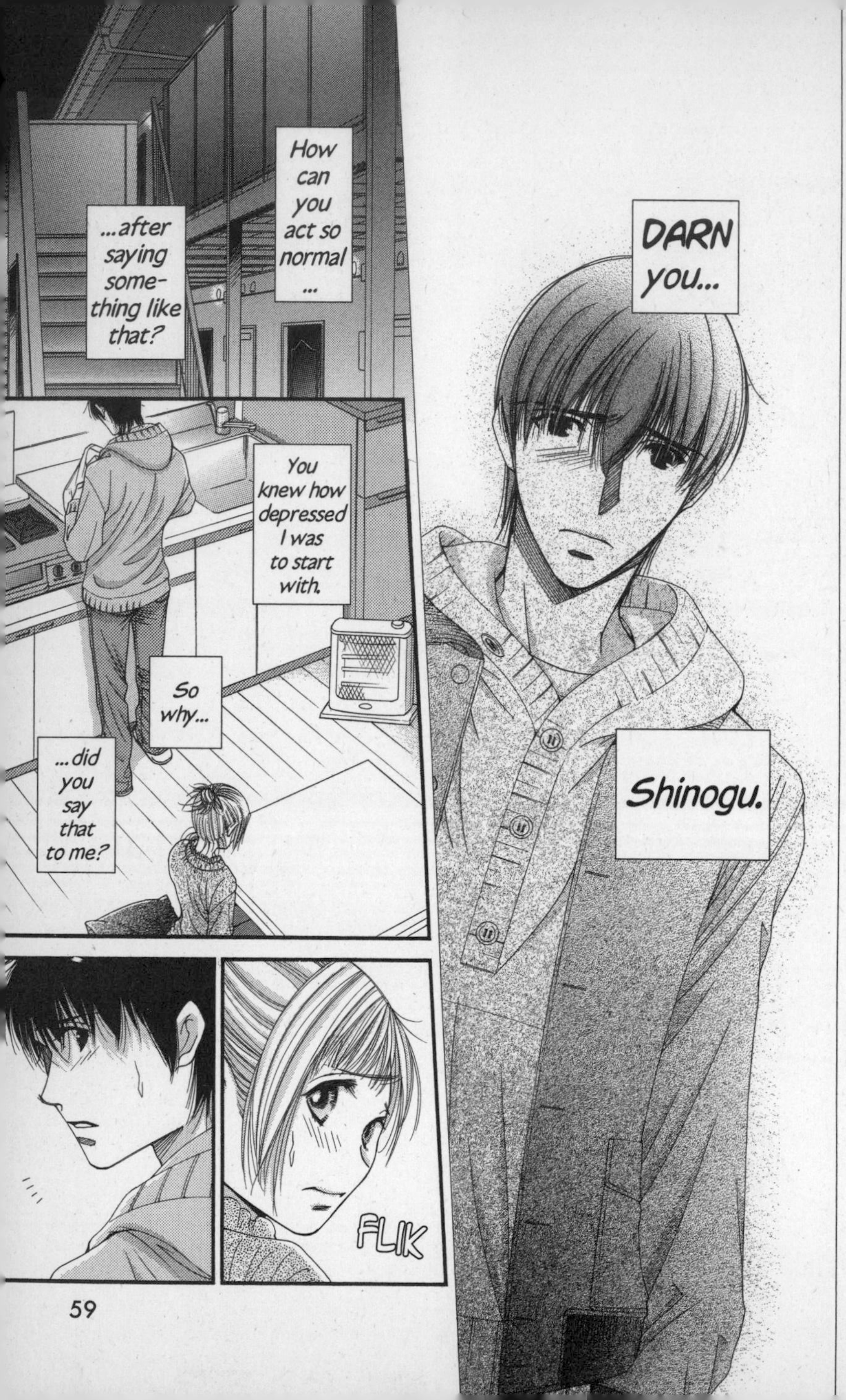
DARN you...
Shinogu.
How can you act so normal ...
...after saying some-thing like that?
You knew how depressed I was to start with.
So why...
...did you say that to me?
FLIK

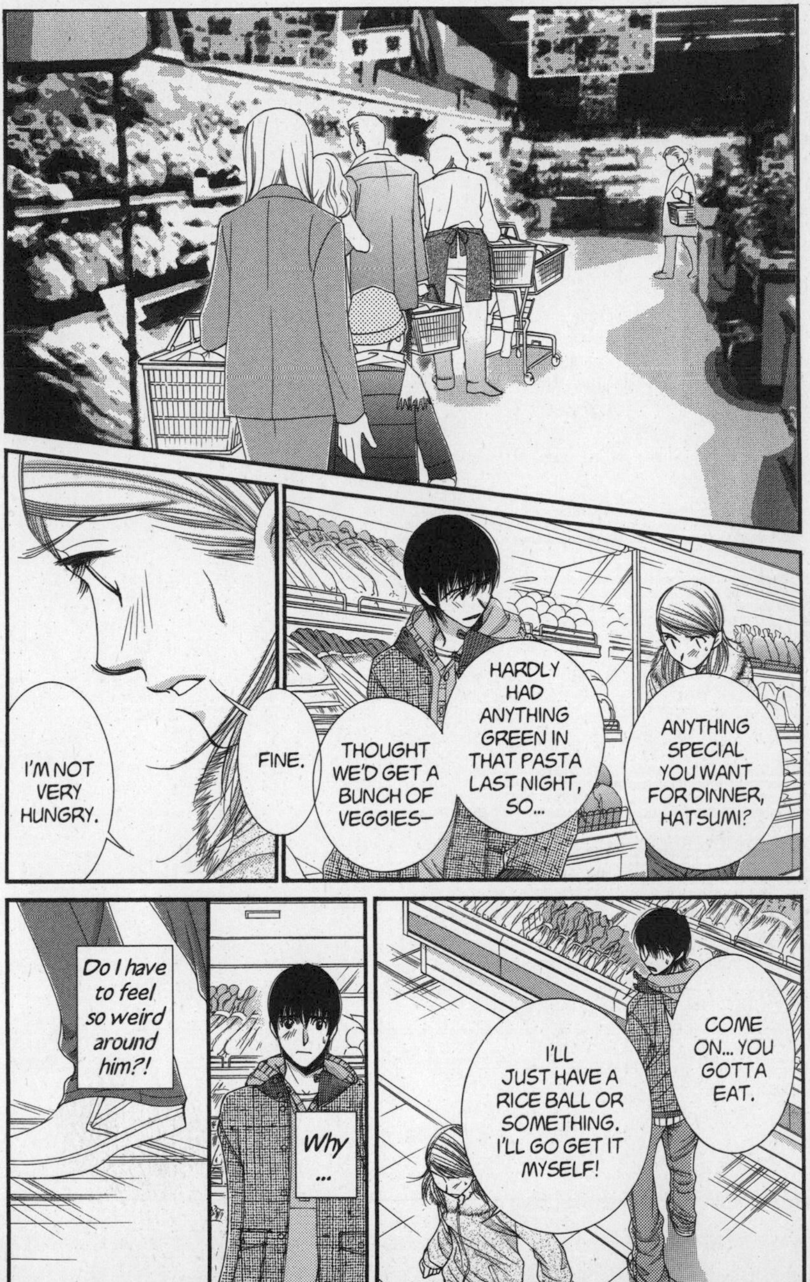
ANYTHING SPECIAL YOU WANT FOR DINNER, HATSUMI?
HARDLY HAD ANYTHING GREEN IN THAT PASTA LAST NIGHT, SO...
THOUGHT WE'D GET A BUNCH OF VEGGIES—
FINE.
I'M NOT VERY HUNGRY.
COME ON... YOU GOTTA EAT.
I'LL JUST HAVE A RICE BALL OR SOMETHING. I'LL GO GET IT MYSELF!
Why ...
Do I have to feel so weird around him?!

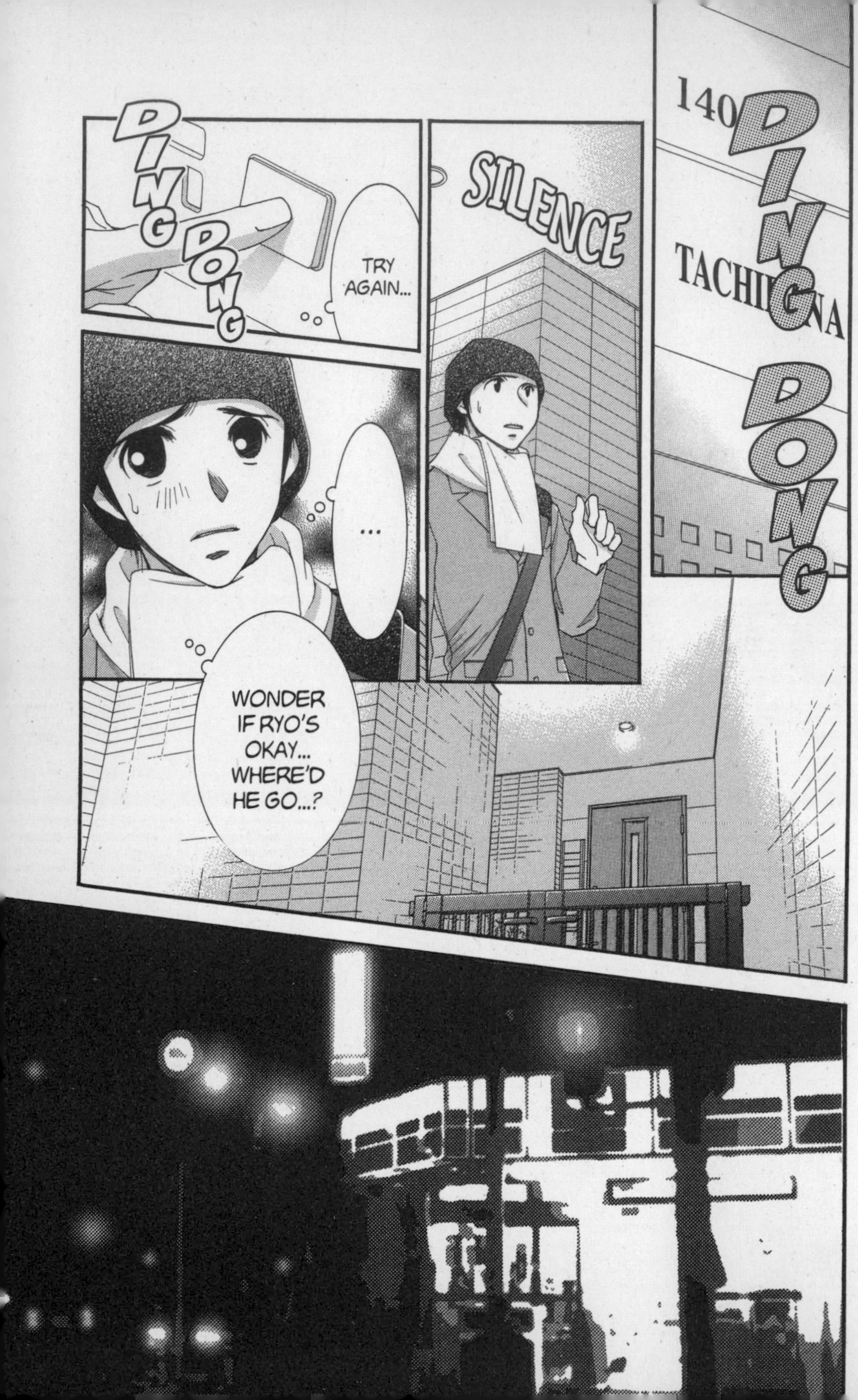
140
DING DONG
SILENCE
DING DONG
TRY AGAIN...
...
WONDER IF RYO'S OKAY... WHERE'D HE GO...?

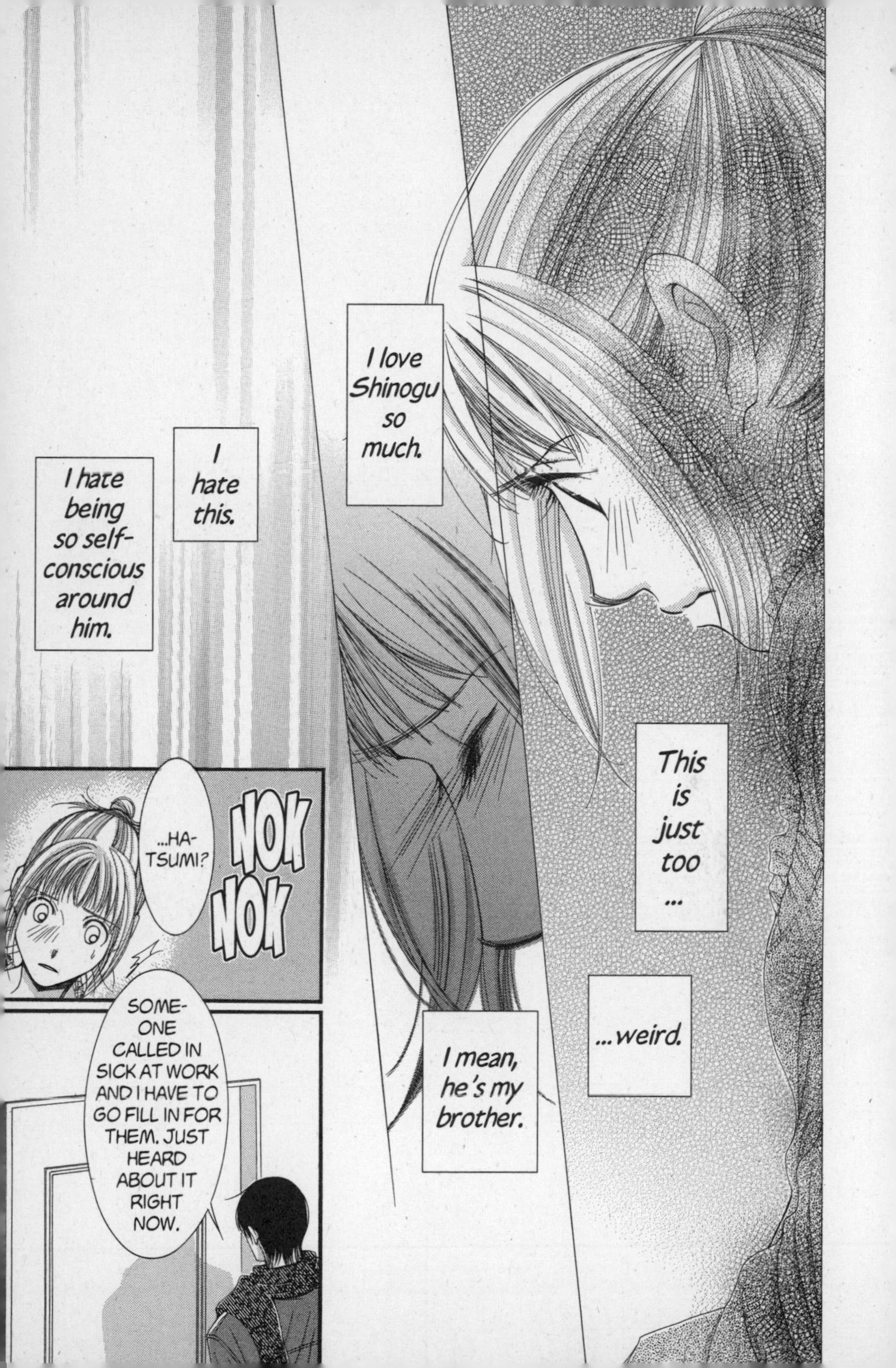
I love Shinogu so much.
This is just too ...
...weird.
I mean, he's my brother.
I hate this.
I hate being so self-conscious around him.
NOK NOK
...HA-TSUMI?
SOME-ONE CALLED IN SICK AT WORK AND I HAVE TO GO FILL IN FOR THEM. JUST HEARD ABOUT IT RIGHT NOW.

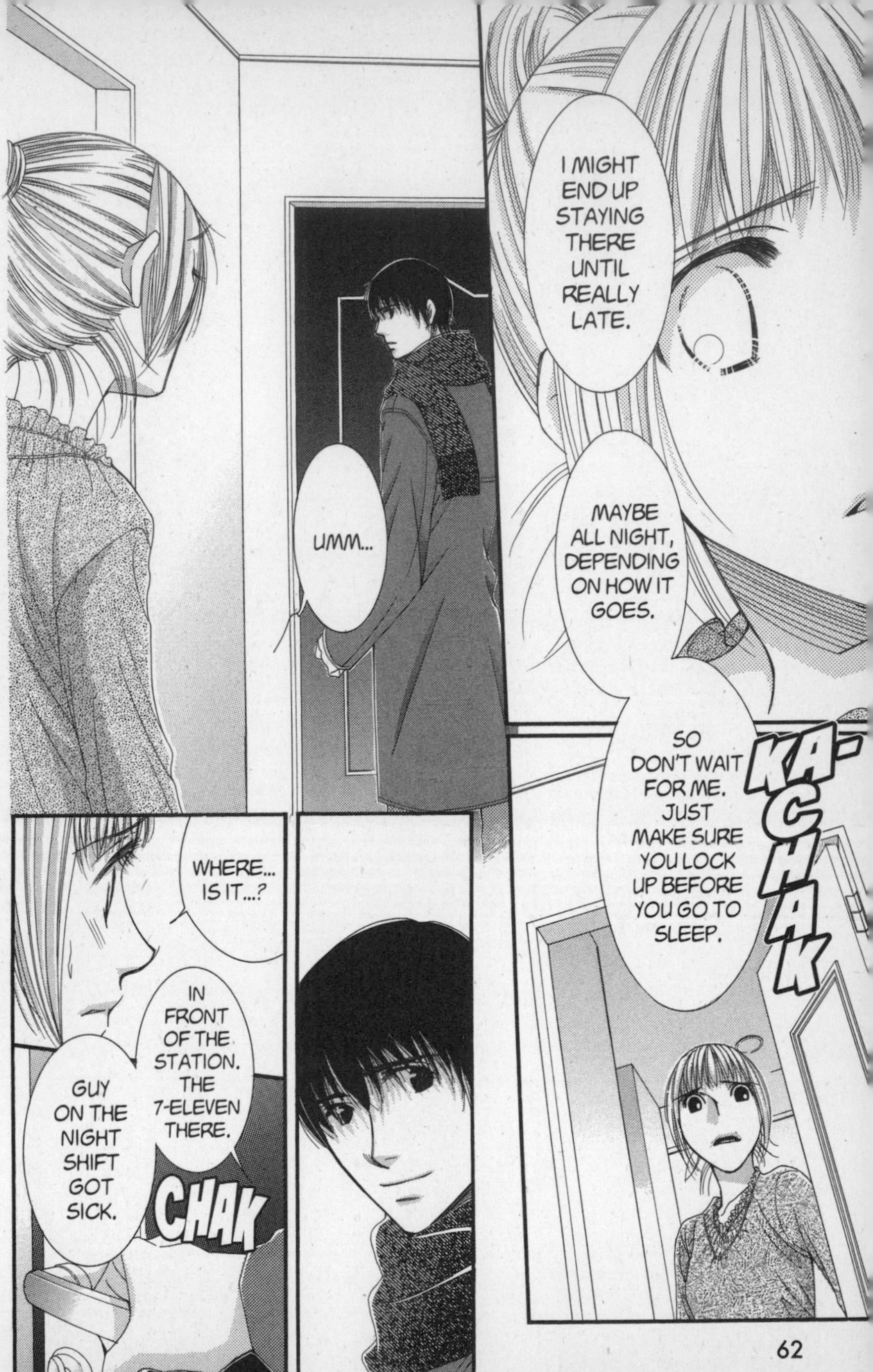
I MIGHT END UP STAYING THERE UNTIL REALLY LATE.
MAYBE ALL NIGHT, DEPENDING ON HOW IT GOES.
SO DON'T WAIT FOR ME. JUST MAKE SURE YOU LOCK UP BEFORE YOU GO TO SLEEP.
KA-CHAK
UMM...
WHERE... IS IT...?
IN FRONT OF THE STATION. THE 7-ELEVEN THERE.
GUY ON THE NIGHT SHIFT GOT SICK.
CHAK

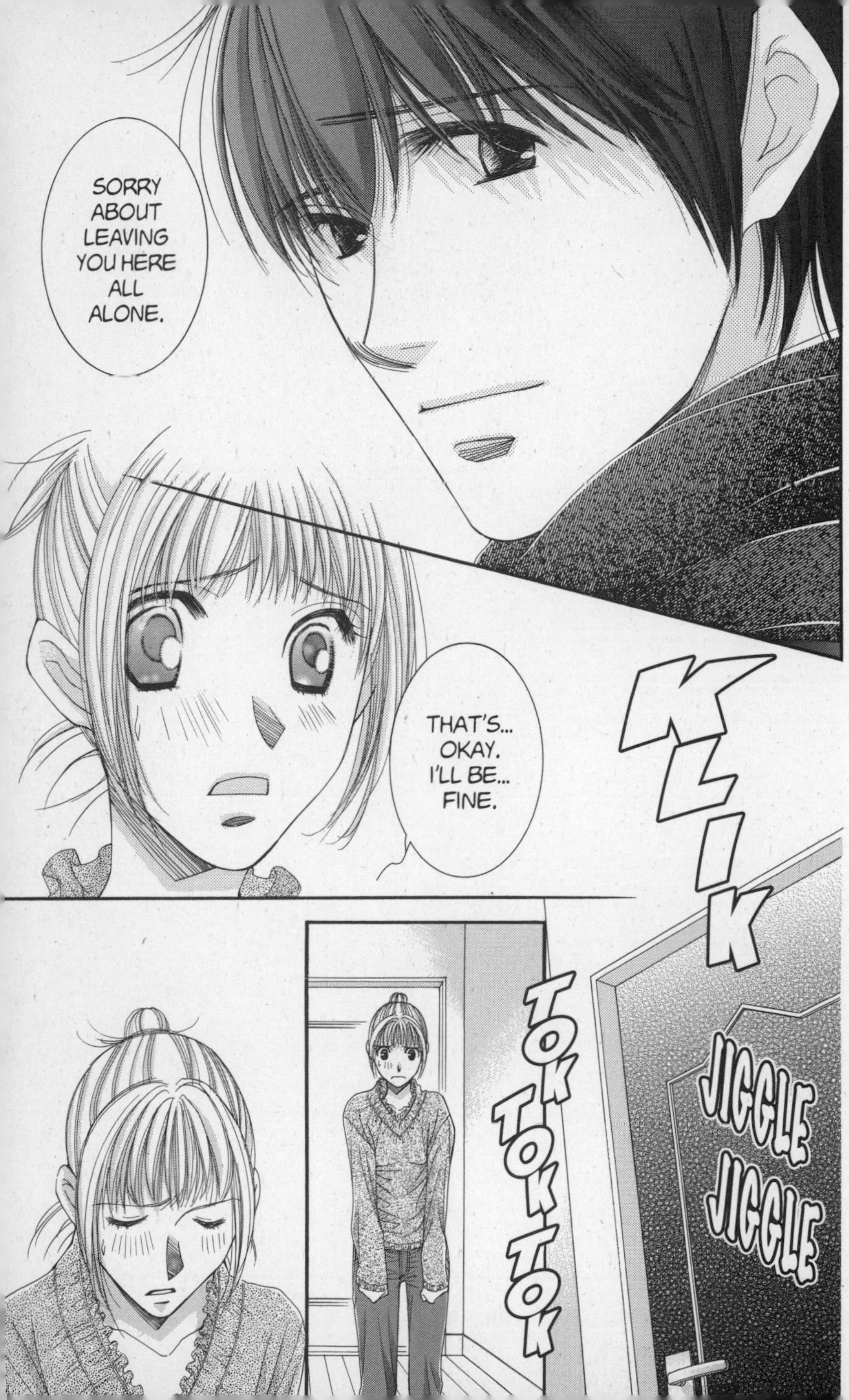
SORRY ABOUT LEAVING YOU HERE ALL ALONE.
THAT'S... OKAY. I'LL BE... FINE.
KLIK
JIGGLE JIGGLE
TOK TOK TOK TOK

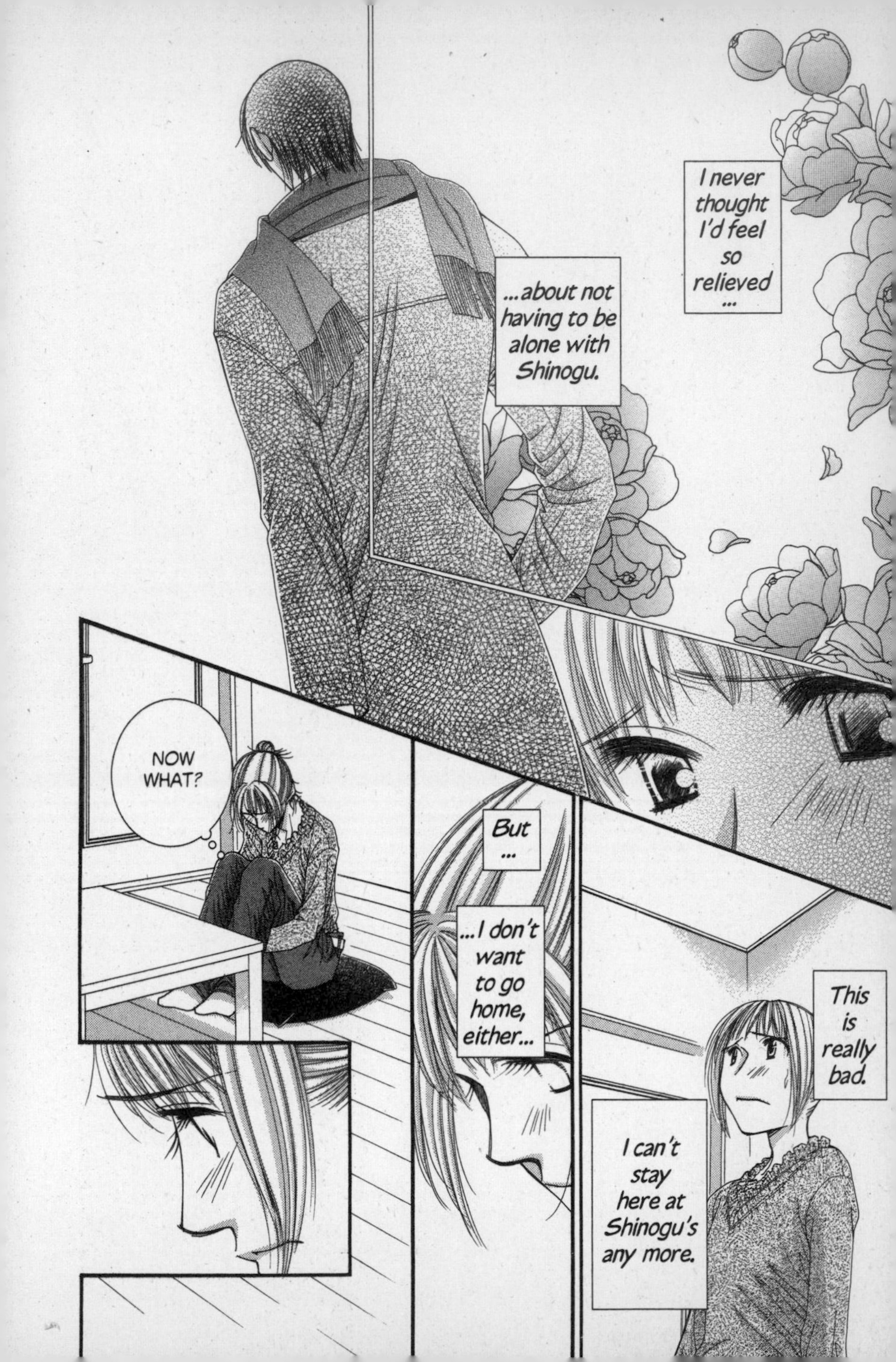
I never thought I'd feel so relieved ...
...about not having to be alone with Shinogu.
This is really bad.
I can't stay here at Shinogu's any more.
But ...
...I don't want to go home, either...
NOW WHAT?

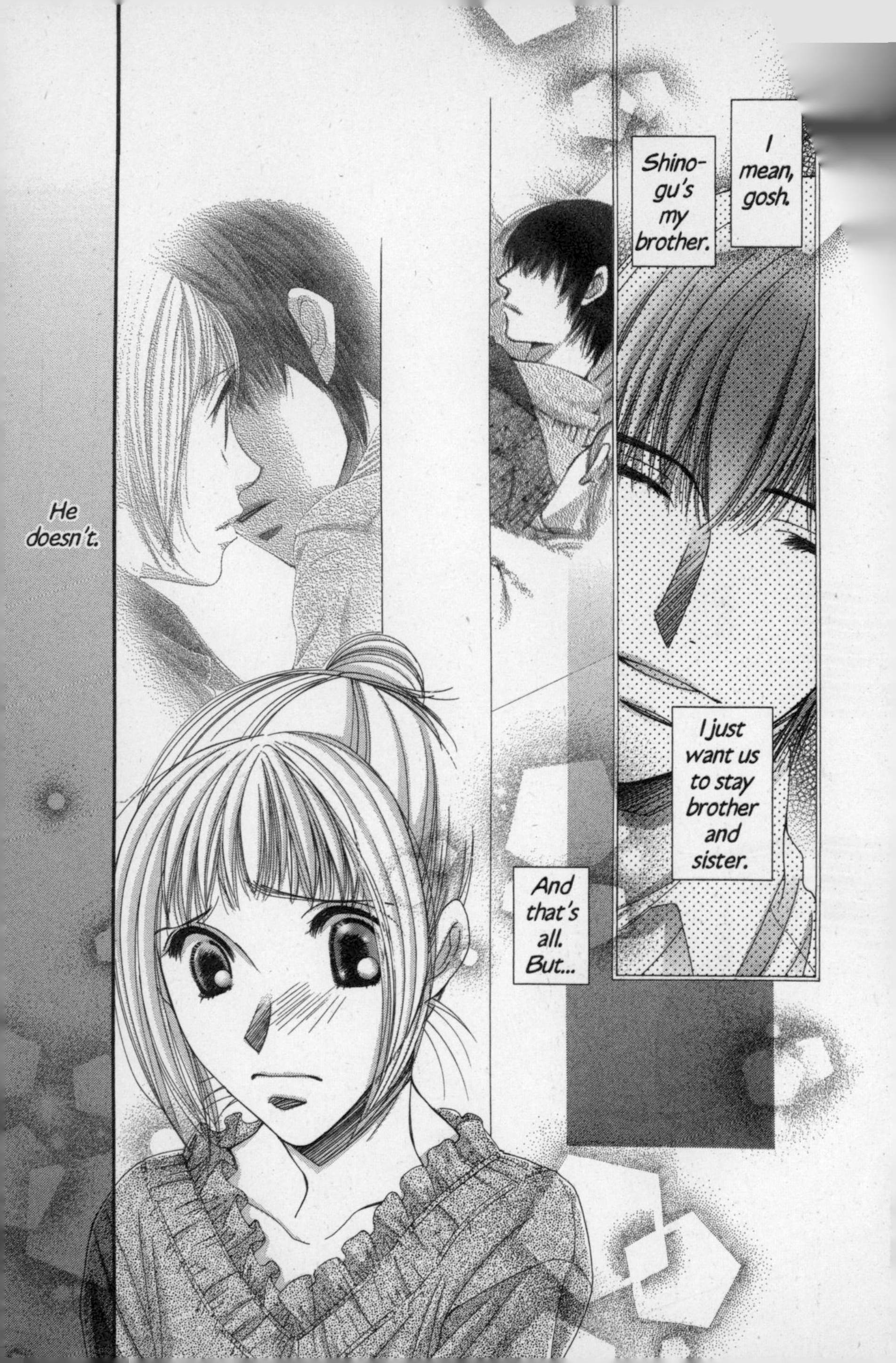
I mean, gosh.
Shinogu's my brother.
I just want us to stay brother and sister.
And that's all. But...
He doesn't.

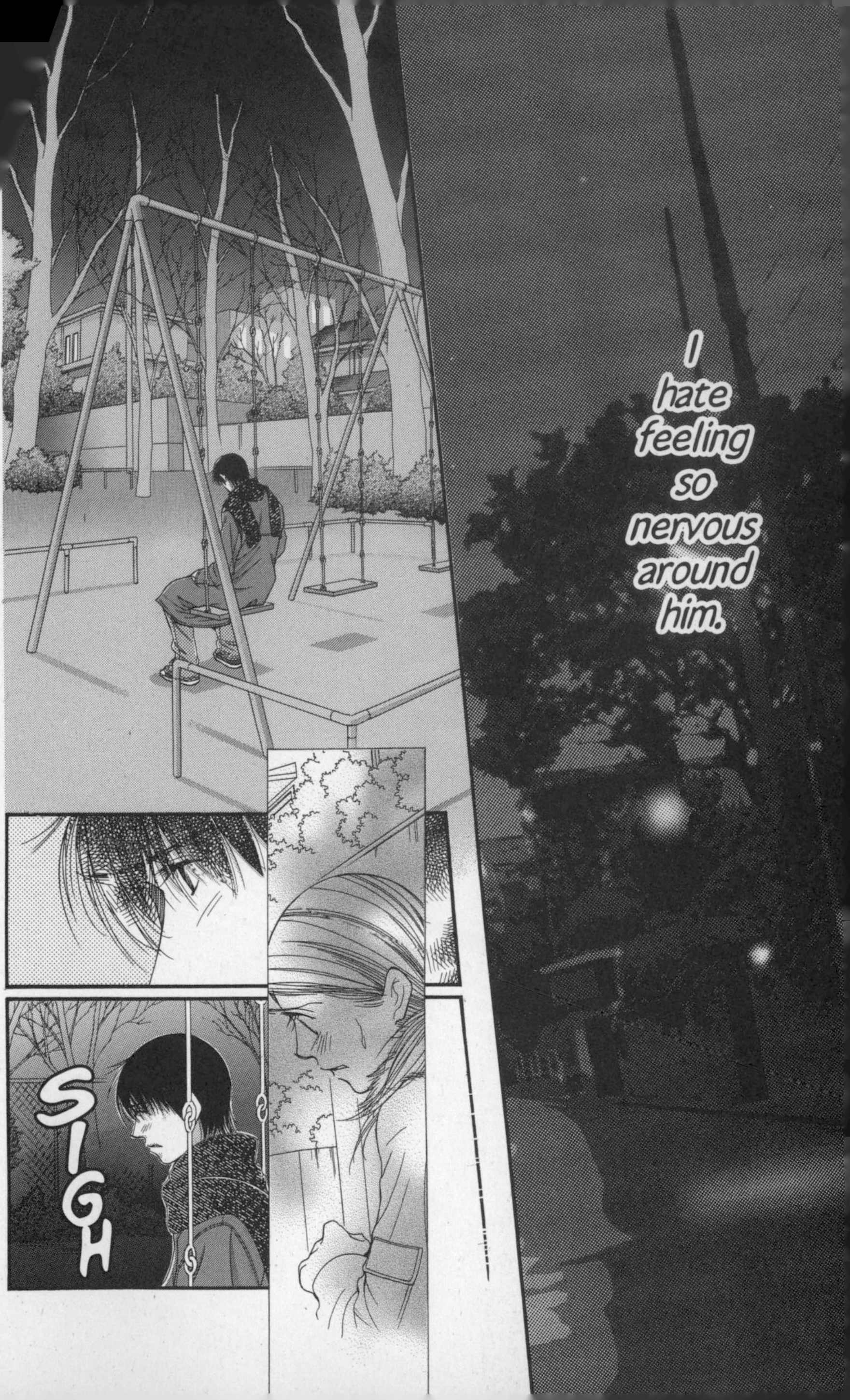
I hate feeling so nervous around him.
SIGH

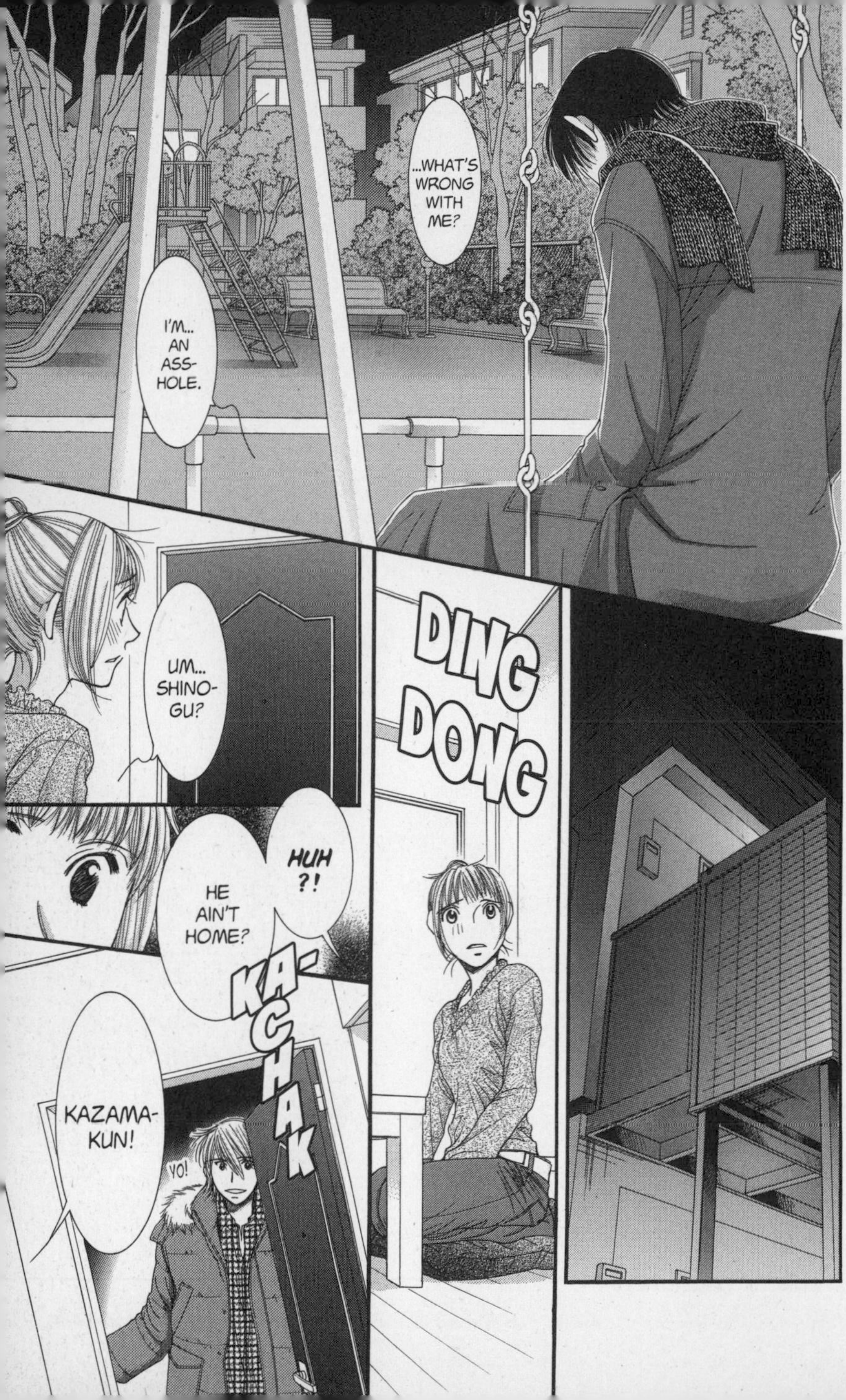
...WHAT'S WRONG WITH ME?
I'M... AN ASS-HOLE.
DING DONG
UM... SHINOGU?
HUH?!
HE AIN'T HOME?
KA-CHAK
KAZAMA-KUN!
YO!

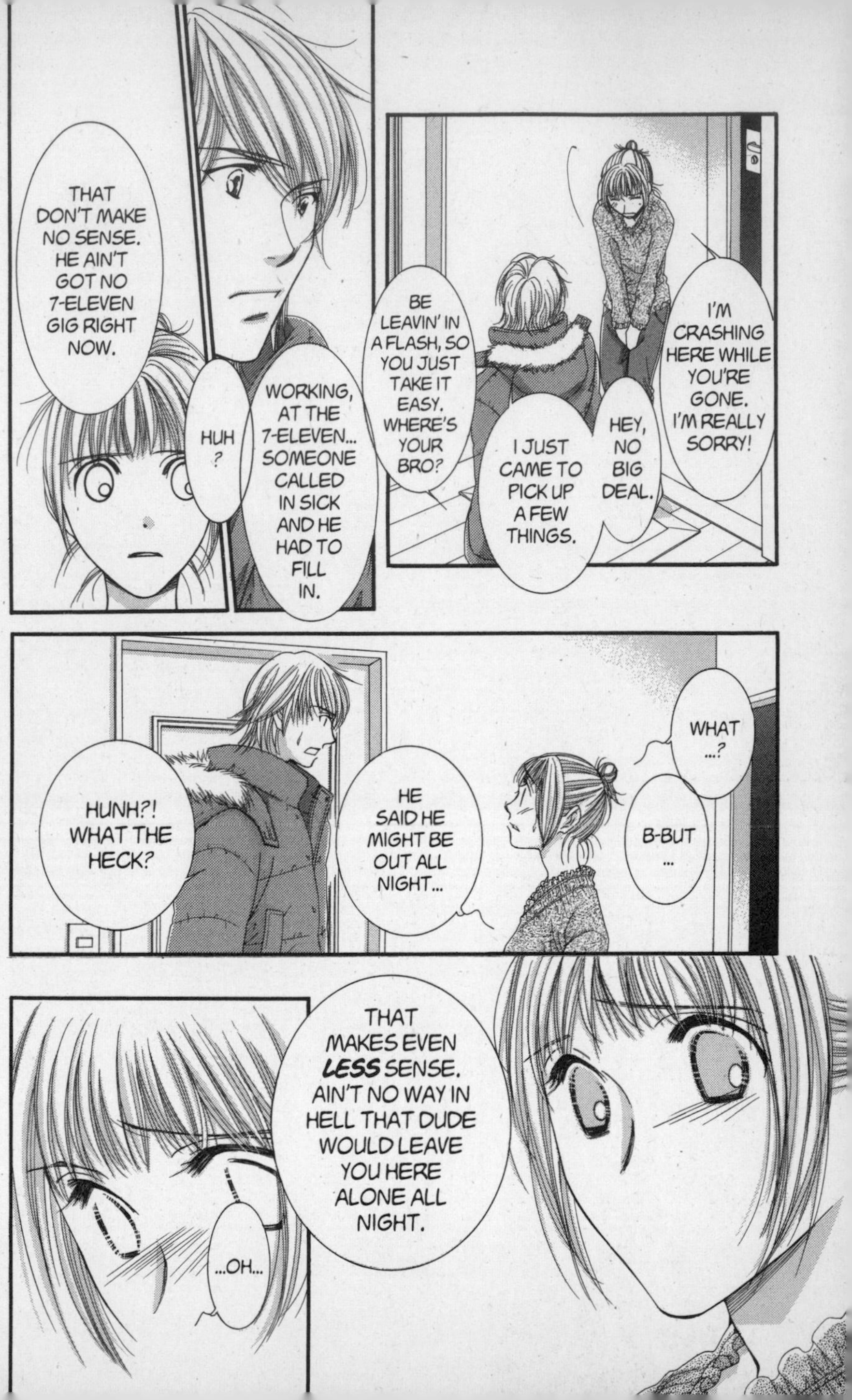
I'M CRASHING HERE WHILE YOU'RE GONE. I'M REALLY SORRY!
HEY, NO BIG DEAL.
I JUST CAME TO PICK UP A FEW THINGS.
BE LEAVIN' IN A FLASH, SO YOU JUST TAKE IT EASY. WHERE'S YOUR BRO?
WORKING, AT THE 7-ELEVEN... SOMEONE CALLED IN SICK AND HE HAD TO FILL IN.
HUH?
THAT DON'T MAKE NO SENSE. HE AIN'T GOT NO 7-ELEVEN GIG RIGHT NOW.
WHAT ...?
B-BUT ...
HE SAID HE MIGHT BE OUT ALL NIGHT...
HUNH?! WHAT THE HECK?
THAT MAKES EVEN *LESS* SENSE. AIN'T NO WAY IN HELL THAT DUDE WOULD LEAVE YOU HERE ALONE ALL NIGHT.
...OH...

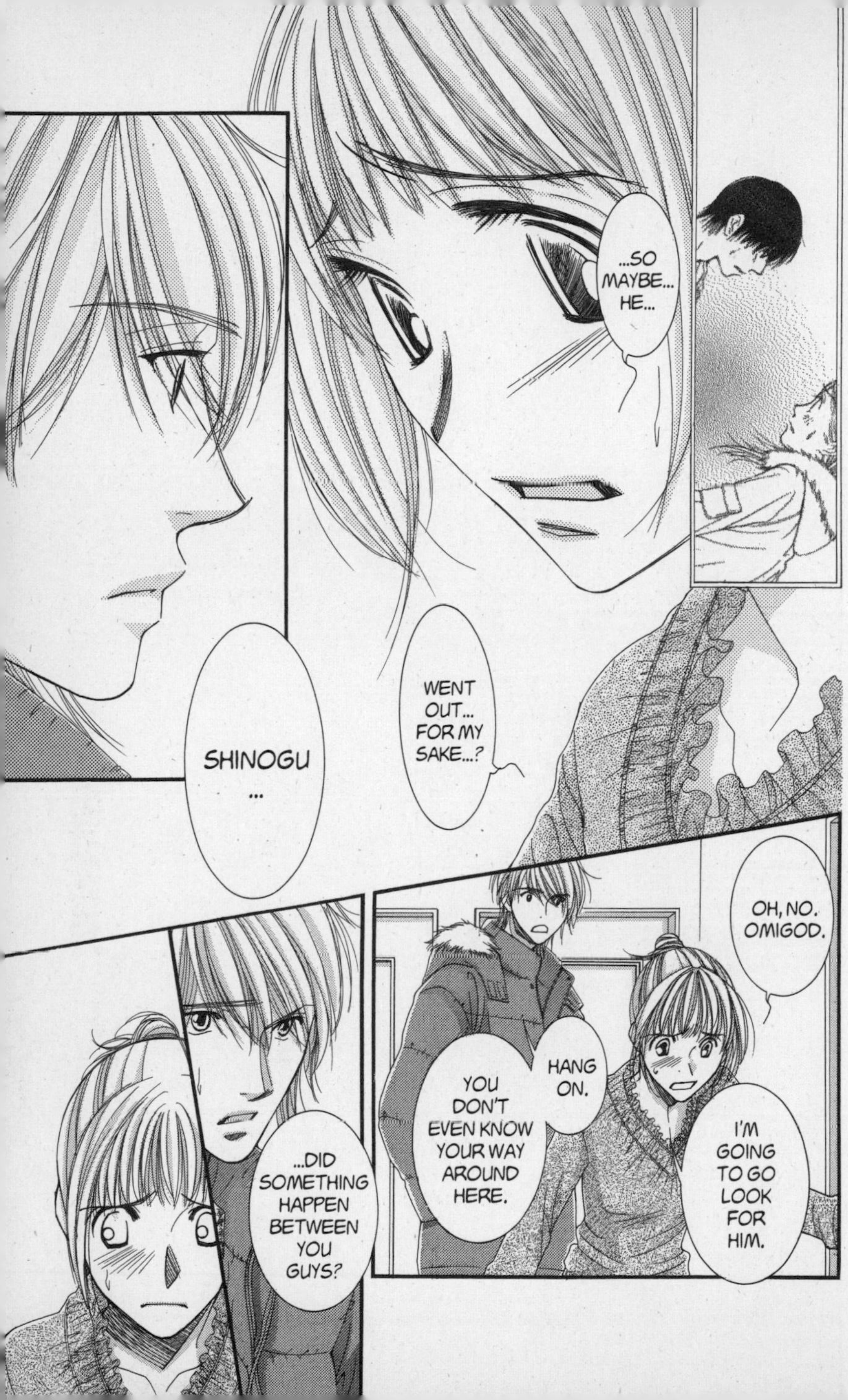
...SO MAYBE... HE...
WENT OUT... FOR MY SAKE...?
SHINOGU ...
OH, NO. OMIGOD.
I'M GOING TO GO LOOK FOR HIM.
HANG ON.
YOU DON'T EVEN KNOW YOUR WAY AROUND HERE.
...DID SOMETHING HAPPEN BETWEEN YOU GUYS?

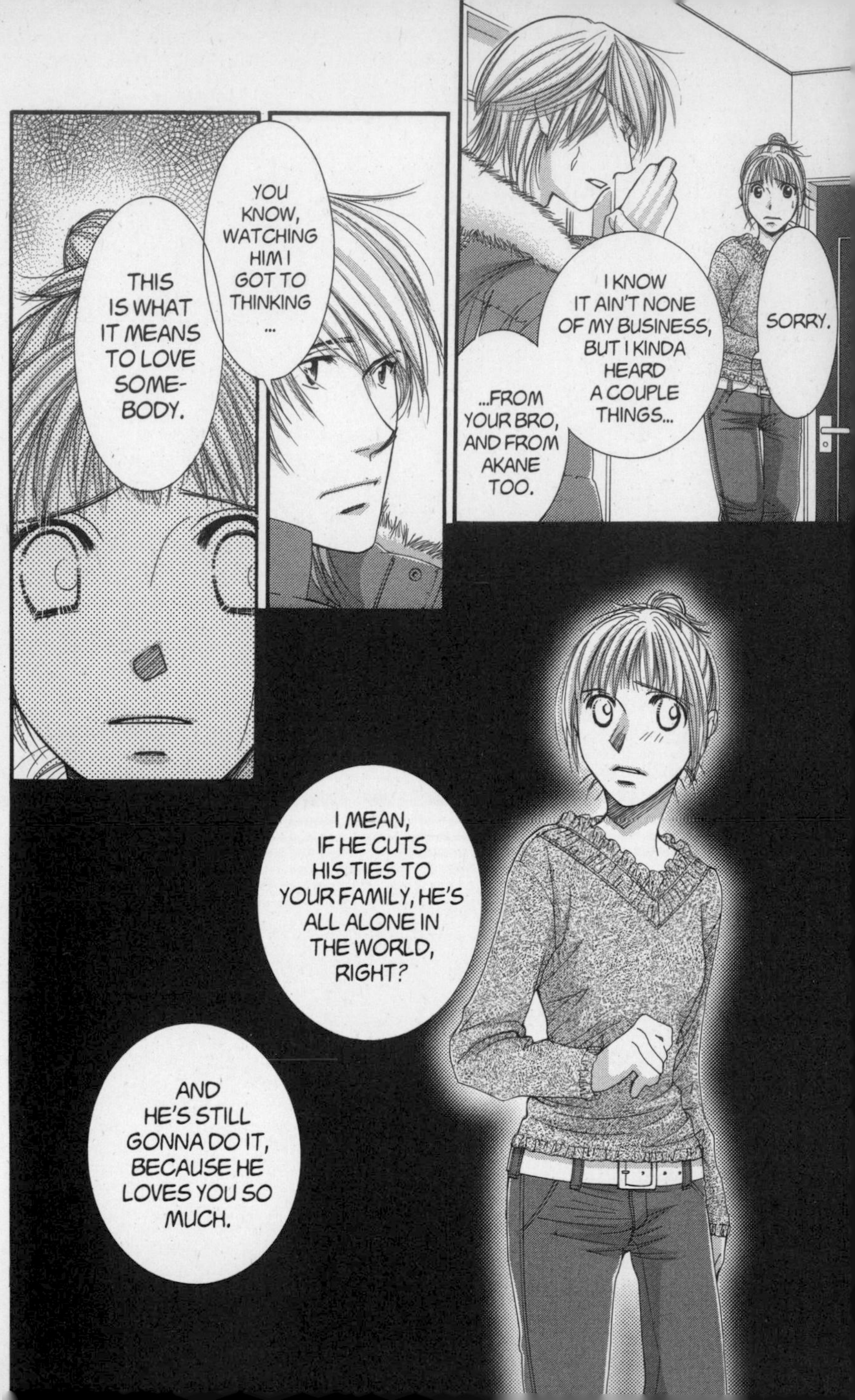
SORRY.
I KNOW IT AIN'T NONE OF MY BUSINESS, BUT I KINDA HEARD A COUPLE THINGS...
...FROM YOUR BRO, AND FROM AKANE TOO.
YOU KNOW, WATCHING HIM I GOT TO THINKING ...
THIS IS WHAT IT MEANS TO LOVE SOME-BODY.
I MEAN, IF HE CUTS HIS TIES TO YOUR FAMILY, HE'S ALL ALONE IN THE WORLD, RIGHT?
AND HE'S STILL GONNA DO IT, BECAUSE HE LOVES YOU SO MUCH.

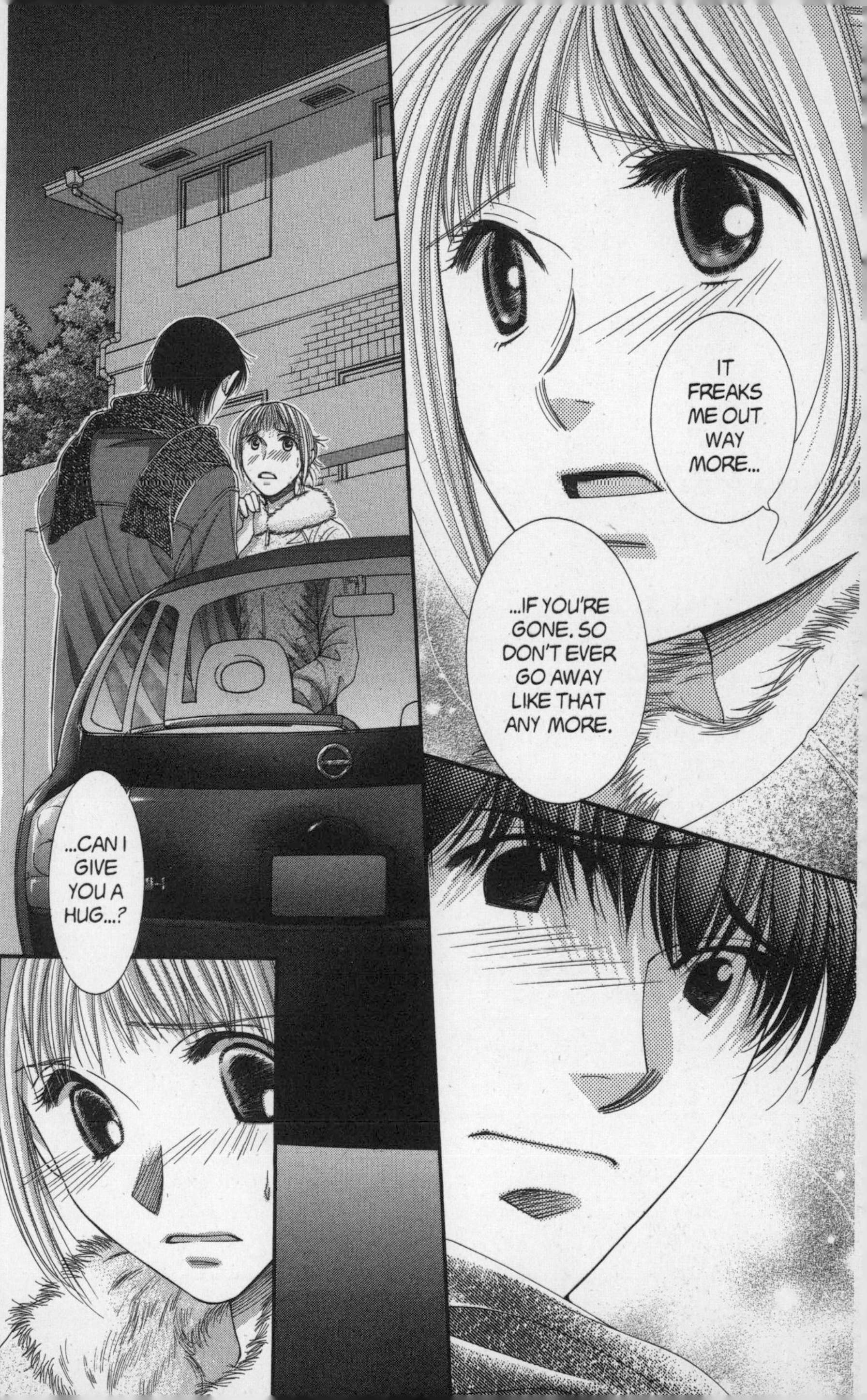
IT FREAKS ME OUT WAY MORE...
...IF YOU'RE GONE. SO DON'T EVER GO AWAY LIKE THAT ANY MORE.
...CAN I GIVE YOU A HUG...?

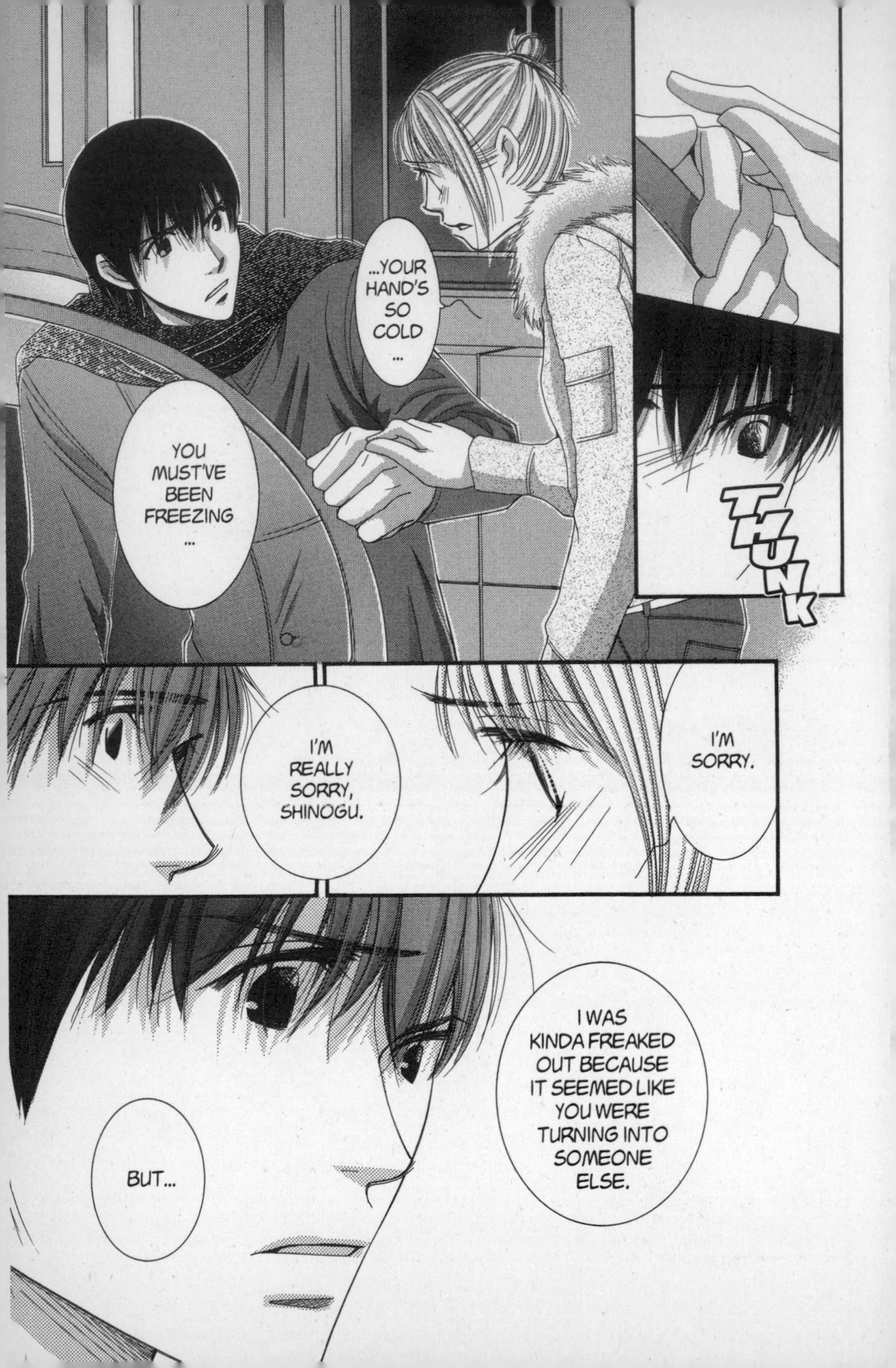
THUNK
...YOUR HAND'S SO COLD ...
YOU MUST'VE BEEN FREEZING ...
I'M SORRY.
I'M REALLY SORRY, SHINOGU.
I WAS KINDA FREAKED OUT BECAUSE IT SEEMED LIKE YOU WERE TURNING INTO SOMEONE ELSE.
BUT...

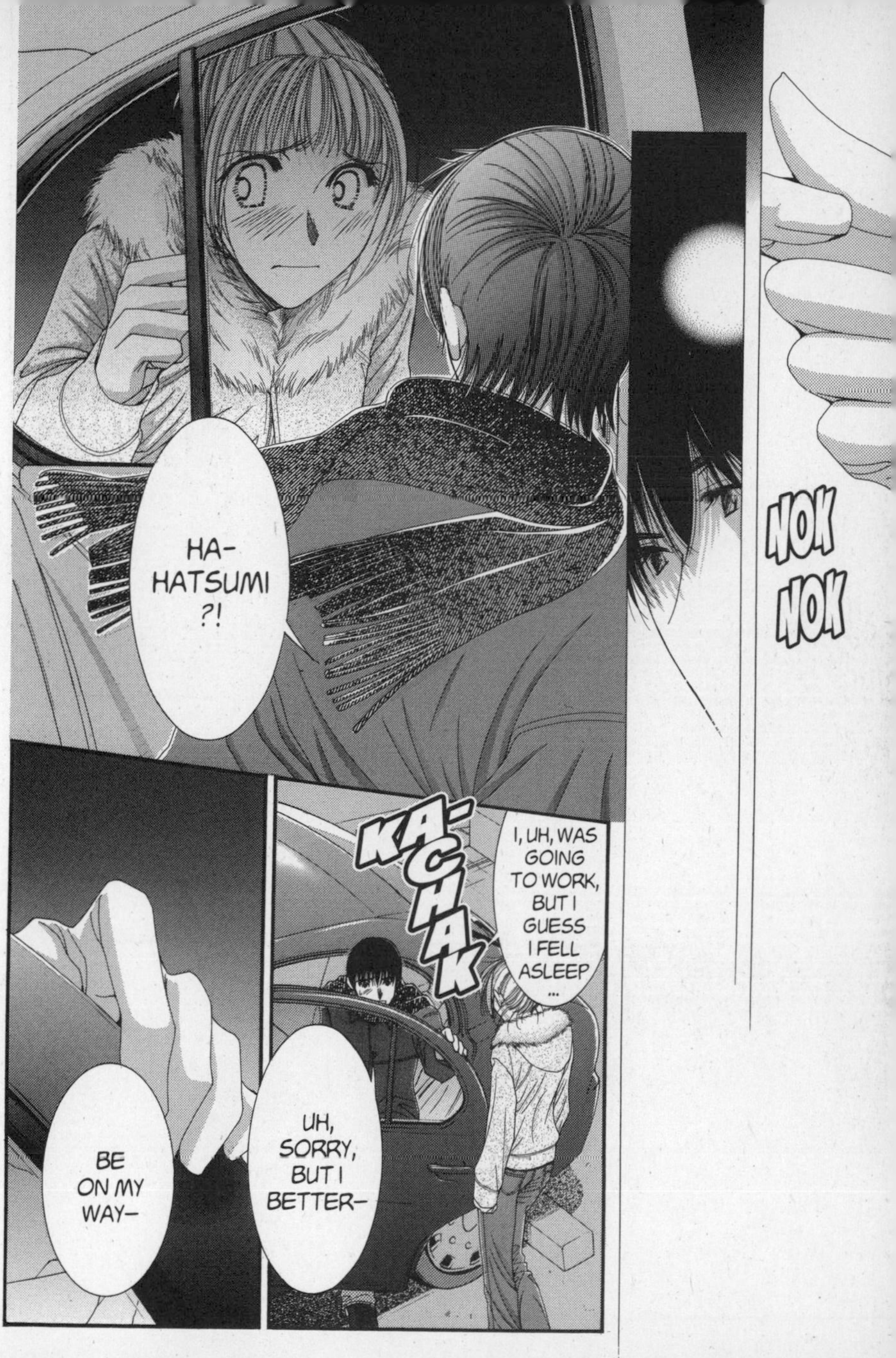
NOK NOK
HA-HATSUMI?!
KA-CHAK
I, UH, WAS GOING TO WORK, BUT I GUESS I FELL ASLEEP...
UH, SORRY, BUT I BETTER–
BE ON MY WAY–

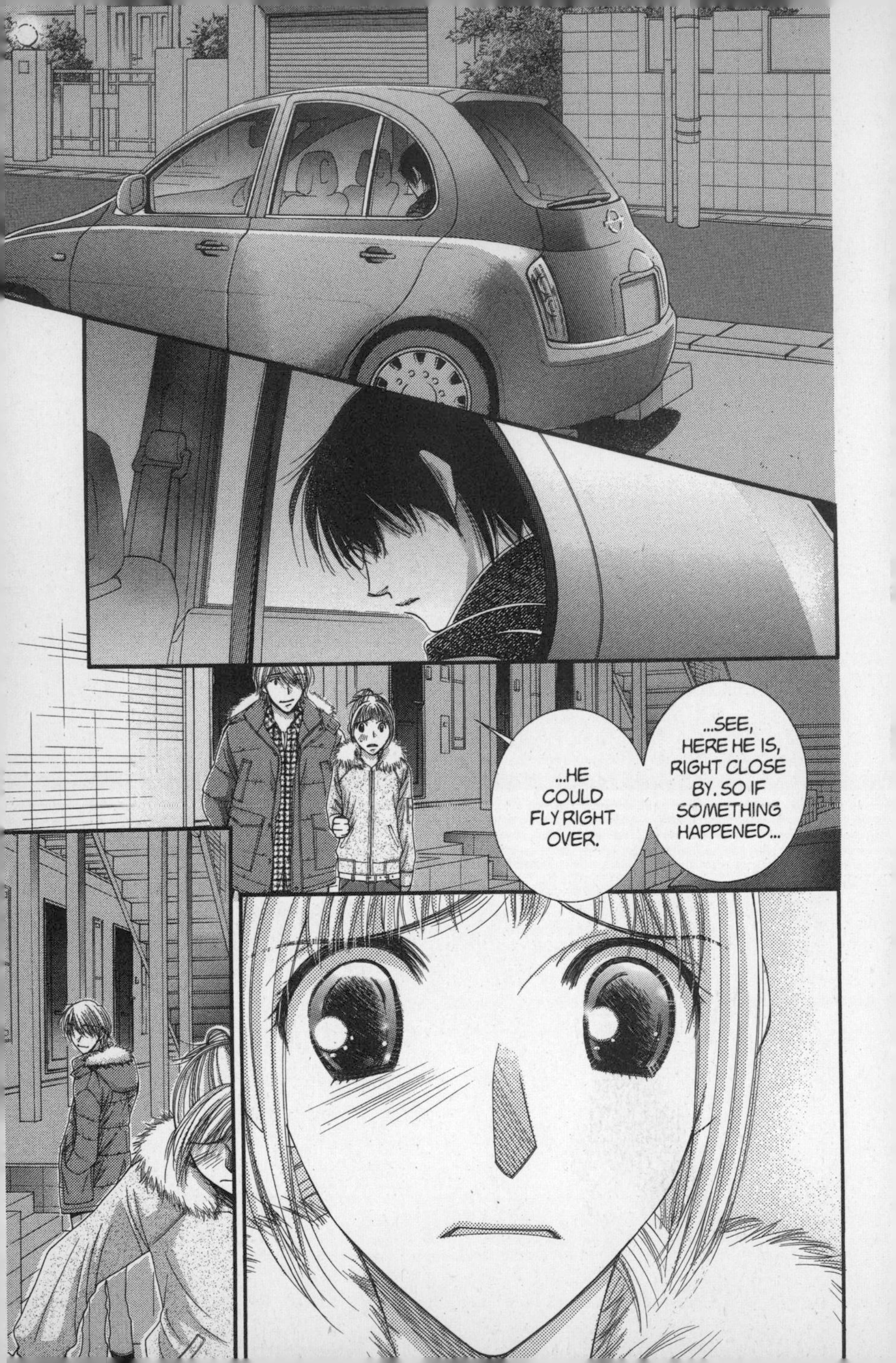
...SEE, HERE HE IS, RIGHT CLOSE BY. SO IF SOMETHING HAPPENED...
...HE COULD FLY RIGHT OVER.

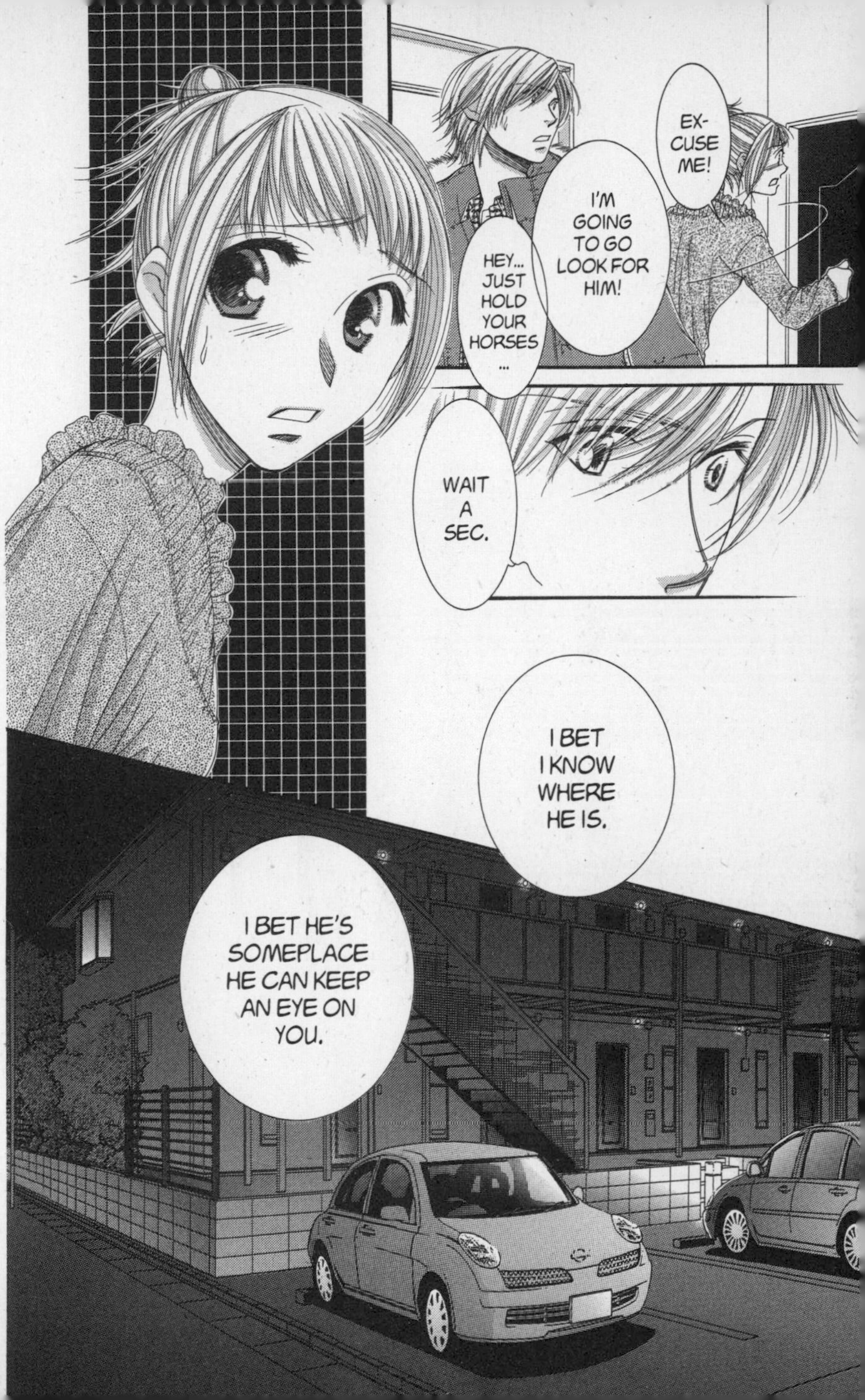
EX-CUSE ME!
I'M GOING TO GO LOOK FOR HIM!
HEY... JUST HOLD YOUR HORSES...
WAIT A SEC.
I BET I KNOW WHERE HE IS.
I BET HE'S SOMEPLACE HE CAN KEEP AN EYE ON YOU.

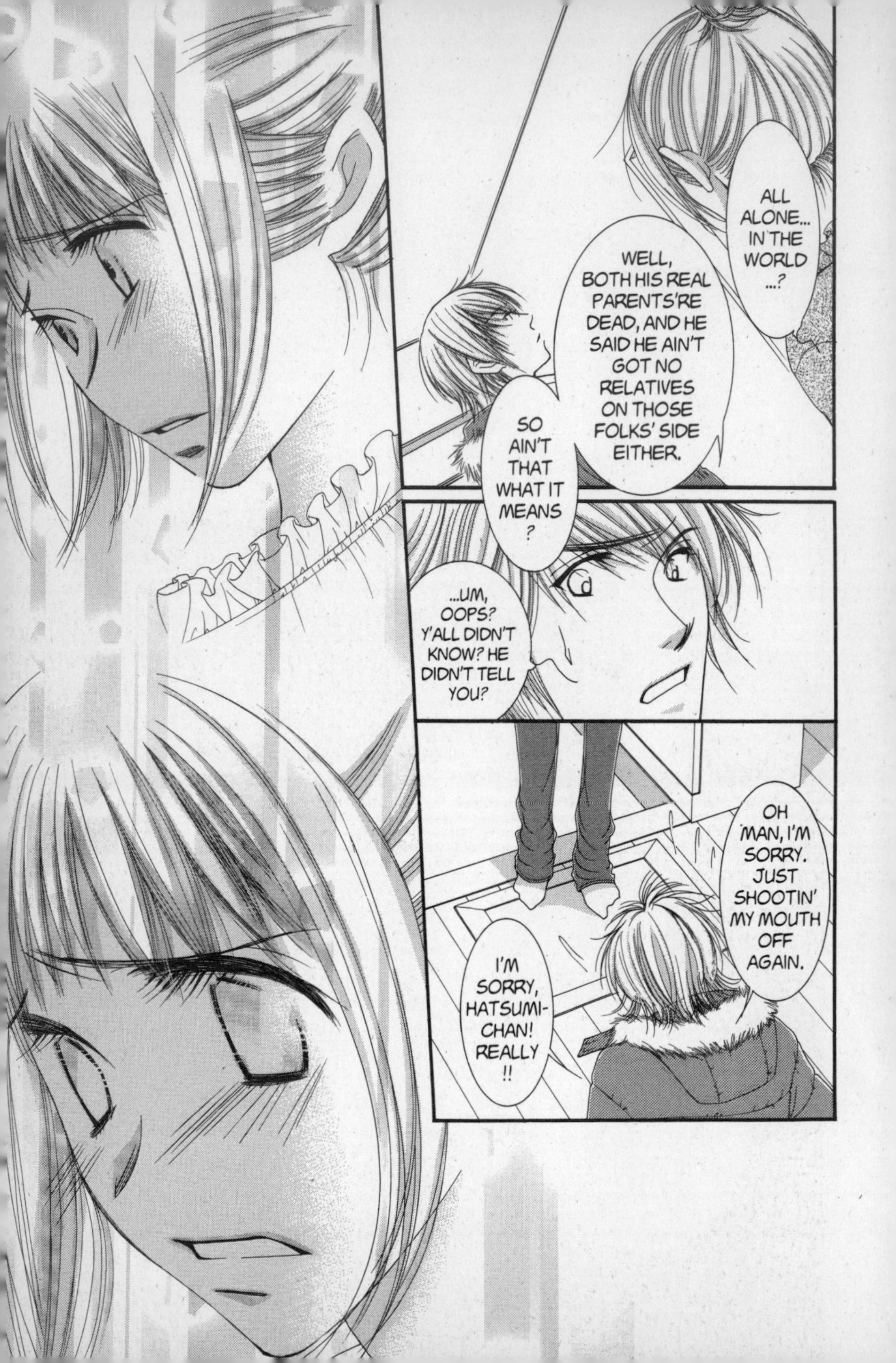
ALL ALONE... IN THE WORLD ...?
WELL, BOTH HIS REAL PARENTS'RE DEAD, AND HE SAID HE AIN'T GOT NO RELATIVES ON THOSE FOLKS' SIDE EITHER.
SO AIN'T THAT WHAT IT MEANS ?
...UM, OOPS? Y'ALL DIDN'T KNOW? HE DIDN'T TELL YOU?
OH MAN, I'M SORRY. JUST SHOOTIN' MY MOUTH OFF AGAIN.
I'M SORRY, HATSUMI-CHAN! REALLY !!

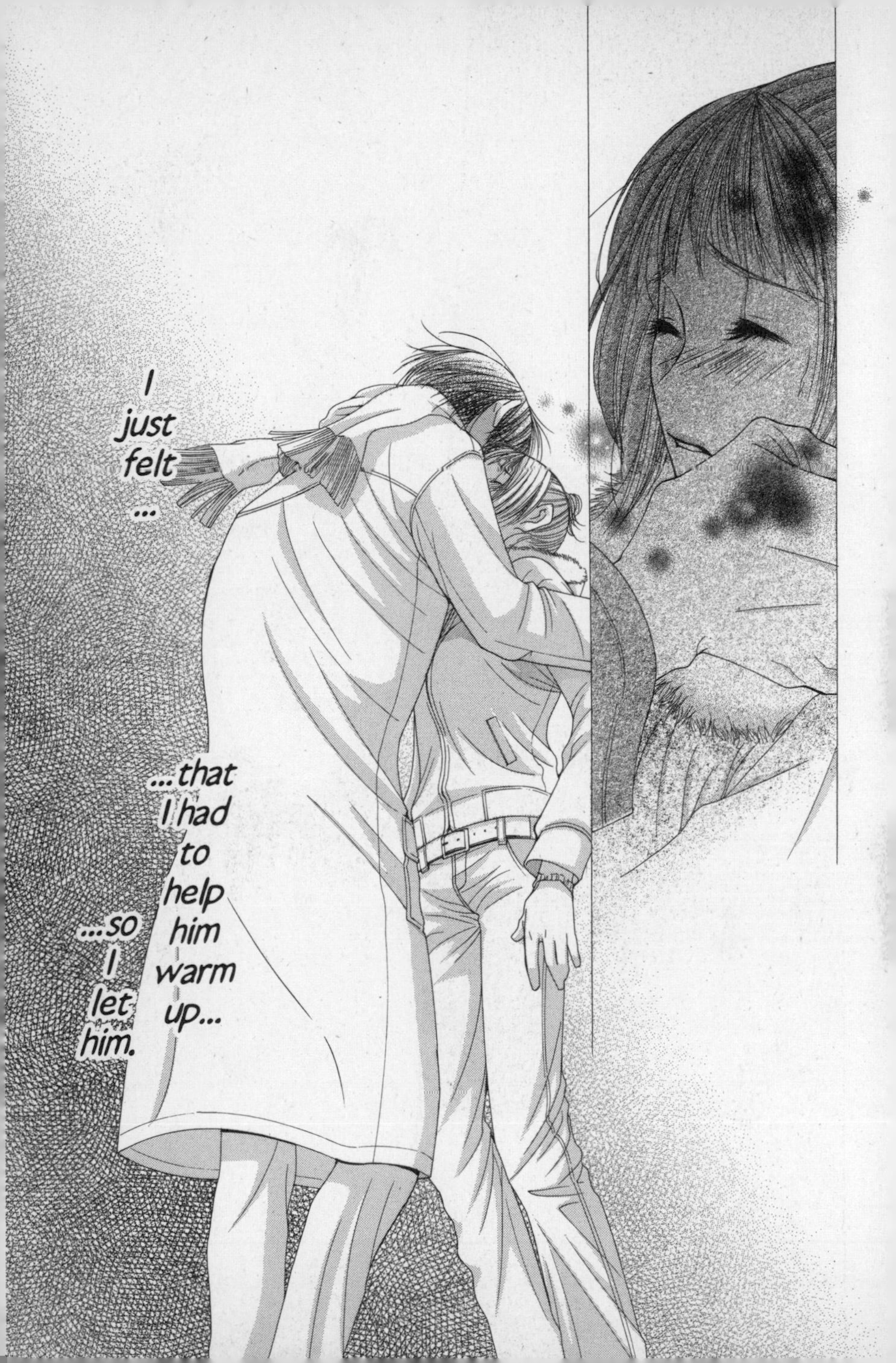
I just felt...
...that I had to help him warm up...
...so I let him.

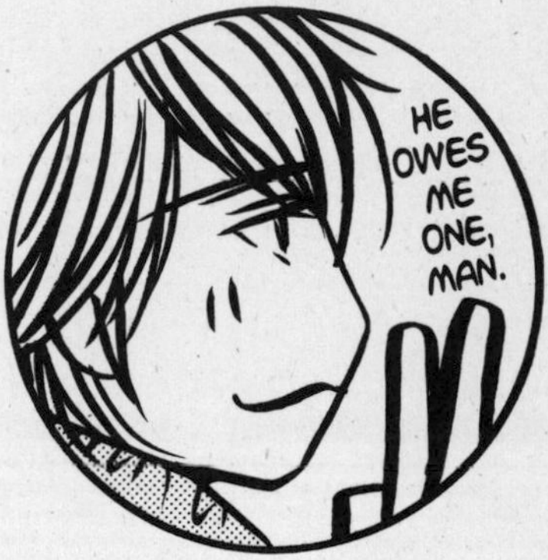
HE OWES ME ONE, MAN.

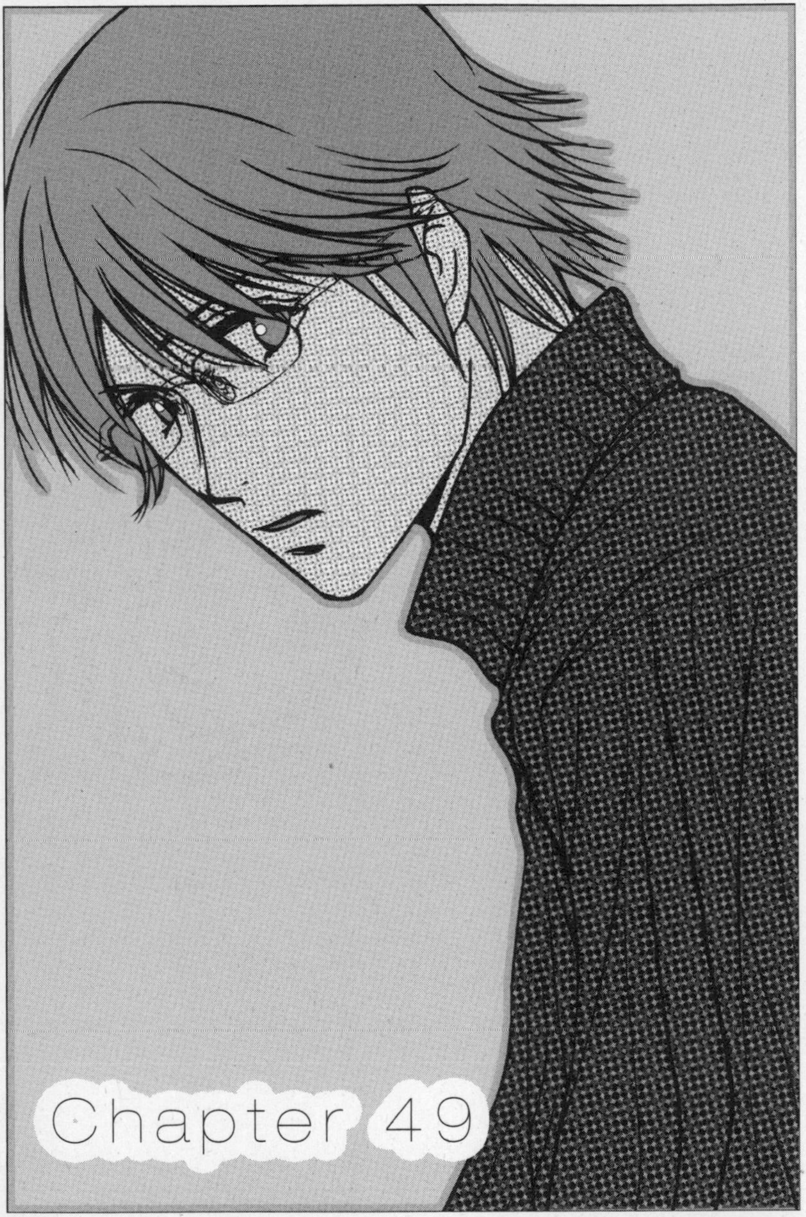
Chapter 49

hot gimmick

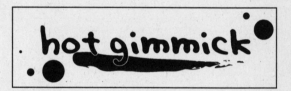

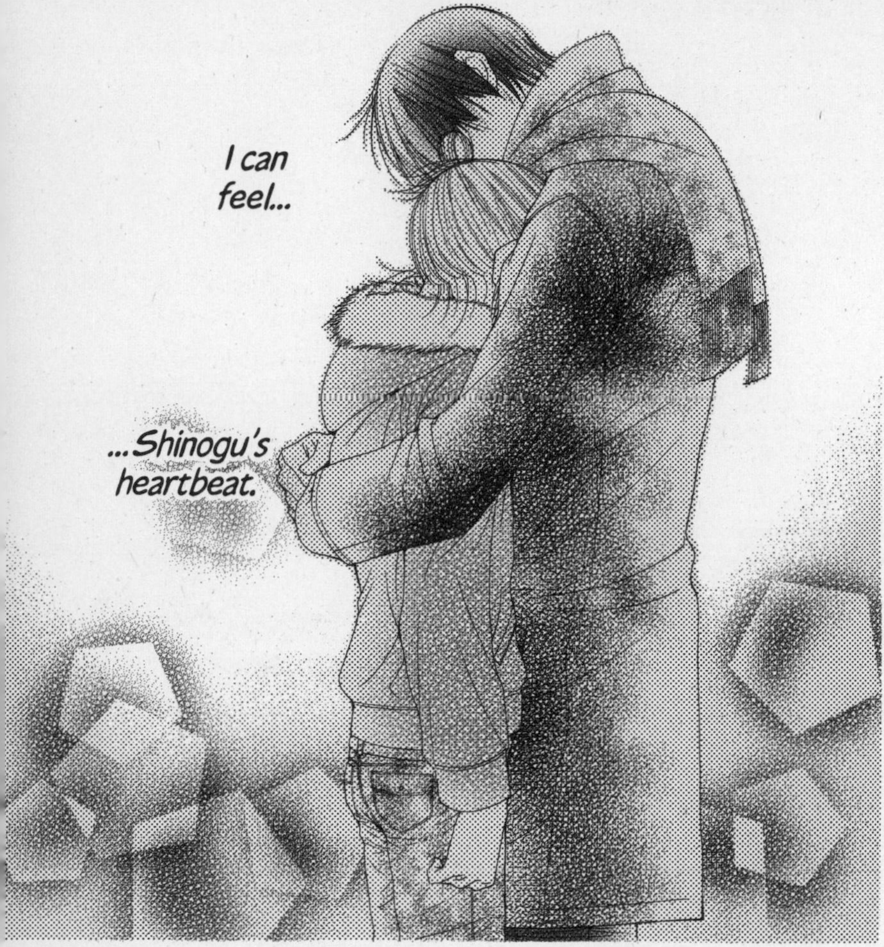
I can feel...
...Shinogu's heartbeat.

hot gimmick

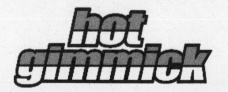

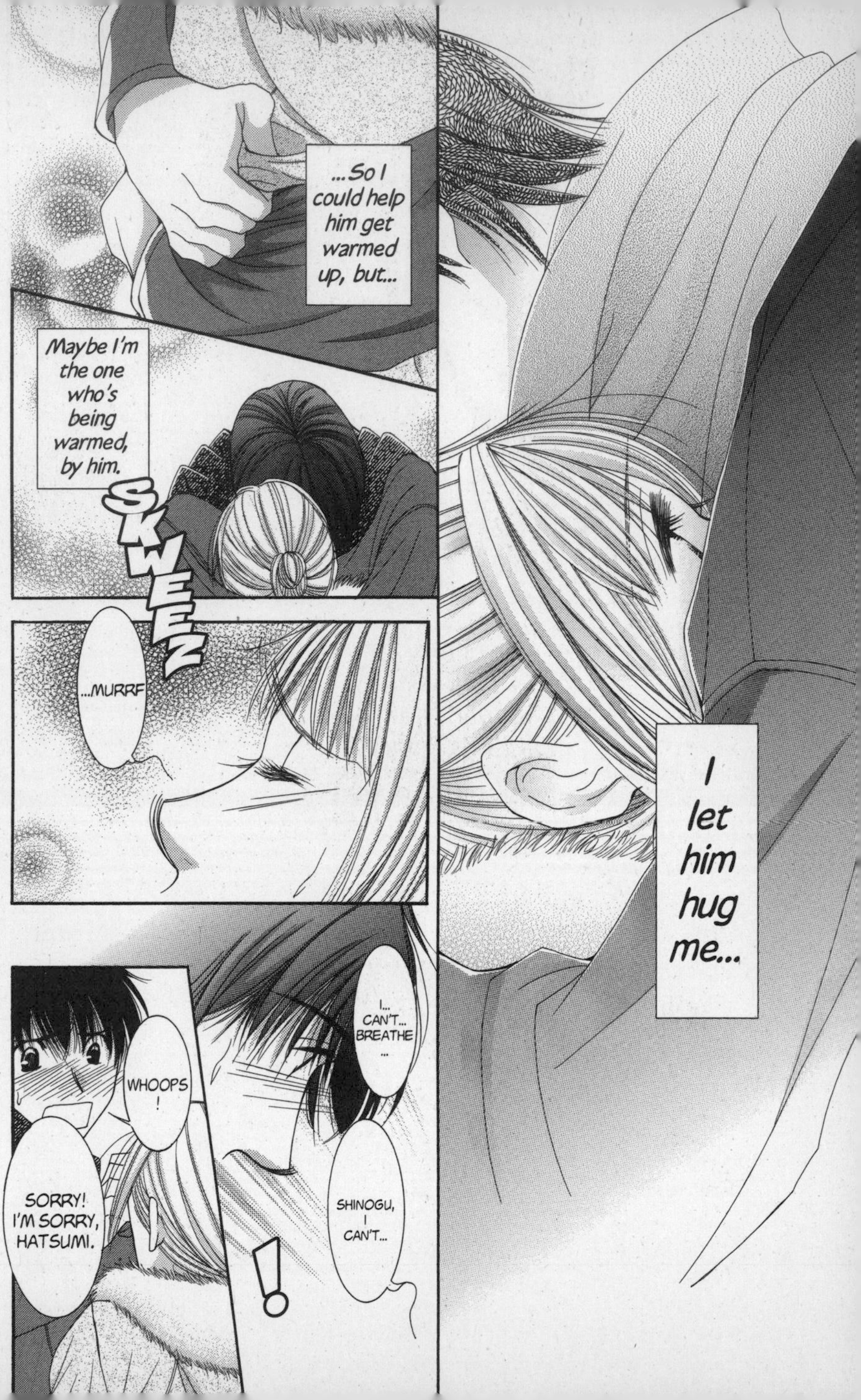
I let him hug me...
...So I could help him get warmed up, but...
Maybe I'm the one who's being warmed, by him.
SKWEEZ
...MURRF
I... CAN'T... BREATHE...
WHOOPS!
SHINOGU, I CAN'T...
!
SORRY! I'M SORRY, HATSUMI.

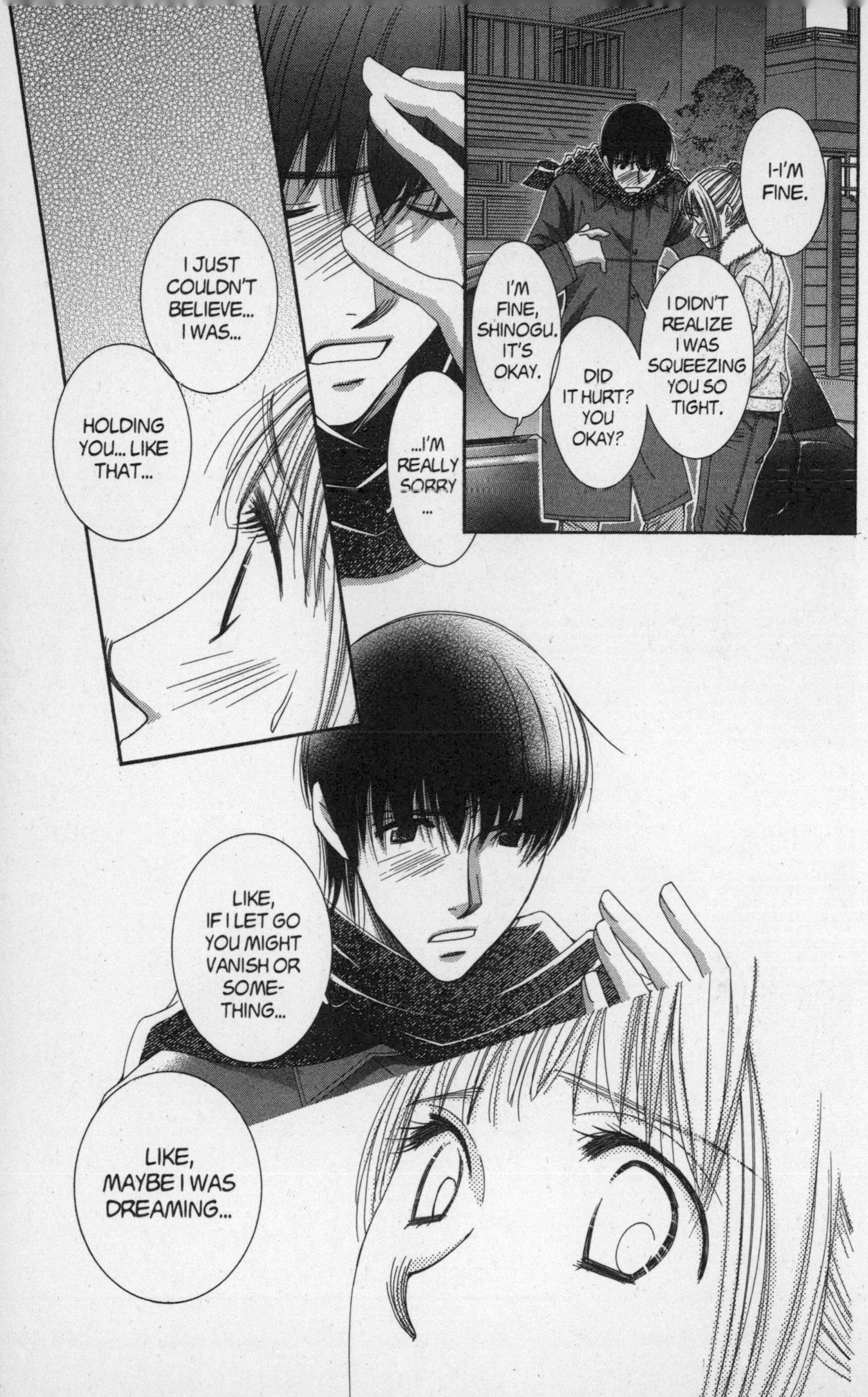
I-I'M FINE.
I DIDN'T REALIZE I WAS SQUEEZING YOU SO TIGHT.
DID IT HURT? YOU OKAY?
I'M FINE, SHINOGU. IT'S OKAY.
...I'M REALLY SORRY...
I JUST COULDN'T BELIEVE... I WAS...
HOLDING YOU... LIKE THAT...
LIKE, IF I LET GO YOU MIGHT VANISH OR SOME-THING...
LIKE, MAYBE I WAS DREAMING...

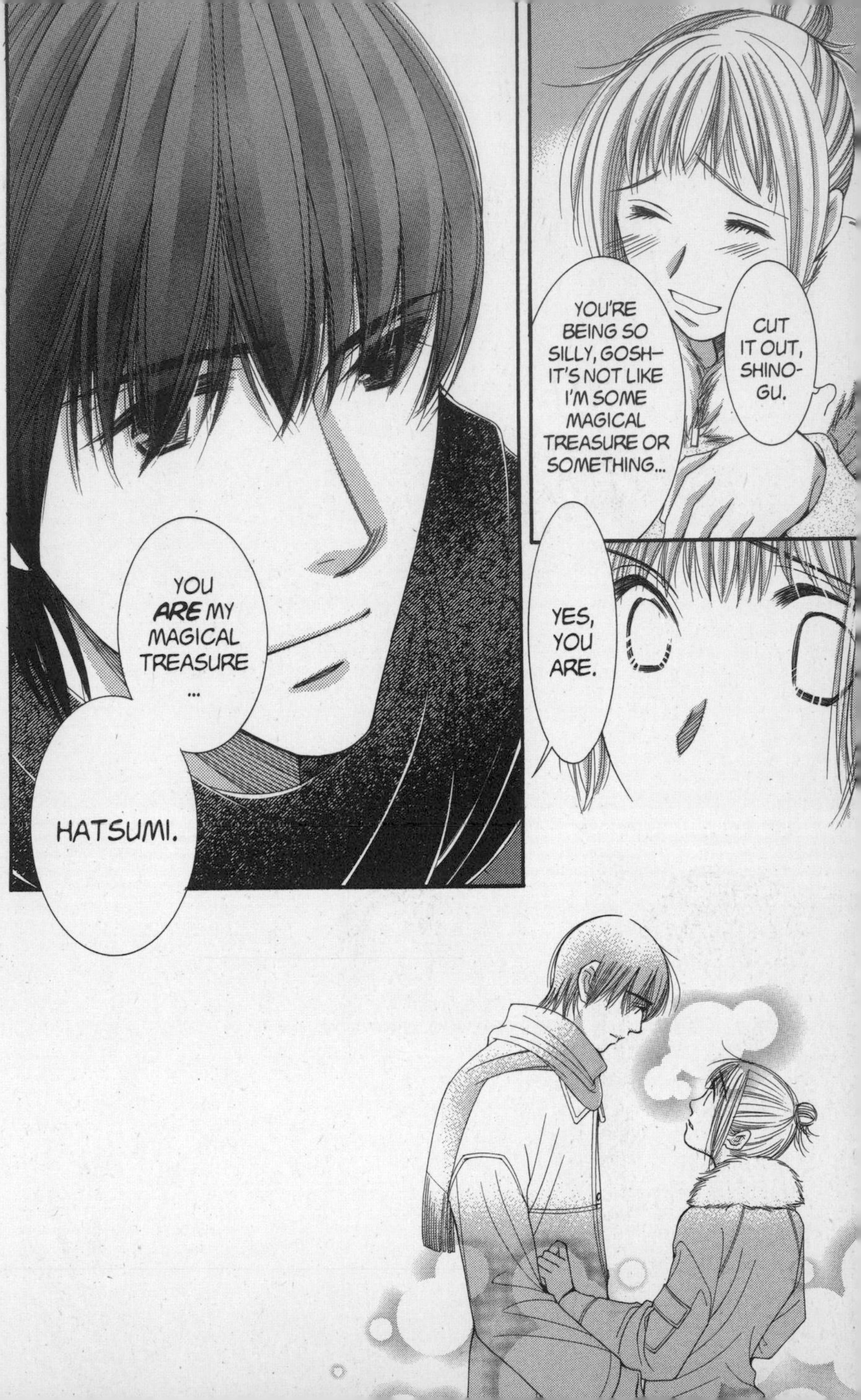
CUT IT OUT, SHINOGU.
YOU'RE BEING SO SILLY, GOSH— IT'S NOT LIKE I'M SOME MAGICAL TREASURE OR SOMETHING...
YES, YOU ARE.
YOU **ARE** MY MAGICAL TREASURE ...
HATSUMI.

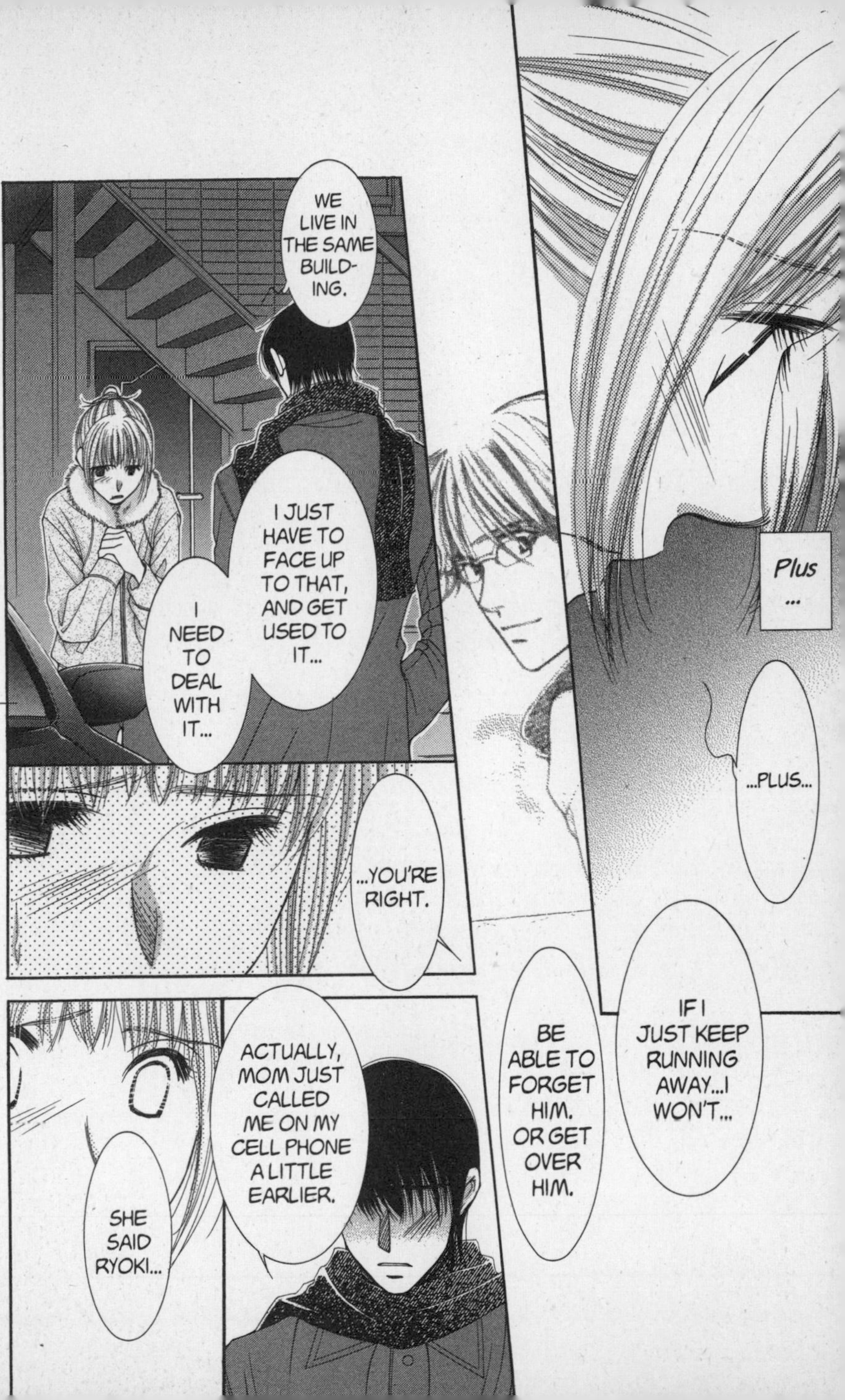
WE LIVE IN THE SAME BUILD-ING.
I JUST HAVE TO FACE UP TO THAT, AND GET USED TO IT...
I NEED TO DEAL WITH IT...
...YOU'RE RIGHT.
Plus ...
...PLUS...
IF I JUST KEEP RUNNING AWAY...I WON'T...
BE ABLE TO FORGET HIM. OR GET OVER HIM.
ACTUALLY, MOM JUST CALLED ME ON MY CELL PHONE A LITTLE EARLIER.
SHE SAID RYOKI...

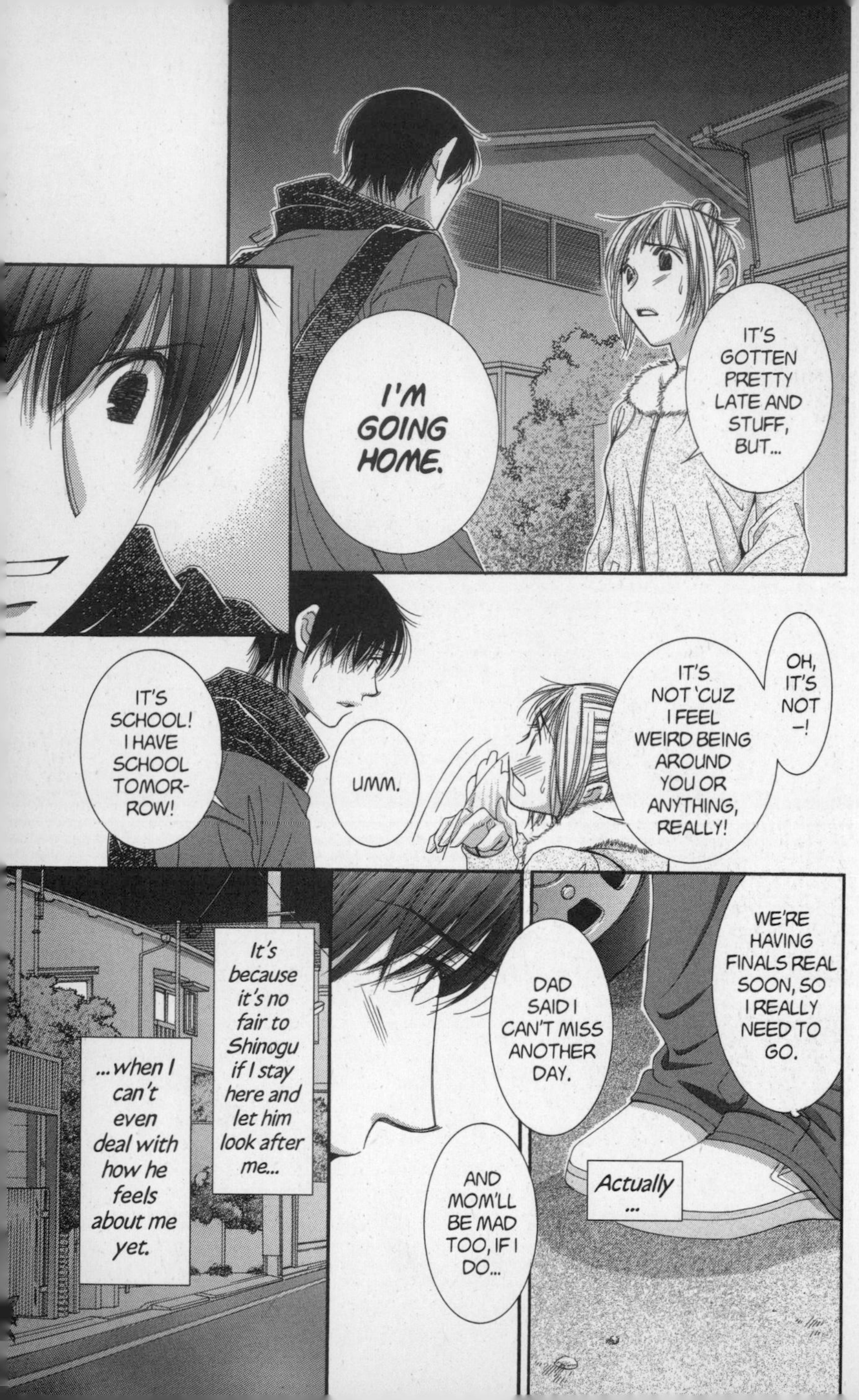
IT'S GOTTEN PRETTY LATE AND STUFF, BUT...
I'M GOING HOME.
OH, IT'S NOT—!
IT'S NOT 'CUZ I FEEL WEIRD BEING AROUND YOU OR ANYTHING, REALLY!
UMM.
IT'S SCHOOL! I HAVE SCHOOL TOMORROW!
WE'RE HAVING FINALS REAL SOON, SO I REALLY NEED TO GO.
DAD SAID I CAN'T MISS ANOTHER DAY.
AND MOM'LL BE MAD TOO, IF I DO...
Actually...
It's because it's no fair to Shinogu if I stay here and let him look after me...
...when I can't even deal with how he feels about me yet.

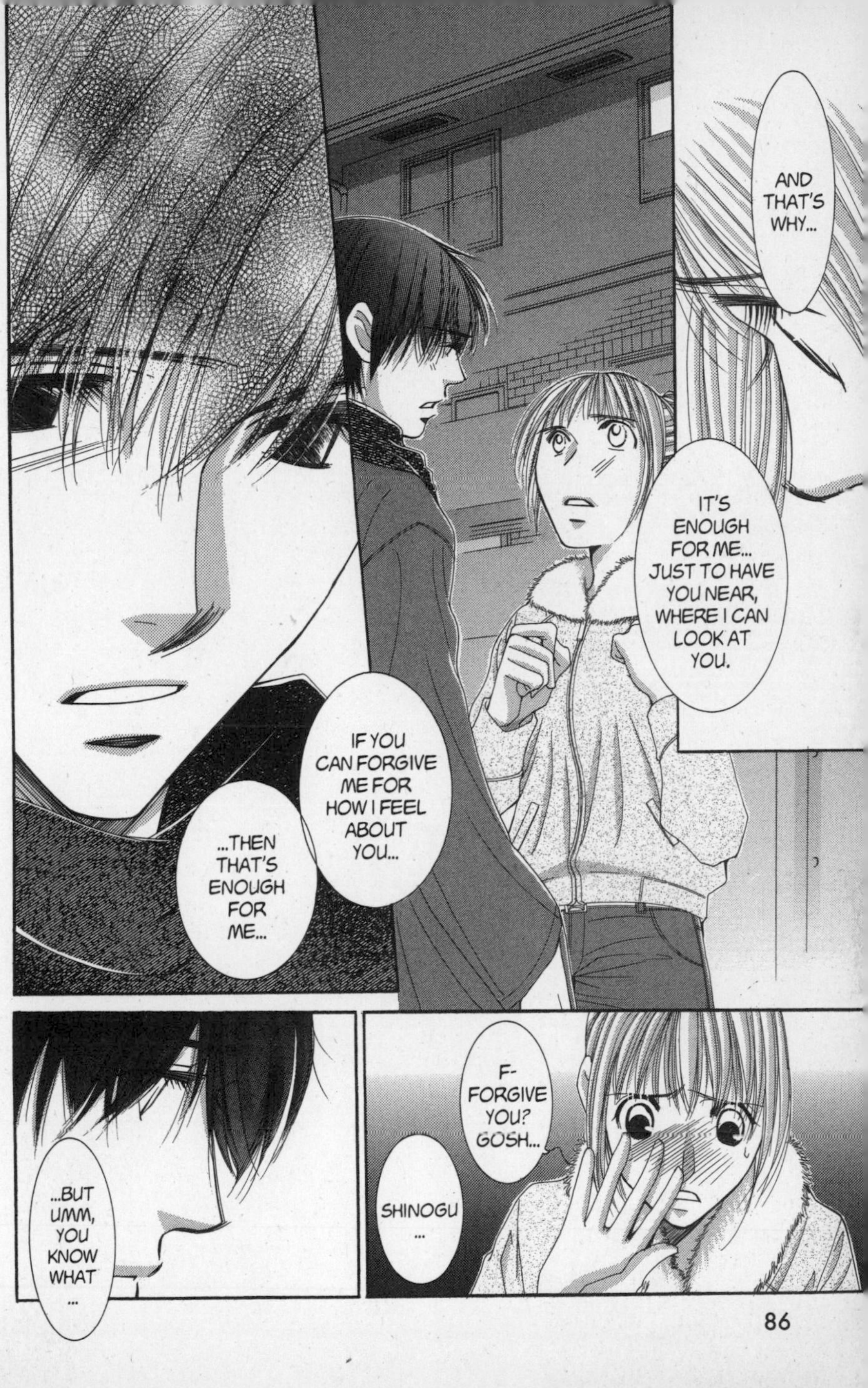
AND THAT'S WHY...
IT'S ENOUGH FOR ME... JUST TO HAVE YOU NEAR, WHERE I CAN LOOK AT YOU.
IF YOU CAN FORGIVE ME FOR HOW I FEEL ABOUT YOU...
...THEN THAT'S ENOUGH FOR ME...
F-FORGIVE YOU? GOSH...
SHINOGU...
...BUT UMM, YOU KNOW WHAT...

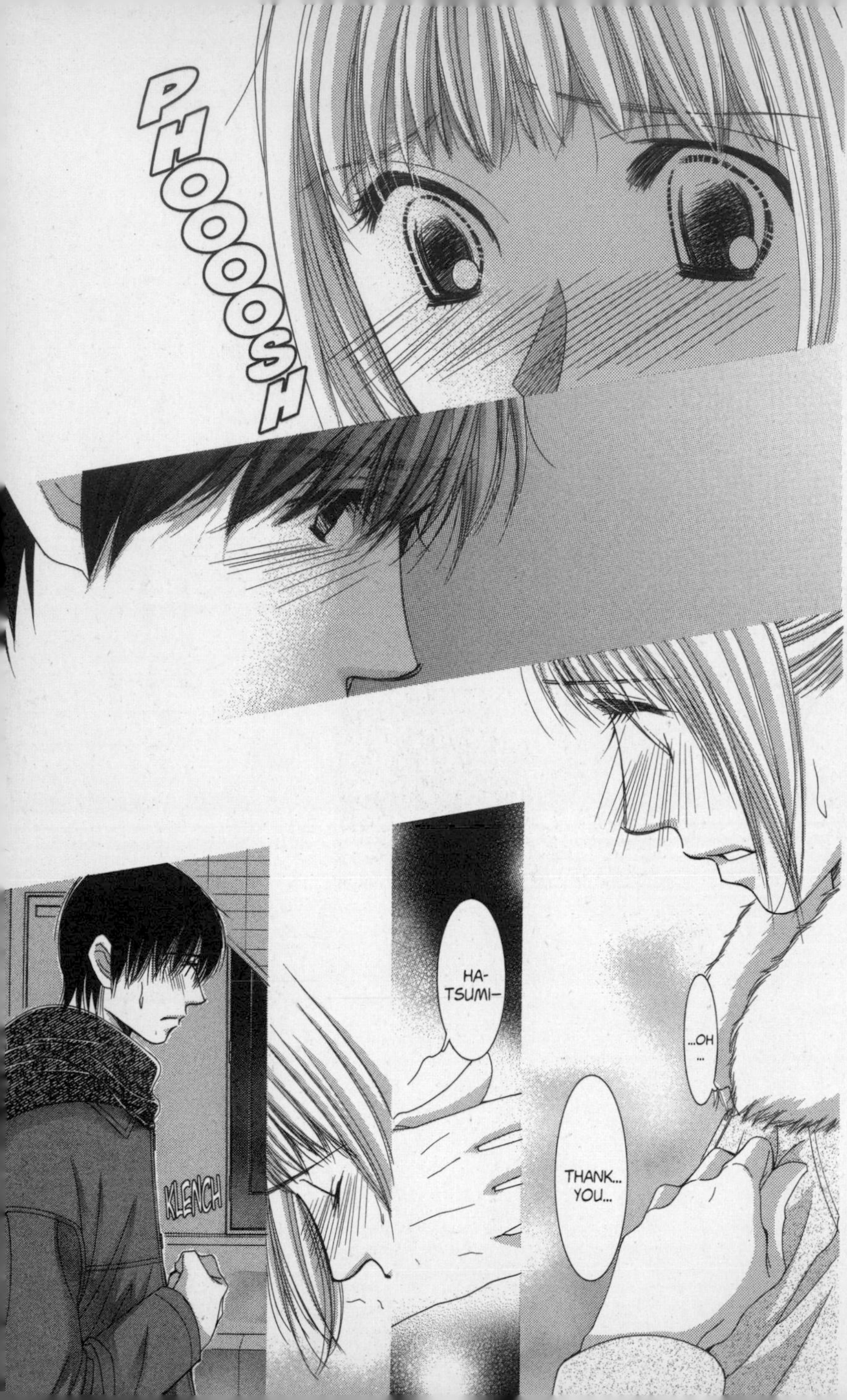
PHOOOOSH
...OH ...
THANK... YOU...
HA-TSUMI-
KLENCH

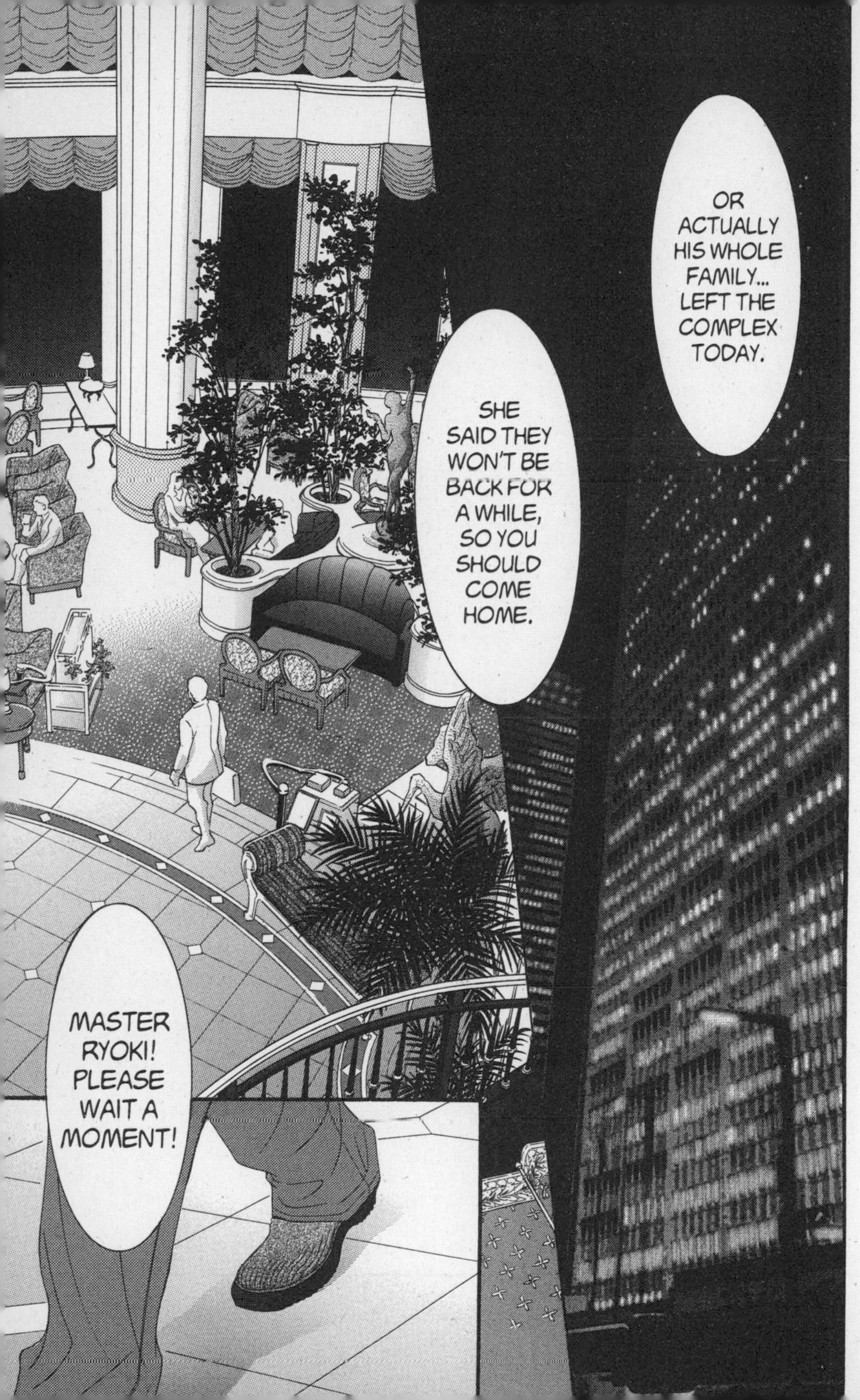
OR ACTUALLY HIS WHOLE FAMILY... LEFT THE COMPLEX TODAY.
SHE SAID THEY WON'T BE BACK FOR A WHILE, SO YOU SHOULD COME HOME.
MASTER RYOKI! PLEASE WAIT A MOMENT!

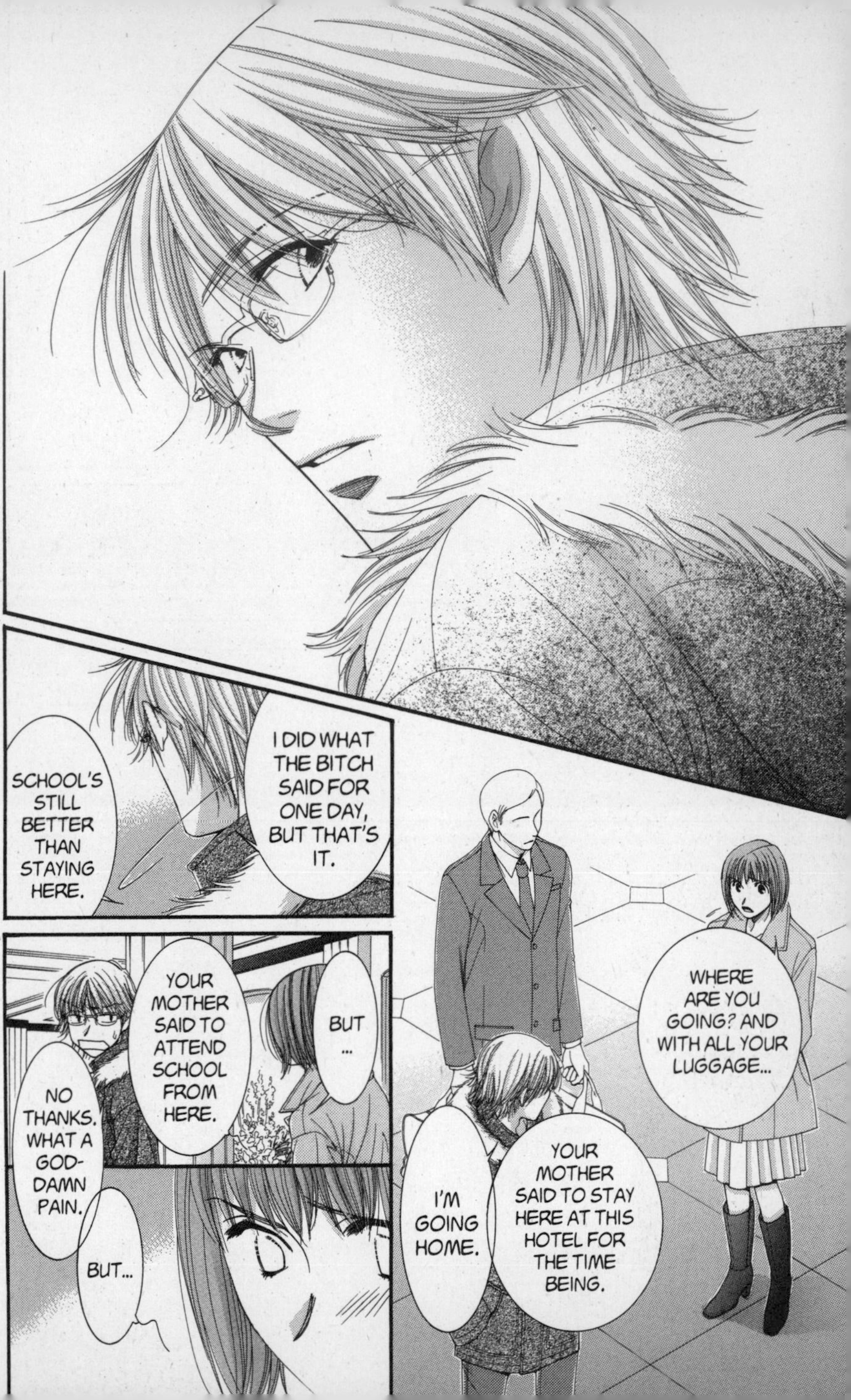
WHERE ARE YOU GOING? AND WITH ALL YOUR LUGGAGE...
YOUR MOTHER SAID TO STAY HERE AT THIS HOTEL FOR THE TIME BEING.
I'M GOING HOME.
I DID WHAT THE BITCH SAID FOR ONE DAY, BUT THAT'S IT.
SCHOOL'S STILL BETTER THAN STAYING HERE.
BUT ...
YOUR MOTHER SAID TO ATTEND SCHOOL FROM HERE.
NO THANKS. WHAT A GOD-DAMN PAIN.
BUT...

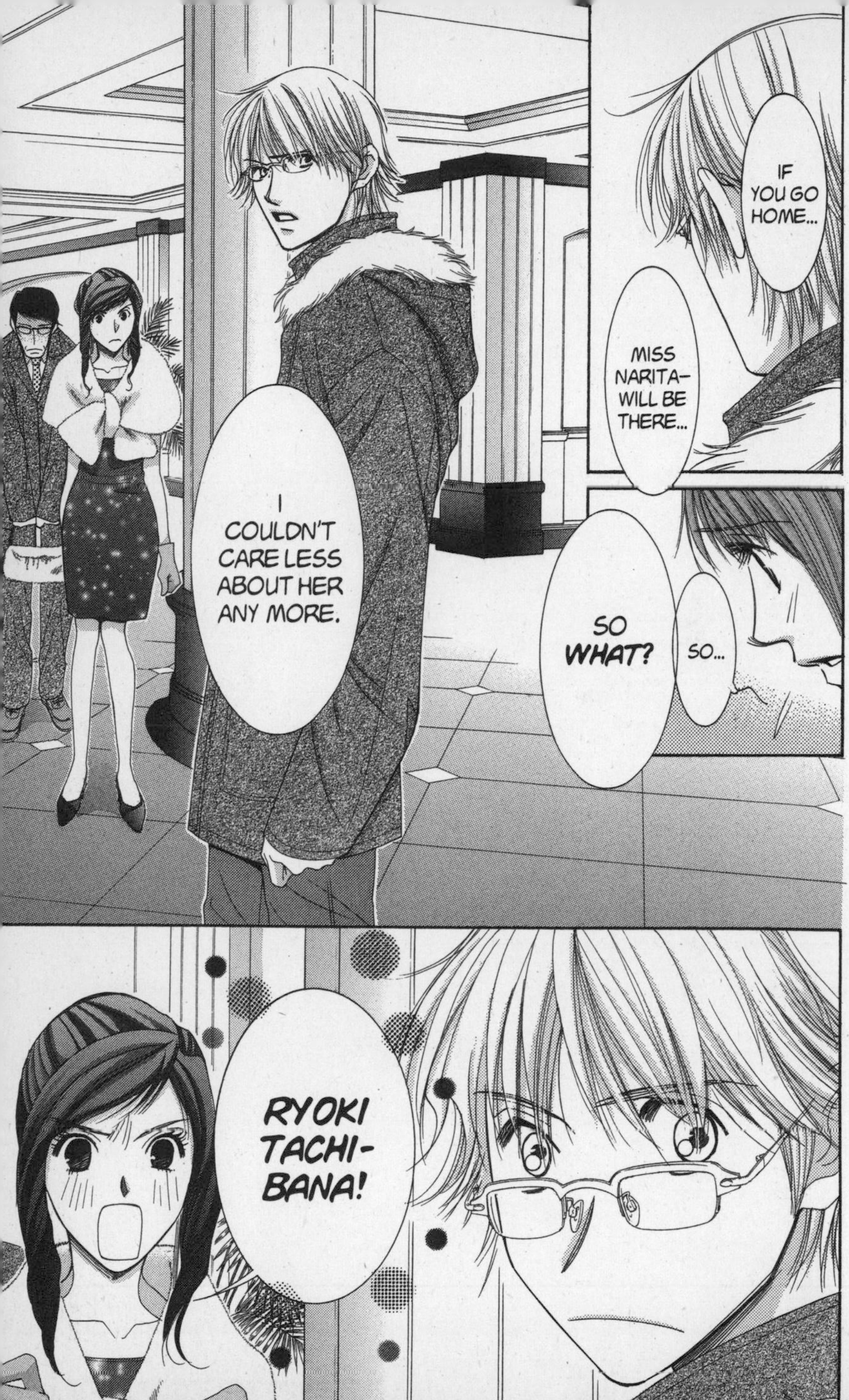
IF YOU GO HOME...
MISS NARITA-WILL BE THERE...
SO...
SO WHAT?
I COULDN'T CARE LESS ABOUT HER ANY MORE.
RYOKI TACHI-BANA!

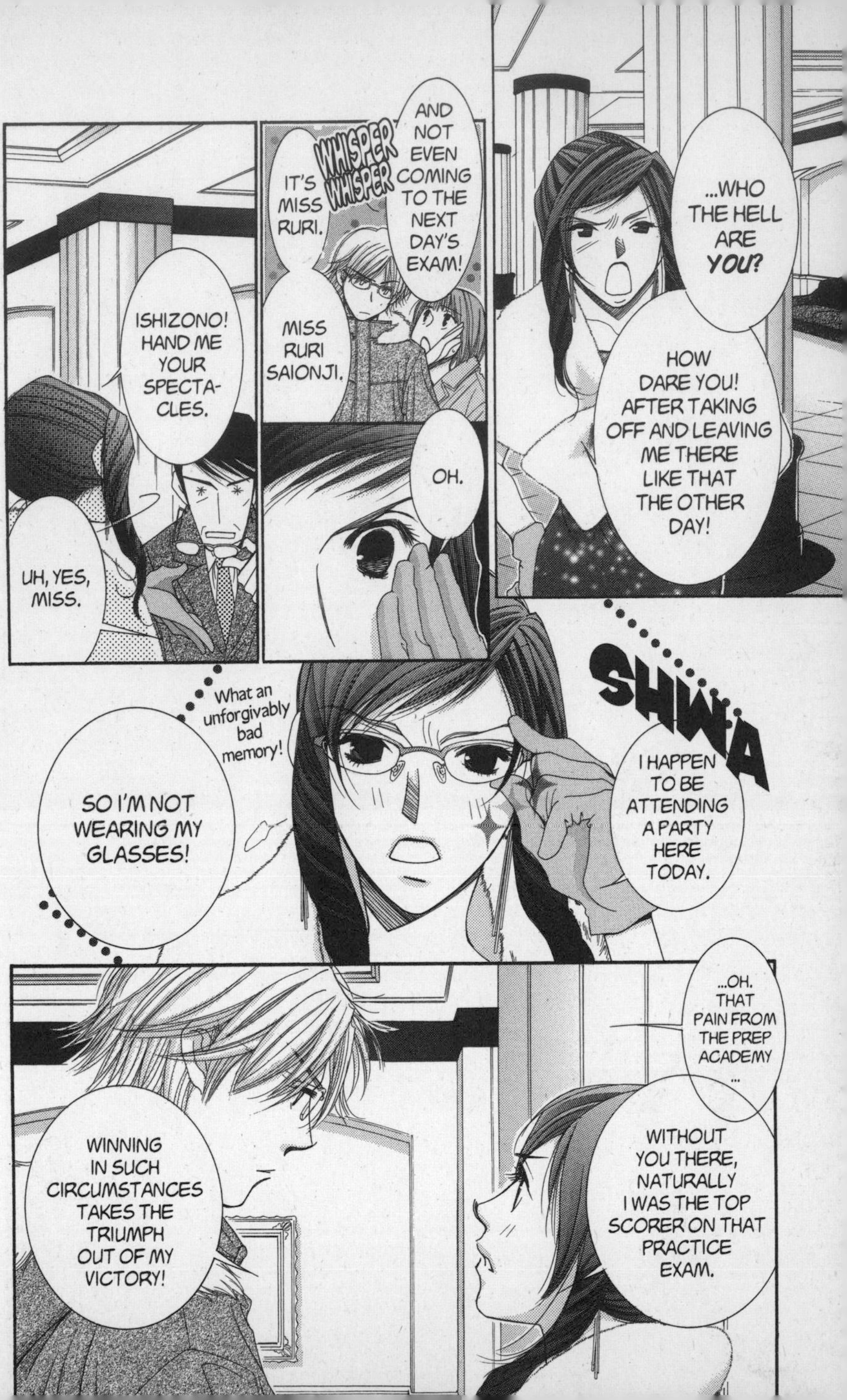
...WHO THE HELL ARE YOU?
HOW DARE YOU! AFTER TAKING OFF AND LEAVING ME THERE LIKE THAT THE OTHER DAY!
AND NOT EVEN COMING TO THE NEXT DAY'S EXAM!
WHISPER WHISPER
IT'S MISS RURI.
MISS RURI SAIONJI.
OH.
ISHIZONO! HAND ME YOUR SPECTACLES.
UH, YES, MISS.
SHWA
I HAPPEN TO BE ATTENDING A PARTY HERE TODAY.
What an unforgivably bad memory!
SO I'M NOT WEARING MY GLASSES!
...OH. THAT PAIN FROM THE PREP ACADEMY ...
WITHOUT YOU THERE, NATURALLY I WAS THE TOP SCORER ON THAT PRACTICE EXAM.
WINNING IN SUCH CIRCUMSTANCES TAKES THE TRIUMPH OUT OF MY VICTORY!

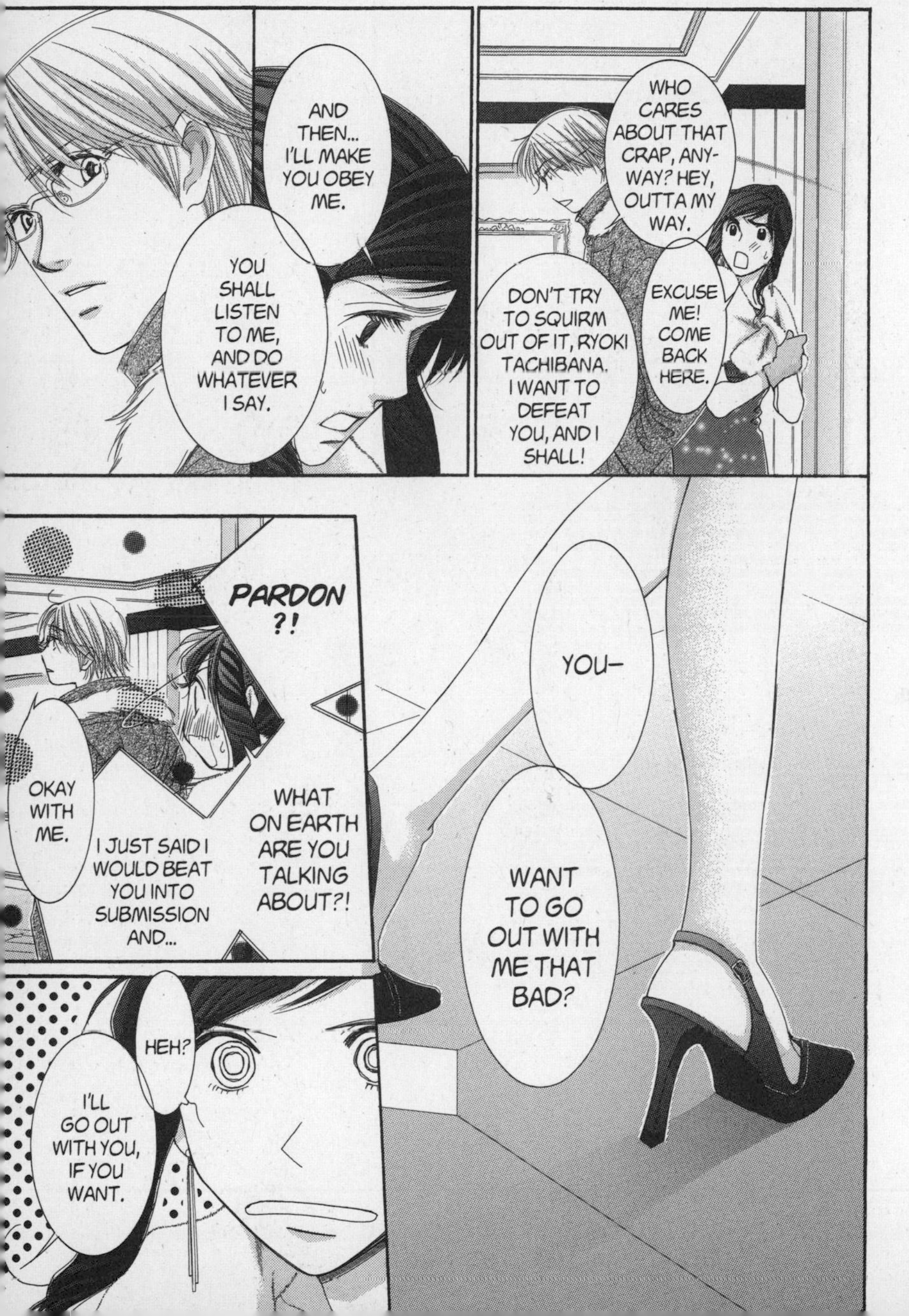
WHO CARES ABOUT THAT CRAP, ANY-WAY? HEY, OUTTA MY WAY.
EXCUSE ME! COME BACK HERE.
DON'T TRY TO SQUIRM OUT OF IT, RYOKI TACHIBANA. I WANT TO DEFEAT YOU, AND I SHALL!
AND THEN... I'LL MAKE YOU OBEY ME.
YOU SHALL LISTEN TO ME, AND DO WHATEVER I SAY.
YOU—
WANT TO GO OUT WITH ME THAT BAD?
PARDON?!
WHAT ON EARTH ARE YOU TALKING ABOUT?!
I JUST SAID I WOULD BEAT YOU INTO SUBMISSION AND...
OKAY WITH ME.
HEH?
I'LL GO OUT WITH YOU, IF YOU WANT.

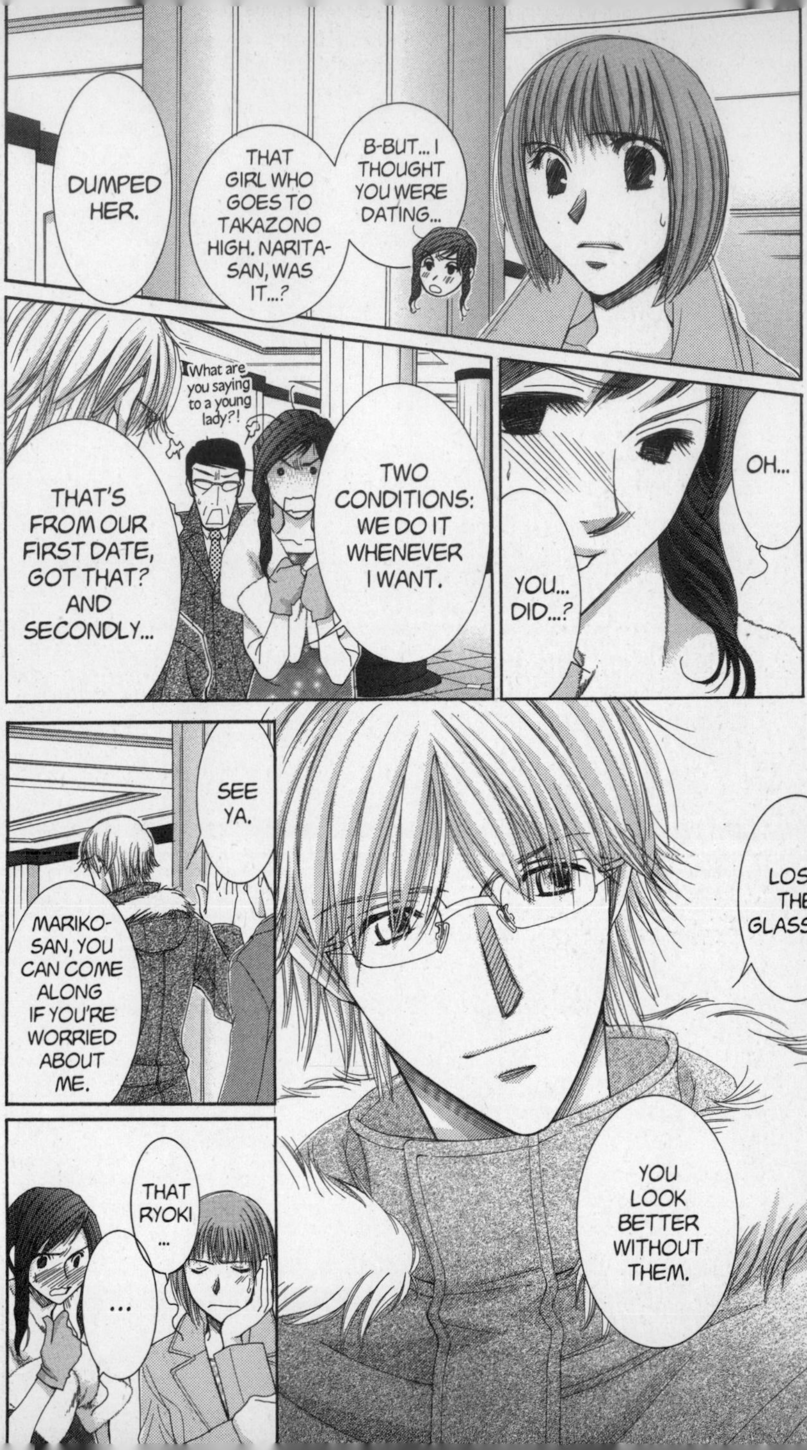
B-BUT... I THOUGHT YOU WERE DATING...
THAT GIRL WHO GOES TO TAKAZONO HIGH. NARITA-SAN, WAS IT...?
DUMPED HER.
OH...
YOU... DID...?
TWO CONDITIONS: WE DO IT WHENEVER I WANT.
What are you saying to a young lady?!
THAT'S FROM OUR FIRST DATE, GOT THAT? AND SECONDLY...
LOSE THE GLASSES.
YOU LOOK BETTER WITHOUT THEM.
SEE YA.
MARIKO-SAN, YOU CAN COME ALONG IF YOU'RE WORRIED ABOUT ME.
THAT RYOKI ...
...

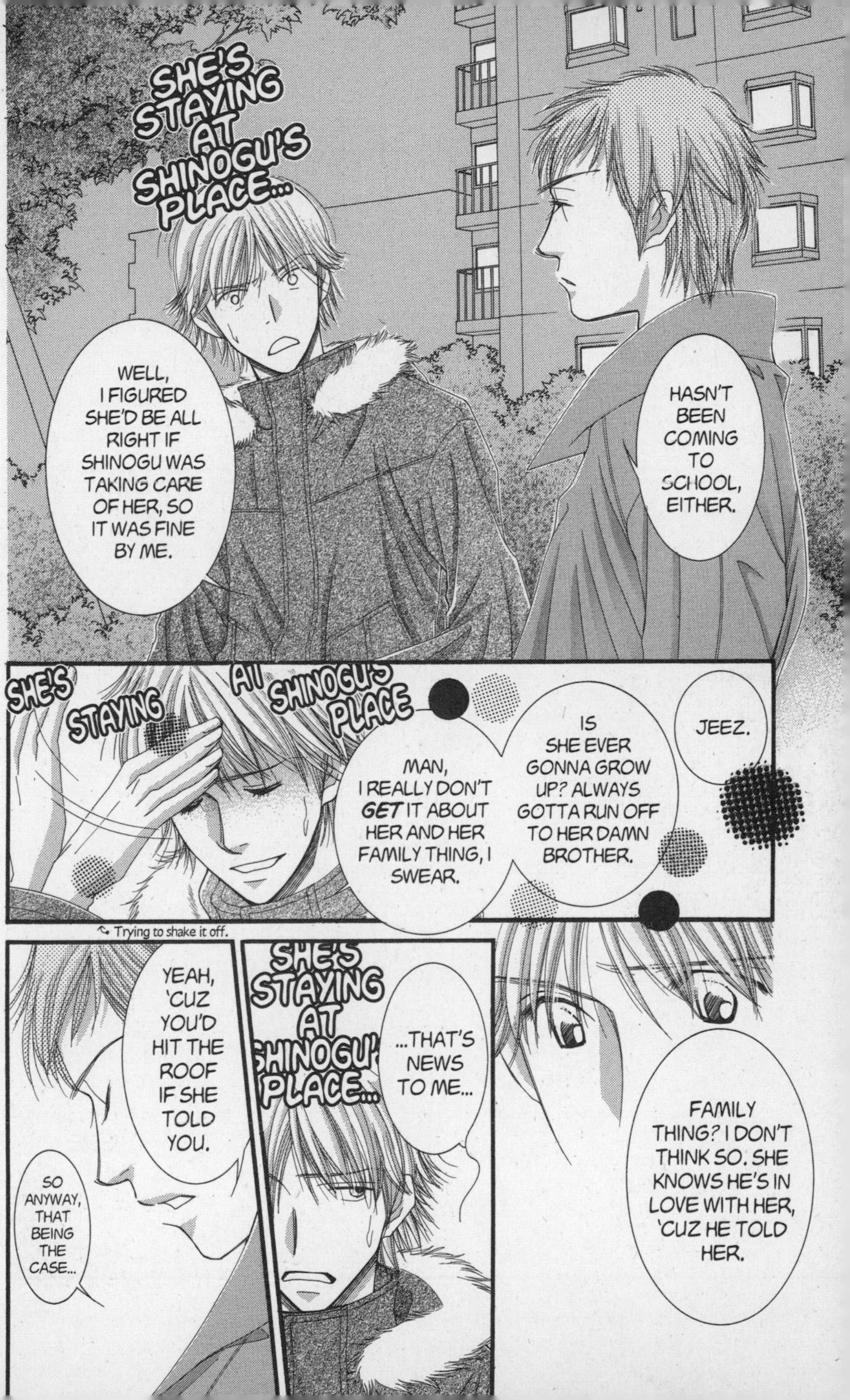
SHE'S STAYING AT SHINOGU'S PLACE...
HASN'T BEEN COMING TO SCHOOL, EITHER.
WELL, I FIGURED SHE'D BE ALL RIGHT IF SHINOGU WAS TAKING CARE OF HER, SO IT WAS FINE BY ME.
JEEZ.
IS SHE EVER GONNA GROW UP? ALWAYS GOTTA RUN OFF TO HER DAMN BROTHER.
MAN, I REALLY DON'T GET IT ABOUT HER AND HER FAMILY THING, I SWEAR.
SHE'S STAYING AT SHINOGU'S PLACE
Trying to shake it off.
FAMILY THING? I DON'T THINK SO. SHE KNOWS HE'S IN LOVE WITH HER, 'CUZ HE TOLD HER.
...THAT'S NEWS TO ME...
SHE'S STAYING AT SHINOGU'S PLACE...
YEAH, 'CUZ YOU'D HIT THE ROOF IF SHE TOLD YOU.
SO ANYWAY, THAT BEING THE CASE...

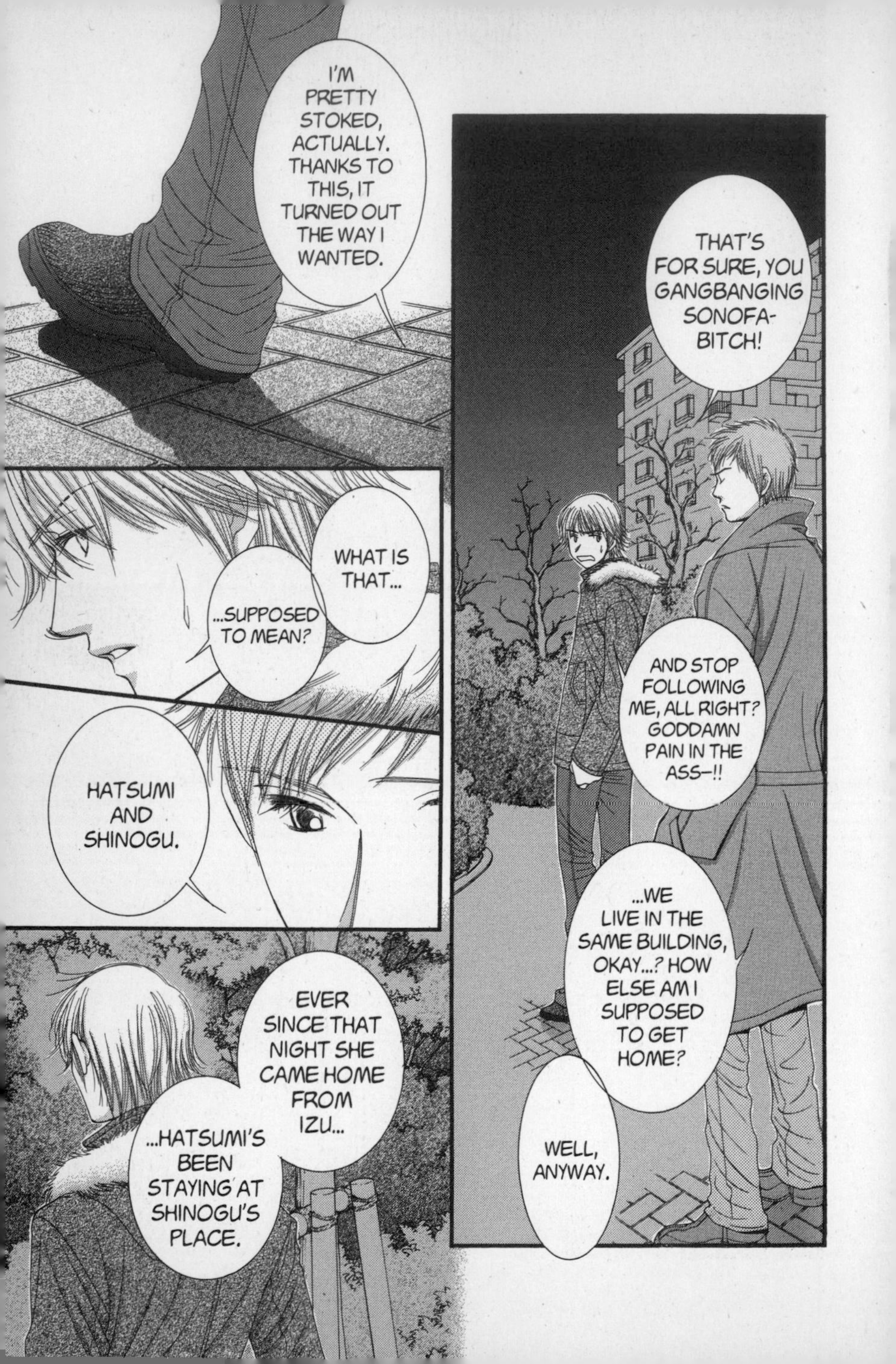
THAT'S FOR SURE, YOU GANGBANGING SONOFA-BITCH!
AND STOP FOLLOWING ME, ALL RIGHT? GODDAMN PAIN IN THE ASS—!!
...WE LIVE IN THE SAME BUILDING, OKAY...? HOW ELSE AM I SUPPOSED TO GET HOME?
WELL, ANYWAY.
I'M PRETTY STOKED, ACTUALLY. THANKS TO THIS, IT TURNED OUT THE WAY I WANTED.
WHAT IS THAT...
...SUPPOSED TO MEAN?
HATSUMI AND SHINOGU.
EVER SINCE THAT NIGHT SHE CAME HOME FROM IZU...
...HATSUMI'S BEEN STAYING AT SHINOGU'S PLACE.

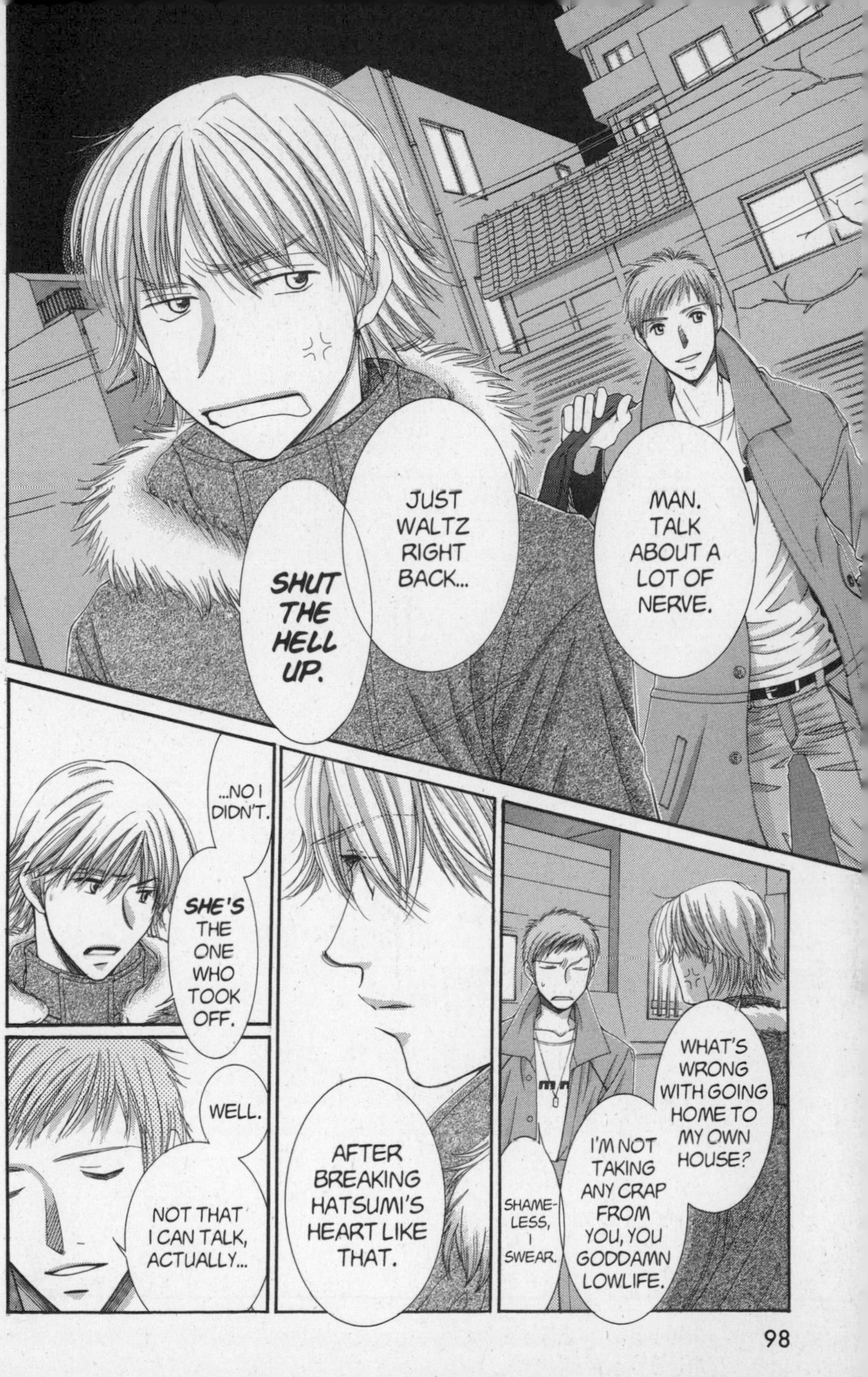
MAN. TALK ABOUT A LOT OF NERVE.
JUST WALTZ RIGHT BACK...
SHUT THE HELL UP.
WHAT'S WRONG WITH GOING HOME TO MY OWN HOUSE?
I'M NOT TAKING ANY CRAP FROM YOU, YOU GODDAMN LOWLIFE.
SHAME-LESS, I SWEAR.
AFTER BREAKING HATSUMI'S HEART LIKE THAT.
...NO I DIDN'T.
SHE'S THE ONE WHO TOOK OFF.
WELL.
NOT THAT I CAN TALK, ACTUALLY...

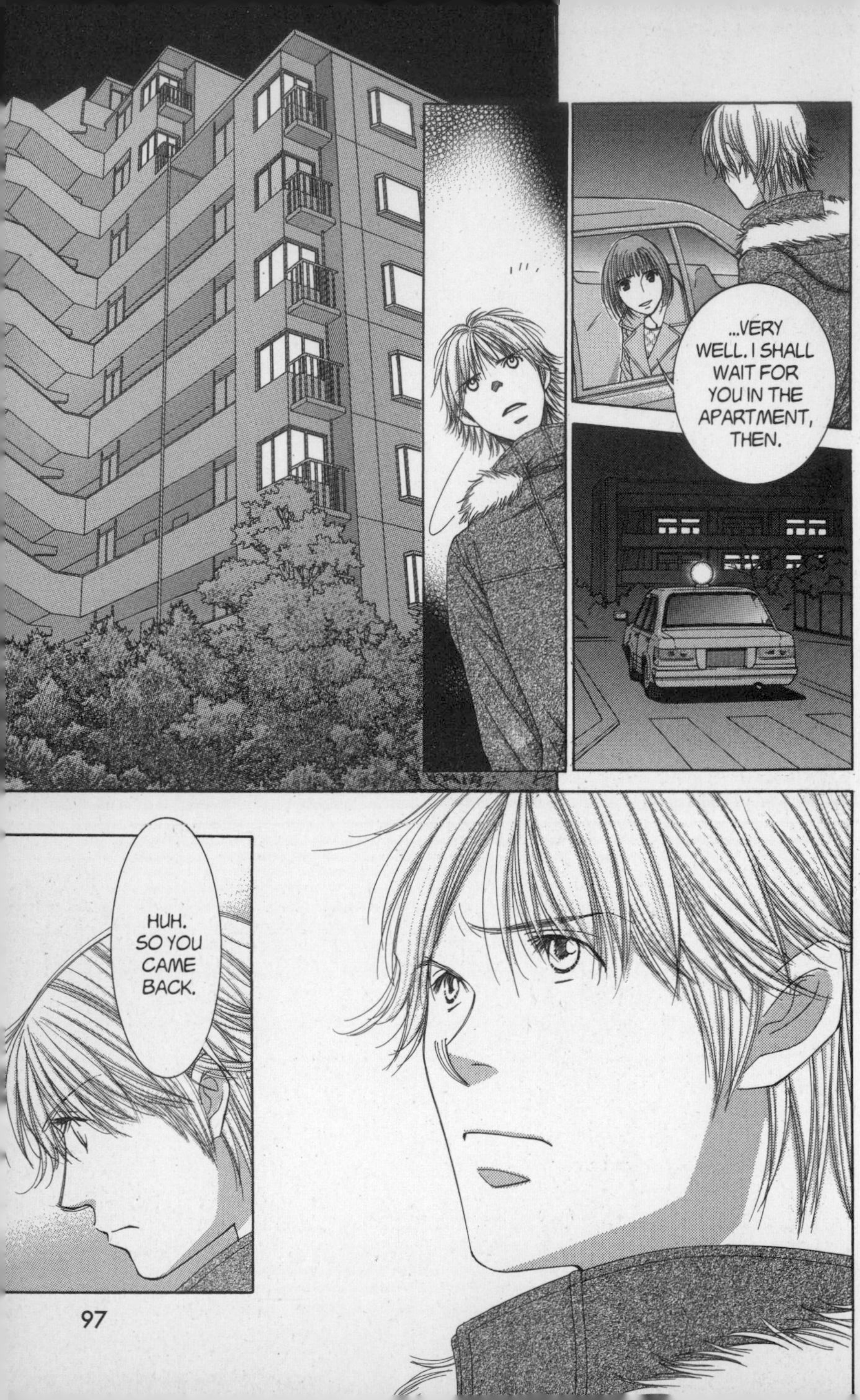
...VERY WELL. I SHALL WAIT FOR YOU IN THE APARTMENT, THEN.
HUH. SO YOU CAME BACK.

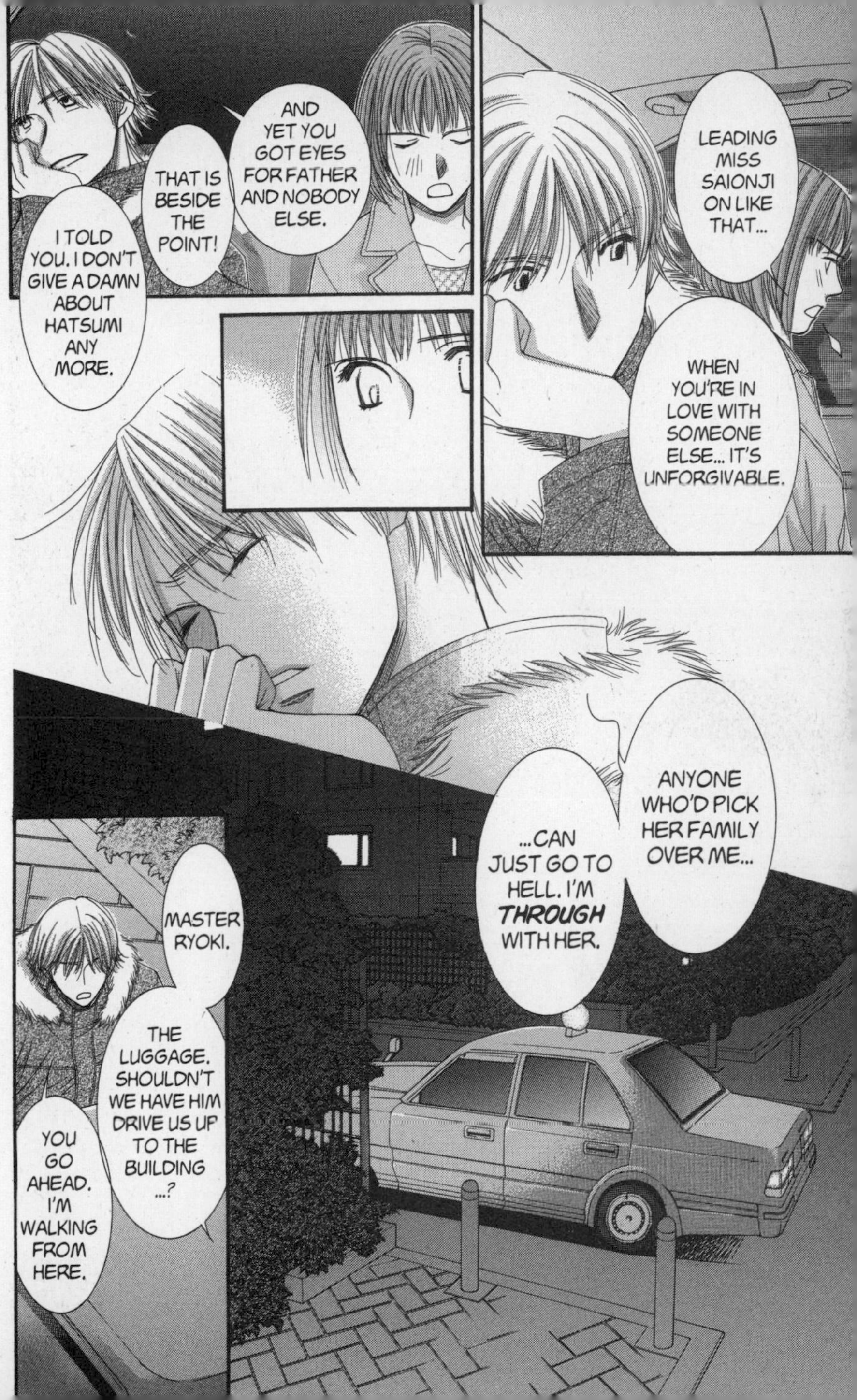

LEADING MISS SAIONJI ON LIKE THAT...
WHEN YOU'RE IN LOVE WITH SOMEONE ELSE... IT'S UNFORGIVABLE.
AND YET YOU GOT EYES FOR FATHER AND NOBODY ELSE.
THAT IS BESIDE THE POINT!
I TOLD YOU. I DON'T GIVE A DAMN ABOUT HATSUMI ANY MORE.
ANYONE WHO'D PICK HER FAMILY OVER ME...
...CAN JUST GO TO HELL. I'M ***THROUGH*** WITH HER.
MASTER RYOKI.
THE LUGGAGE. SHOULDN'T WE HAVE HIM DRIVE US UP TO THE BUILDING ...?
YOU GO AHEAD. I'M WALKING FROM HERE.

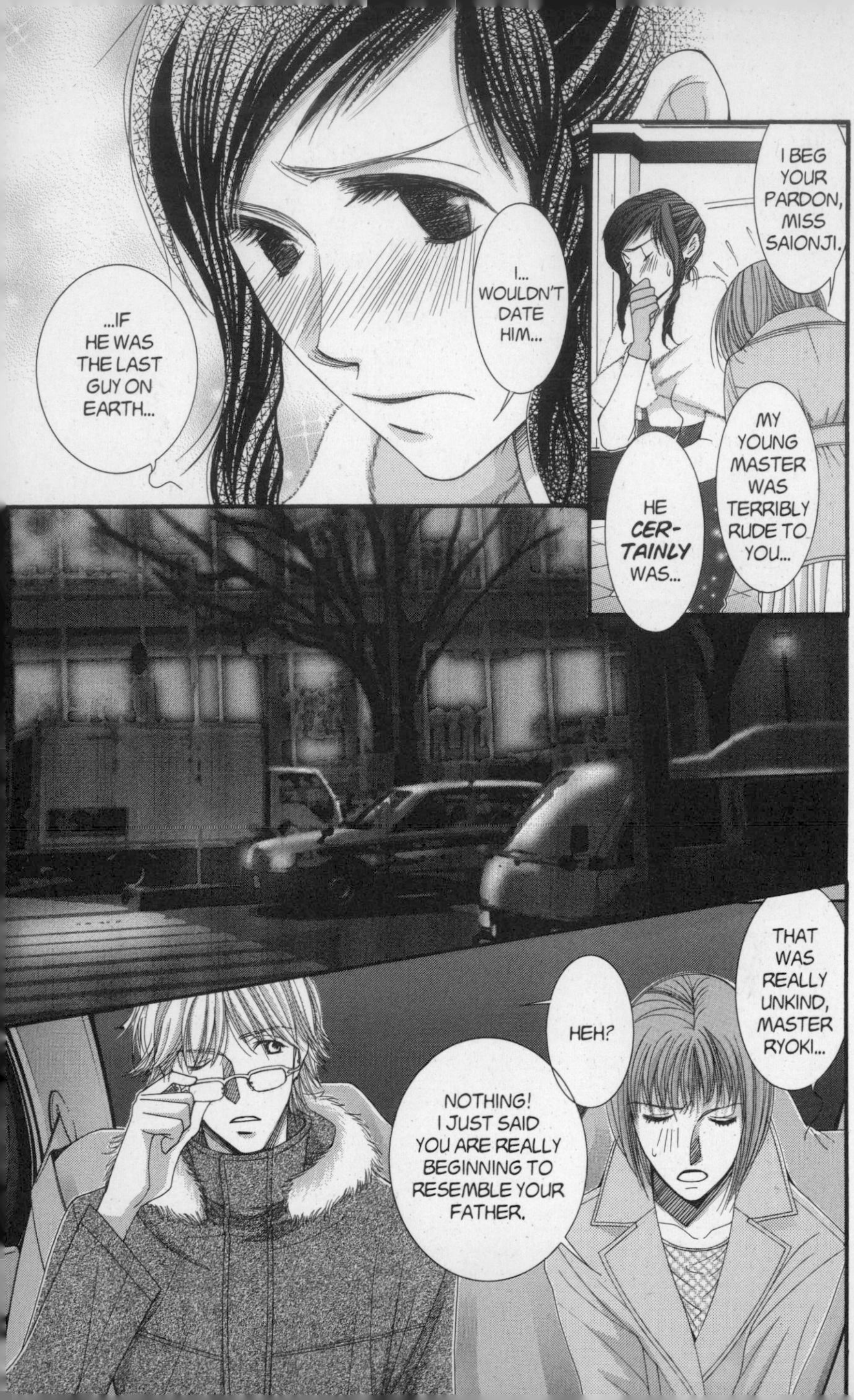
I BEG YOUR PARDON, MISS SAIONJI.
MY YOUNG MASTER WAS TERRIBLY RUDE TO YOU...
HE *CERTAINLY* WAS...
I... WOULDN'T DATE HIM...
...IF HE WAS THE LAST GUY ON EARTH...
THAT WAS REALLY UNKIND, MASTER RYOKI...
HEH?
NOTHING! I JUST SAID YOU ARE REALLY BEGINNING TO RESEMBLE YOUR FATHER.

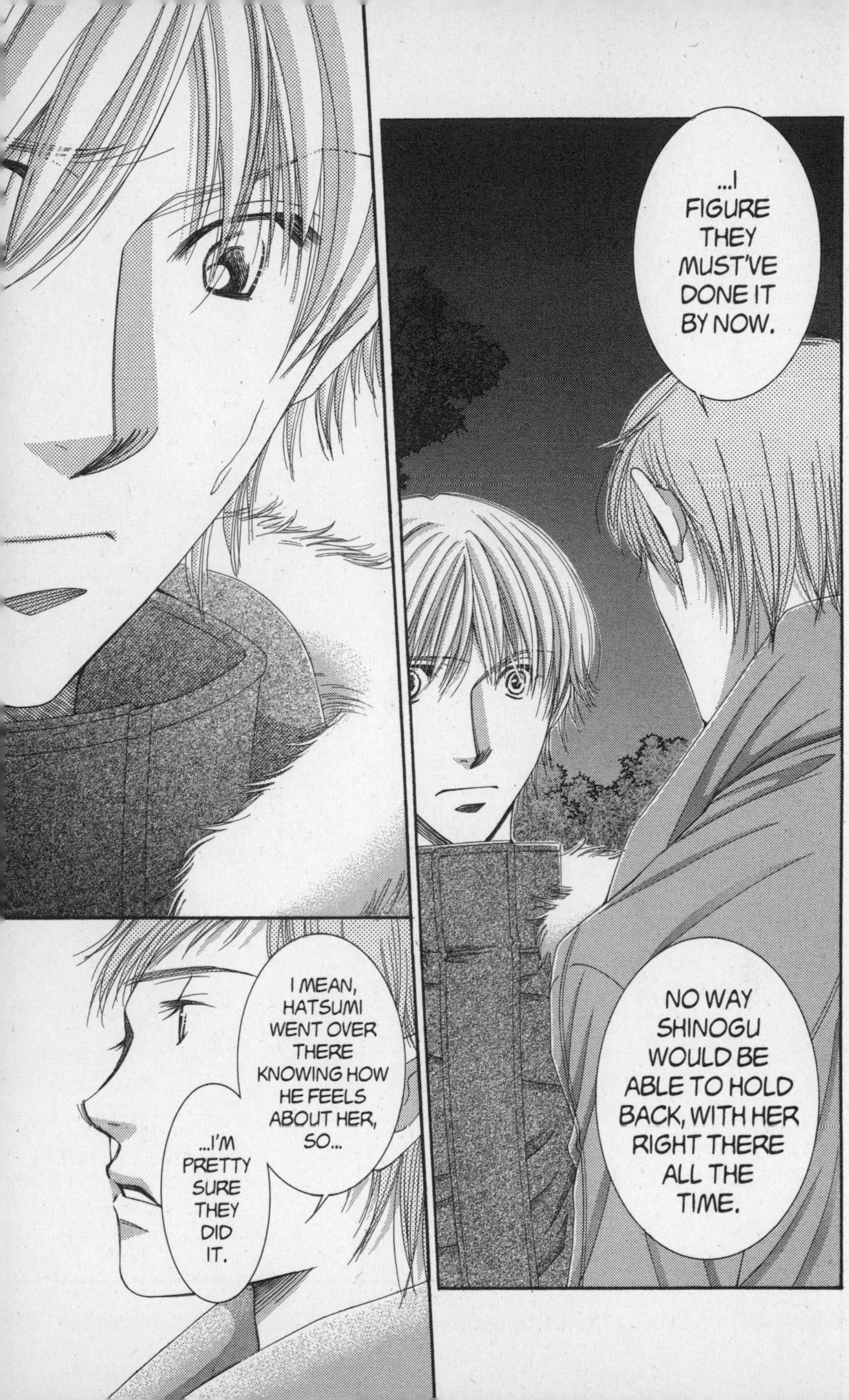
...I FIGURE THEY MUST'VE DONE IT BY NOW.
NO WAY SHINOGU WOULD BE ABLE TO HOLD BACK, WITH HER RIGHT THERE ALL THE TIME.
I MEAN, HATSUMI WENT OVER THERE KNOWING HOW HE FEELS ABOUT HER, SO...
...I'M PRETTY SURE THEY DID IT.

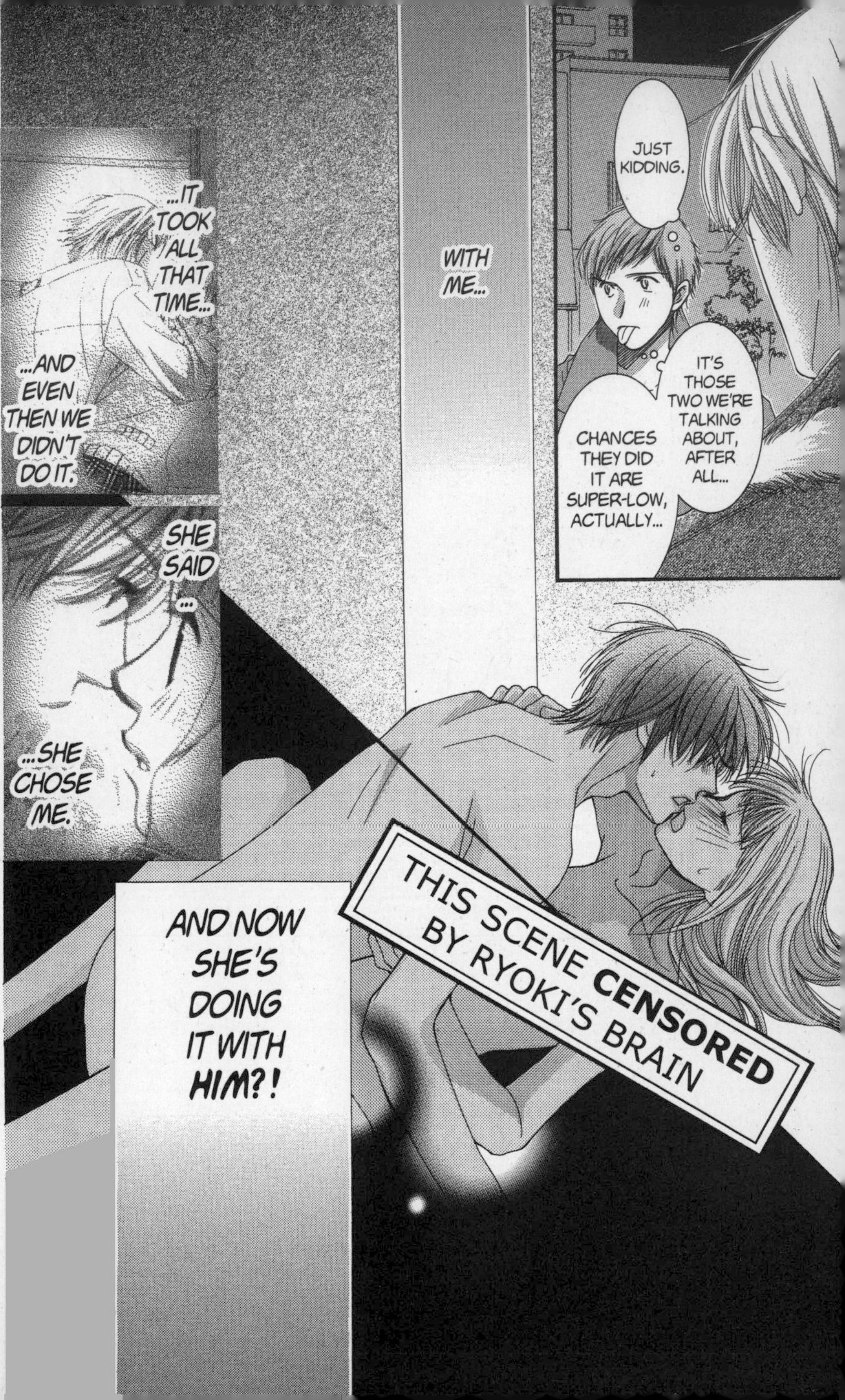
JUST KIDDING.
IT'S THOSE TWO WE'RE TALKING ABOUT, AFTER ALL...
CHANCES THEY DID IT ARE SUPER-LOW, ACTUALLY...
WITH ME...
...IT TOOK ALL THAT TIME...
...AND EVEN THEN WE DIDN'T DO IT.
SHE SAID...
...SHE CHOSE ME.
THIS SCENE **CENSORED** BY RYOKI'S BRAIN
AND NOW SHE'S DOING IT WITH **HIM?!**

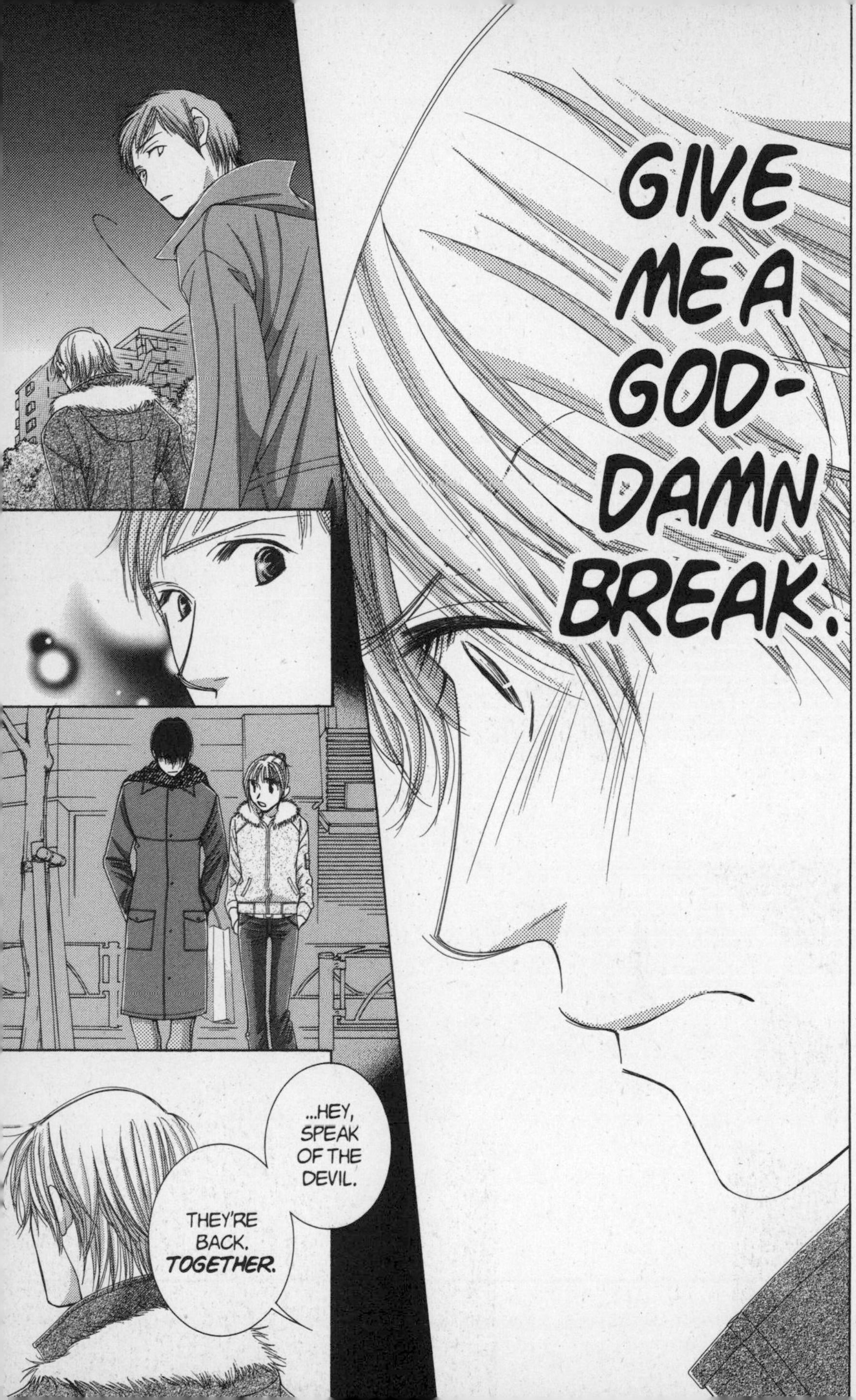
GIVE ME A GOD-DAMN BREAK.
...HEY, SPEAK OF THE DEVIL.
THEY'RE BACK. *TOGETHER.*

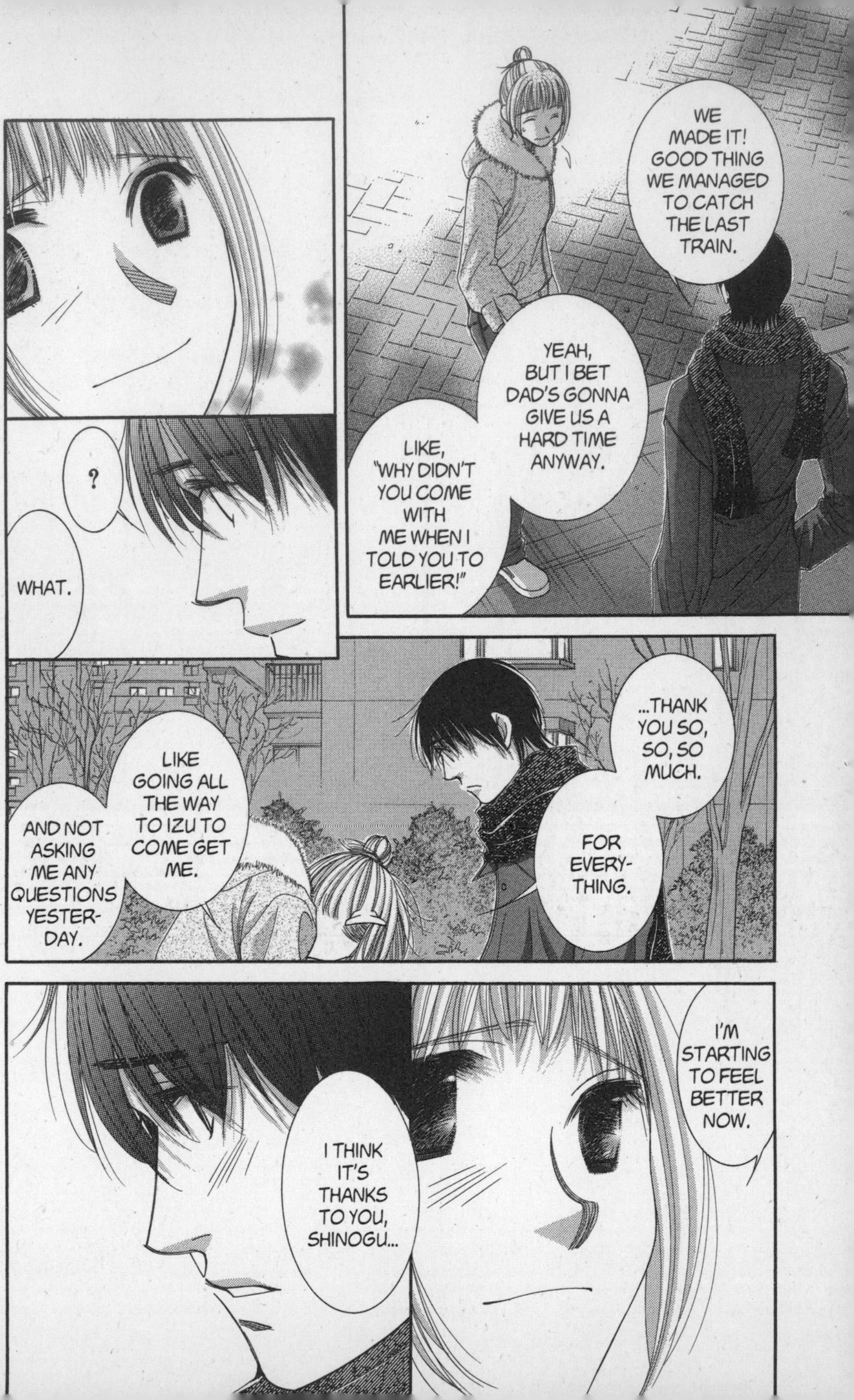
WE MADE IT! GOOD THING WE MANAGED TO CATCH THE LAST TRAIN.
YEAH, BUT I BET DAD'S GONNA GIVE US A HARD TIME ANYWAY.
LIKE, "WHY DIDN'T YOU COME WITH ME WHEN I TOLD YOU TO EARLIER!"
?
WHAT.
...THANK YOU SO, SO, SO MUCH.
FOR EVERYTHING.
LIKE GOING ALL THE WAY TO IZU TO COME GET ME.
AND NOT ASKING ME ANY QUESTIONS YESTERDAY.
I'M STARTING TO FEEL BETTER NOW.
I THINK IT'S THANKS TO YOU, SHINOGU...

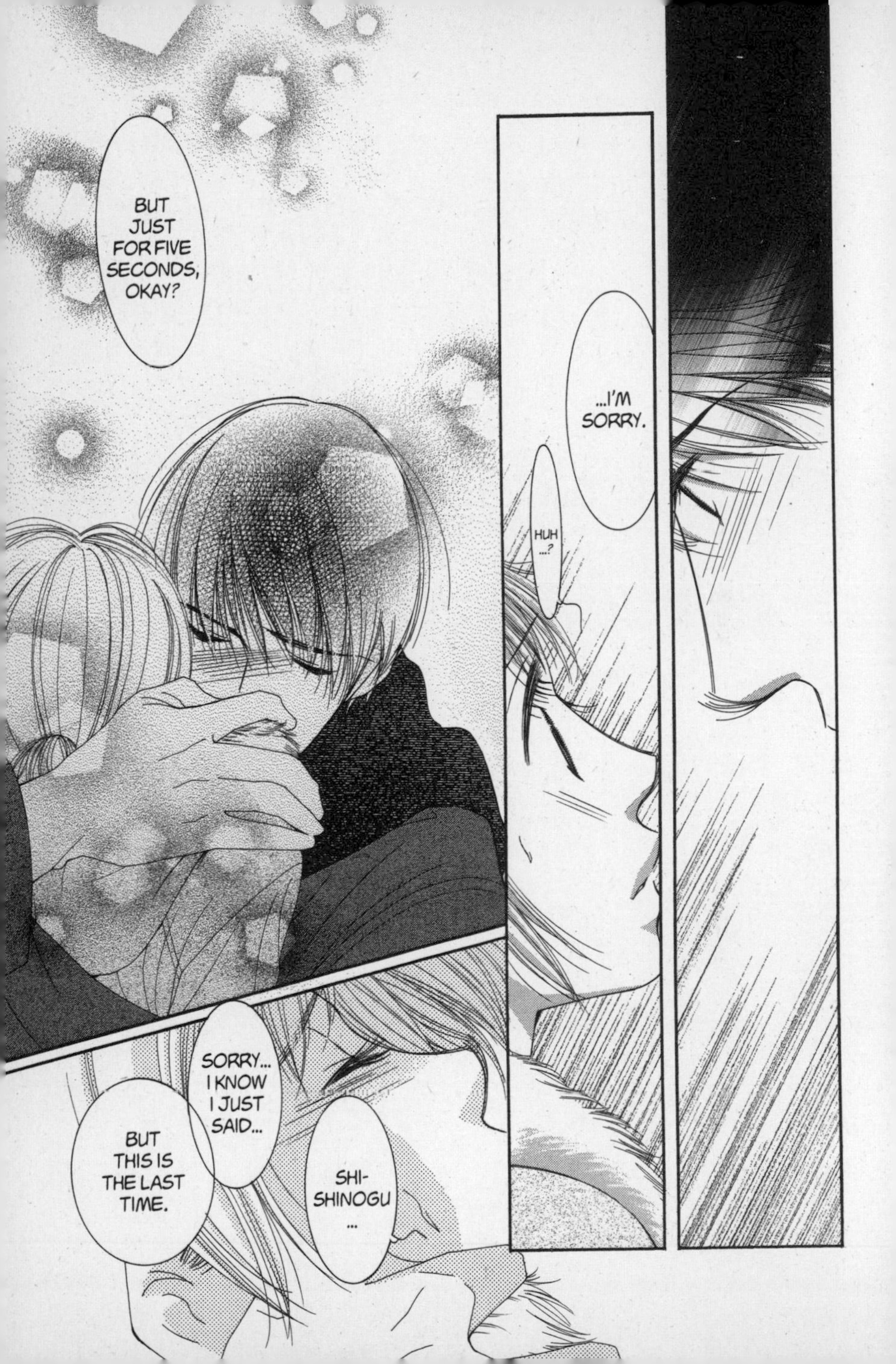
...I'M SORRY.
HUH ...?
BUT JUST FOR FIVE SECONDS, OKAY?
SHI-SHINOGU ...
SORRY... I KNOW I JUST SAID...
BUT THIS IS THE LAST TIME.

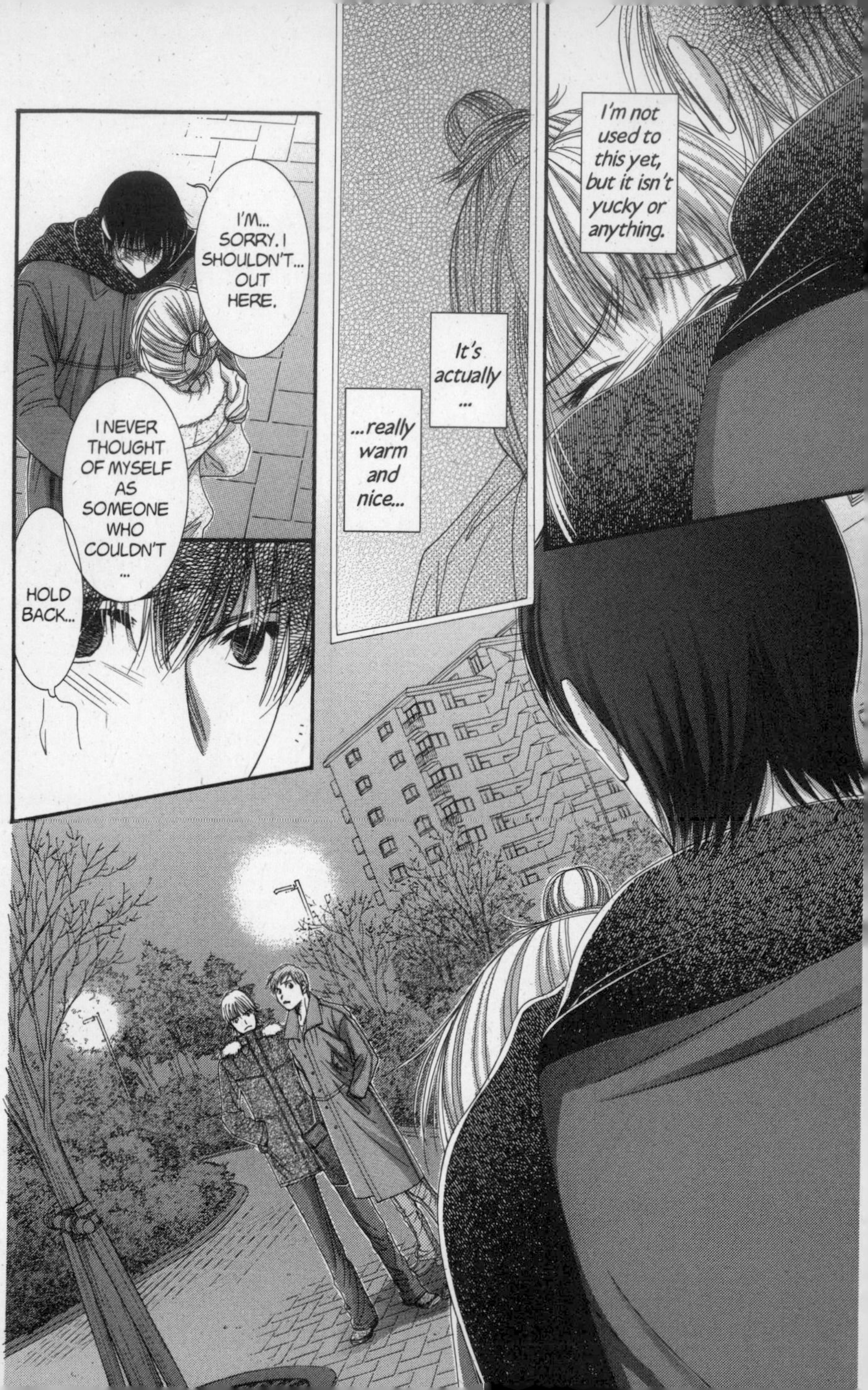
I'm not used to this yet, but it isn't yucky or anything.
It's actually ...
...really warm and nice...
I'M... SORRY. I SHOULDN'T... OUT HERE.
I NEVER THOUGHT OF MYSELF AS SOMEONE WHO COULDN'T ...
HOLD BACK...

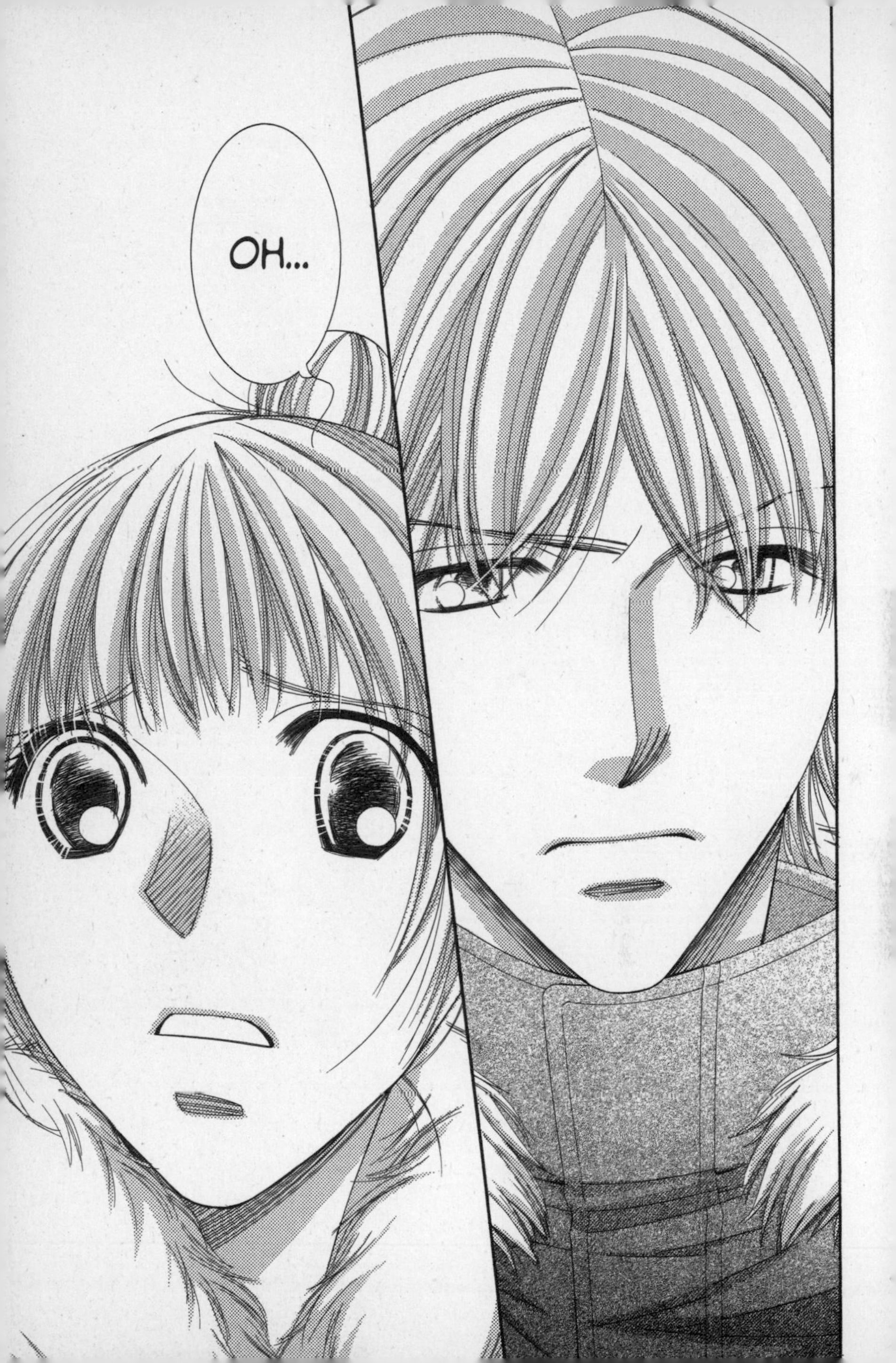
OH...

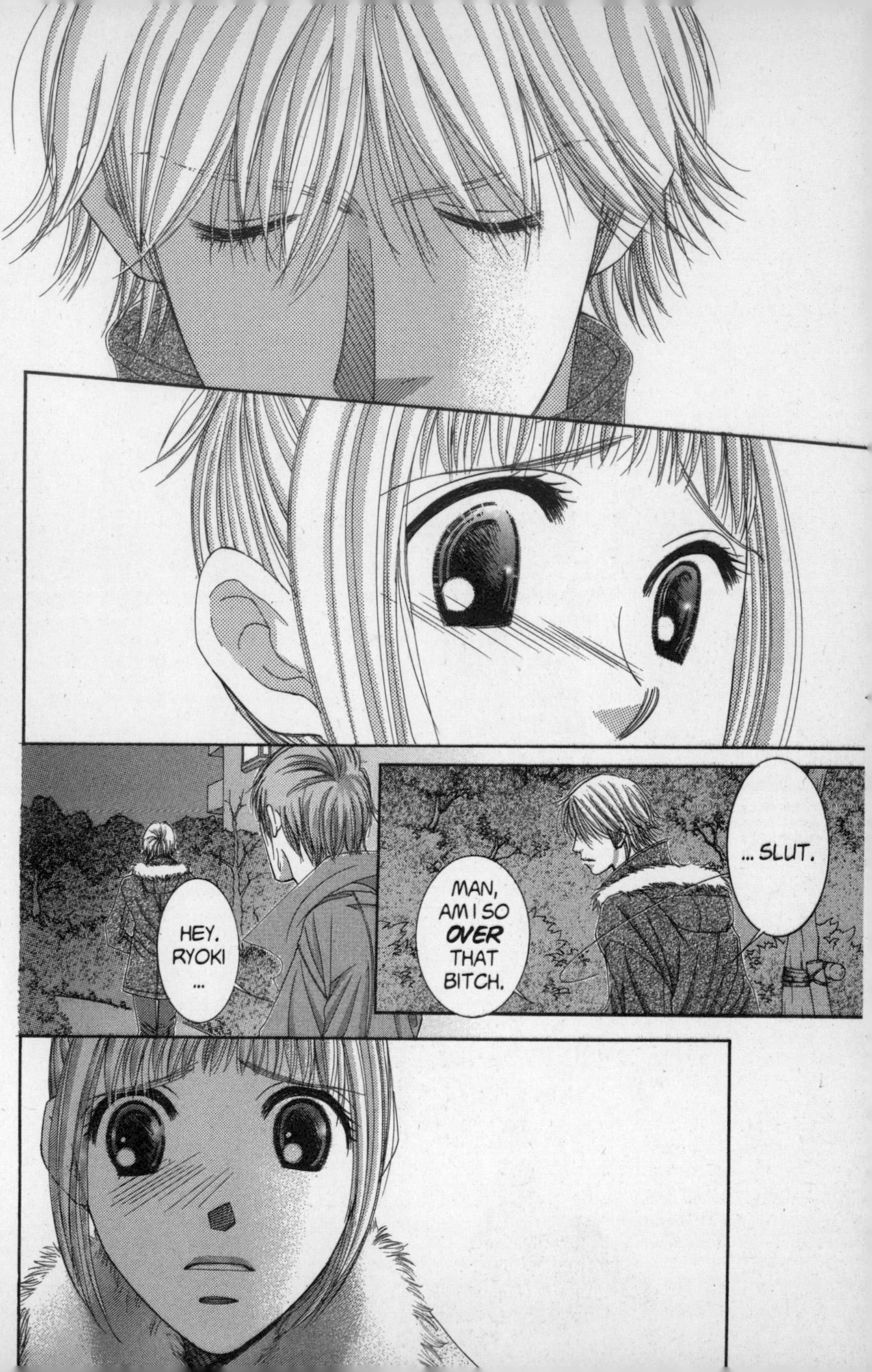
... SLUT.
MAN, AM I SO **OVER** THAT BITCH.
HEY. RYOKI ...

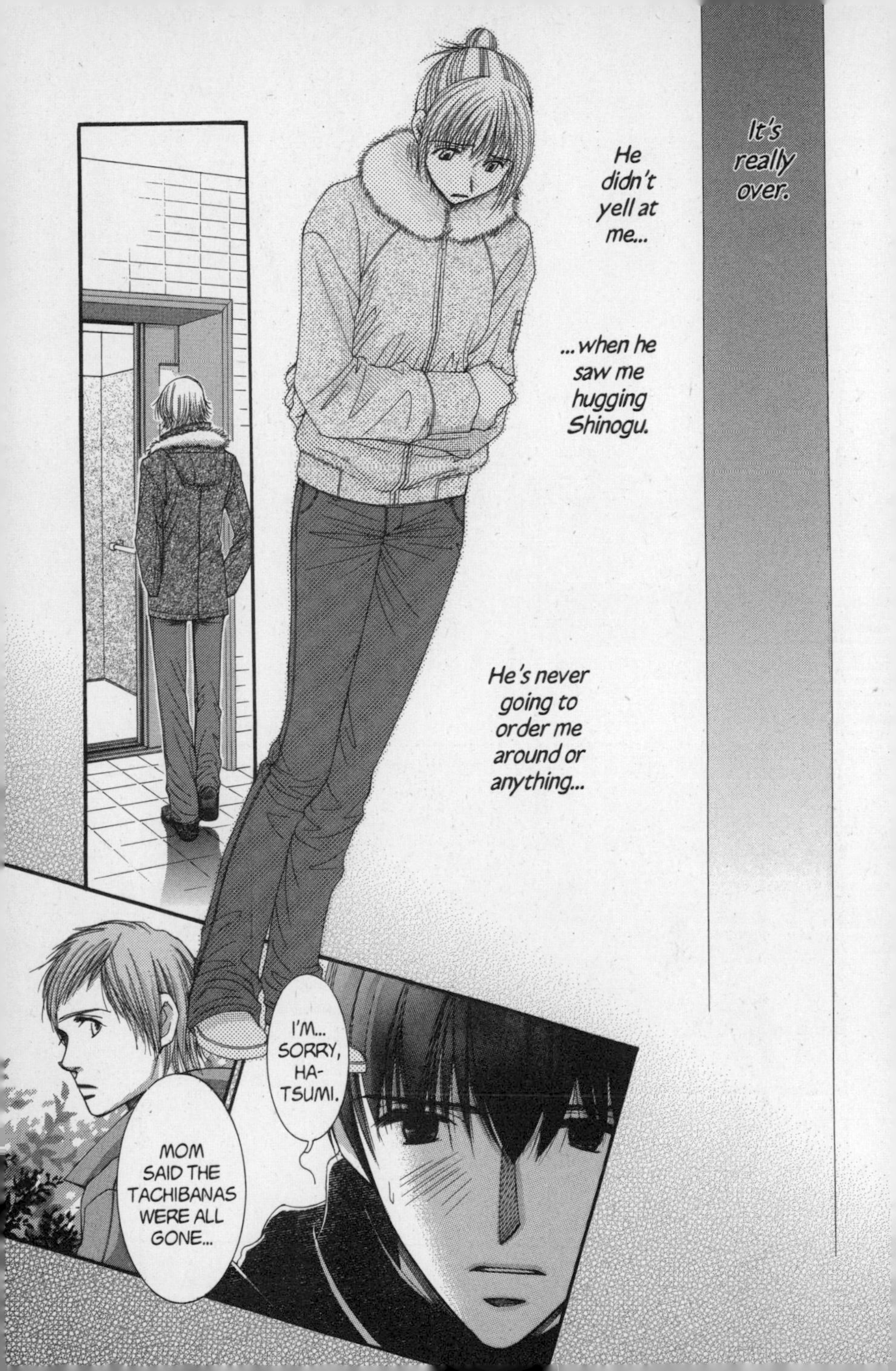
It's really over.
He didn't yell at me...
...when he saw me hugging Shinogu.
He's never going to order me around or anything...
I'M... SORRY, HA-TSUMI.
MOM SAID THE TACHIBANAS WERE ALL GONE...

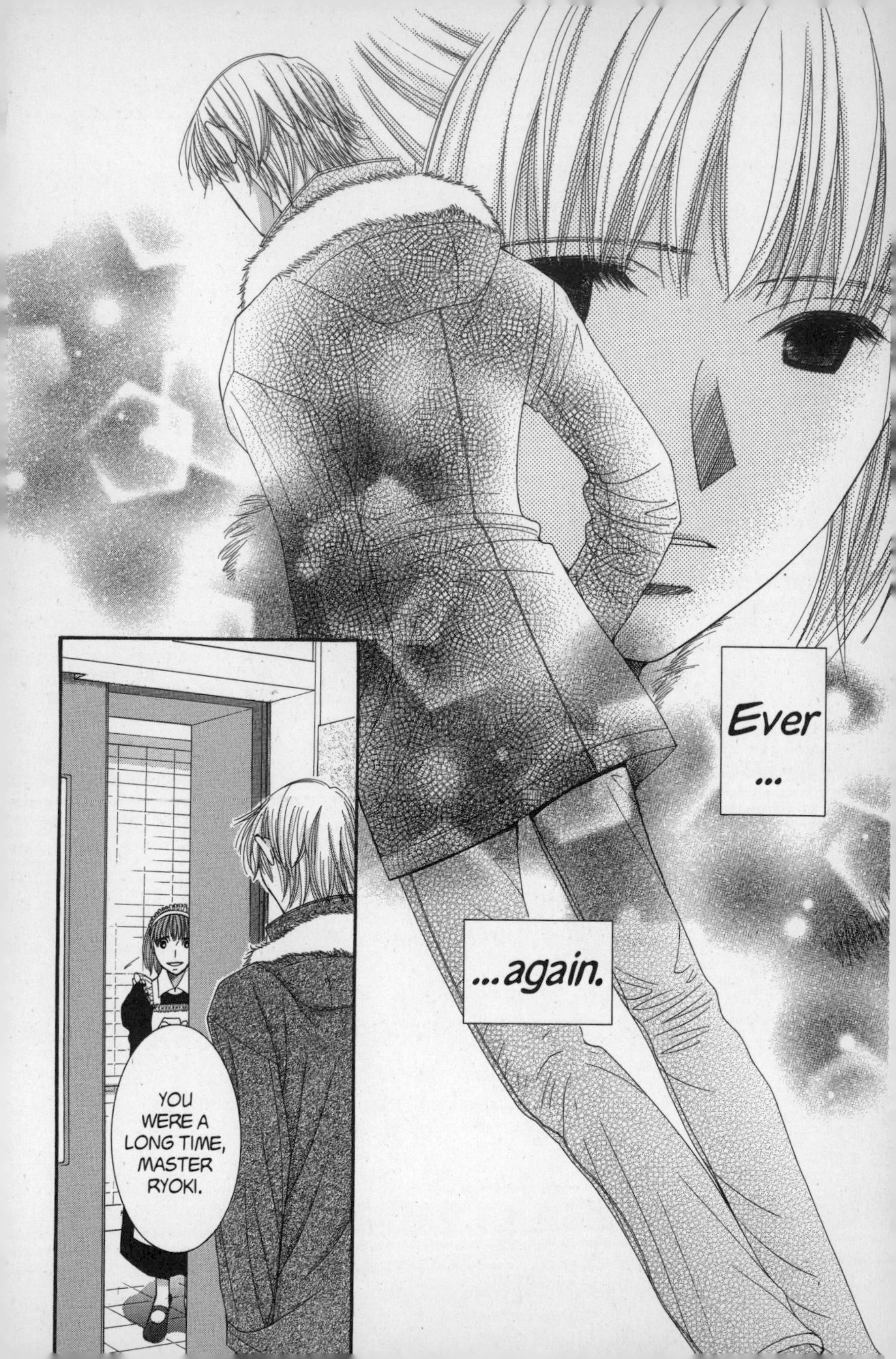
Ever ...
...again.
YOU WERE A LONG TIME, MASTER RYOKI.

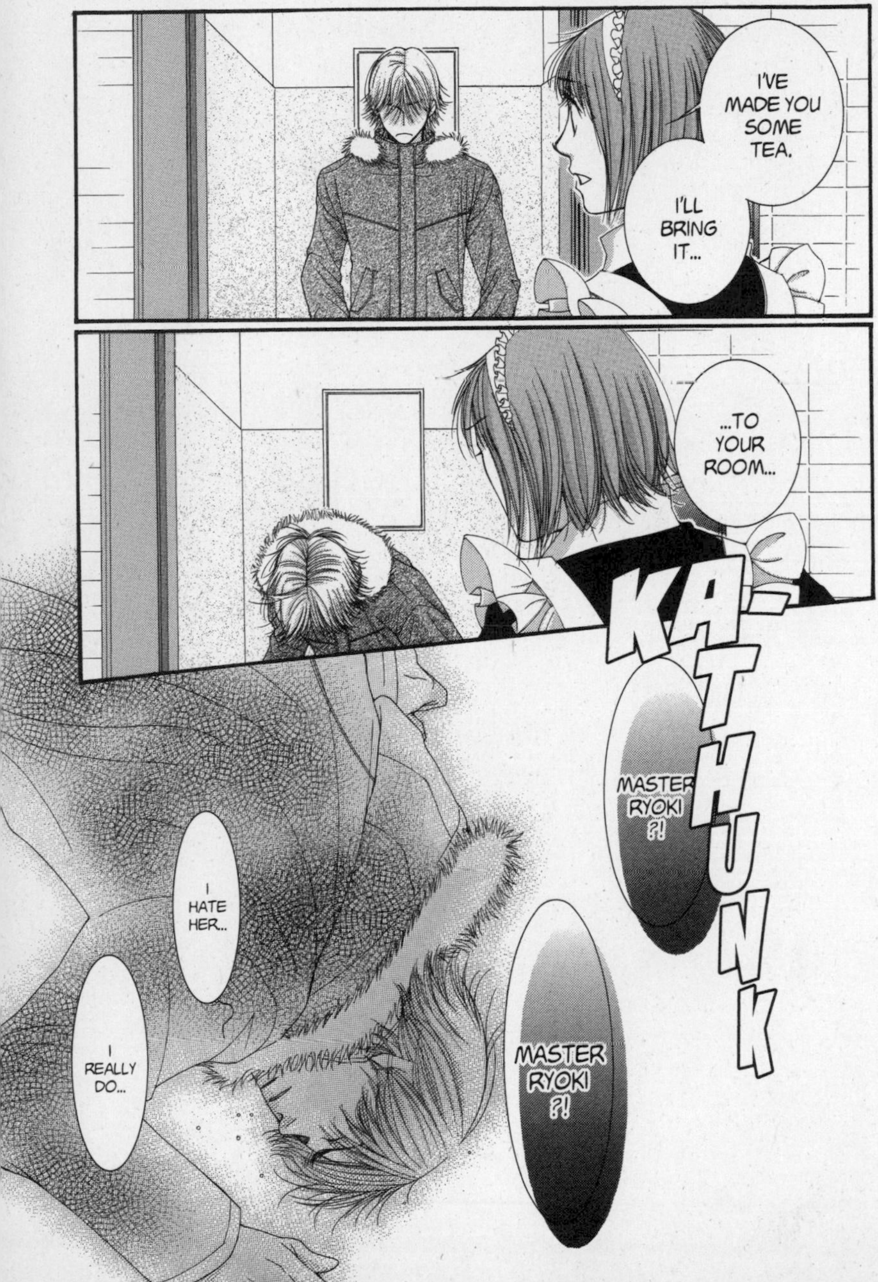
I'VE MADE YOU SOME TEA.
I'LL BRING IT...
...TO YOUR ROOM...
KA-THUNK
MASTER RYOKI ?!
MASTER RYOKI ?!
I HATE HER...
I REALLY DO...

Chapter 50

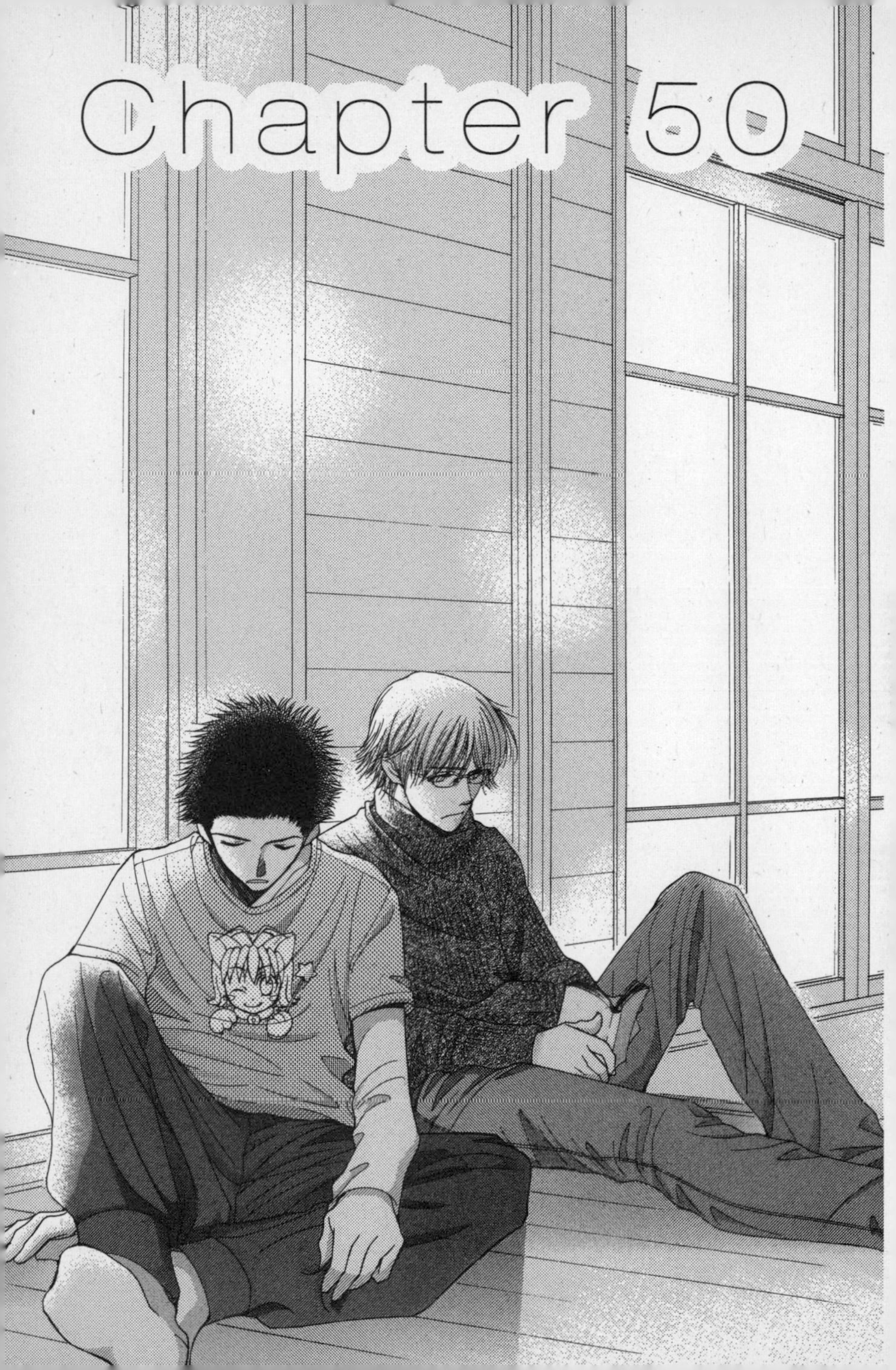

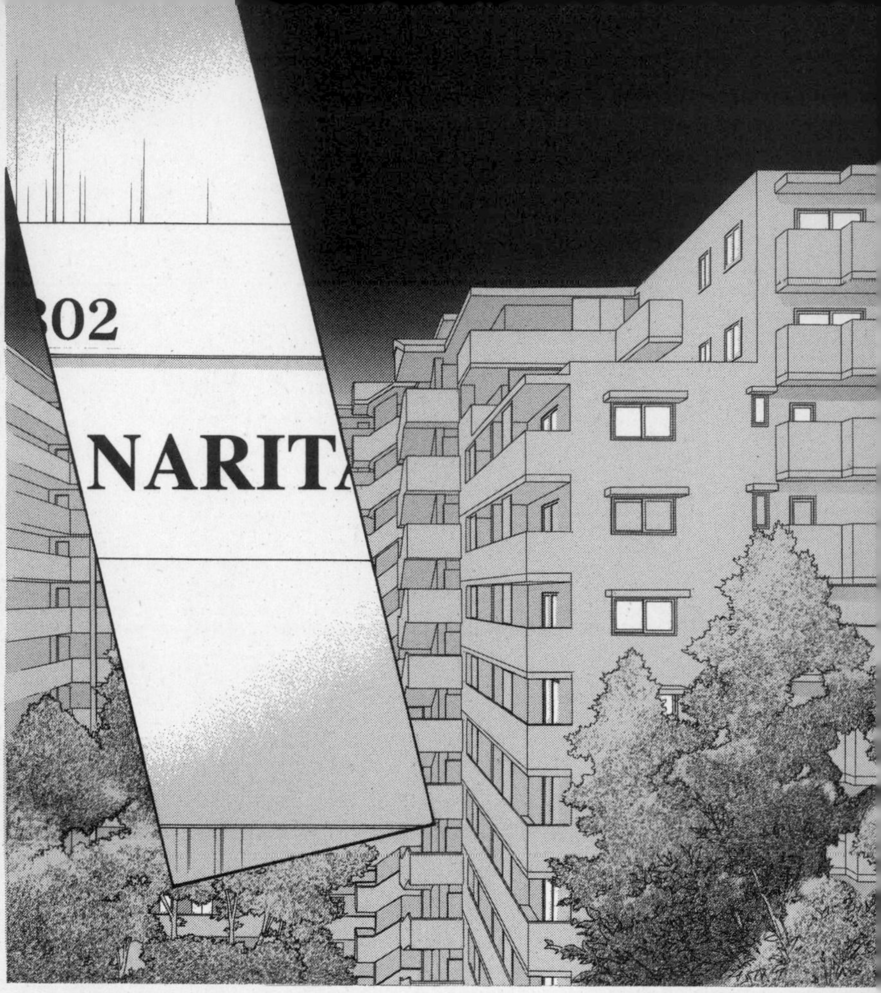
302
NARITA

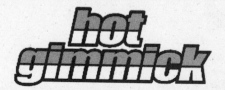

hot gimmick

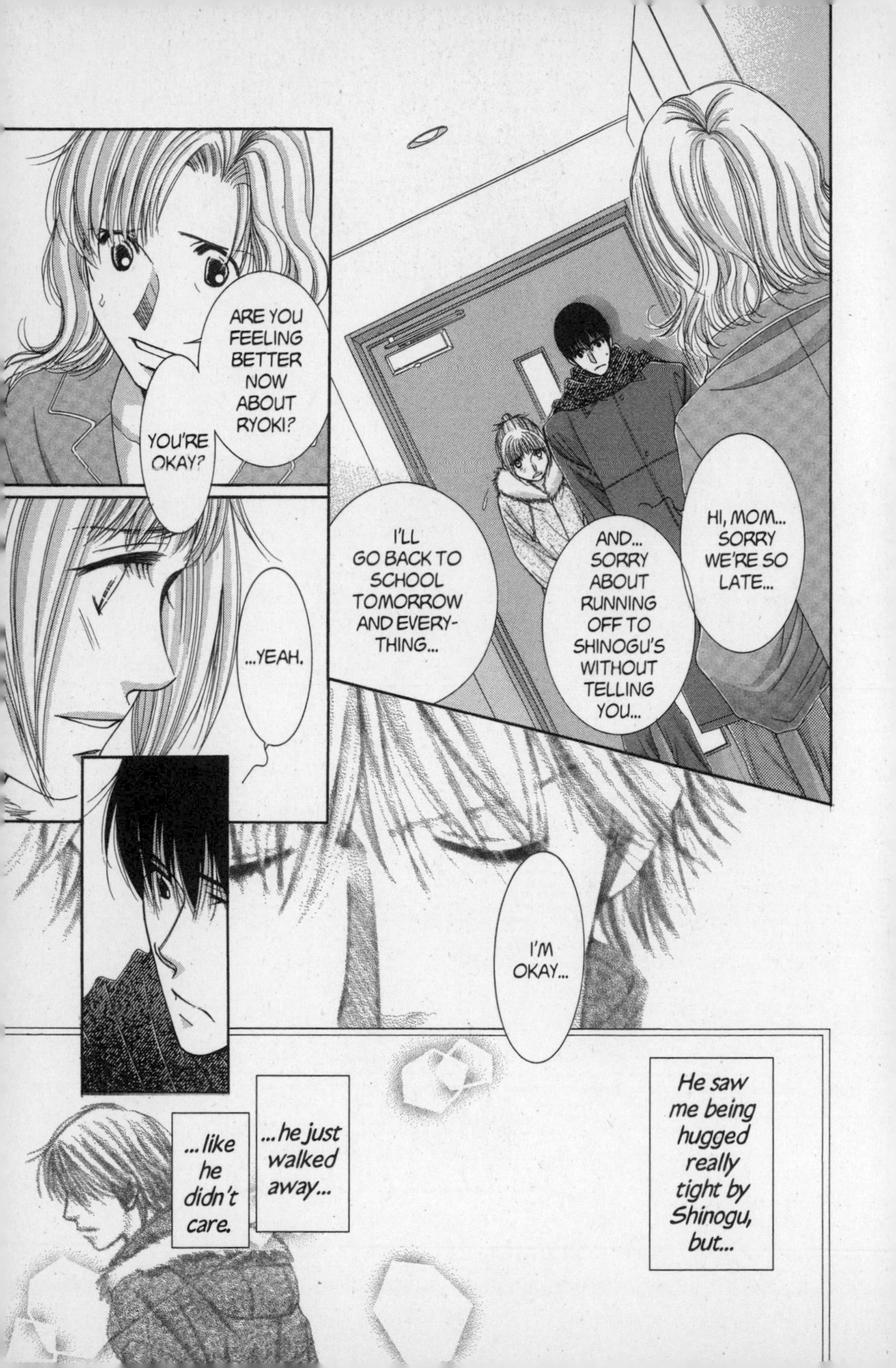
HI, MOM... SORRY WE'RE SO LATE...
AND... SORRY ABOUT RUNNING OFF TO SHINOGU'S WITHOUT TELLING YOU...
I'LL GO BACK TO SCHOOL TOMORROW AND EVERY-THING...
ARE YOU FEELING BETTER NOW ABOUT RYOKI?
YOU'RE OKAY?
...YEAH.
I'M OKAY...
He saw me being hugged really tight by Shinogu, but...
...he just walked away...
...like he didn't care.

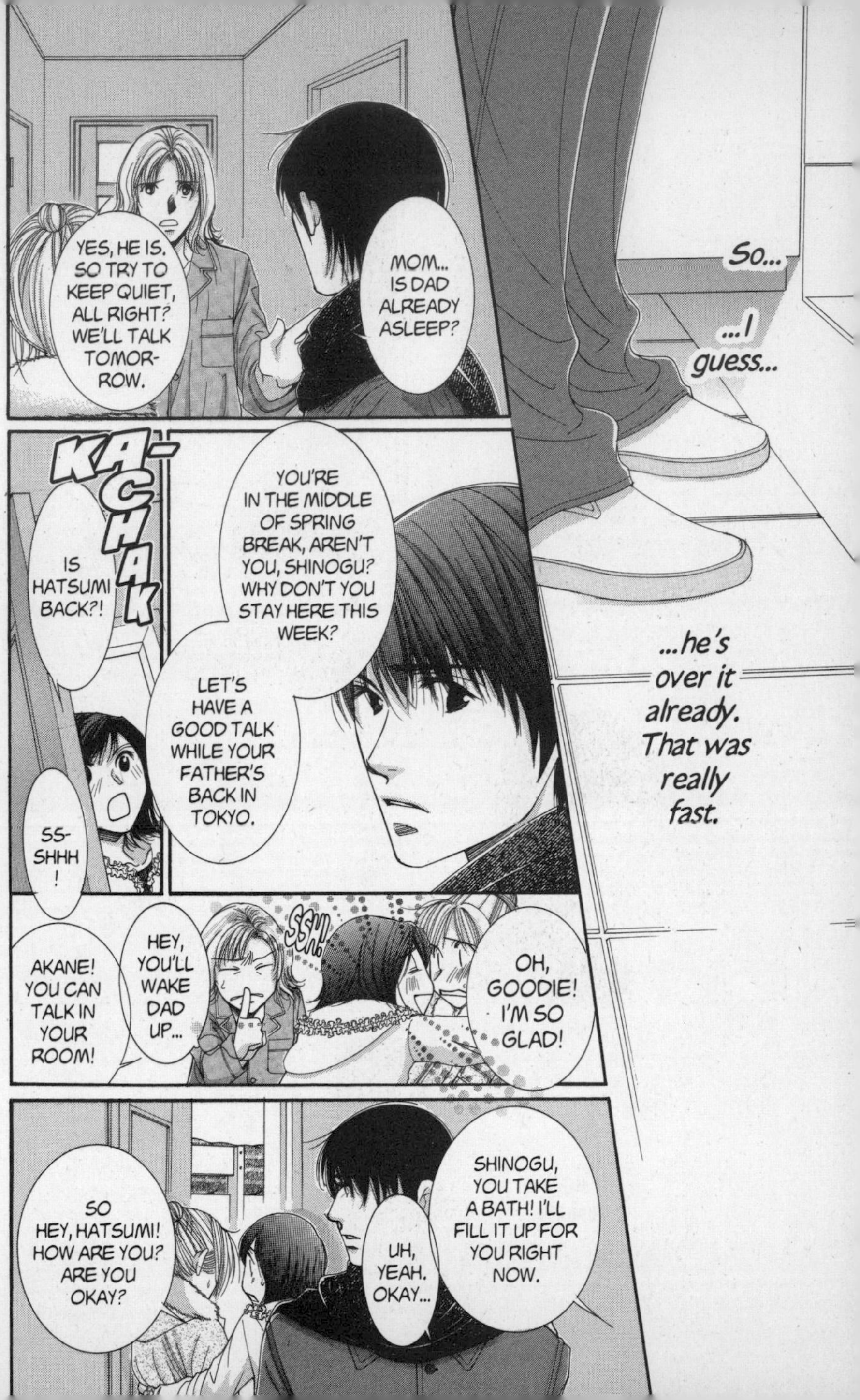
So...
...I guess...
...he's over it already. That was really fast.
MOM... IS DAD ALREADY ASLEEP?
YES, HE IS. SO TRY TO KEEP QUIET, ALL RIGHT? WE'LL TALK TOMOR-ROW.
YOU'RE IN THE MIDDLE OF SPRING BREAK, AREN'T YOU, SHINOGU? WHY DON'T YOU STAY HERE THIS WEEK?
LET'S HAVE A GOOD TALK WHILE YOUR FATHER'S BACK IN TOKYO.
KA-CHAK
IS HATSUMI BACK?!
SS-SHHH!
OH, GOODIE! I'M SO GLAD!
SSH!
HEY, YOU'LL WAKE DAD UP...
AKANE! YOU CAN TALK IN YOUR ROOM!
SHINOGU, YOU TAKE A BATH! I'LL FILL IT UP FOR YOU RIGHT NOW.
UH, YEAH. OKAY...
SO HEY, HATSUMI! HOW ARE YOU? ARE YOU OKAY?

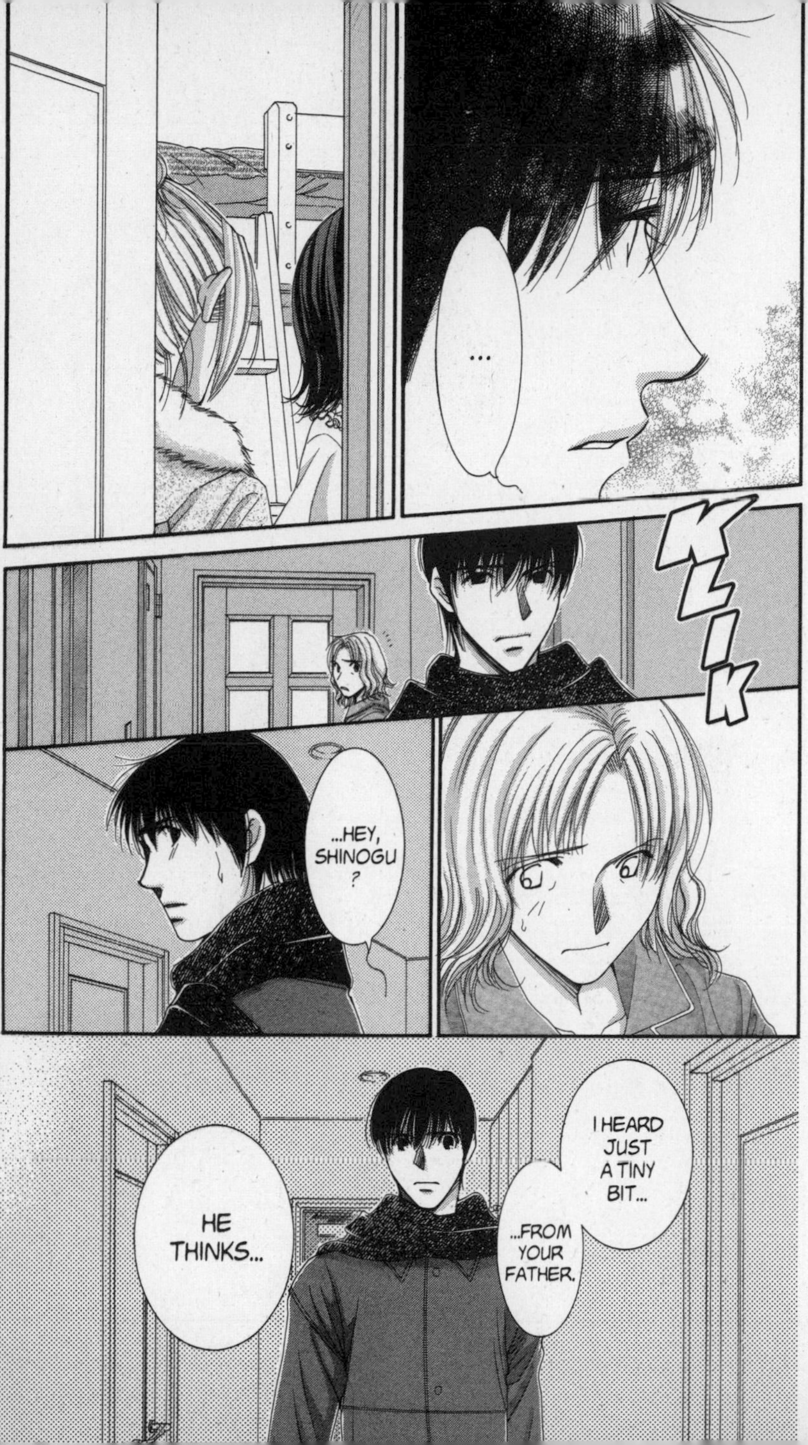
...
KLIK
...HEY, SHINOGU?
I HEARD JUST A TINY BIT...
...FROM YOUR FATHER.
HE THINKS...

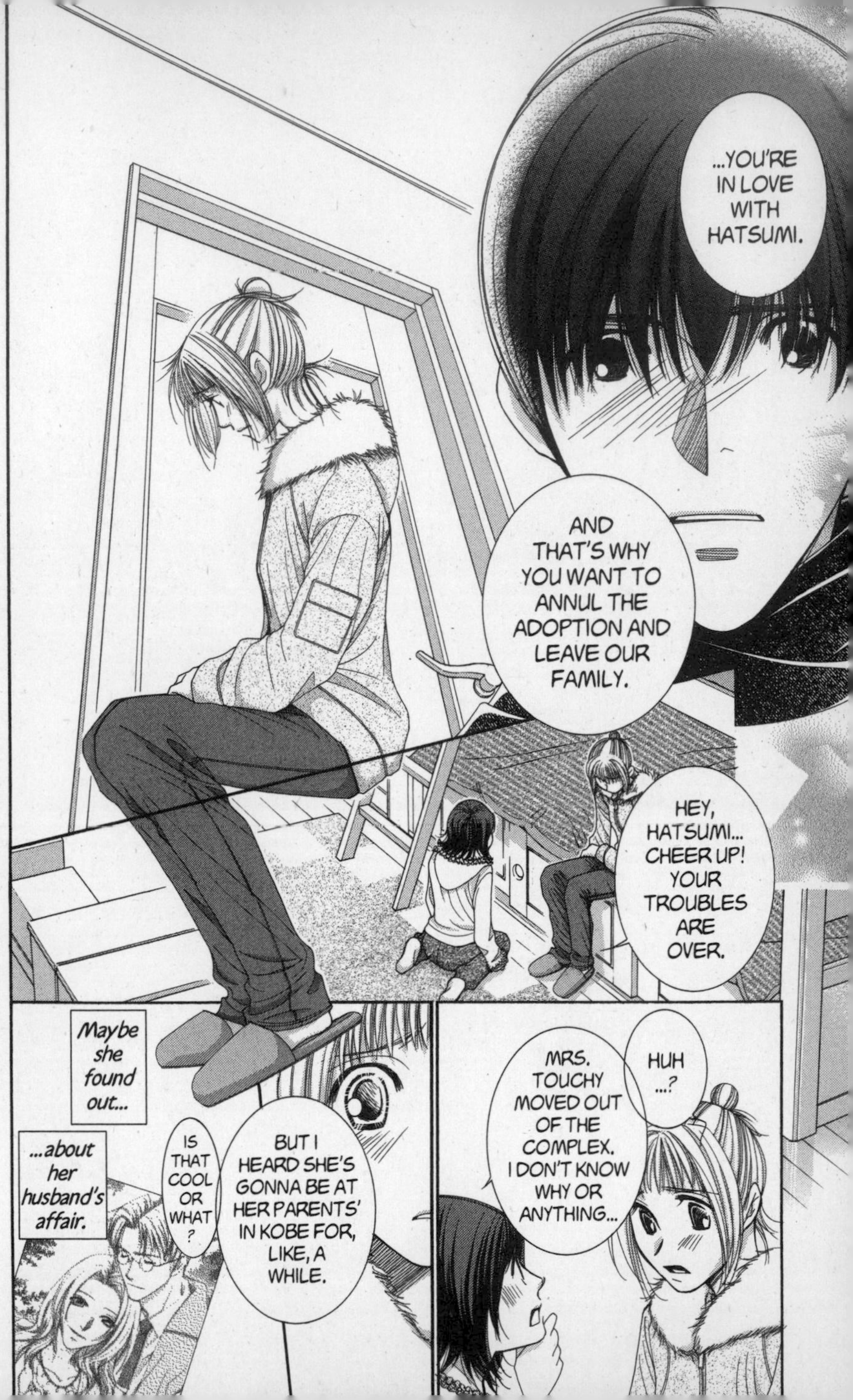
...YOU'RE IN LOVE WITH HATSUMI.
AND THAT'S WHY YOU WANT TO ANNUL THE ADOPTION AND LEAVE OUR FAMILY.
HEY, HATSUMI... CHEER UP! YOUR TROUBLES ARE OVER.
HUH ...?
MRS. TOUCHY MOVED OUT OF THE COMPLEX. I DON'T KNOW WHY OR ANYTHING...
BUT I HEARD SHE'S GONNA BE AT HER PARENTS' IN KOBE FOR, LIKE, A WHILE.
IS THAT COOL OR WHAT?
Maybe she found out...
...about her husband's affair.

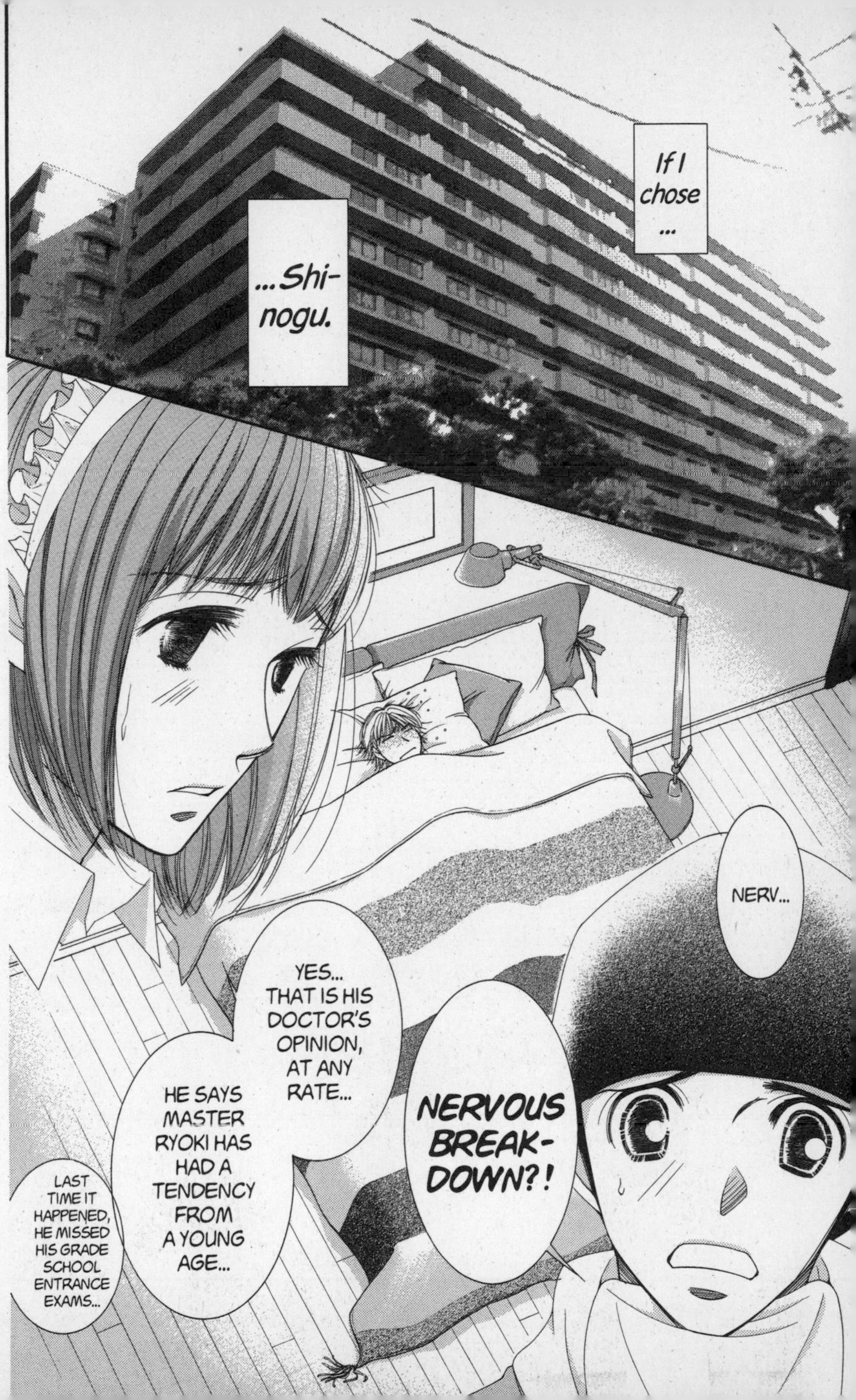
If I chose ...
...Shi-nogu.
NERV...
NERVOUS BREAK-DOWN?!
YES... THAT IS HIS DOCTOR'S OPINION, AT ANY RATE...
HE SAYS MASTER RYOKI HAS HAD A TENDENCY FROM A YOUNG AGE...
LAST TIME IT HAPPENED, HE MISSED HIS GRADE SCHOOL ENTRANCE EXAMS...

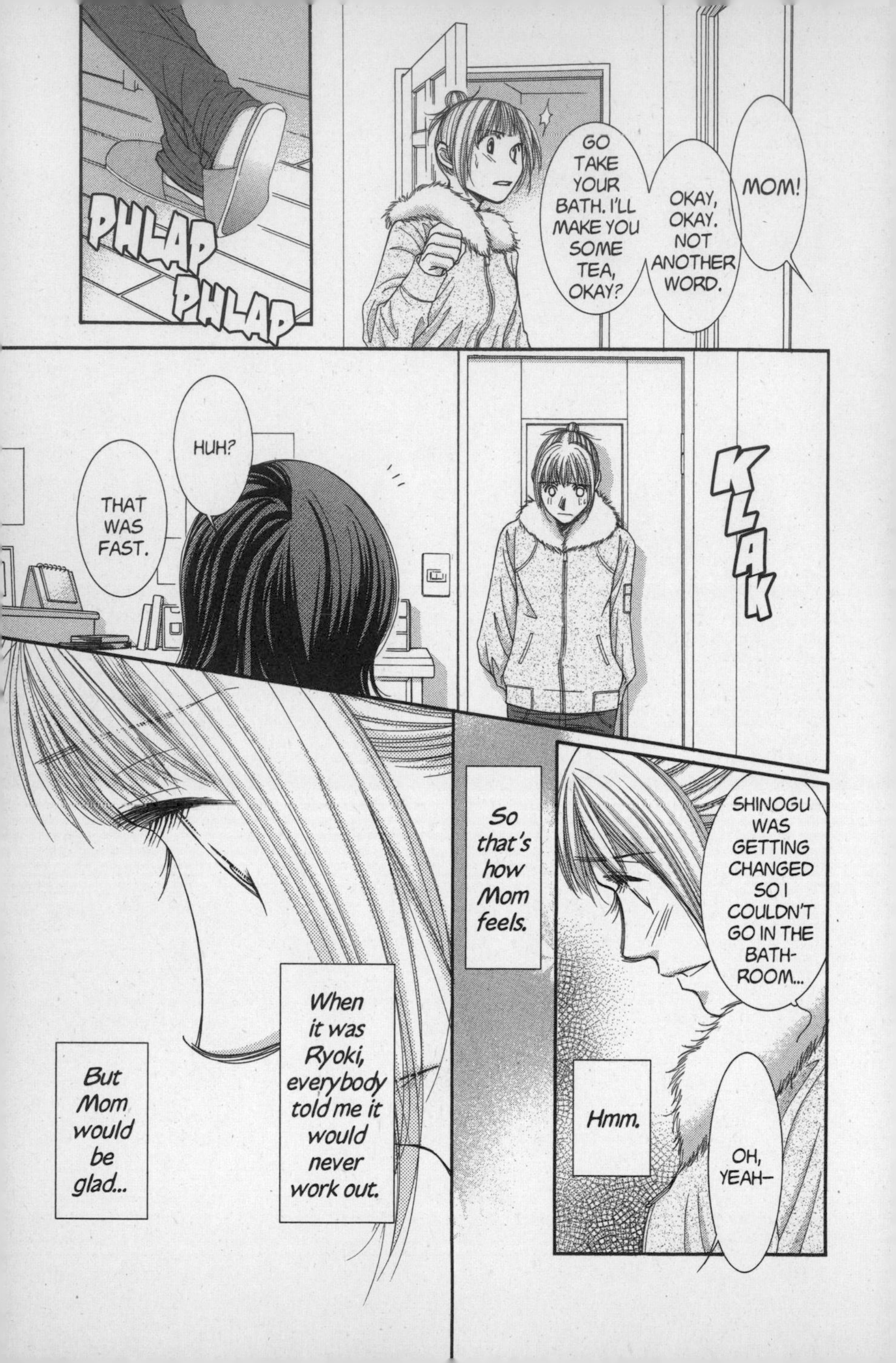
MOM!
OKAY, OKAY. NOT ANOTHER WORD.
GO TAKE YOUR BATH. I'LL MAKE YOU SOME TEA, OKAY?
PHLAP PHLAP
KLAK
HUH?
THAT WAS FAST.
SHINOGU WAS GETTING CHANGED SO I COULDN'T GO IN THE BATH-ROOM...
OH, YEAH—
Hmm.
So that's how Mom feels.
When it was Ryoki, everybody told me it would never work out.
But Mom would be glad...

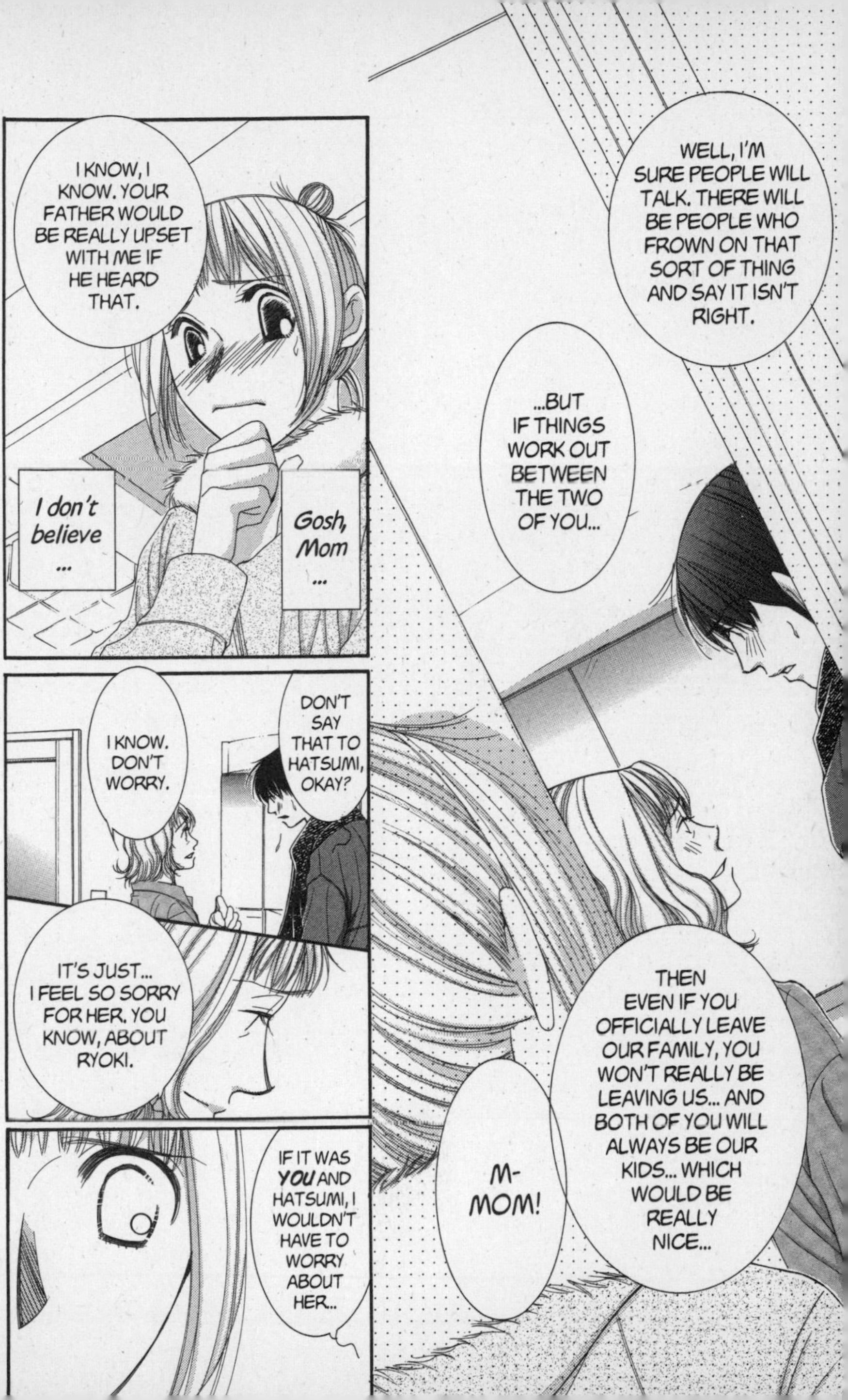
WELL, I'M SURE PEOPLE WILL TALK. THERE WILL BE PEOPLE WHO FROWN ON THAT SORT OF THING AND SAY IT ISN'T RIGHT.
...BUT IF THINGS WORK OUT BETWEEN THE TWO OF YOU...
THEN EVEN IF YOU OFFICIALLY LEAVE OUR FAMILY, YOU WON'T REALLY BE LEAVING US... AND BOTH OF YOU WILL ALWAYS BE OUR KIDS... WHICH WOULD BE REALLY NICE...
M-MOM!
I KNOW, I KNOW. YOUR FATHER WOULD BE REALLY UPSET WITH ME IF HE HEARD THAT.
Gosh, Mom ...
I don't believe ...
DON'T SAY THAT TO HATSUMI, OKAY?
I KNOW. DON'T WORRY.
IT'S JUST... I FEEL SO SORRY FOR HER. YOU KNOW, ABOUT RYOKI.
IF IT WAS **YOU** AND HATSUMI, I WOULDN'T HAVE TO WORRY ABOUT HER...

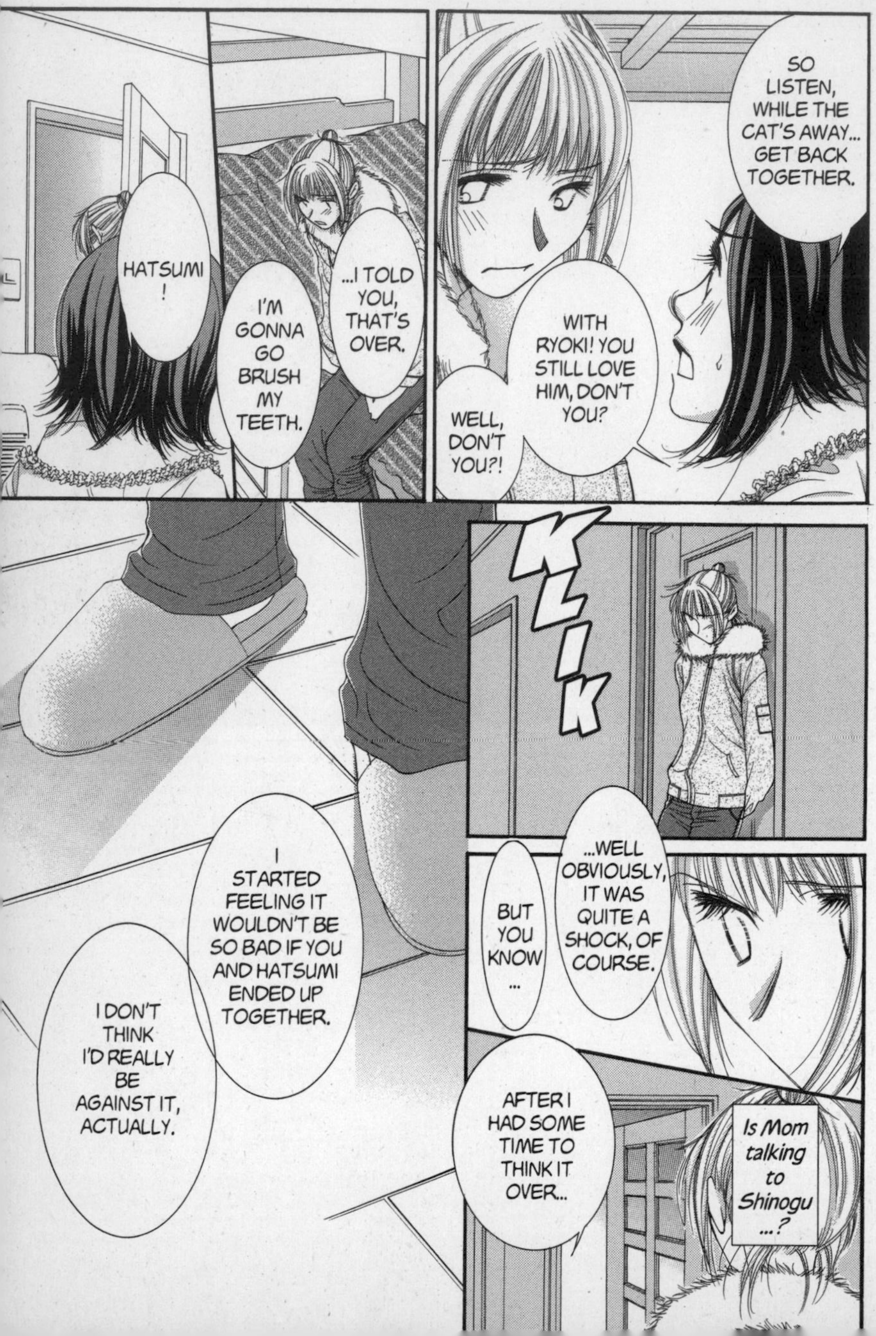
SO LISTEN, WHILE THE CAT'S AWAY... GET BACK TOGETHER.
WITH RYOKI! YOU STILL LOVE HIM, DON'T YOU?
WELL, DON'T YOU?!
...I TOLD YOU, THAT'S OVER.
I'M GONNA GO BRUSH MY TEETH.
HATSUMI!
KLIK
...WELL OBVIOUSLY, IT WAS QUITE A SHOCK, OF COURSE.
BUT YOU KNOW...
AFTER I HAD SOME TIME TO THINK IT OVER...
Is Mom talking to Shinogu...?
I STARTED FEELING IT WOULDN'T BE SO BAD IF YOU AND HATSUMI ENDED UP TOGETHER.
I DON'T THINK I'D REALLY BE AGAINST IT, ACTUALLY.

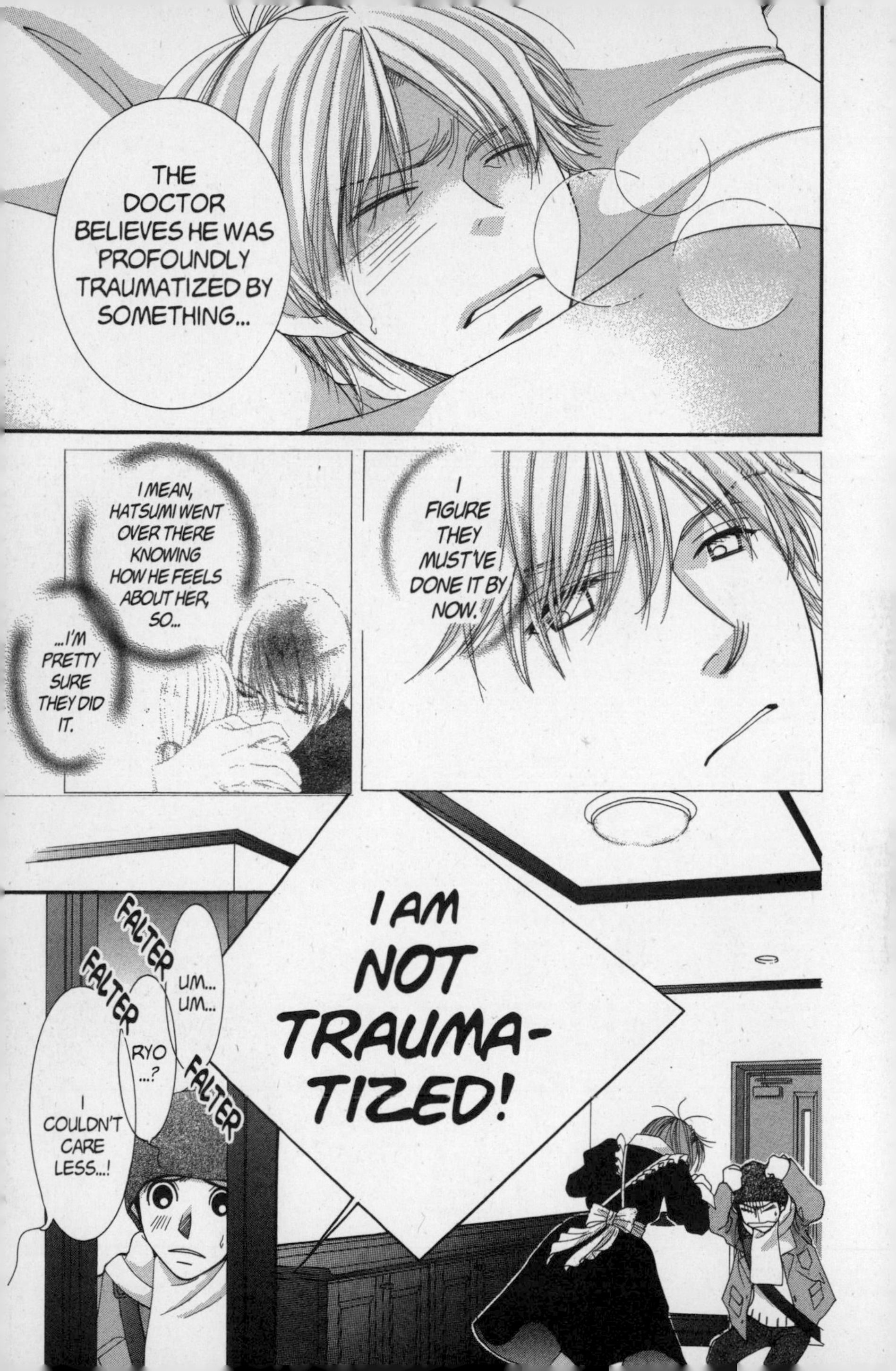
THE DOCTOR BELIEVES HE WAS PROFOUNDLY TRAUMATIZED BY SOMETHING...
I FIGURE THEY MUST'VE DONE IT BY NOW.
I MEAN, HATSUMI WENT OVER THERE KNOWING HOW HE FEELS ABOUT HER, SO...
...I'M PRETTY SURE THEY DID IT.
I AM NOT TRAUMA-TIZED!
FALTER
UM... UM...
FALTER
RYO ...?
FALTER
I COULDN'T CARE LESS...!

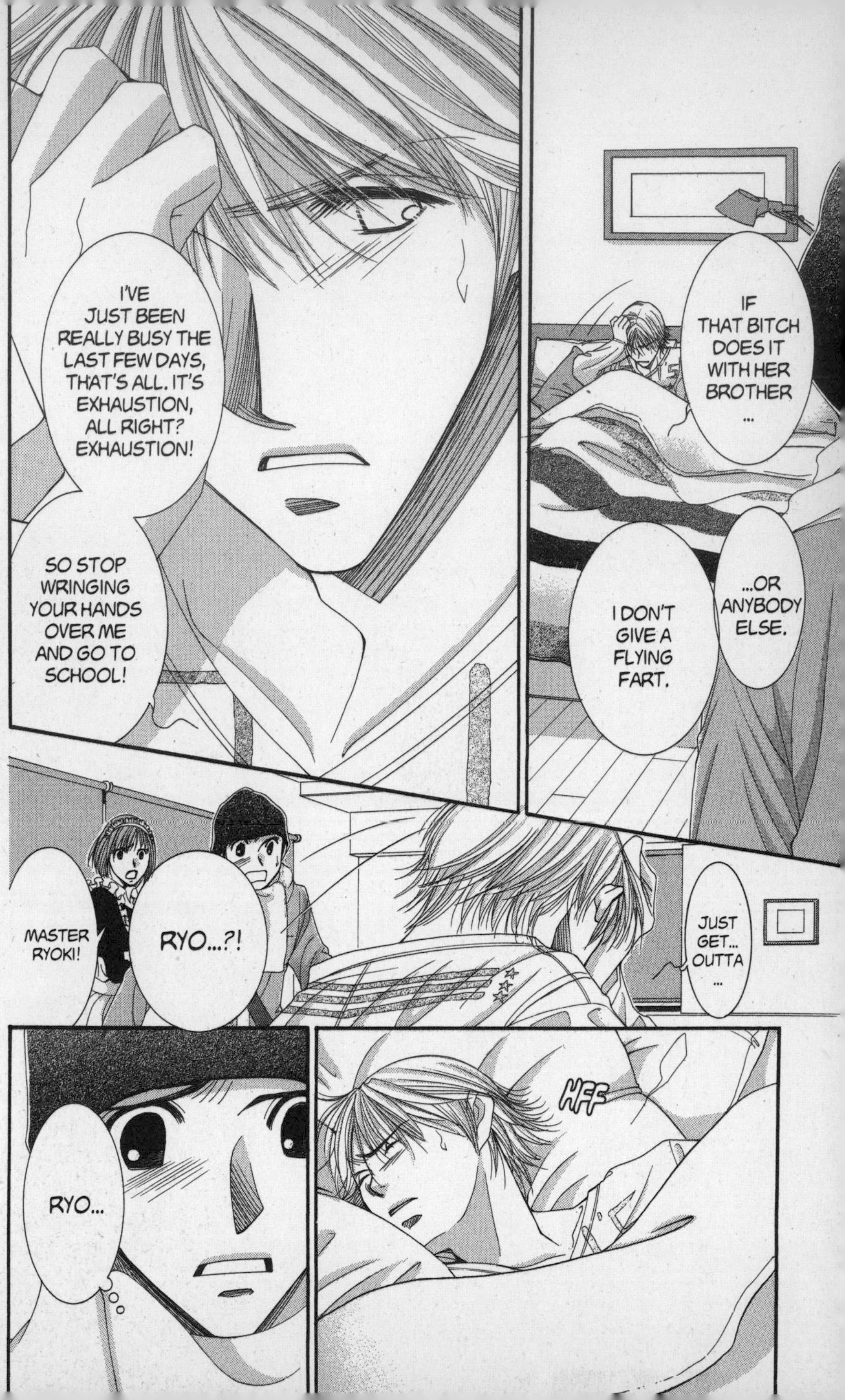
IF THAT BITCH DOES IT WITH HER BROTHER ...
...OR ANYBODY ELSE.
I DON'T GIVE A FLYING FART.
I'VE JUST BEEN REALLY BUSY THE LAST FEW DAYS, THAT'S ALL. IT'S EXHAUSTION, ALL RIGHT? EXHAUSTION!
SO STOP WRINGING YOUR HANDS OVER ME AND GO TO SCHOOL!
JUST GET... OUTTA ...
RYO...?!
MASTER RYOKI!
HFF
RYO...

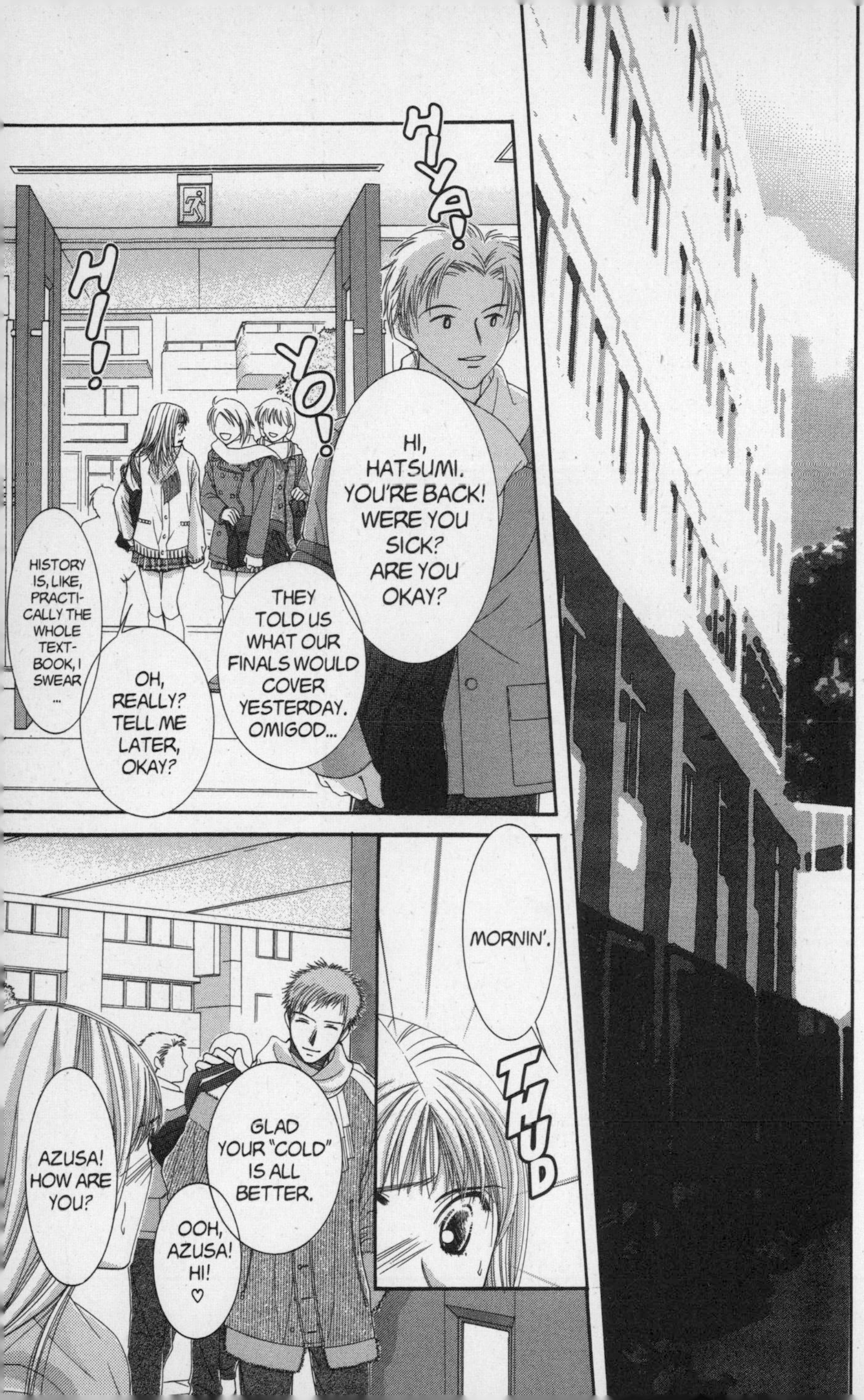
HIYA!
HI, HATSUMI. YOU'RE BACK! WERE YOU SICK? ARE YOU OKAY?
YO!
HI!
THEY TOLD US WHAT OUR FINALS WOULD COVER YESTERDAY. OMIGOD...
HISTORY IS, LIKE, PRACTICALLY THE WHOLE TEXTBOOK, I SWEAR ...
OH, REALLY? TELL ME LATER, OKAY?
MORNIN'.
THUD
GLAD YOUR "COLD" IS ALL BETTER.
AZUSA! HOW ARE YOU?
OOH, AZUSA! HI! ♡

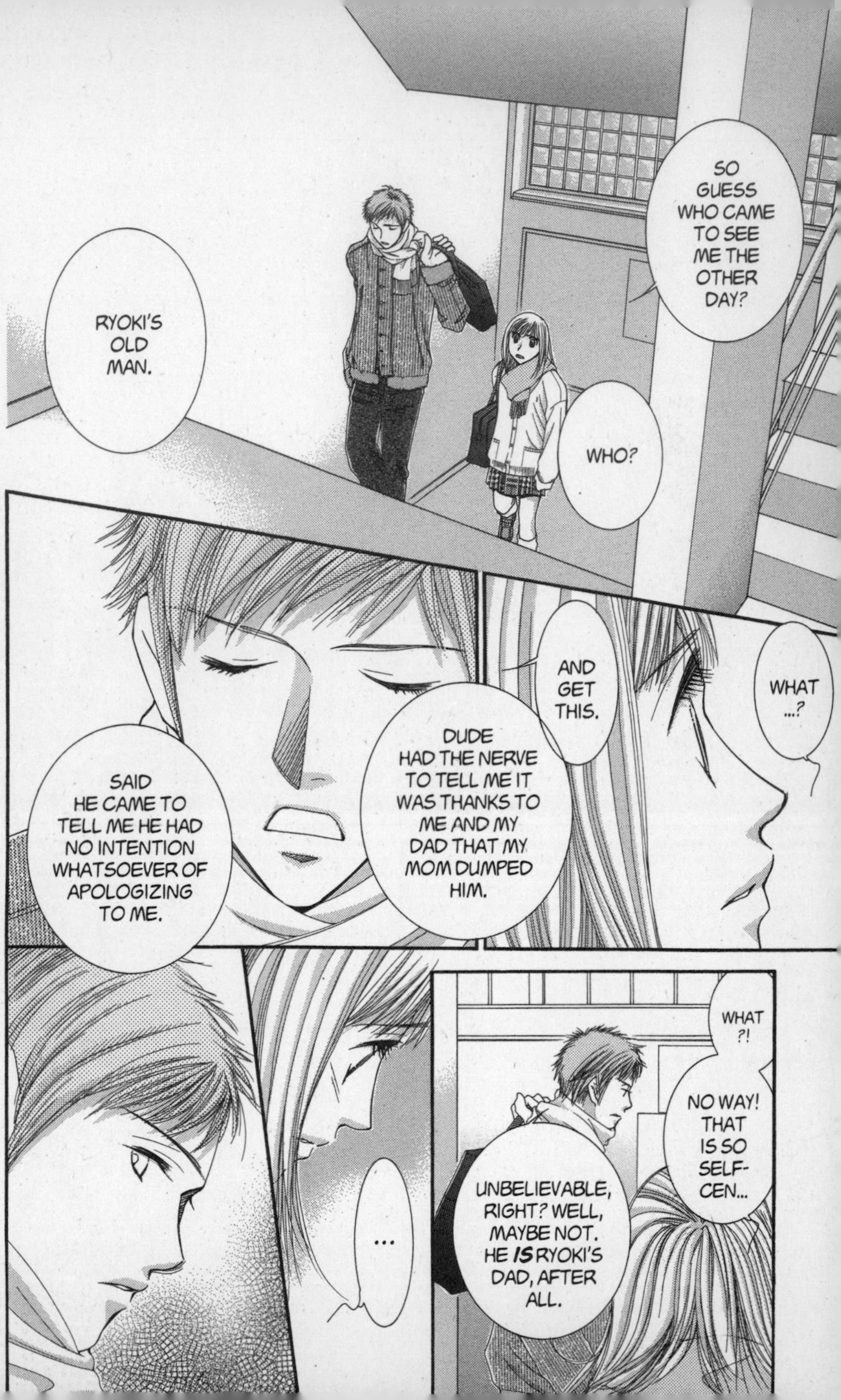
SO GUESS WHO CAME TO SEE ME THE OTHER DAY?
WHO?
RYOKI'S OLD MAN.
WHAT ...?
AND GET THIS.
DUDE HAD THE NERVE TO TELL ME IT WAS THANKS TO ME AND MY DAD THAT MY MOM DUMPED HIM.
SAID HE CAME TO TELL ME HE HAD NO INTENTION WHATSOEVER OF APOLOGIZING TO ME.
WHAT ?!
NO WAY! THAT IS SO SELF-CEN...
UNBELIEVABLE, RIGHT? WELL, MAYBE NOT. HE ***IS*** RYOKI'S DAD, AFTER ALL.
...

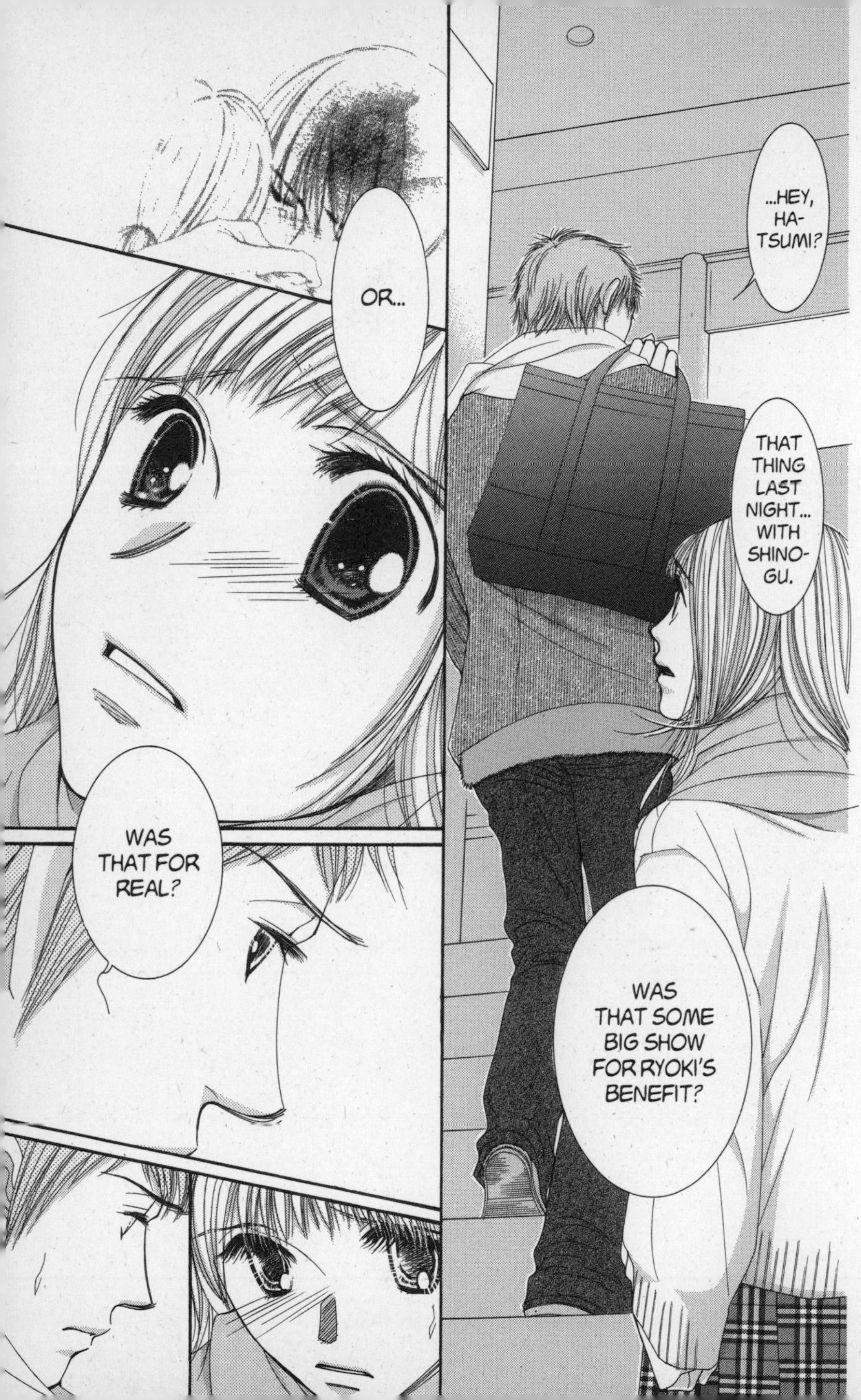
...HEY, HA-TSUMI?
THAT THING LAST NIGHT... WITH SHINO-GU.
WAS THAT SOME BIG SHOW FOR RYOKI'S BENEFIT?
OR...
WAS THAT FOR REAL?

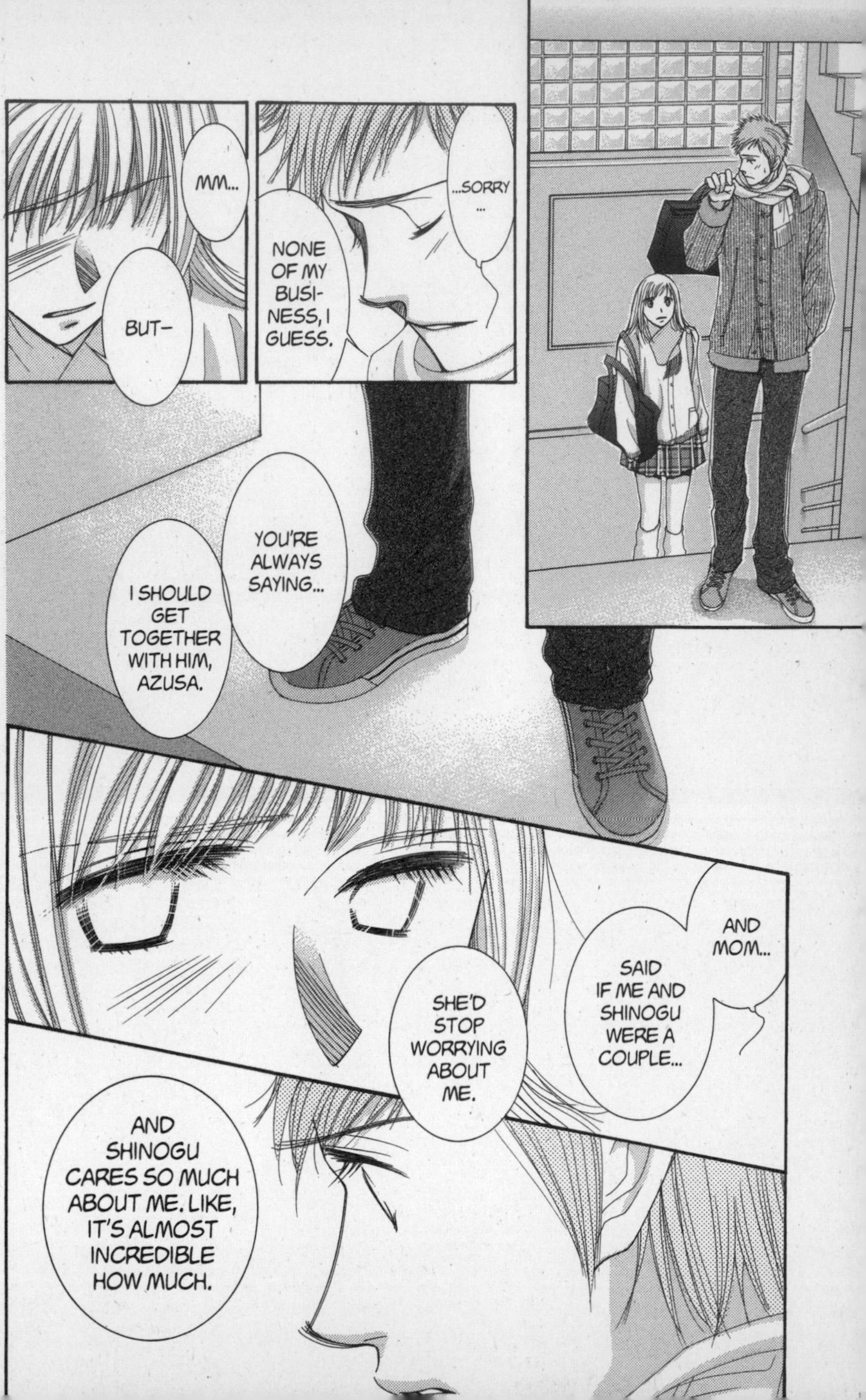
...SORRY ...
NONE OF MY BUSINESS, I GUESS.
MM...
BUT–
YOU'RE ALWAYS SAYING...
I SHOULD GET TOGETHER WITH HIM, AZUSA.
AND MOM...
SAID IF ME AND SHINOGU WERE A COUPLE...
SHE'D STOP WORRYING ABOUT ME.
AND SHINOGU CARES SO MUCH ABOUT ME. LIKE, IT'S ALMOST INCREDIBLE HOW MUCH.

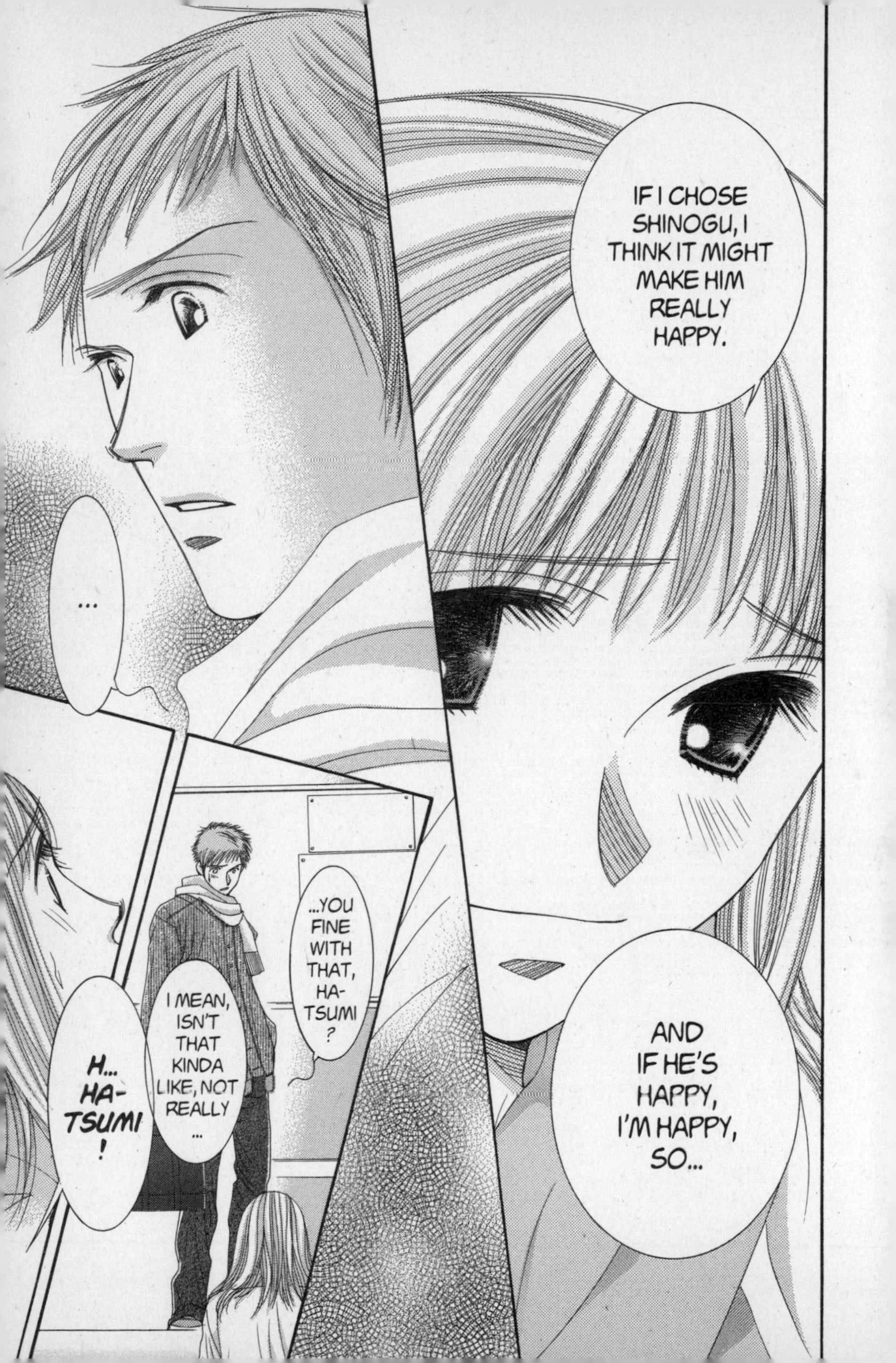
IF I CHOSE SHINOGU, I THINK IT MIGHT MAKE HIM REALLY HAPPY.
AND IF HE'S HAPPY, I'M HAPPY, SO...
...
...YOU FINE WITH THAT, HA-TSUMI?
I MEAN, ISN'T THAT KINDA LIKE, NOT REALLY...
H... HA-TSUMI!

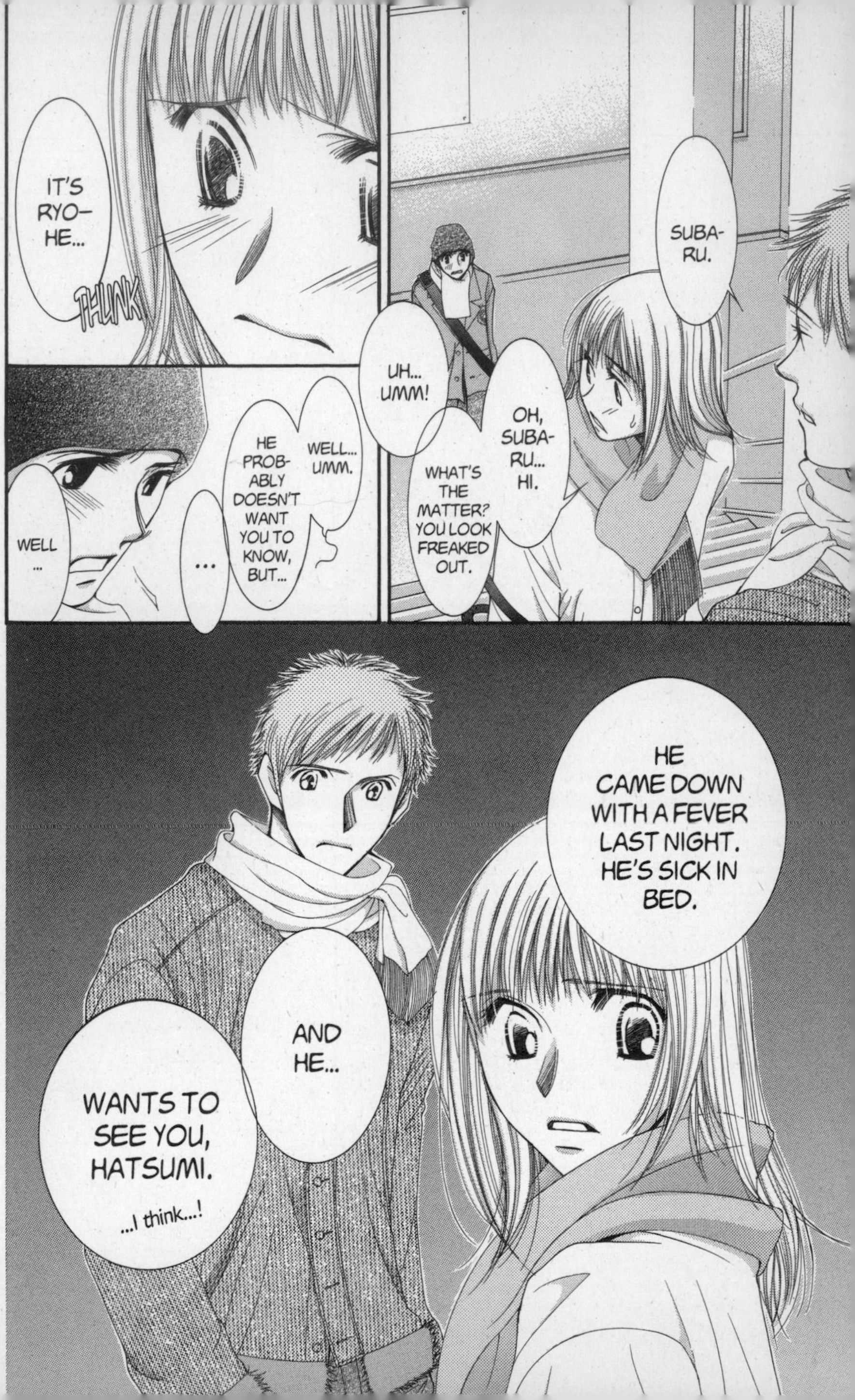
SUBA-RU.
OH, SUBA-RU... HI.
UH... UMM!
WHAT'S THE MATTER? YOU LOOK FREAKED OUT.
IT'S RYO-HE...
THUNK
WELL... UMM.
HE PROBABLY DOESN'T WANT YOU TO KNOW, BUT...
...
WELL ...
HE CAME DOWN WITH A FEVER LAST NIGHT. HE'S SICK IN BED.
AND HE...
WANTS TO SEE YOU, HATSUMI.
...I think...!

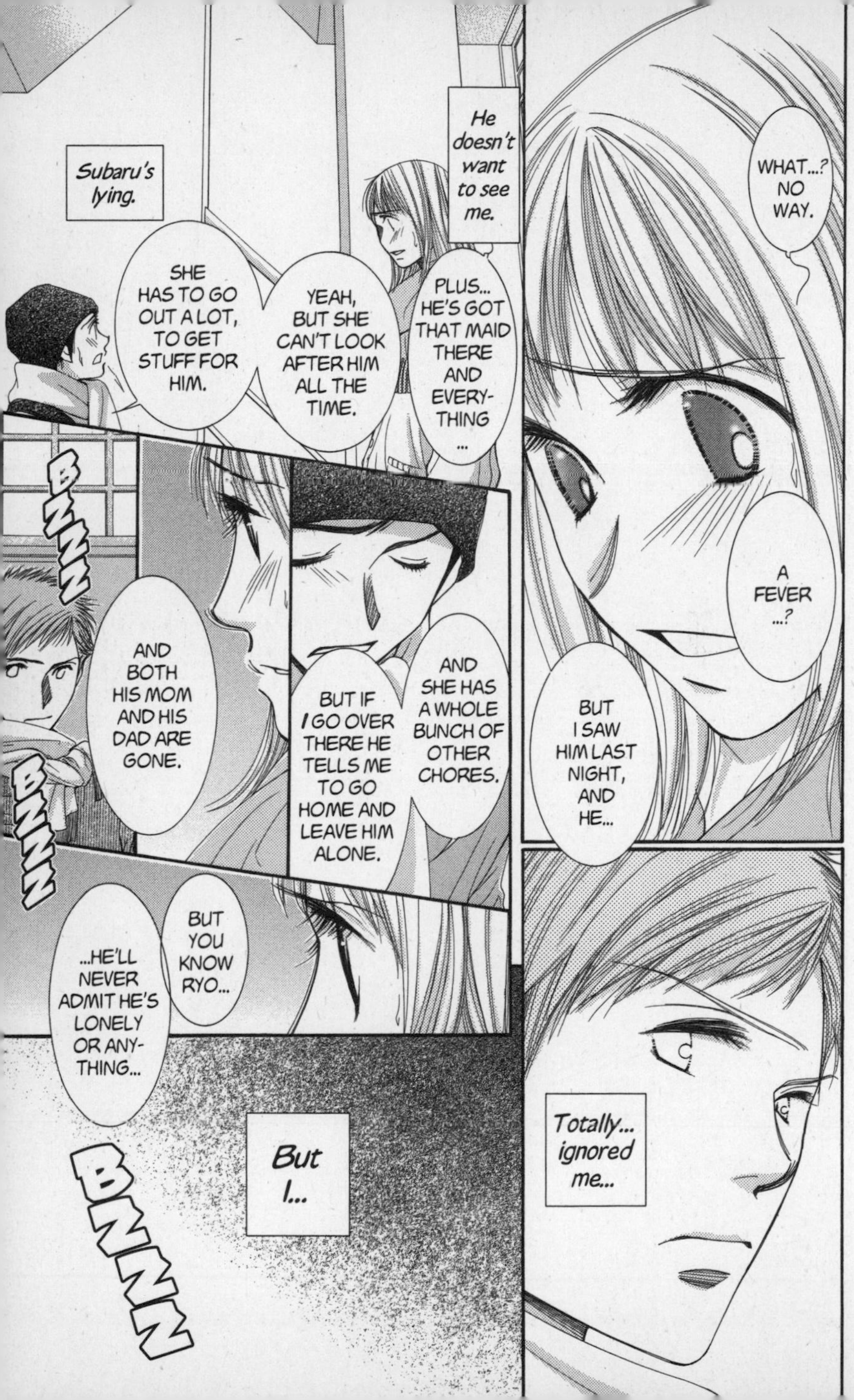
WHAT...? NO WAY.
A FEVER...?
BUT I SAW HIM LAST NIGHT, AND HE...
Totally... ignored me...
He doesn't want to see me.
Subaru's lying.
PLUS... HE'S GOT THAT MAID THERE AND EVERYTHING...
YEAH, BUT SHE CAN'T LOOK AFTER HIM ALL THE TIME.
SHE HAS TO GO OUT A LOT, TO GET STUFF FOR HIM.
AND SHE HAS A WHOLE BUNCH OF OTHER CHORES.
BUT IF I GO OVER THERE HE TELLS ME TO GO HOME AND LEAVE HIM ALONE.
AND BOTH HIS MOM AND HIS DAD ARE GONE.
BNNN
BNNN
BUT YOU KNOW RYO...
...HE'LL NEVER ADMIT HE'S LONELY OR ANYTHING...
But I...
BNNN

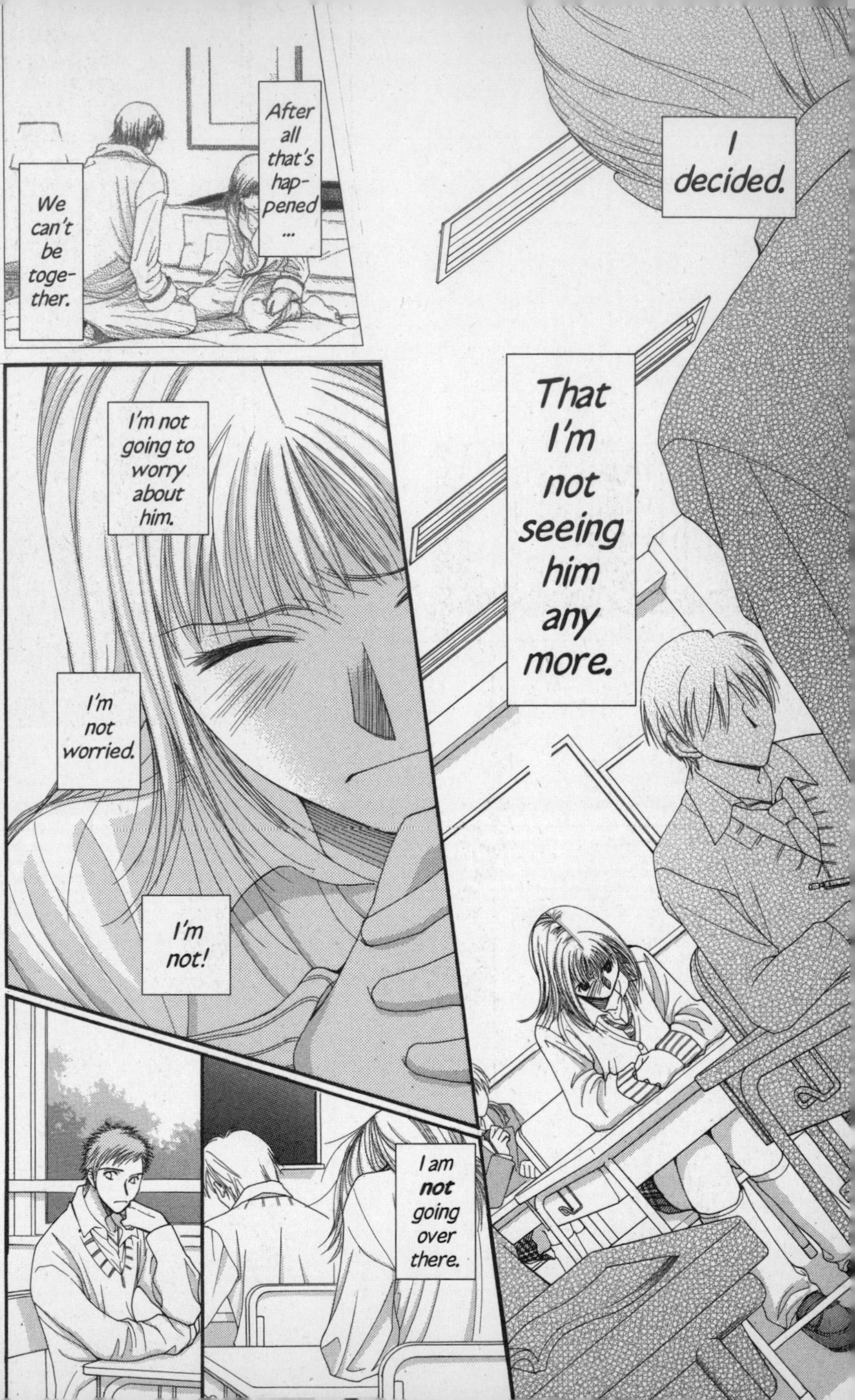
I decided.
That I'm not seeing him any more.
After all that's hap-pened ...
We can't be toge-ther.
I'm not going to worry about him.
I'm not worried.
I'm not!
I am **not** going over there.

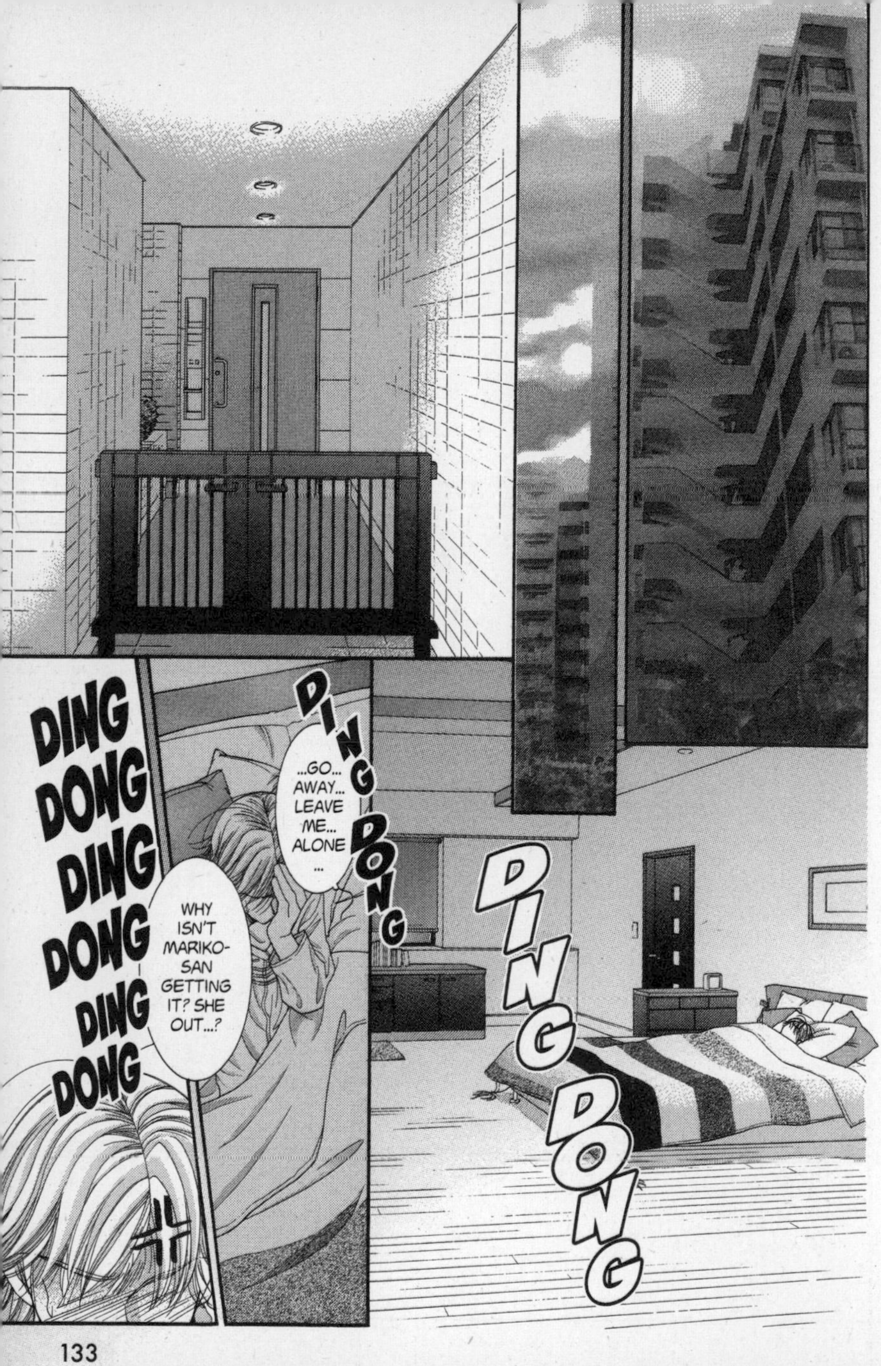
DING DONG
DING DONG
...GO... AWAY... LEAVE ME... ALONE ...
WHY ISN'T MARIKO-SAN GETTING IT? SHE OUT...?
DING DONG DING DONG DING DONG DING DONG

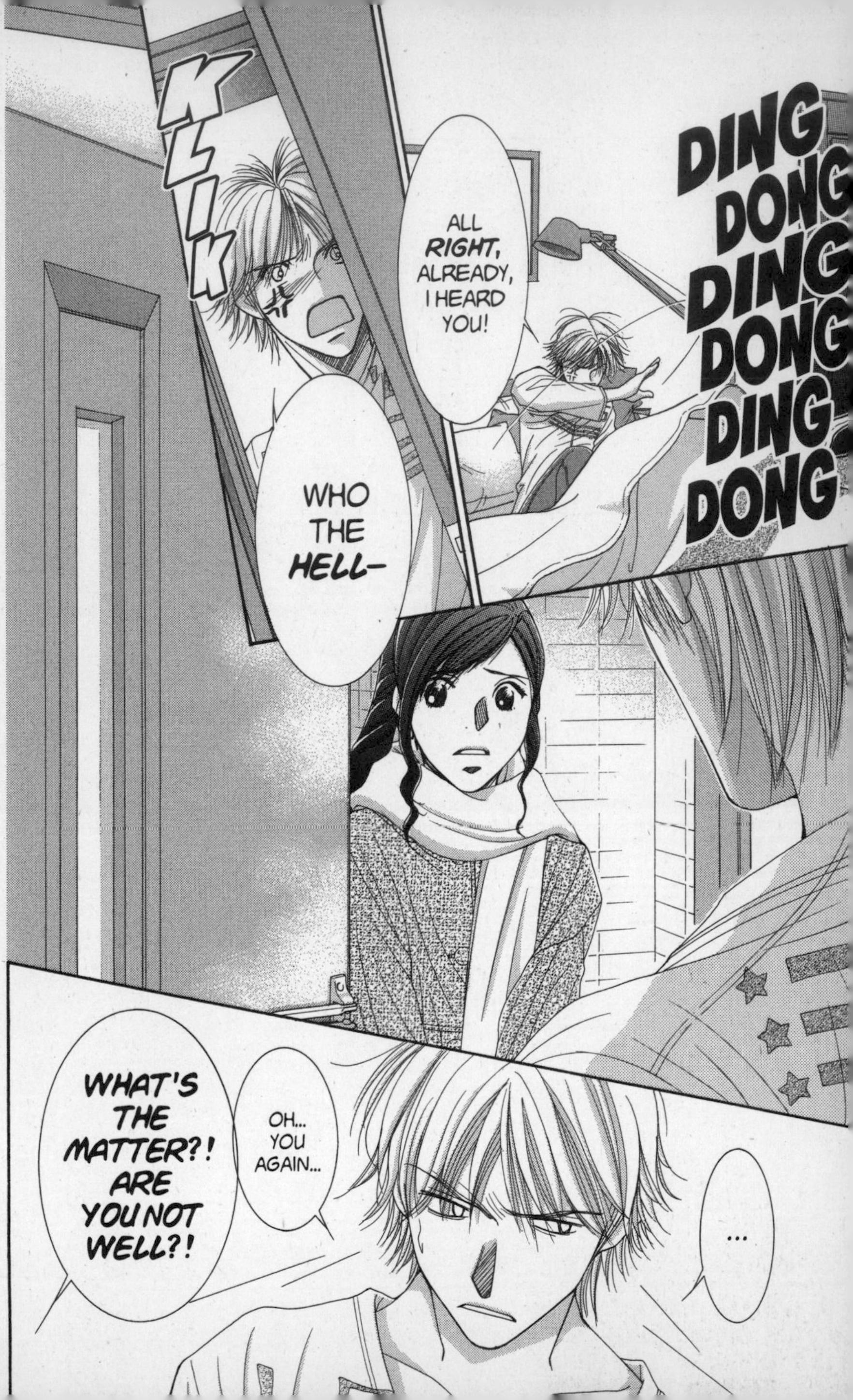
DING DONG DING DONG DING DONG
ALL RIGHT, ALREADY, I HEARD YOU!
KLIK
WHO THE HELL–
...
OH... YOU AGAIN...
WHAT'S THE MATTER?! ARE YOU NOT WELL?!

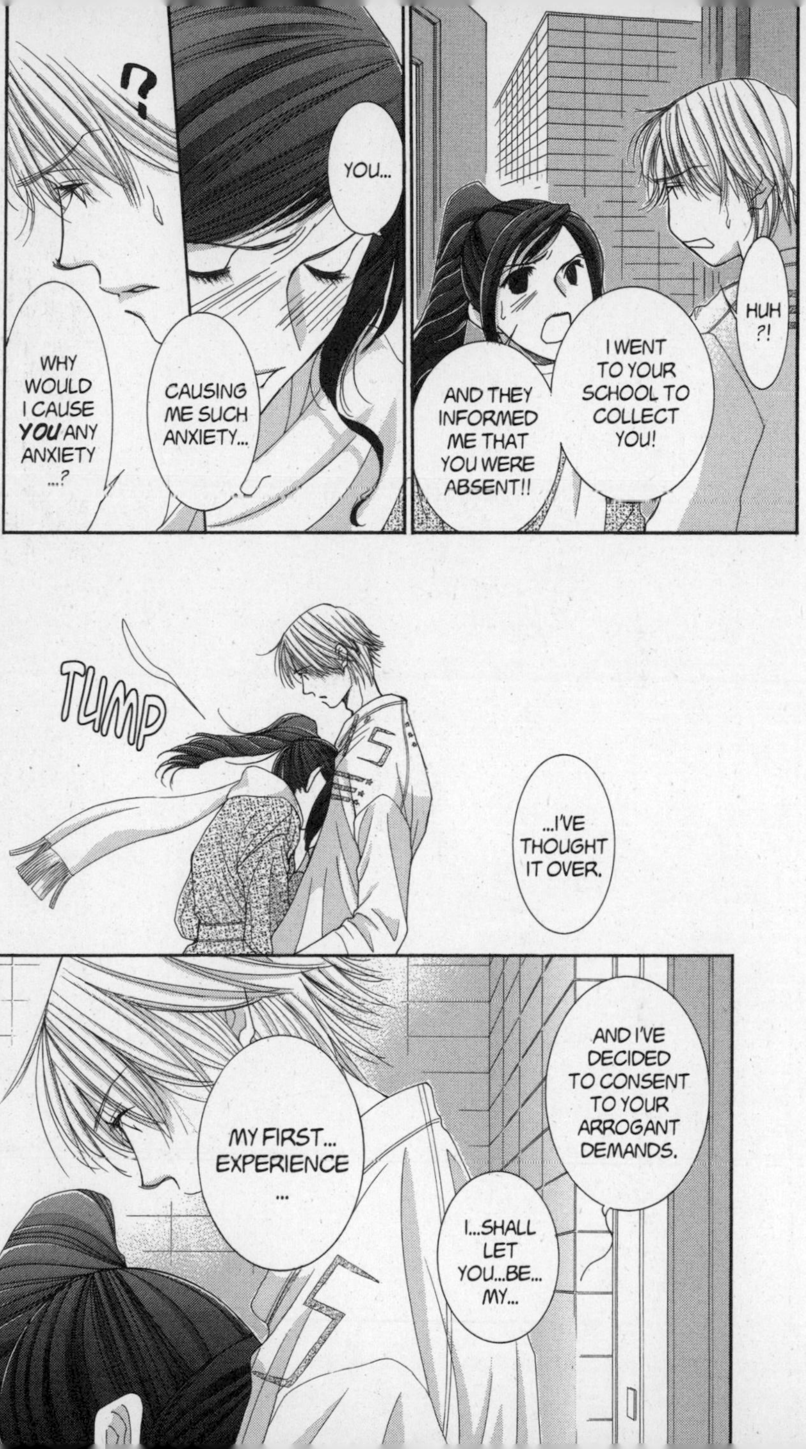
HUH ?!
I WENT TO YOUR SCHOOL TO COLLECT YOU!
AND THEY INFORMED ME THAT YOU WERE ABSENT!!
YOU...
CAUSING ME SUCH ANXIETY...
?
WHY WOULD I CAUSE YOU ANY ANXIETY ...?
TUMP
...I'VE THOUGHT IT OVER.
AND I'VE DECIDED TO CONSENT TO YOUR ARROGANT DEMANDS.
I...SHALL LET YOU...BE... MY...
MY FIRST... EXPERIENCE ...

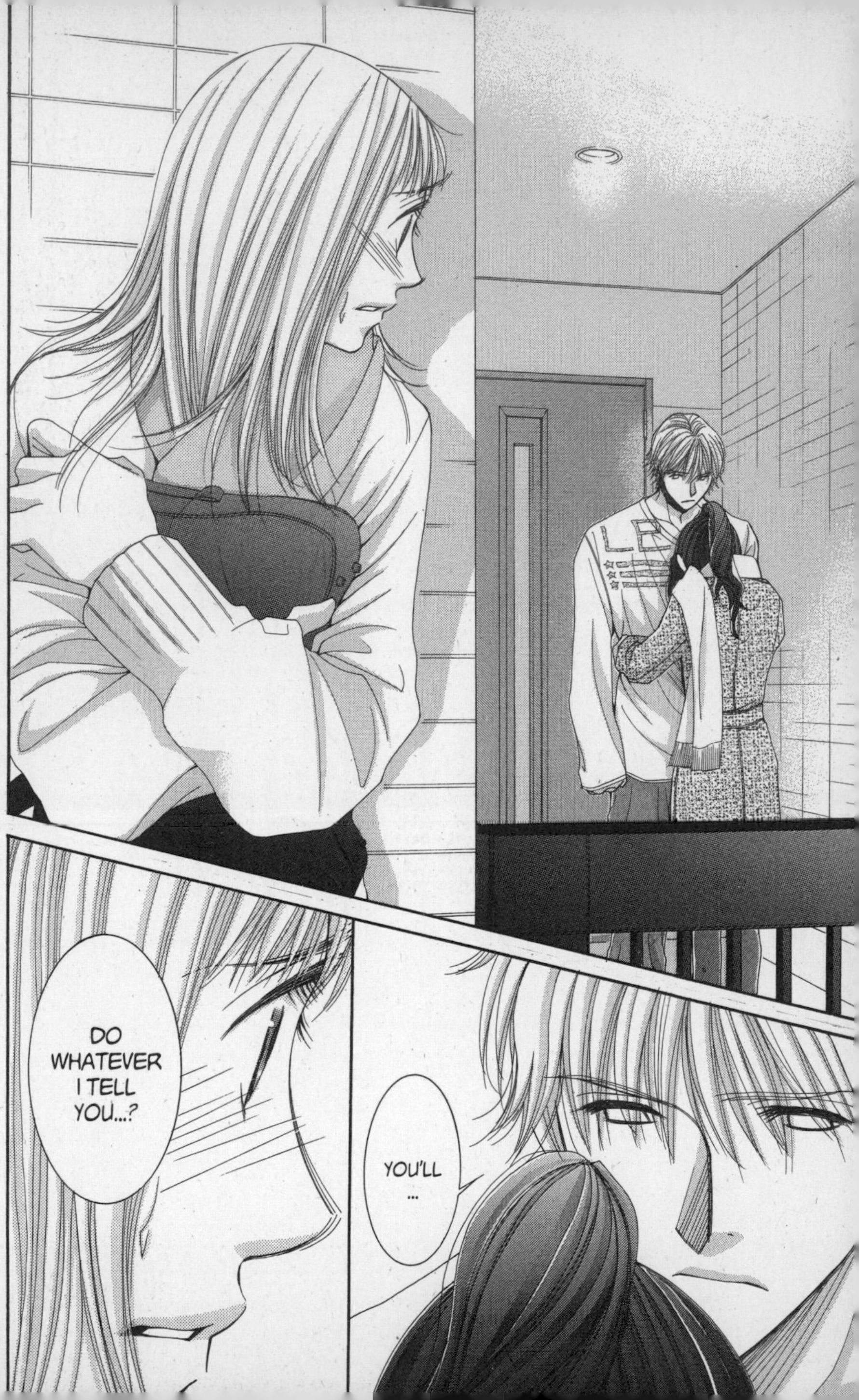
YOU'LL ...
DO WHATEVER I TELL YOU...?

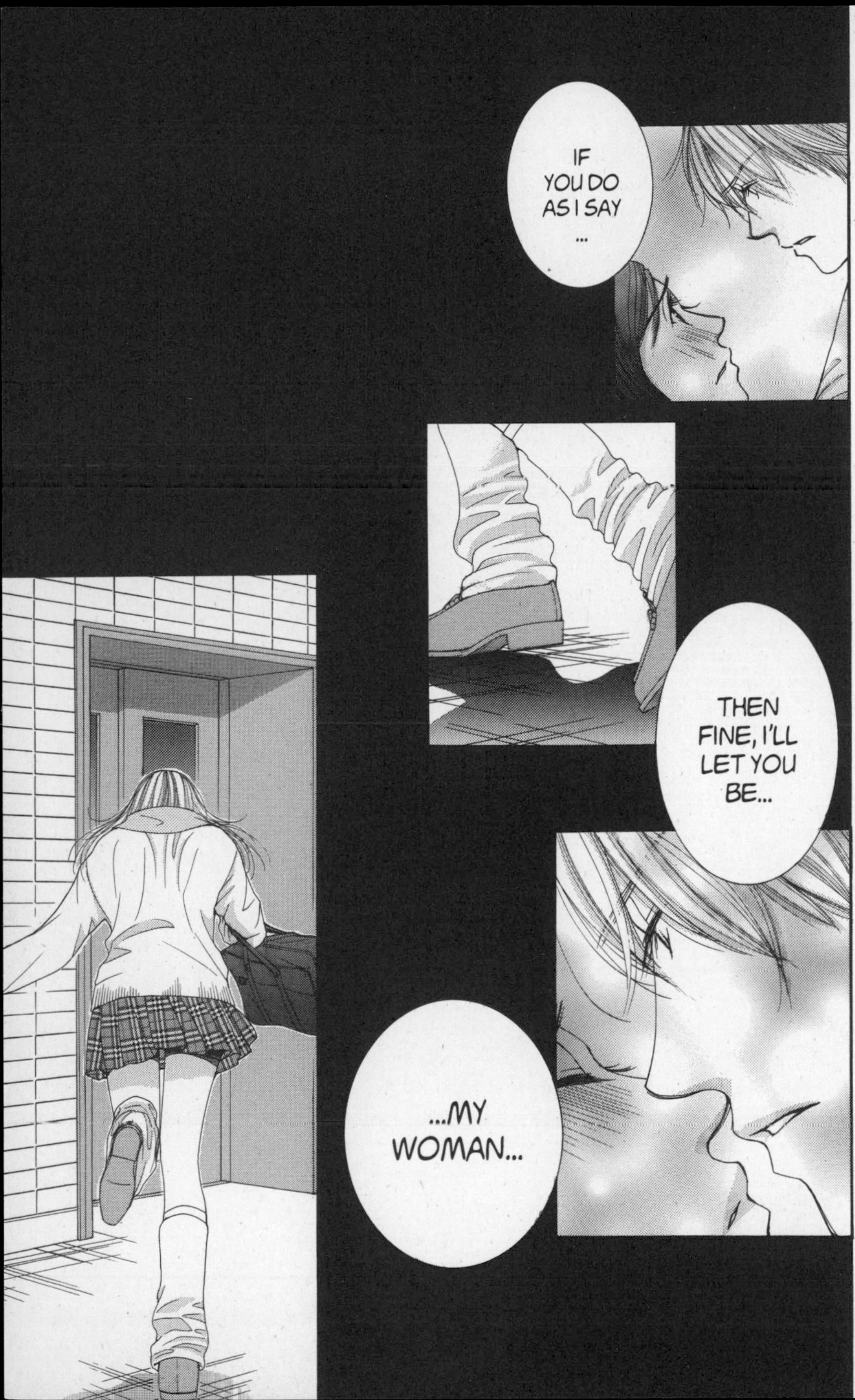
IF YOU DO AS I SAY ...
THEN FINE, I'LL LET YOU BE...
...MY WOMAN...

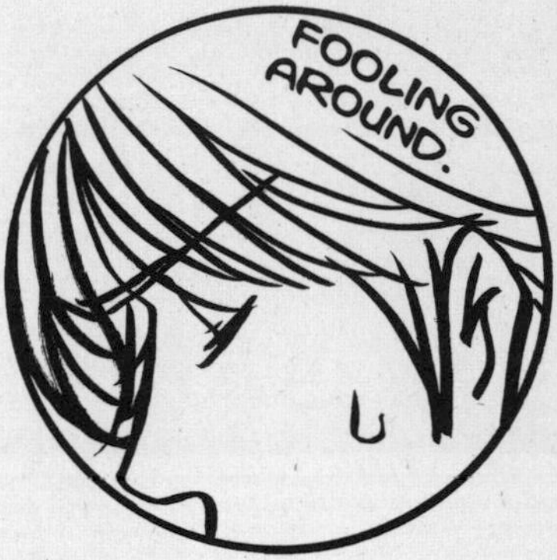
FOOLING AROUND.

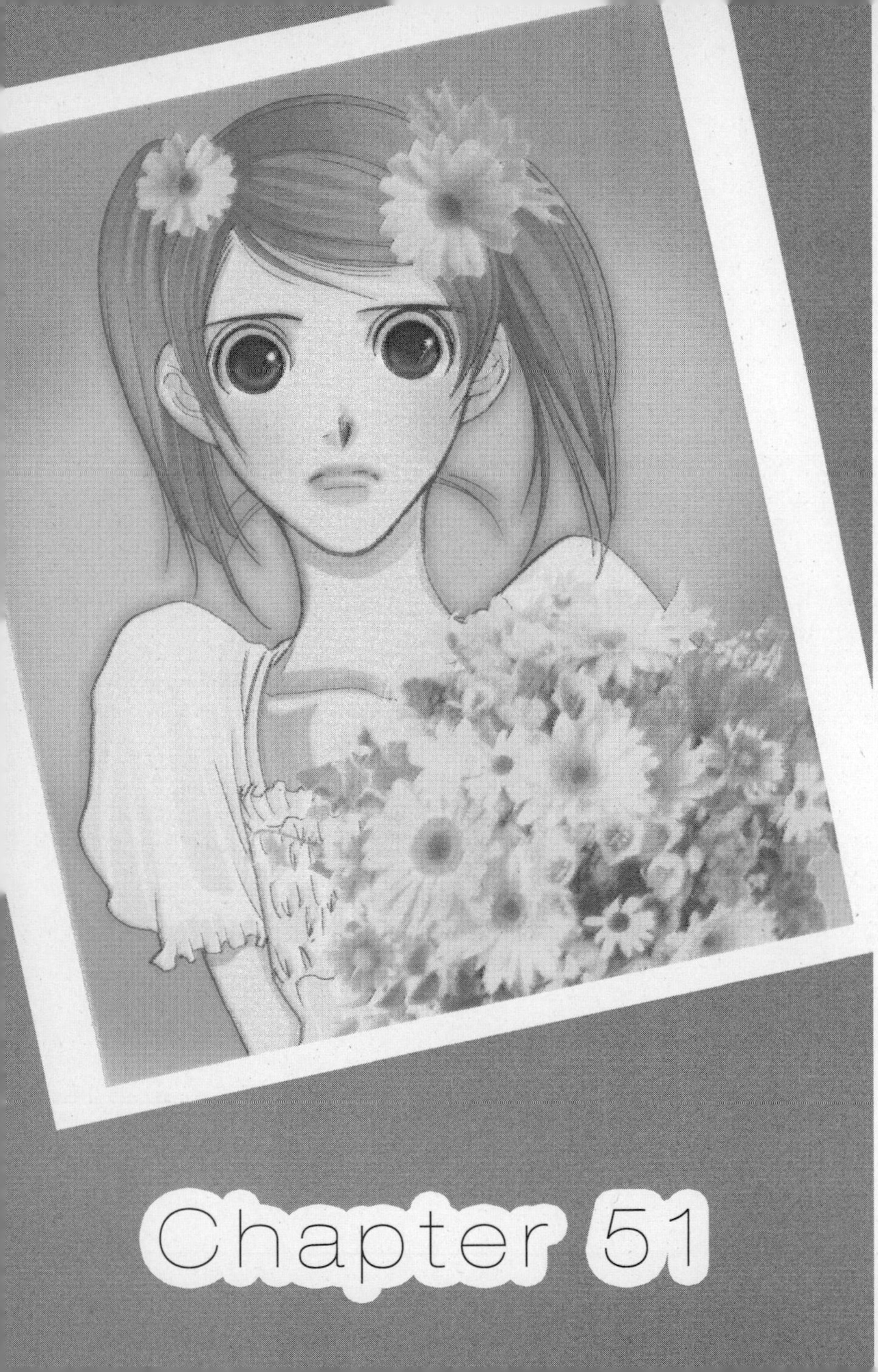

Chapter 51

hot gimmick

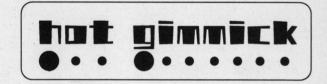

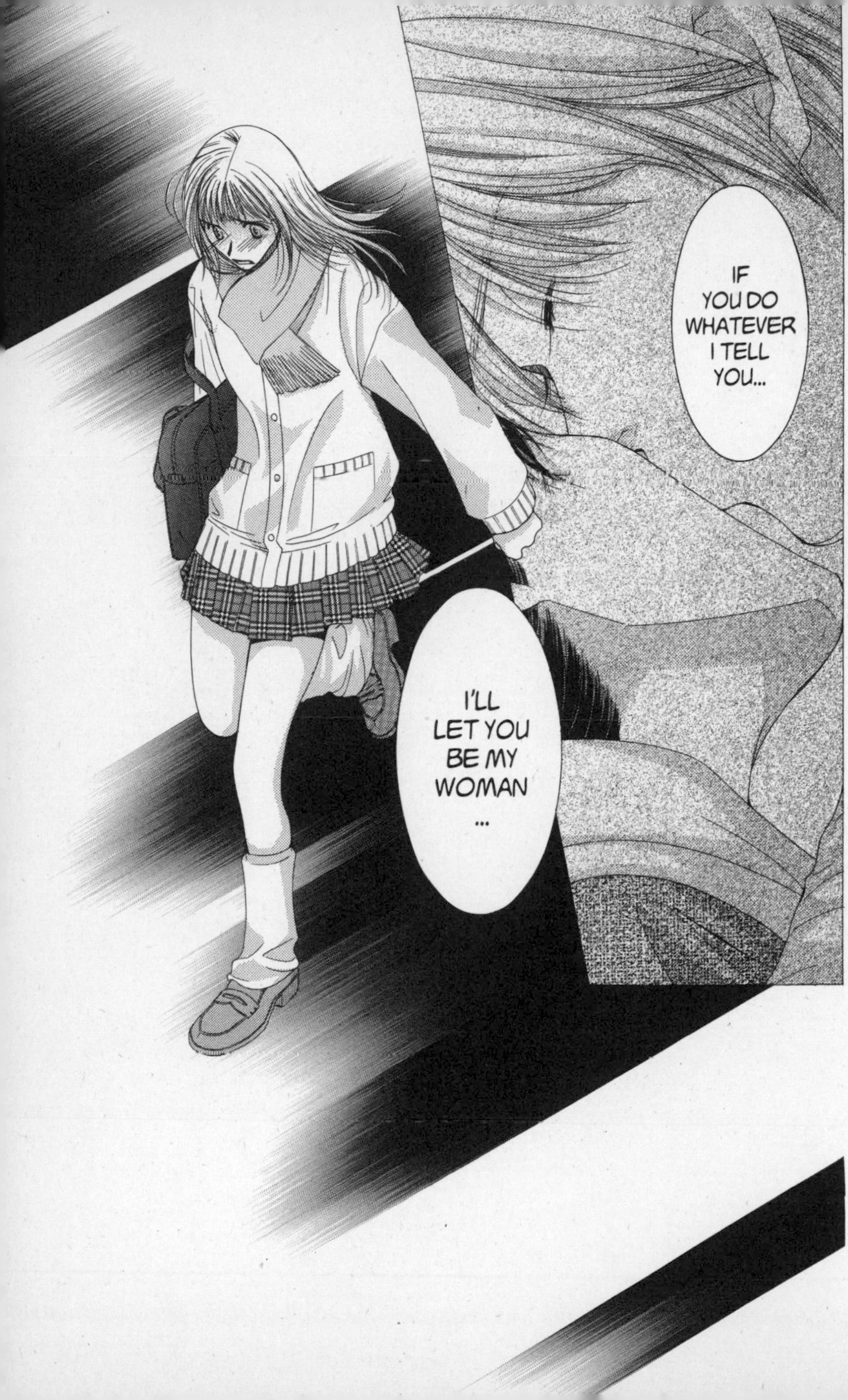
IF YOU DO WHATEVER I TELL YOU...
I'LL LET YOU BE MY WOMAN...

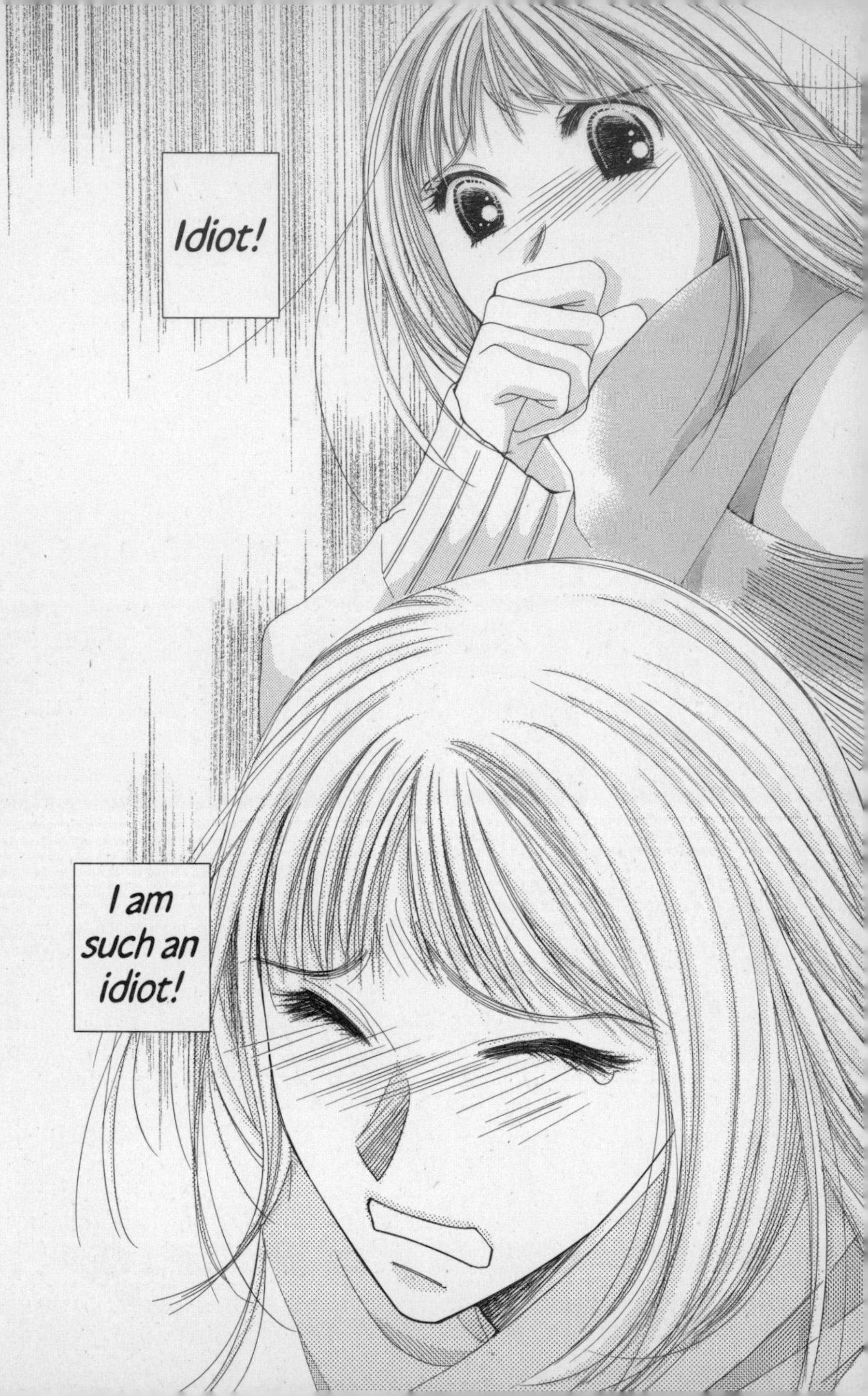
Idiot!
I am such an idiot!

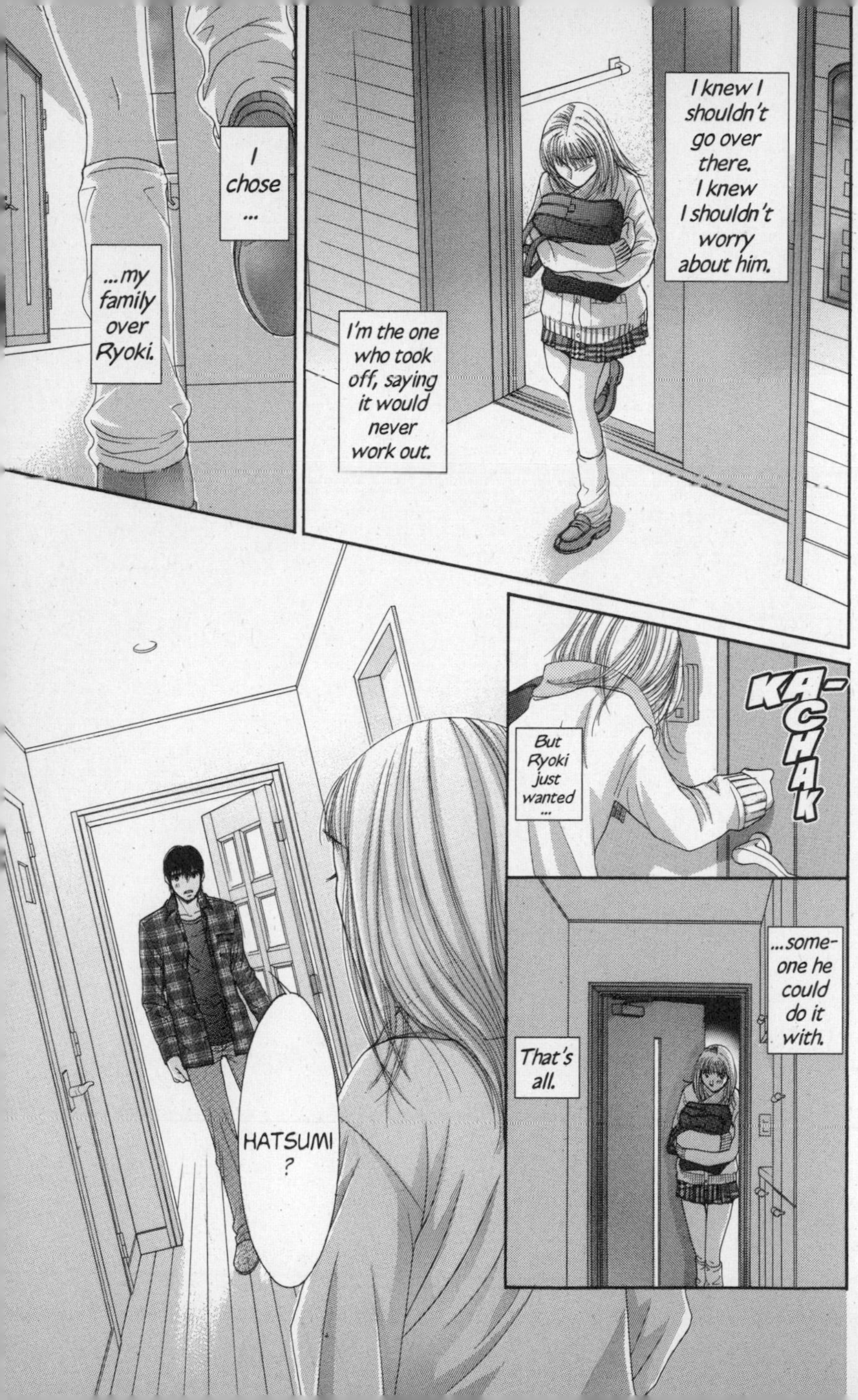
I knew I shouldn't go over there. I knew I shouldn't worry about him.
I'm the one who took off, saying it would never work out.
I chose...
...my family over Ryoki.
KA-CHAK
But Ryoki just wanted...
...some-one he could do it with.
That's all.
HATSUMI?

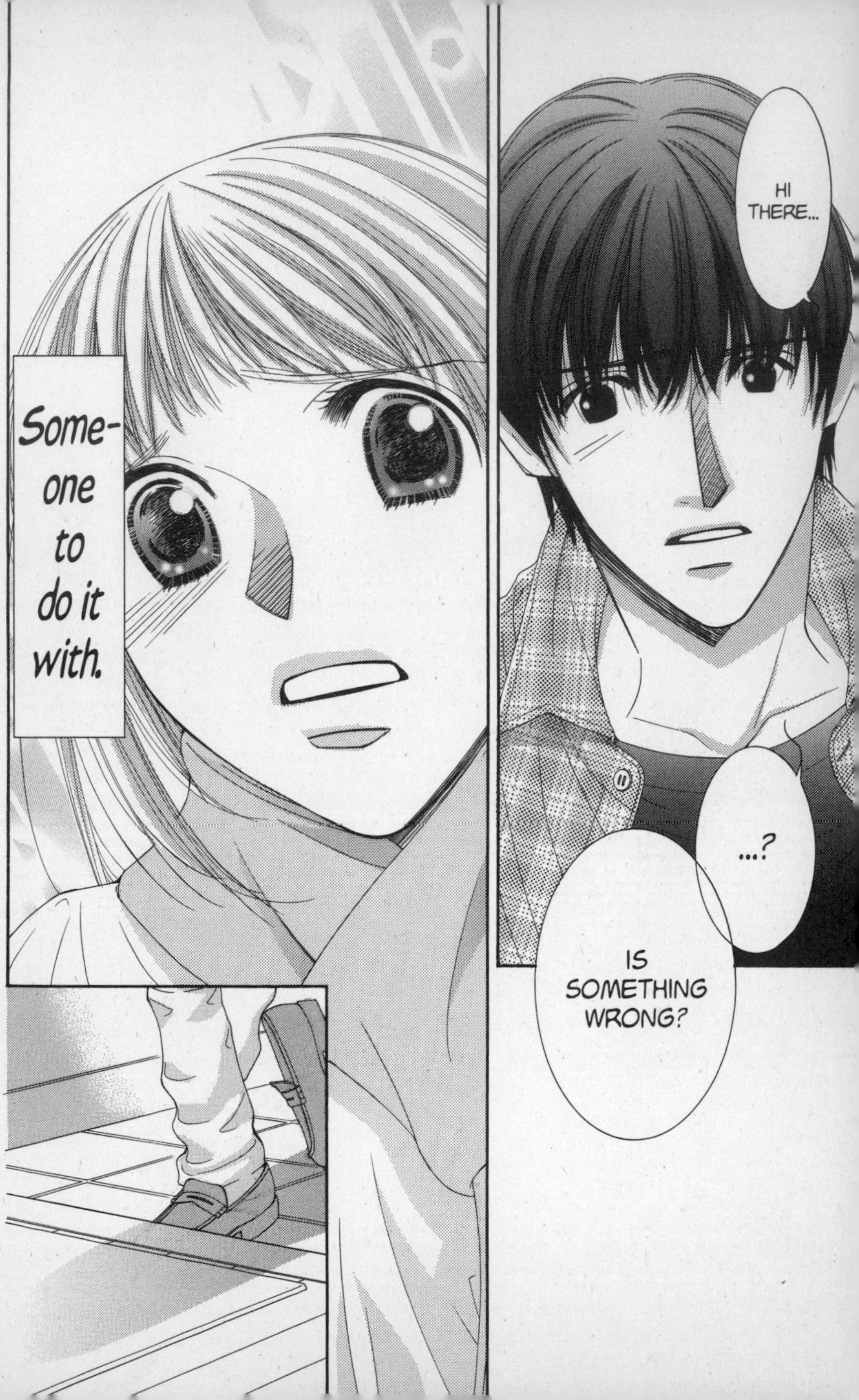
HI THERE...
...?
IS SOMETHING WRONG?
Some-one to do it with.

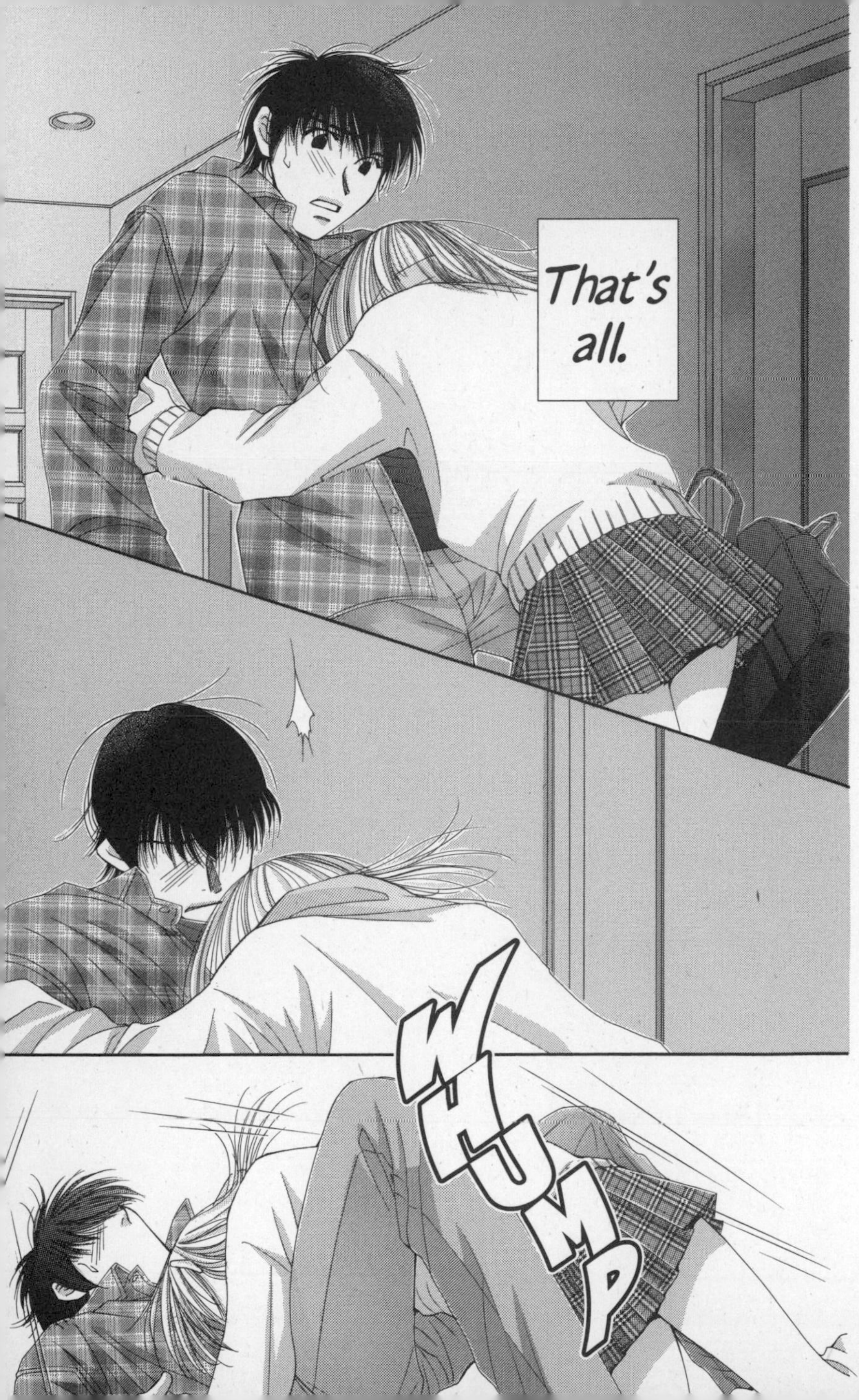
That's all.
WHUMP

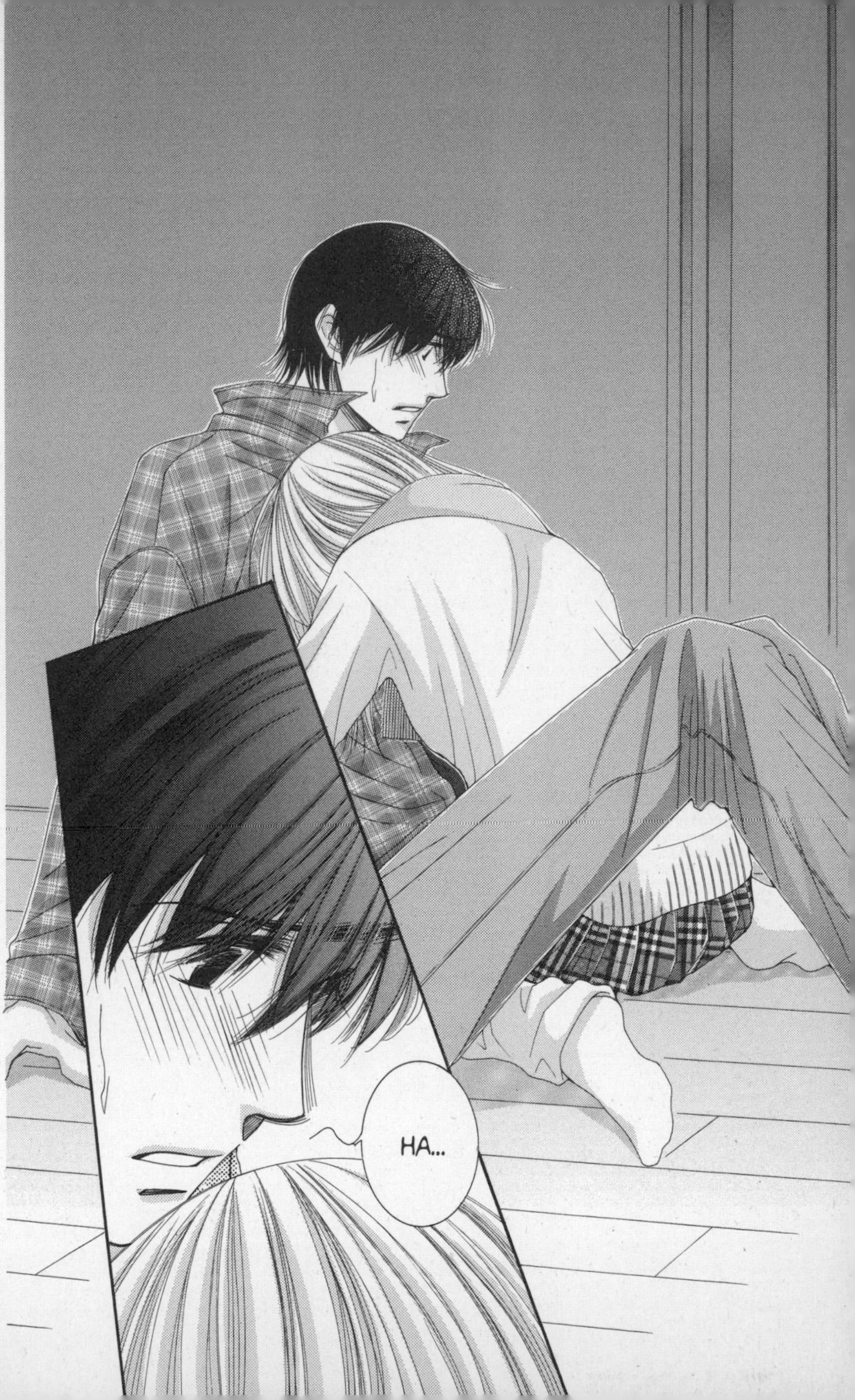
HA...

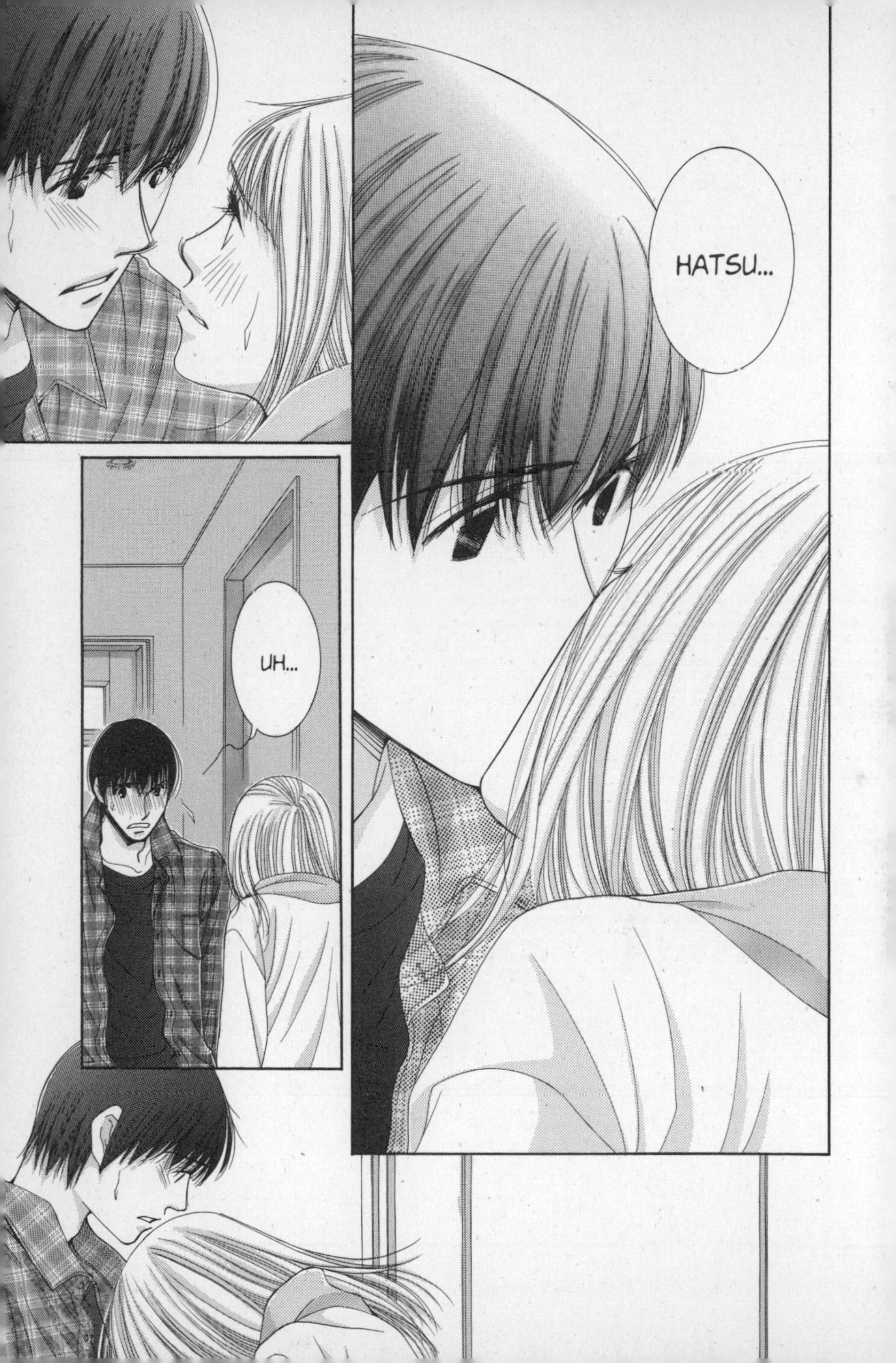
HATSU...
UH...

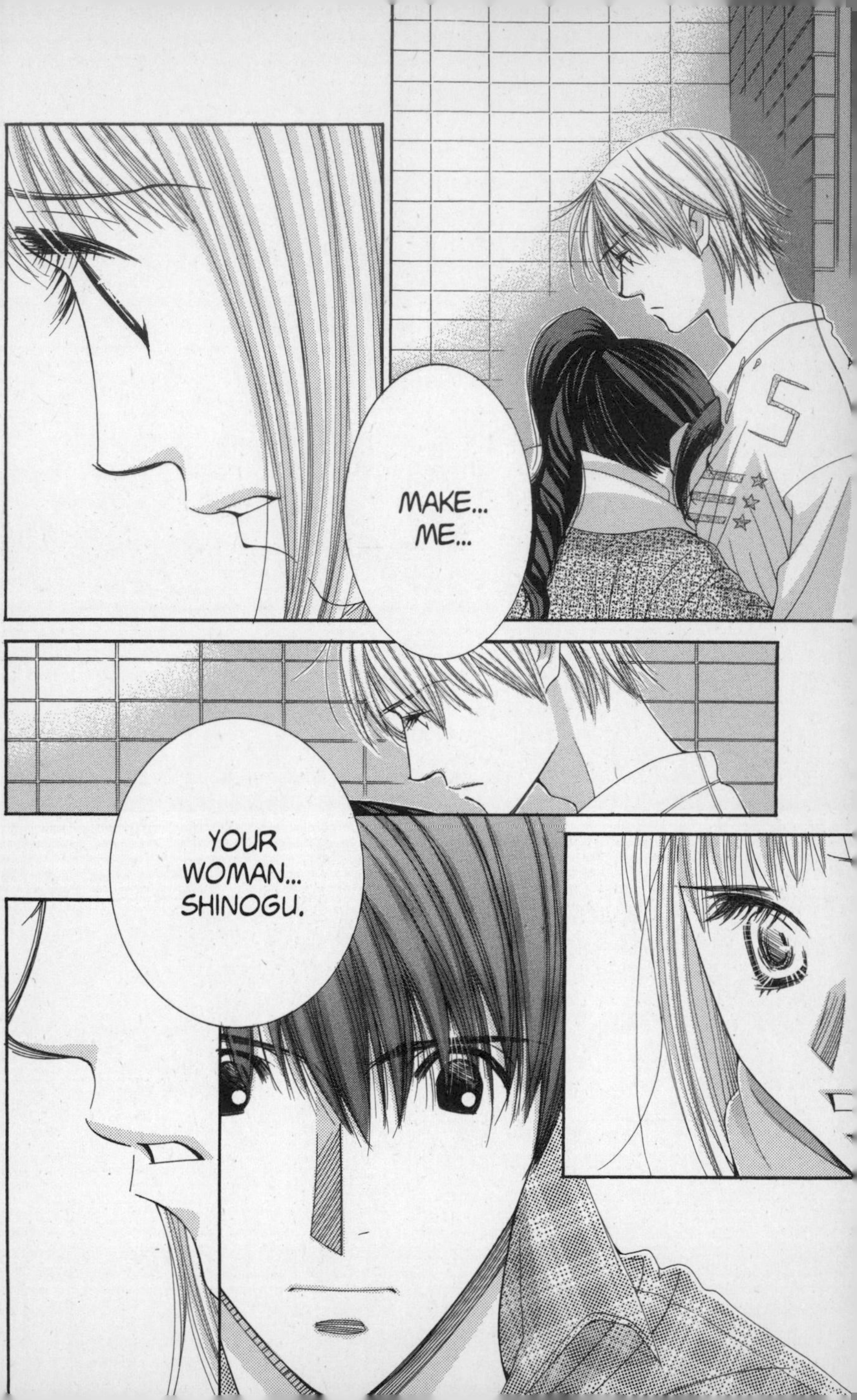
MAKE... ME...
YOUR WOMAN... SHINOGU.

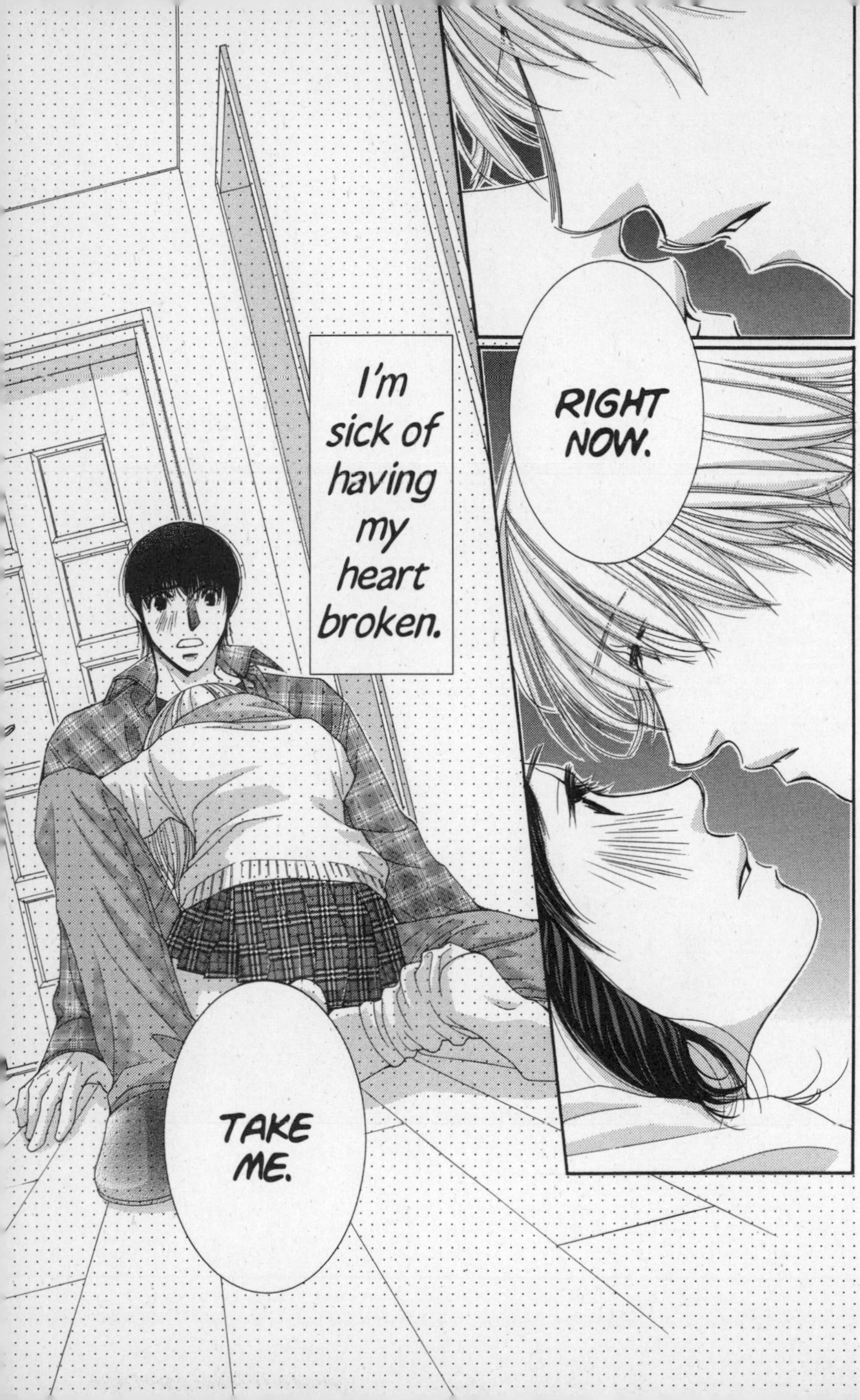
RIGHT NOW.
I'm sick of having my heart broken.
TAKE ME.

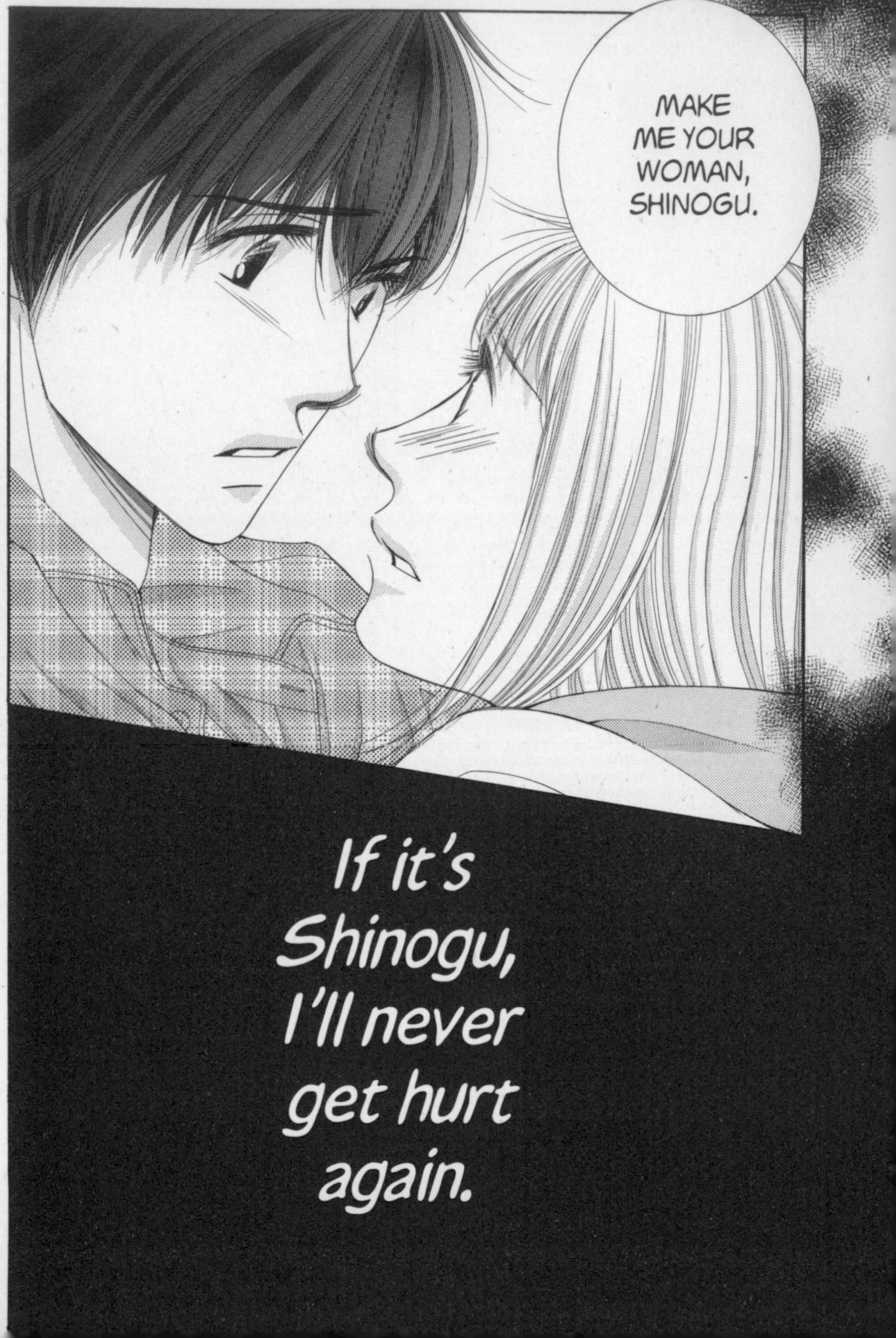
MAKE ME YOUR WOMAN, SHINOGU.
If it's Shinogu, I'll never get hurt again.

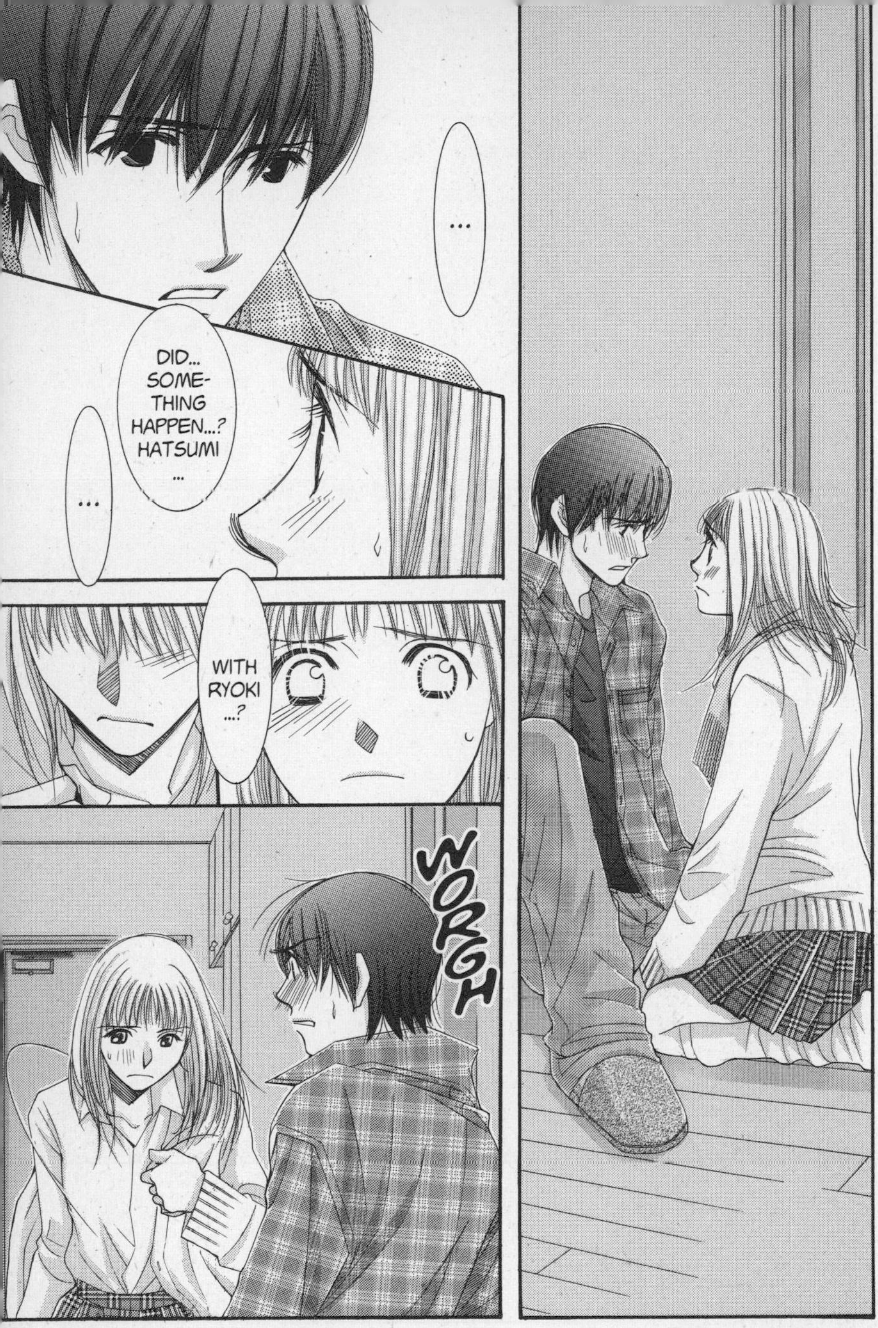
...
DID... SOME-THING HAPPEN...? HATSUMI ...
...
WITH RYOKI ...?
WORGH

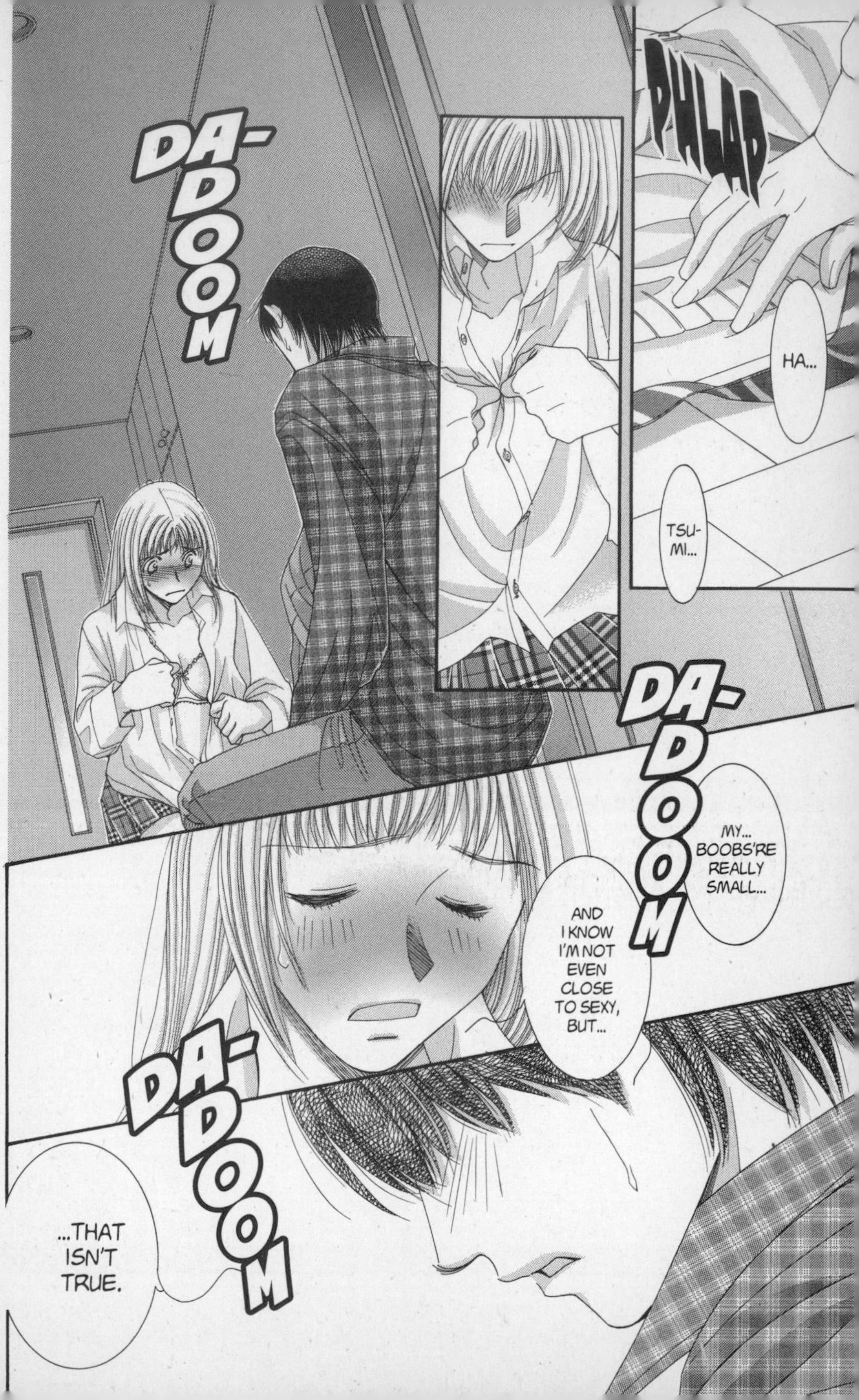
PHLAP
HA...
TSU-MI...
DA-DOOM
DA-DOOM
MY... BOOBS'RE REALLY SMALL...
AND I KNOW I'M NOT EVEN CLOSE TO SEXY, BUT...
DA-DOOM
...THAT ISN'T TRUE.

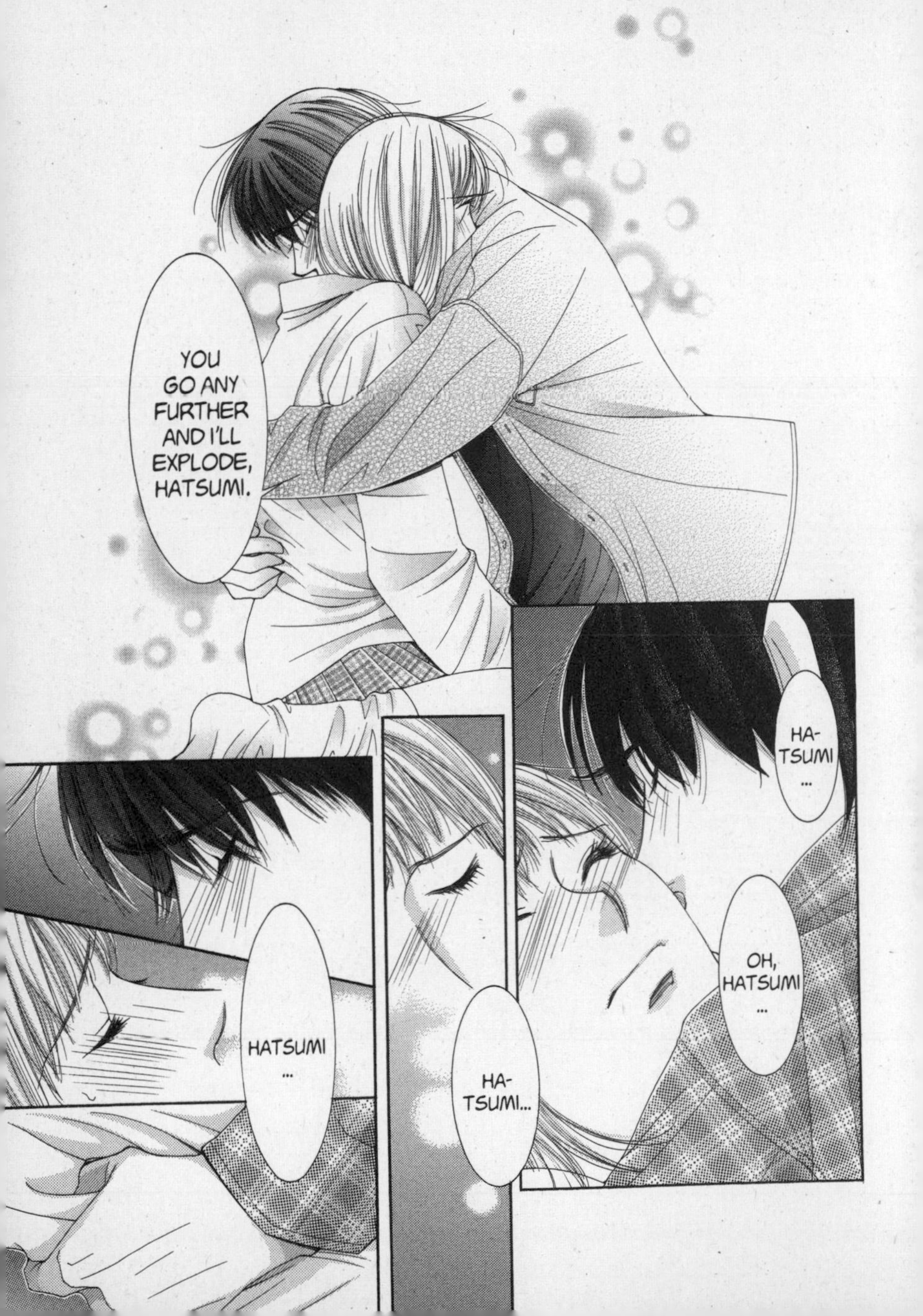
YOU GO ANY FURTHER AND I'LL EXPLODE, HATSUMI.
HA-TSUMI...
OH, HATSUMI...
HA-TSUMI...
HATSUMI...

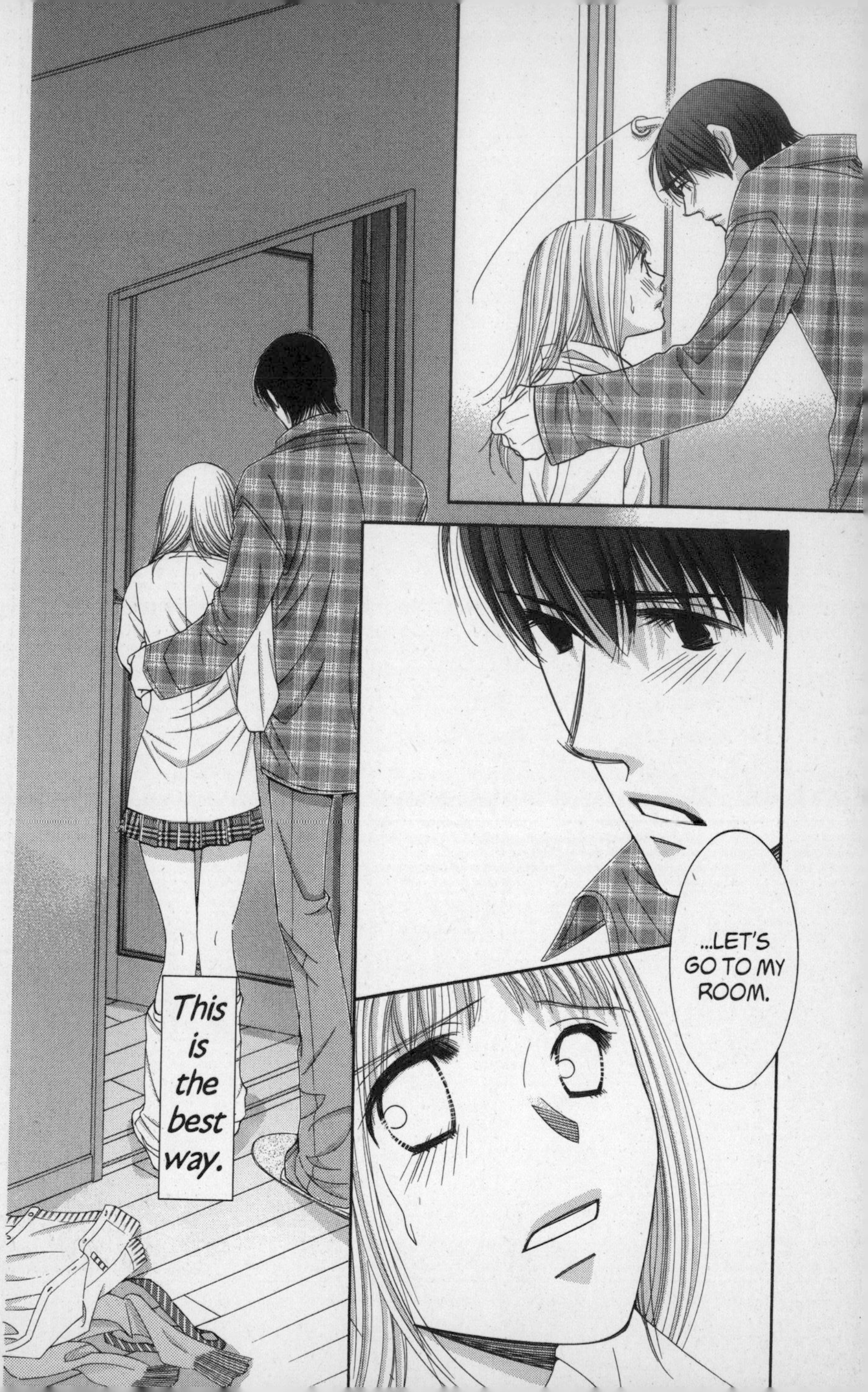
...LET'S GO TO MY ROOM.
This is the best way.

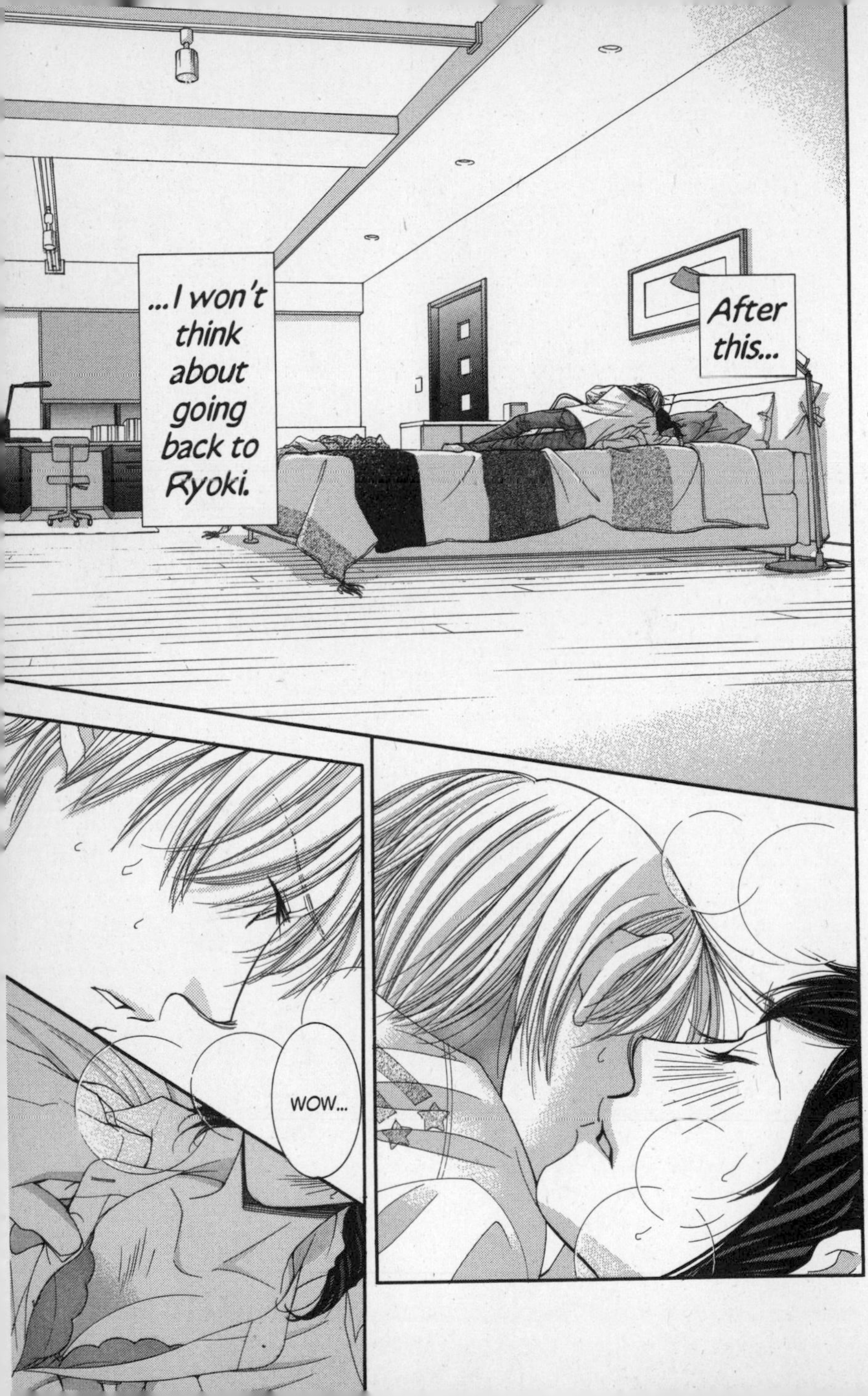
After this...
...I won't think about going back to Ryoki.
WOW...

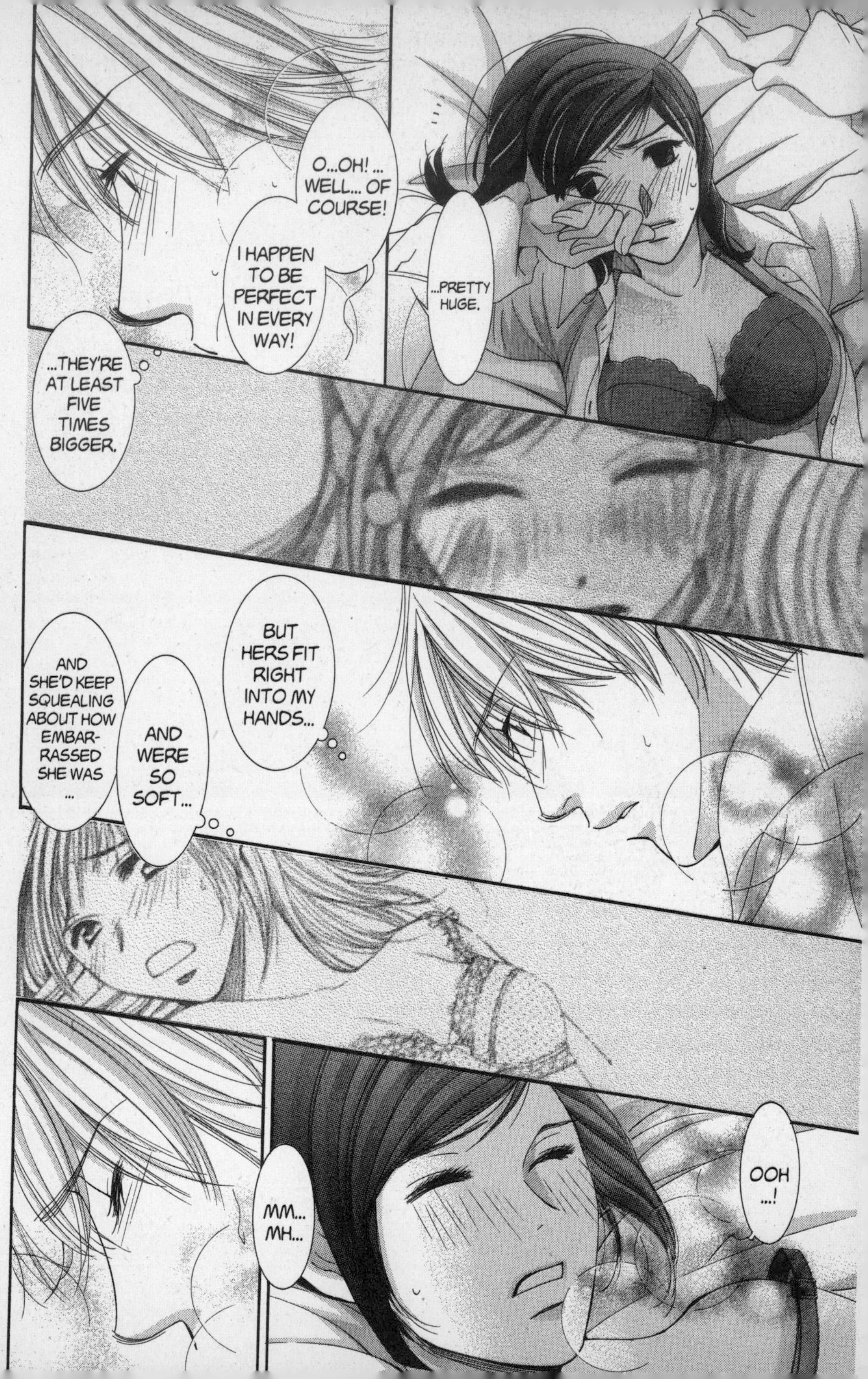
...PRETTY HUGE.
O...OH! ... WELL... OF COURSE!
I HAPPEN TO BE PERFECT IN EVERY WAY!
...THEY'RE AT LEAST FIVE TIMES BIGGER.
BUT HERS FIT RIGHT INTO MY HANDS...
AND WERE SO SOFT...
AND SHE'D KEEP SQUEALING ABOUT HOW EMBAR-RASSED SHE WAS ...
OOH ...!
MM... MH...

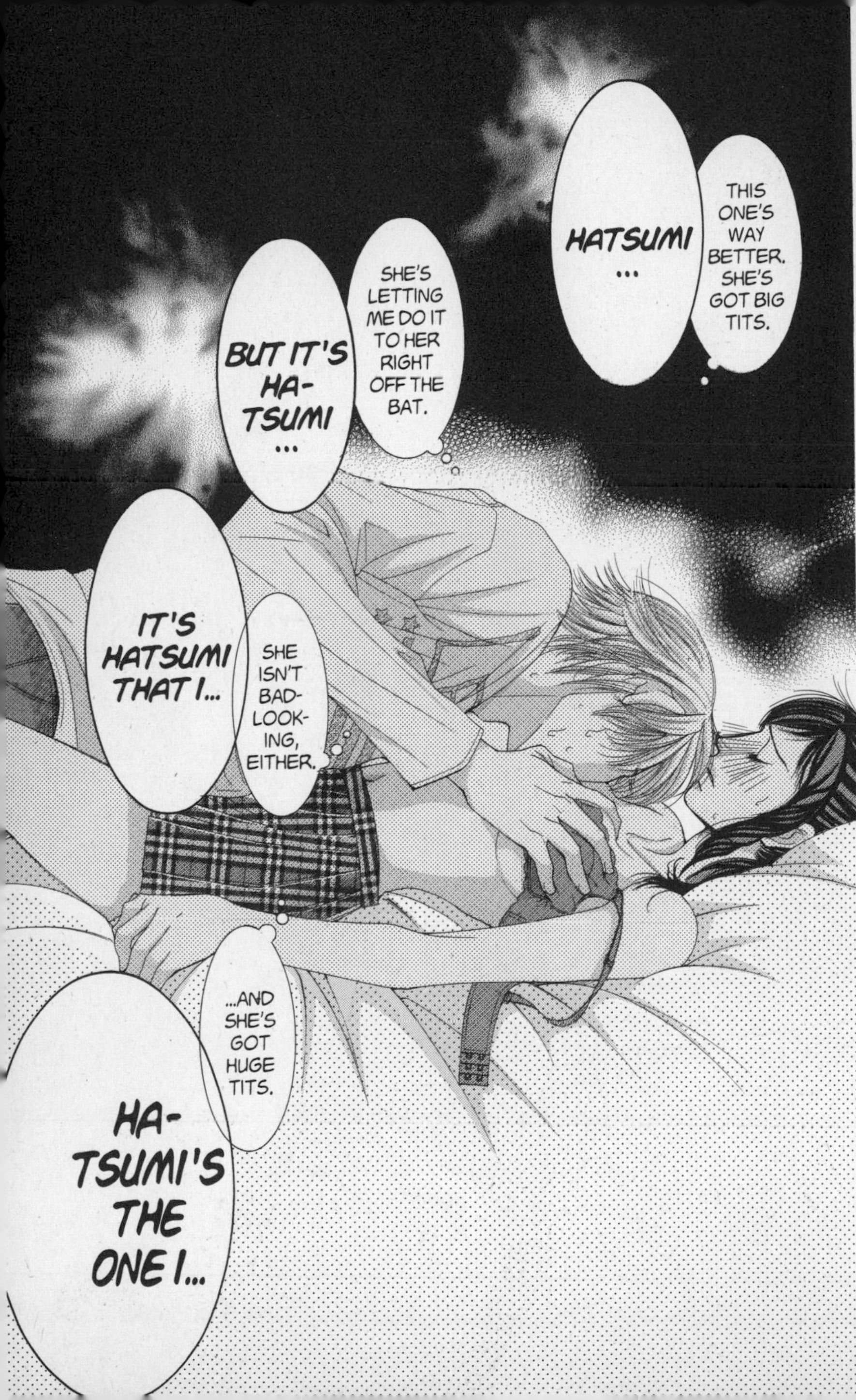
THIS ONE'S WAY BETTER. SHE'S GOT BIG TITS.
HATSUMI...
SHE'S LETTING ME DO IT TO HER RIGHT OFF THE BAT.
BUT IT'S HA-TSUMI...
SHE ISN'T BAD-LOOKING, EITHER.
IT'S HATSUMI THAT I...
...AND SHE'S GOT HUGE TITS.
HA-TSUMI'S THE ONE I...

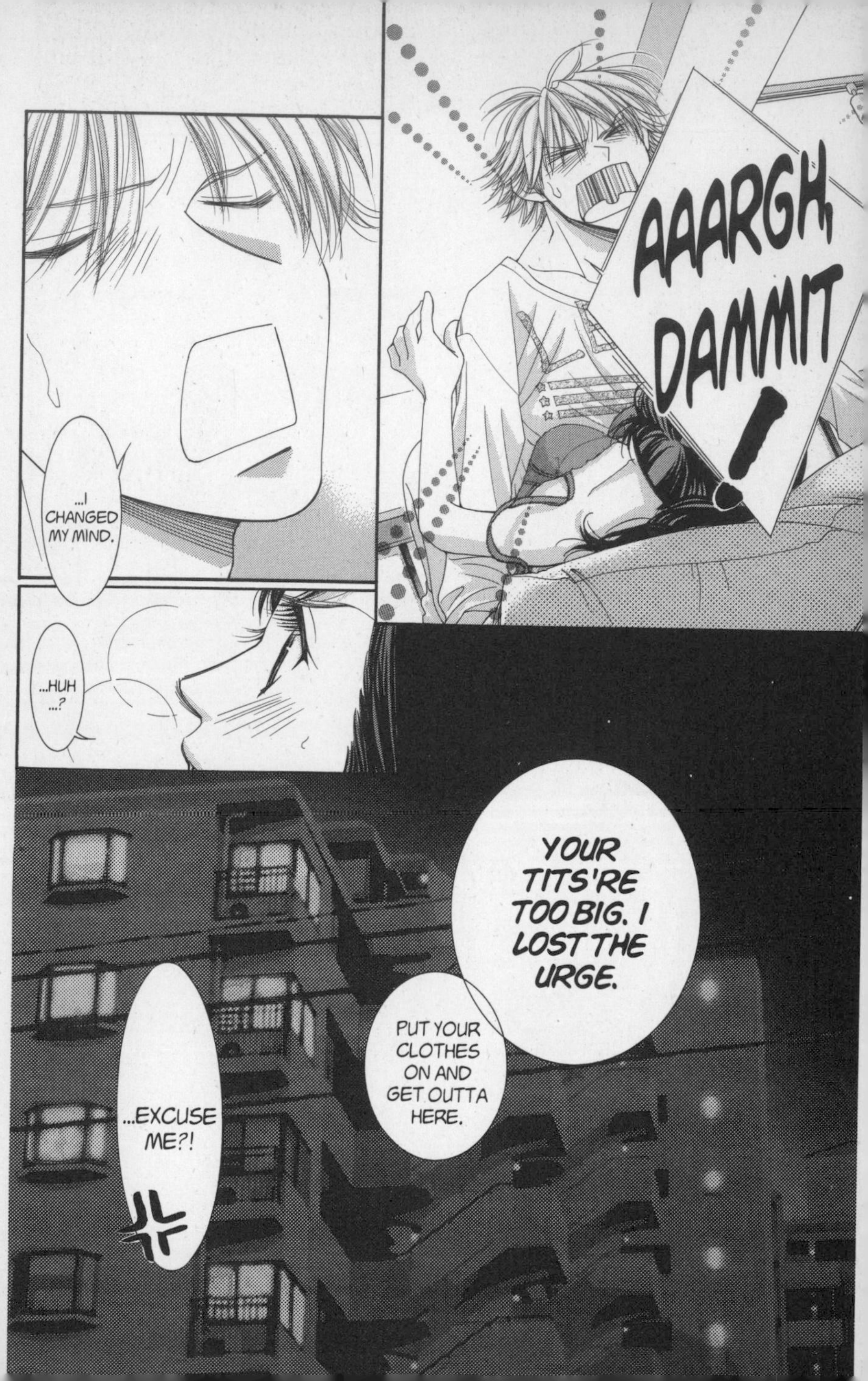
AAARGH, DAMMIT!
...I CHANGED MY MIND.
...HUH ...?
YOUR TITS'RE TOO BIG. I LOST THE URGE.
PUT YOUR CLOTHES ON AND GET OUTTA HERE.
...EXCUSE ME?!

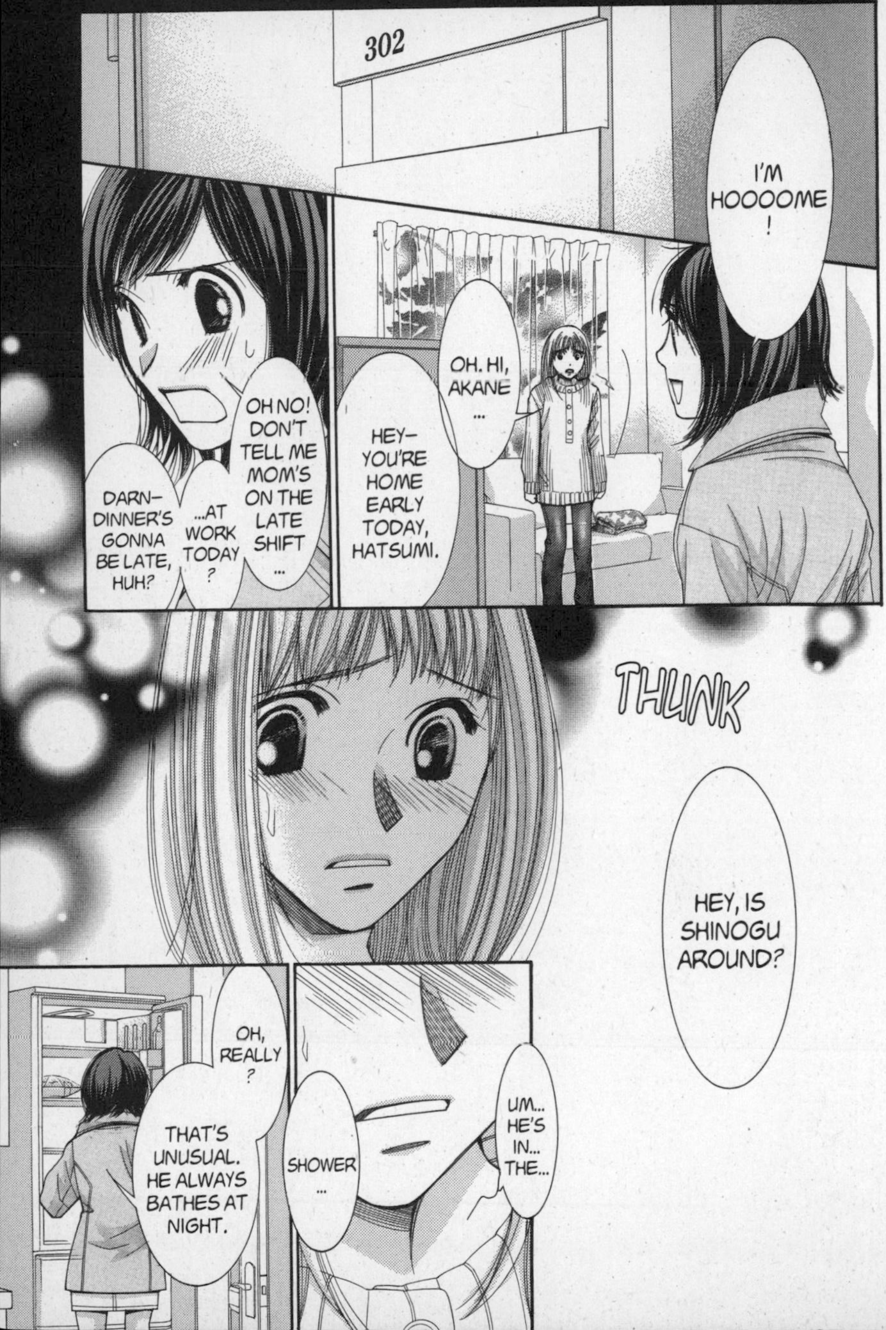
302
I'M HOOOOME!
OH. HI, AKANE...
HEY— YOU'RE HOME EARLY TODAY, HATSUMI.
OH NO! DON'T TELL ME MOM'S ON THE LATE SHIFT...
...AT WORK TODAY?
DARN— DINNER'S GONNA BE LATE, HUH?
THUNK
HEY, IS SHINOGU AROUND?
UM... HE'S IN... THE...
SHOWER...
OH, REALLY?
THAT'S UNUSUAL. HE ALWAYS BATHES AT NIGHT.

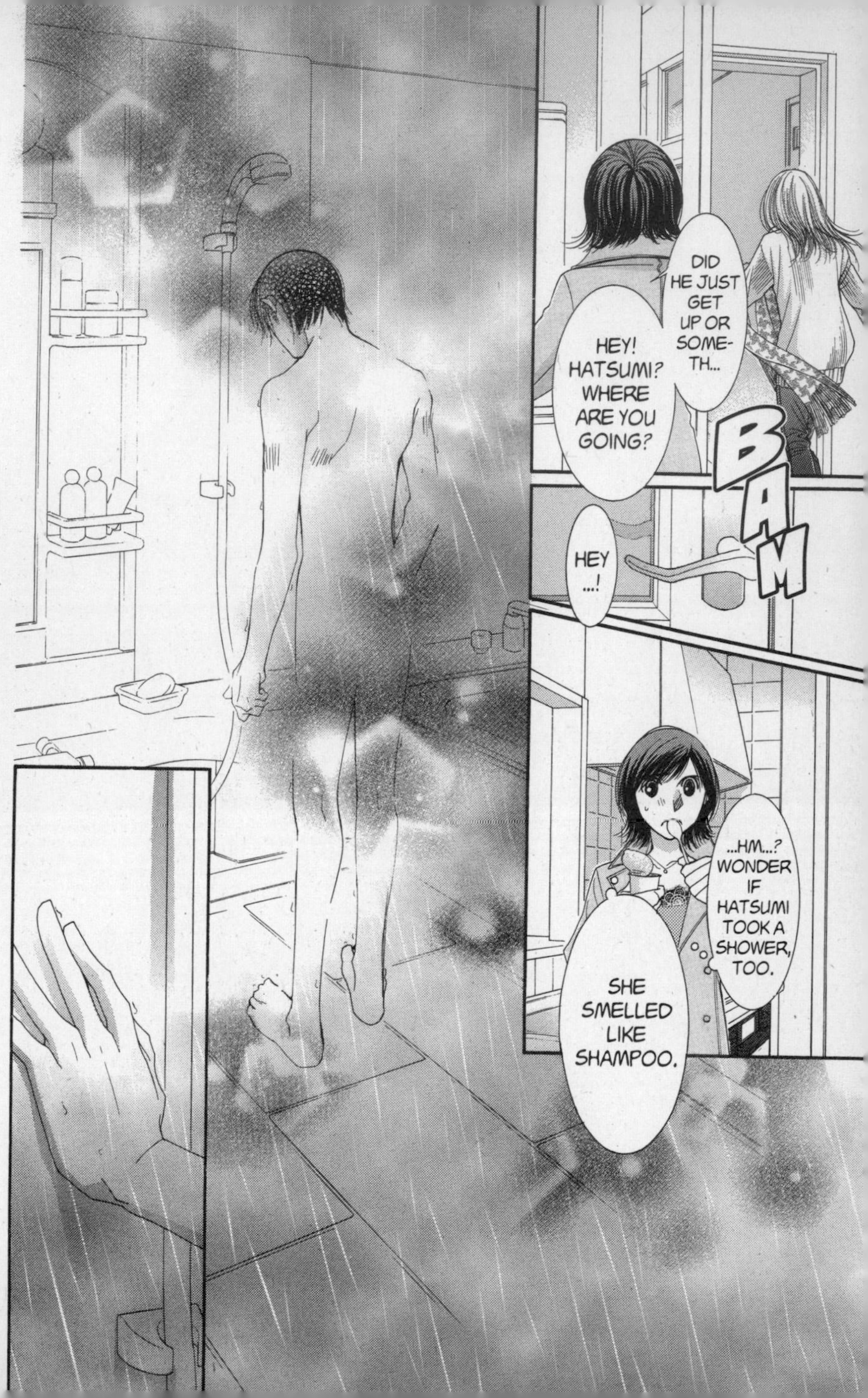
DID HE JUST GET UP OR SOMETH...
HEY! HATSUMI? WHERE ARE YOU GOING?
BAM
HEY ...!
...HM...? WONDER IF HATSUMI TOOK A SHOWER, TOO.
SHE SMELLED LIKE SHAMPOO.

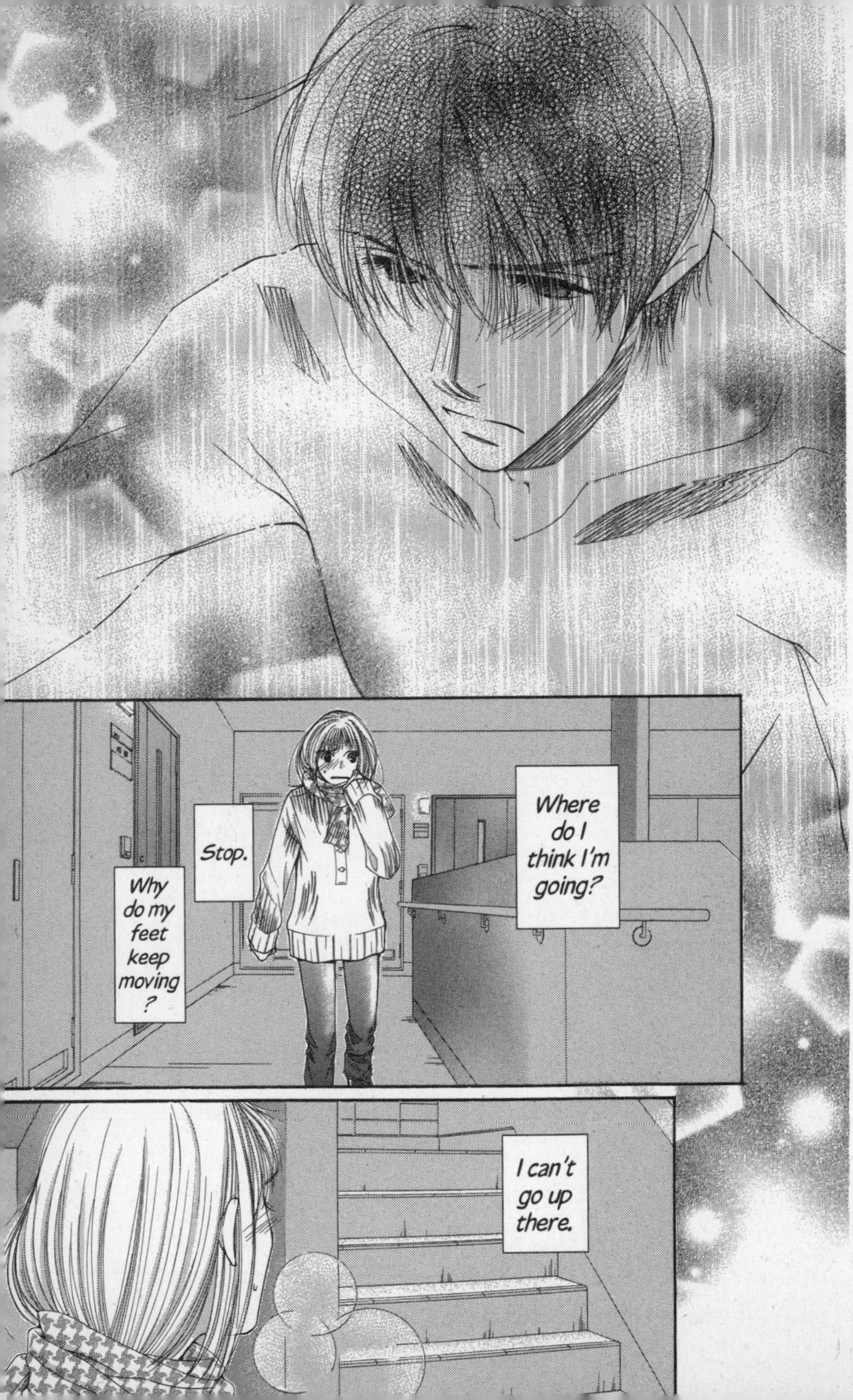
Where do I think I'm going?
Stop.
Why do my feet keep moving?
I can't go up there.

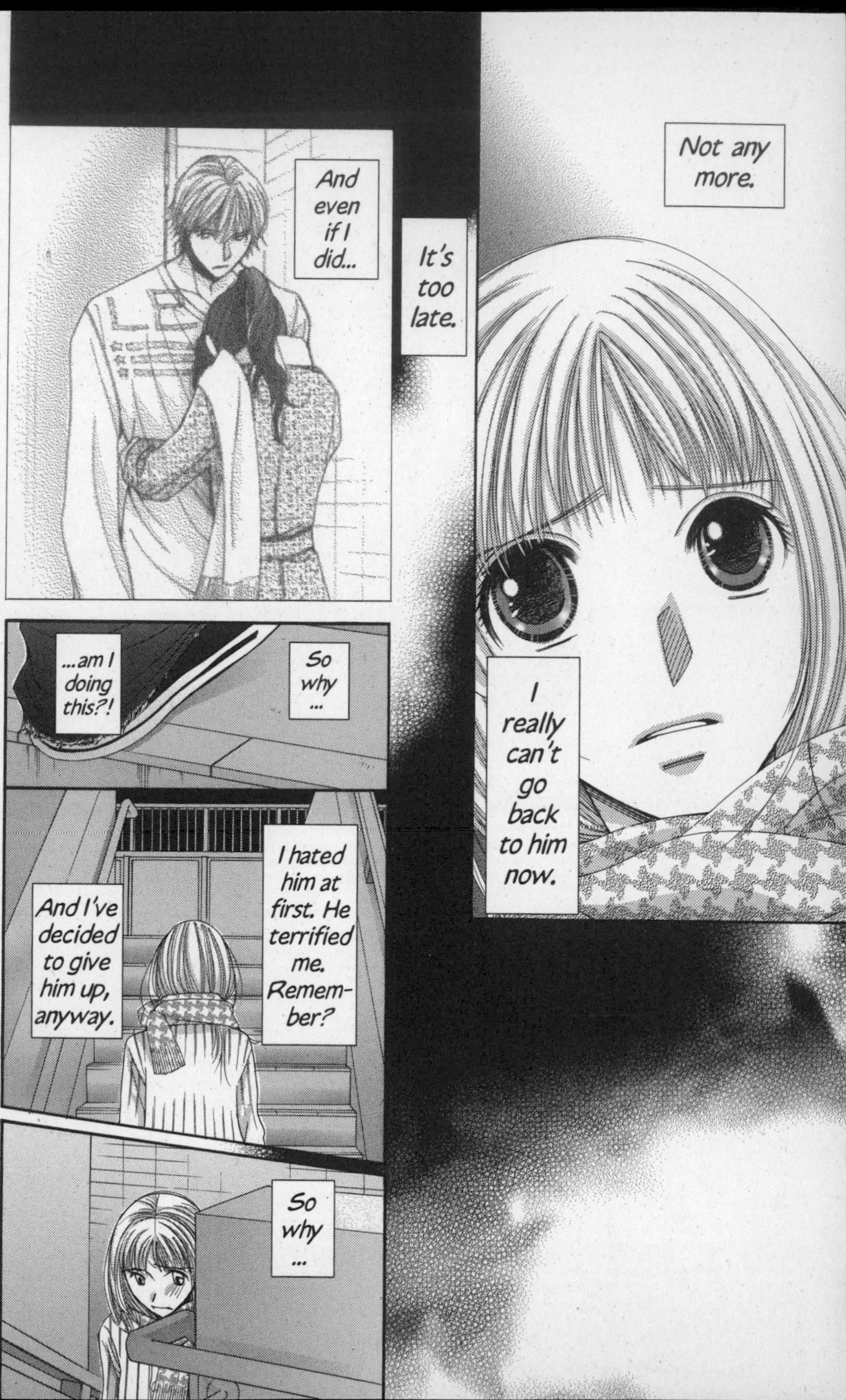
Not any more.
I really can't go back to him now.
It's too late.
And even if I did...
So why...
...am I doing this?!
I hated him at first. He terrified me. Remember?
And I've decided to give him up, anyway.
So why...

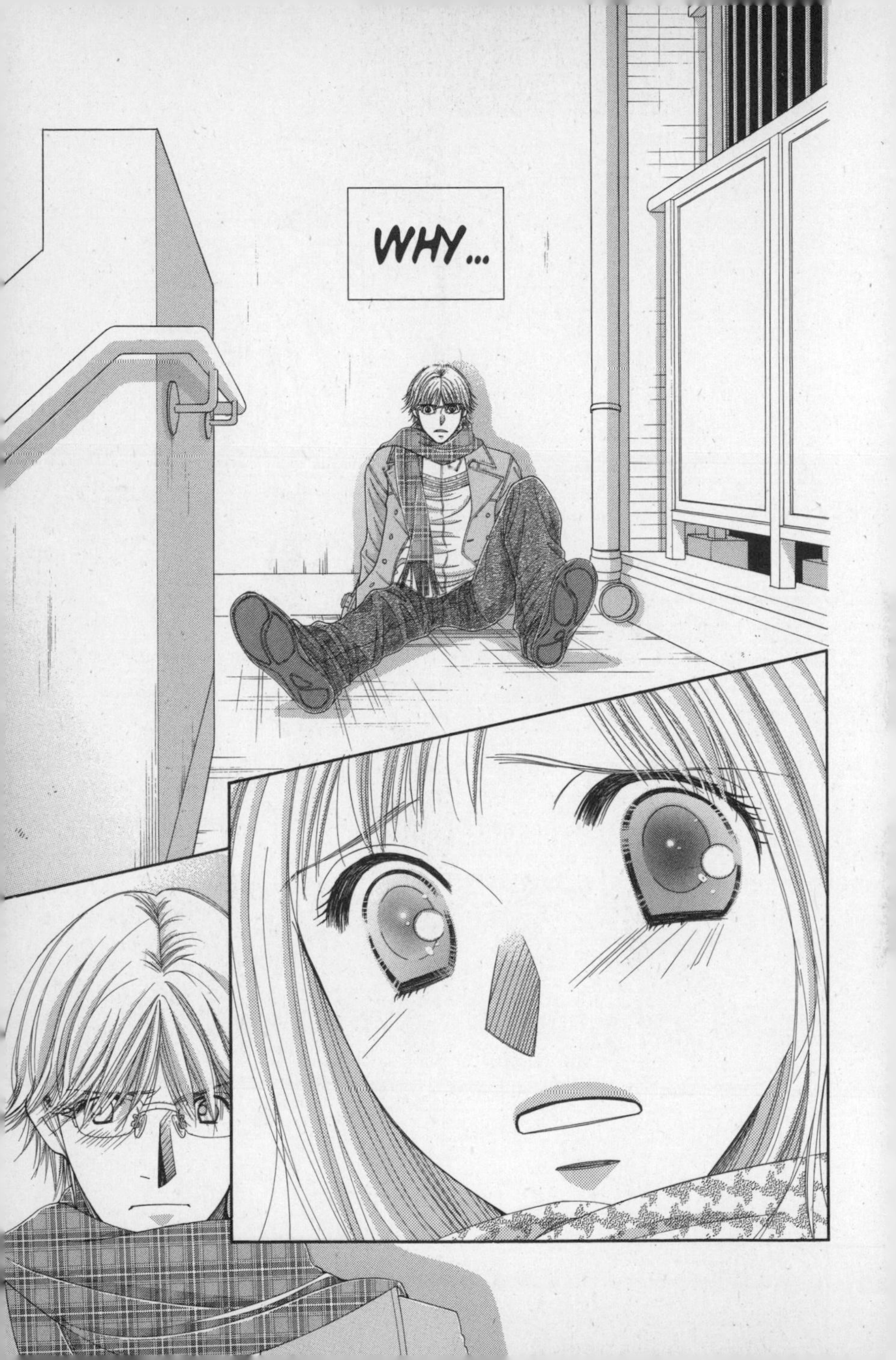
WHY...

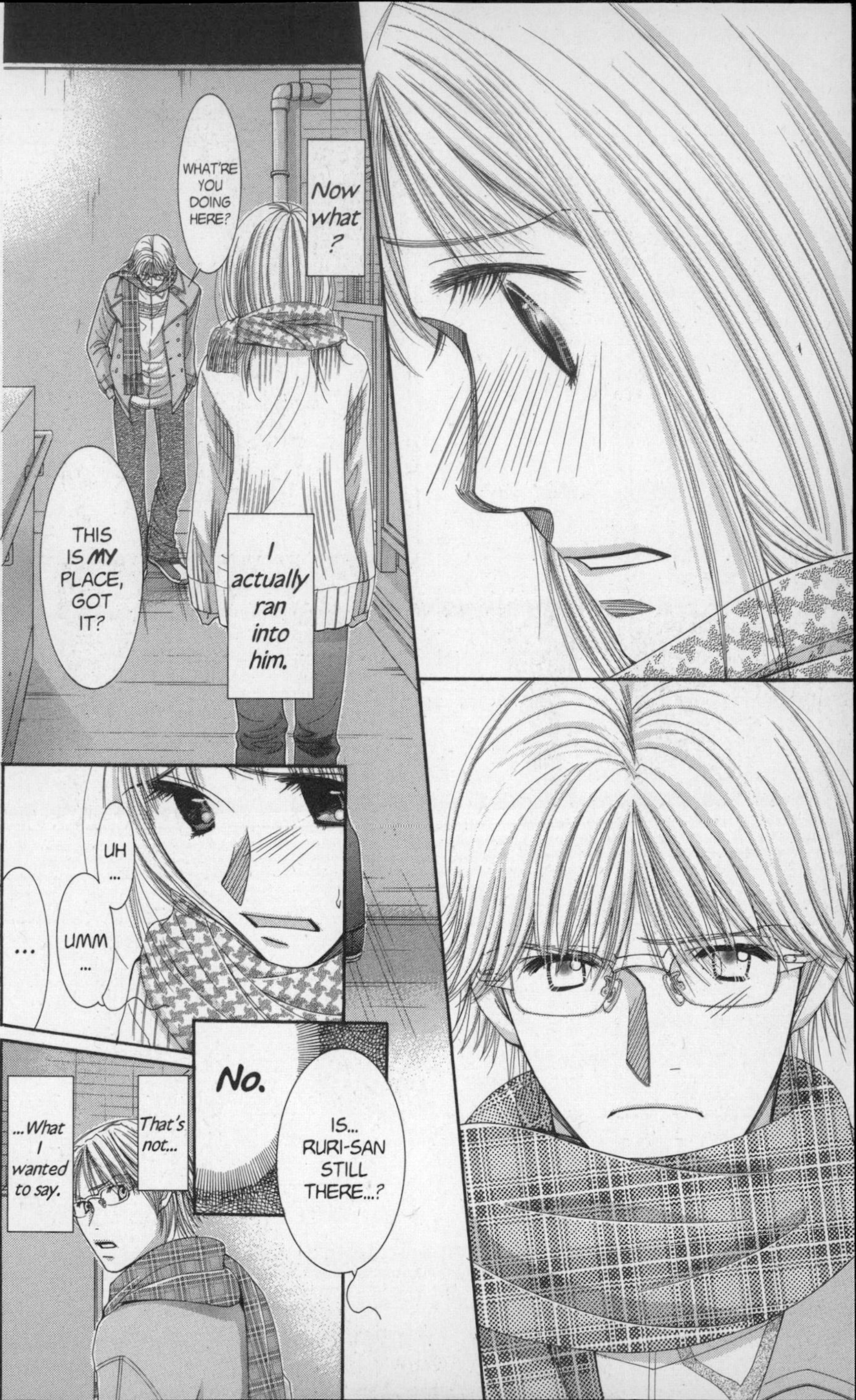
Now what?
WHAT'RE YOU DOING HERE?
I actually ran into him.
THIS IS MY PLACE, GOT IT?
UH...
UMM...
...
No.
IS... RURI-SAN STILL THERE...?
That's not...
...What I wanted to say.

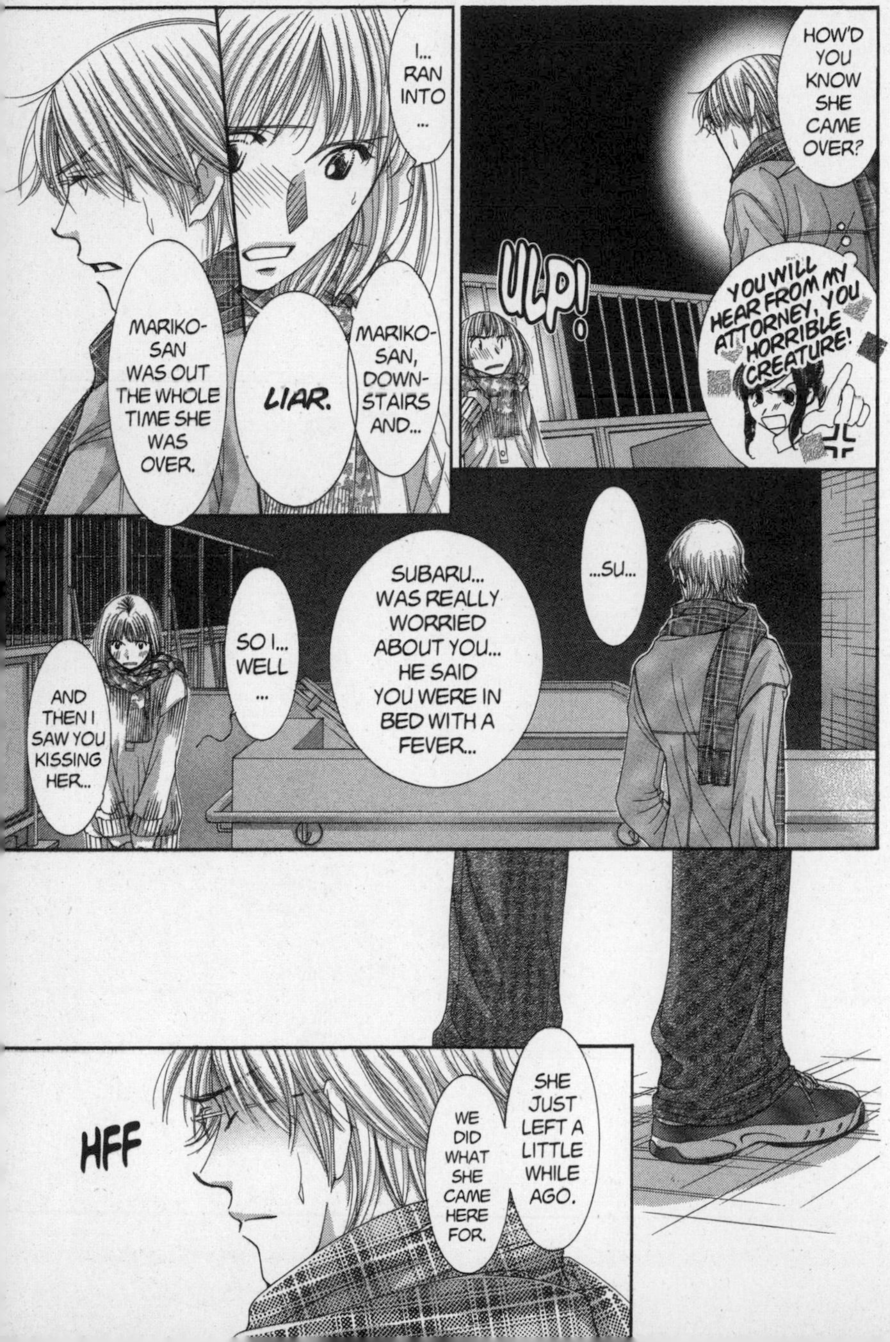
HOW'D YOU KNOW SHE CAME OVER?
ULP!
YOU WILL HEAR FROM MY ATTORNEY, YOU HORRIBLE CREATURE!
I... RAN INTO ...
MARIKO-SAN, DOWN-STAIRS AND...
LIAR.
MARIKO-SAN WAS OUT THE WHOLE TIME SHE WAS OVER.
...SU...
SUBARU... WAS REALLY WORRIED ABOUT YOU... HE SAID YOU WERE IN BED WITH A FEVER...
SO I... WELL ...
AND THEN I SAW YOU KISSING HER...
SHE JUST LEFT A LITTLE WHILE AGO.
WE DID WHAT SHE CAME HERE FOR.
HFF

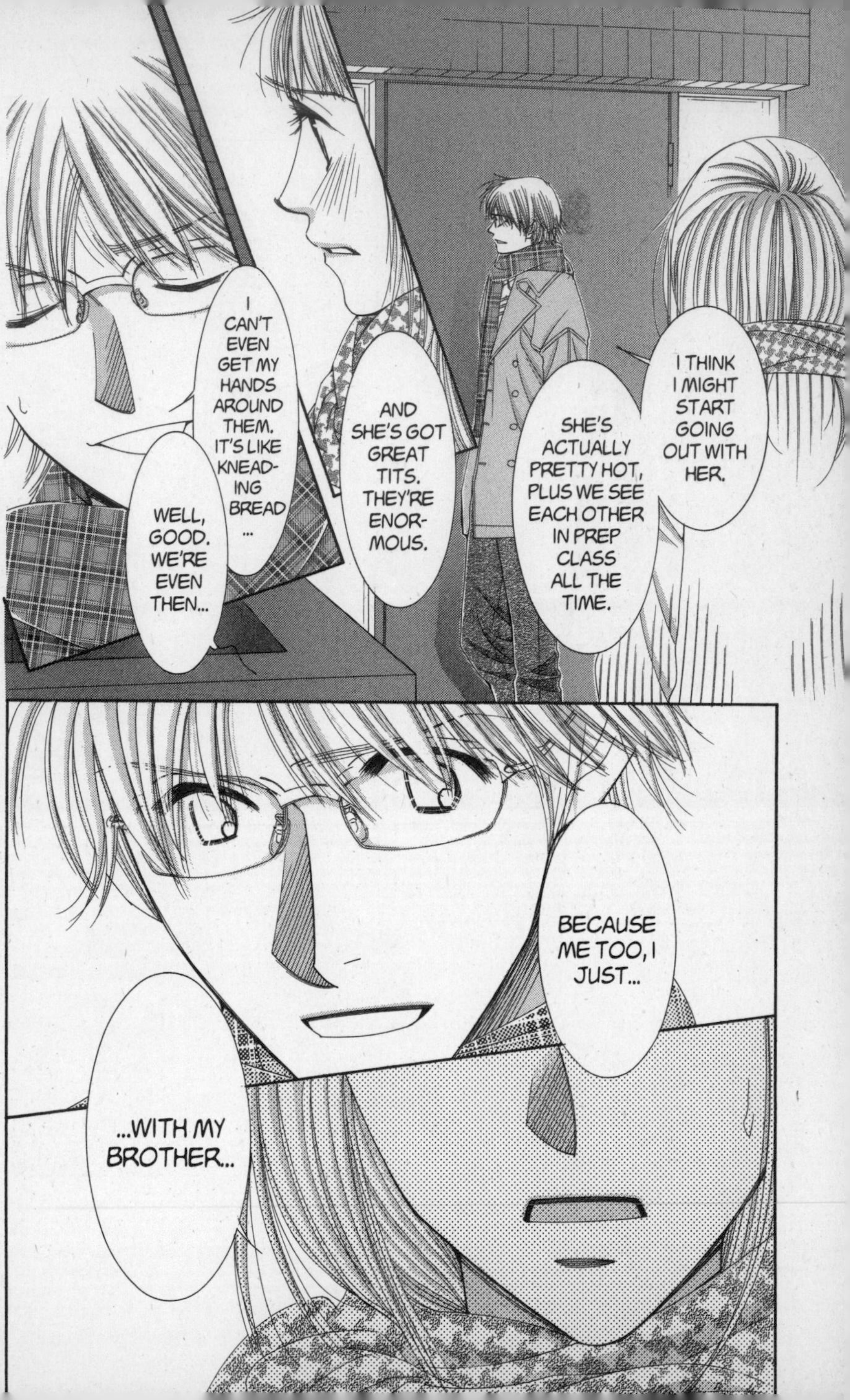
I THINK I MIGHT START GOING OUT WITH HER.
SHE'S ACTUALLY PRETTY HOT, PLUS WE SEE EACH OTHER IN PREP CLASS ALL THE TIME.
AND SHE'S GOT GREAT TITS. THEY'RE ENOR-MOUS.
I CAN'T EVEN GET MY HANDS AROUND THEM. IT'S LIKE KNEAD-ING BREAD ...
WELL, GOOD. WE'RE EVEN THEN...
BECAUSE ME TOO, I JUST...
...WITH MY BROTHER...

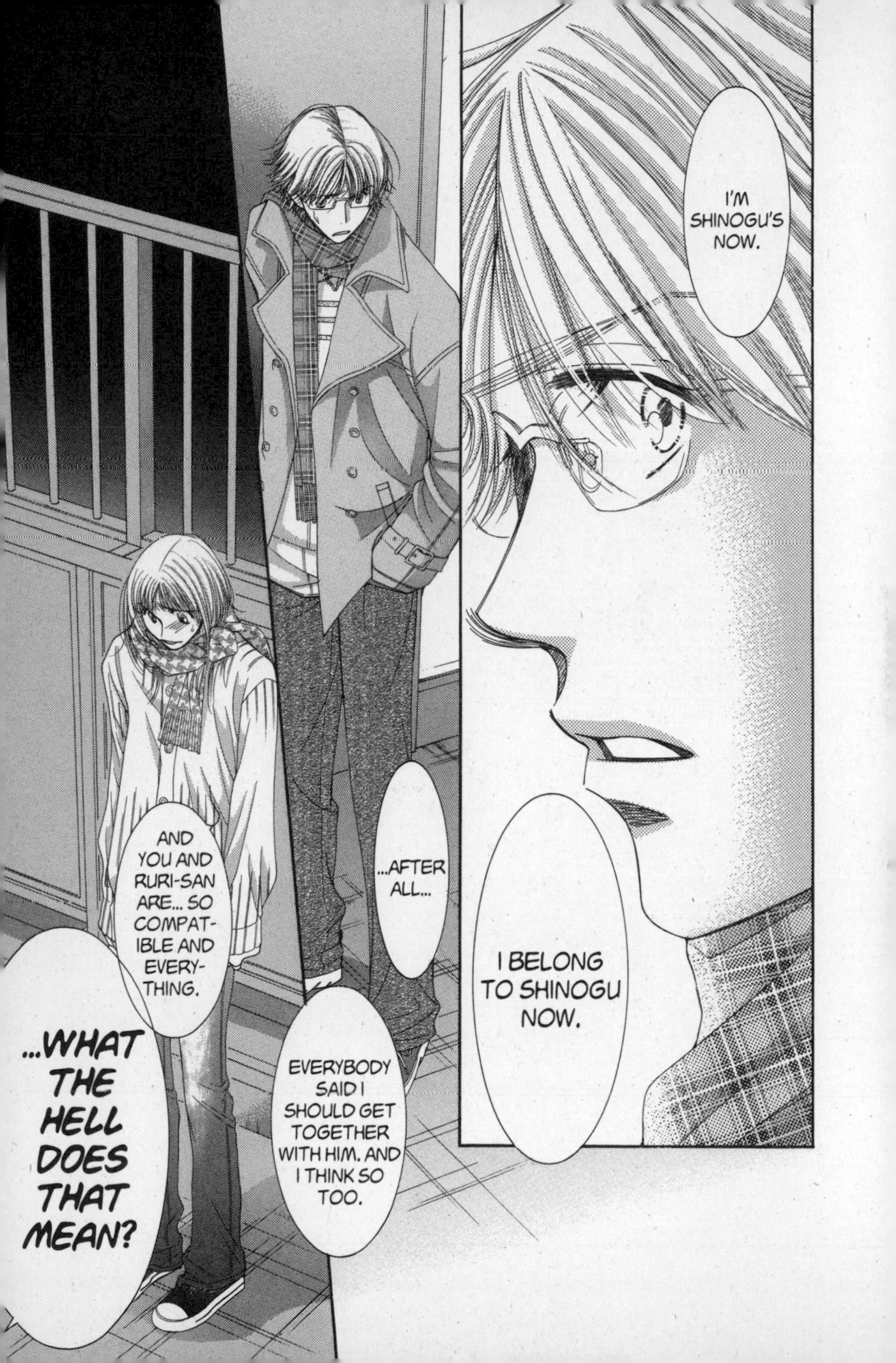
I'M SHINOGU'S NOW.
I BELONG TO SHINOGU NOW.
...AFTER ALL...
AND YOU AND RURI-SAN ARE... SO COMPATIBLE AND EVERYTHING.
EVERYBODY SAID I SHOULD GET TOGETHER WITH HIM. AND I THINK SO TOO.
...WHAT THE HELL DOES THAT MEAN?

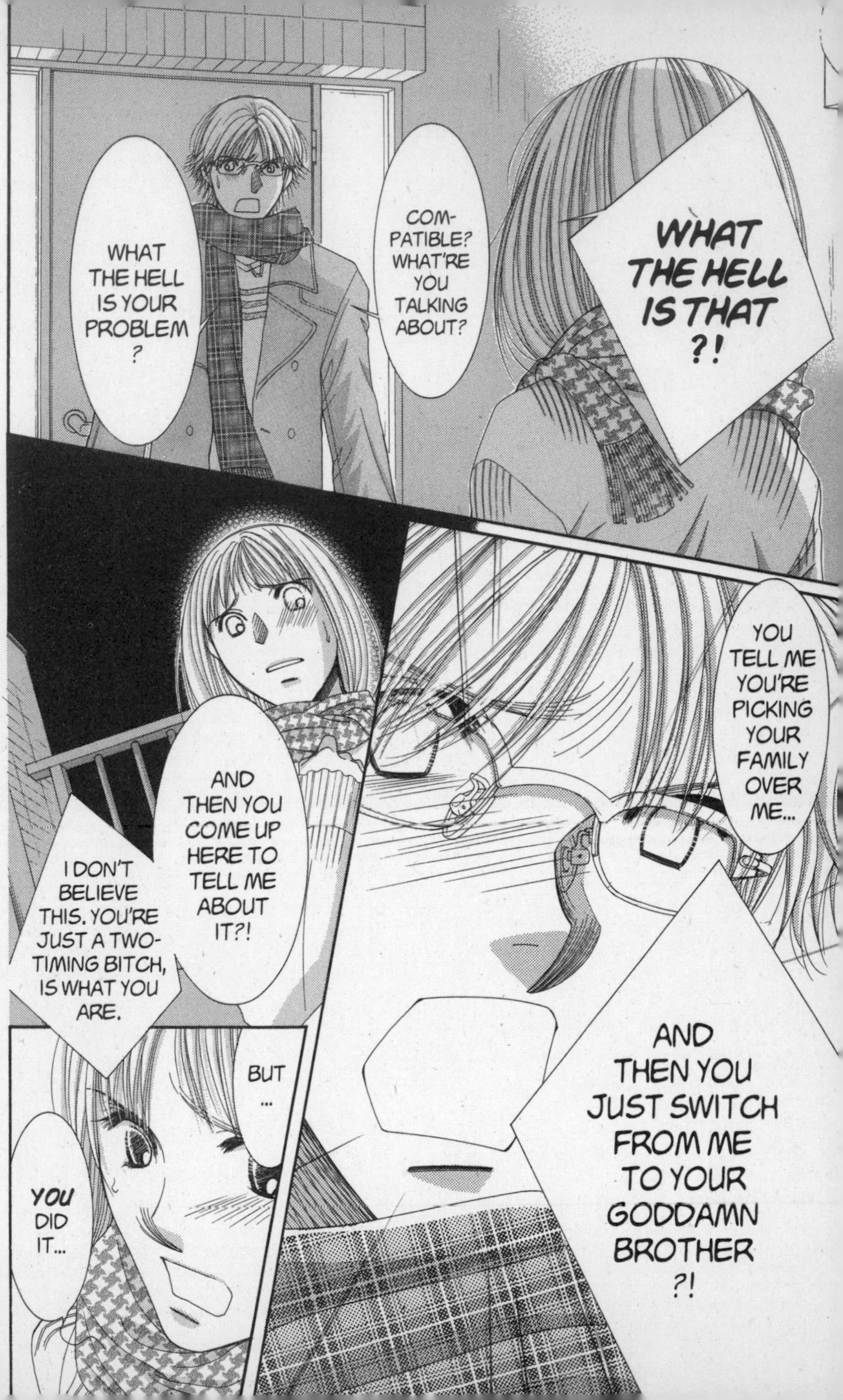
WHAT THE HELL IS THAT ?!
COM-PATIBLE? WHAT'RE YOU TALKING ABOUT?
WHAT THE HELL IS YOUR PROBLEM ?
YOU TELL ME YOU'RE PICKING YOUR FAMILY OVER ME...
AND THEN YOU JUST SWITCH FROM ME TO YOUR GODDAMN BROTHER ?!
AND THEN YOU COME UP HERE TO TELL ME ABOUT IT?!
I DON'T BELIEVE THIS. YOU'RE JUST A TWO-TIMING BITCH, IS WHAT YOU ARE.
BUT ...
YOU DID IT...

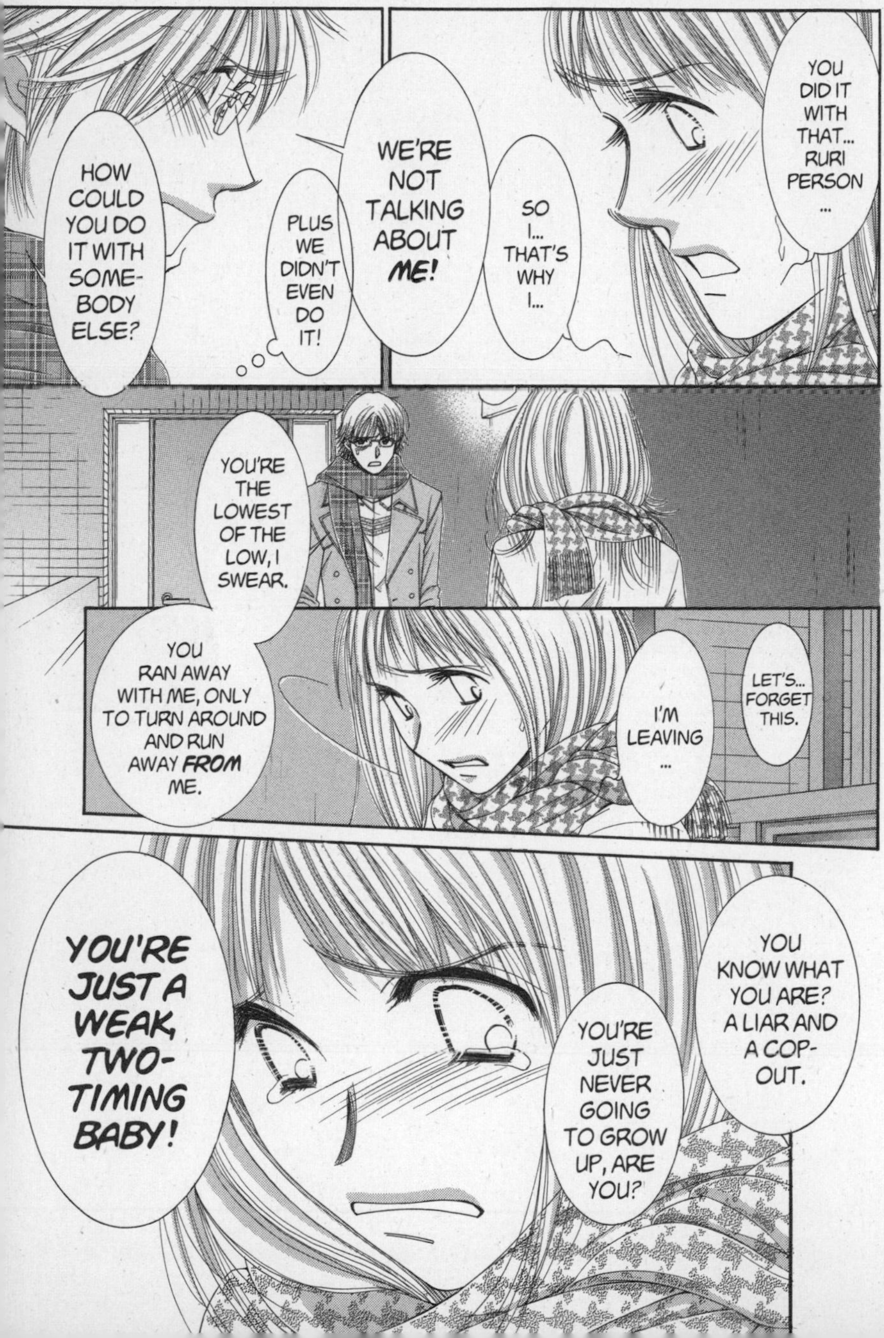
YOU DID IT WITH THAT... RURI PERSON ...
SO I... THAT'S WHY I...
WE'RE NOT TALKING ABOUT *ME!*
PLUS WE DIDN'T EVEN DO IT!
HOW COULD YOU DO IT WITH SOME-BODY ELSE?
YOU'RE THE LOWEST OF THE LOW, I SWEAR.
LET'S... FORGET THIS.
I'M LEAVING ...
YOU RAN AWAY WITH ME, ONLY TO TURN AROUND AND RUN AWAY *FROM* ME.
YOU KNOW WHAT YOU ARE? A LIAR AND A COP-OUT.
YOU'RE JUST NEVER GOING TO GROW UP, ARE YOU?
YOU'RE JUST A WEAK, TWO-TIMING BABY!

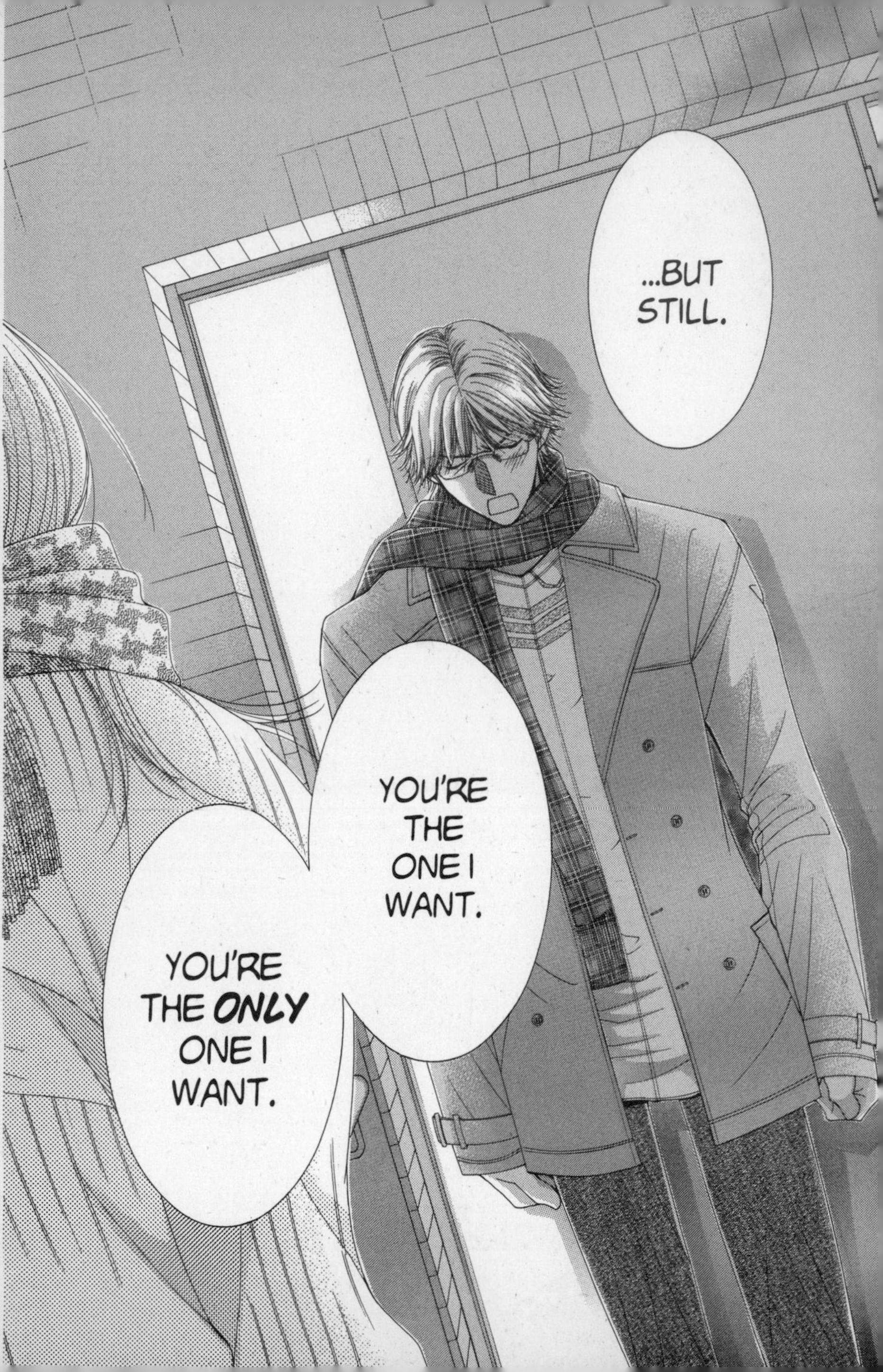
...BUT STILL.
YOU'RE THE ONE I WANT.
YOU'RE THE *ONLY* ONE I WANT.

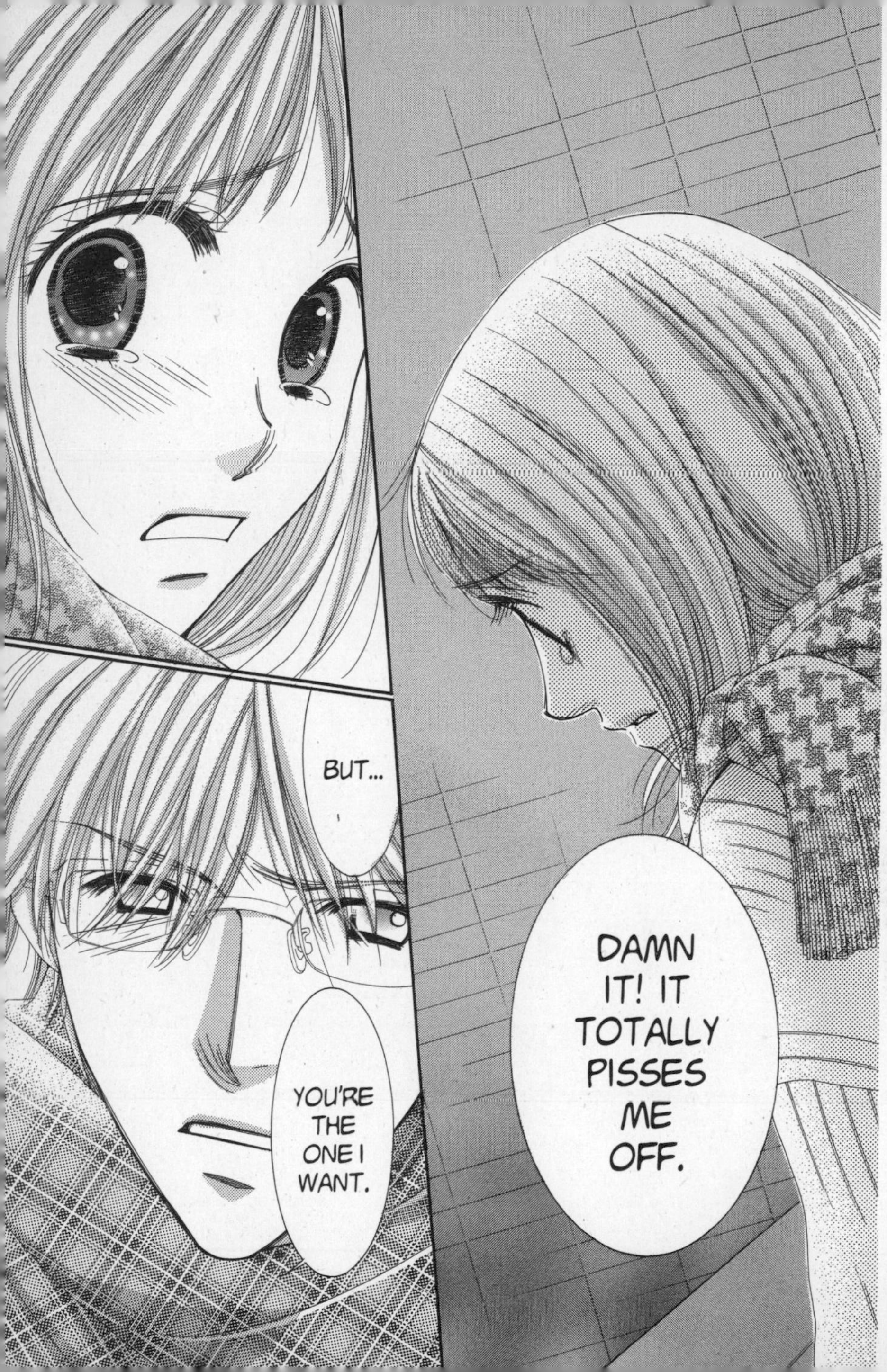
DAMN IT! IT TOTALLY PISSES ME OFF.
BUT...
YOU'RE THE ONE I WANT.

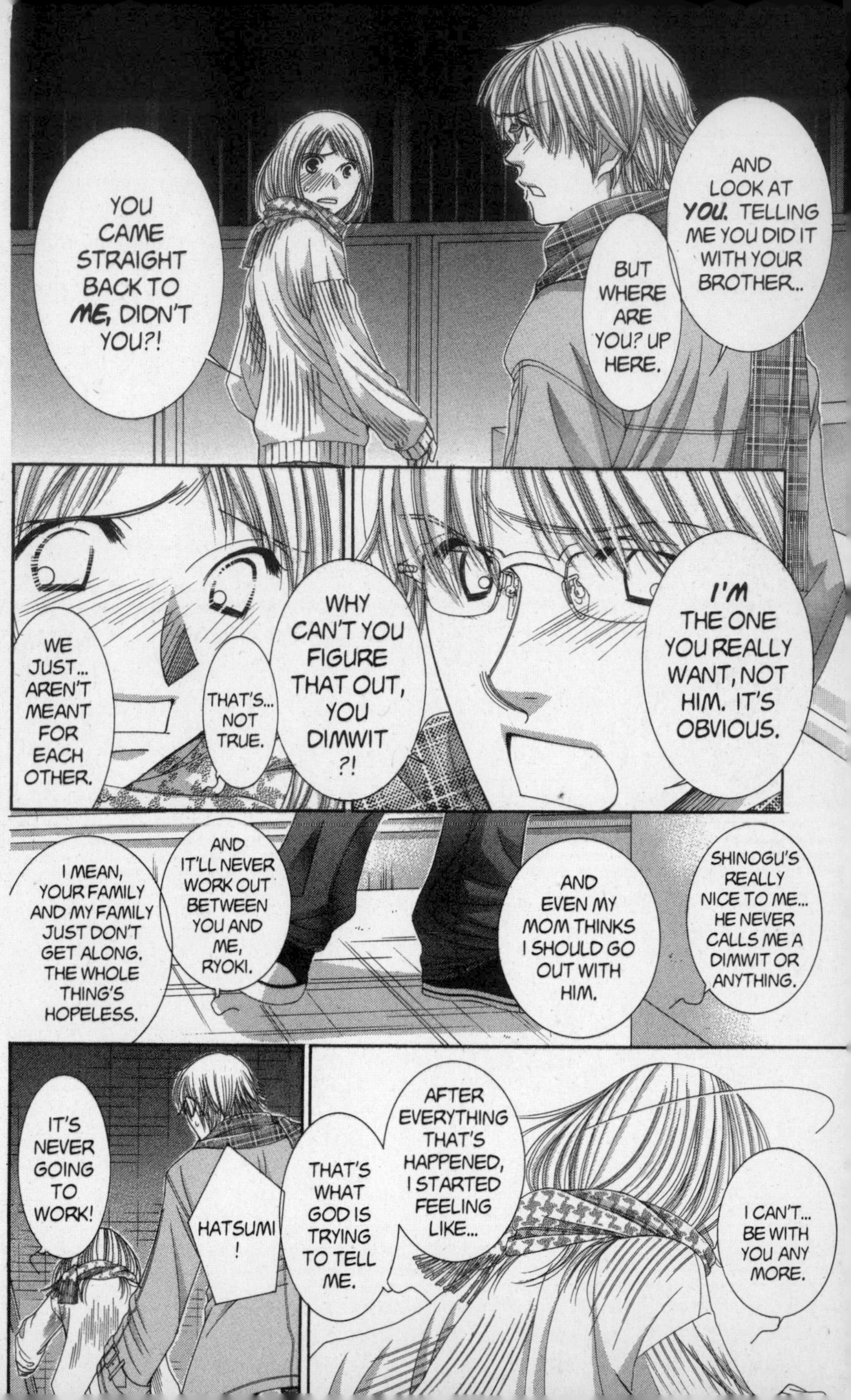
AND LOOK AT YOU. TELLING ME YOU DID IT WITH YOUR BROTHER...
BUT WHERE ARE YOU? UP HERE.
YOU CAME STRAIGHT BACK TO ME, DIDN'T YOU?!
I'M THE ONE YOU REALLY WANT, NOT HIM. IT'S OBVIOUS.
WHY CAN'T YOU FIGURE THAT OUT, YOU DIMWIT?!
THAT'S... NOT TRUE.
WE JUST... AREN'T MEANT FOR EACH OTHER.
SHINOGU'S REALLY NICE TO ME... HE NEVER CALLS ME A DIMWIT OR ANYTHING.
AND EVEN MY MOM THINKS I SHOULD GO OUT WITH HIM.
AND IT'LL NEVER WORK OUT BETWEEN YOU AND ME, RYOKI.
I MEAN, YOUR FAMILY AND MY FAMILY JUST DON'T GET ALONG. THE WHOLE THING'S HOPELESS.
I CAN'T... BE WITH YOU ANY MORE.
AFTER EVERYTHING THAT'S HAPPENED, I STARTED FEELING LIKE...
THAT'S WHAT GOD IS TRYING TO TELL ME.
IT'S NEVER GOING TO WORK!
HATSUMI!

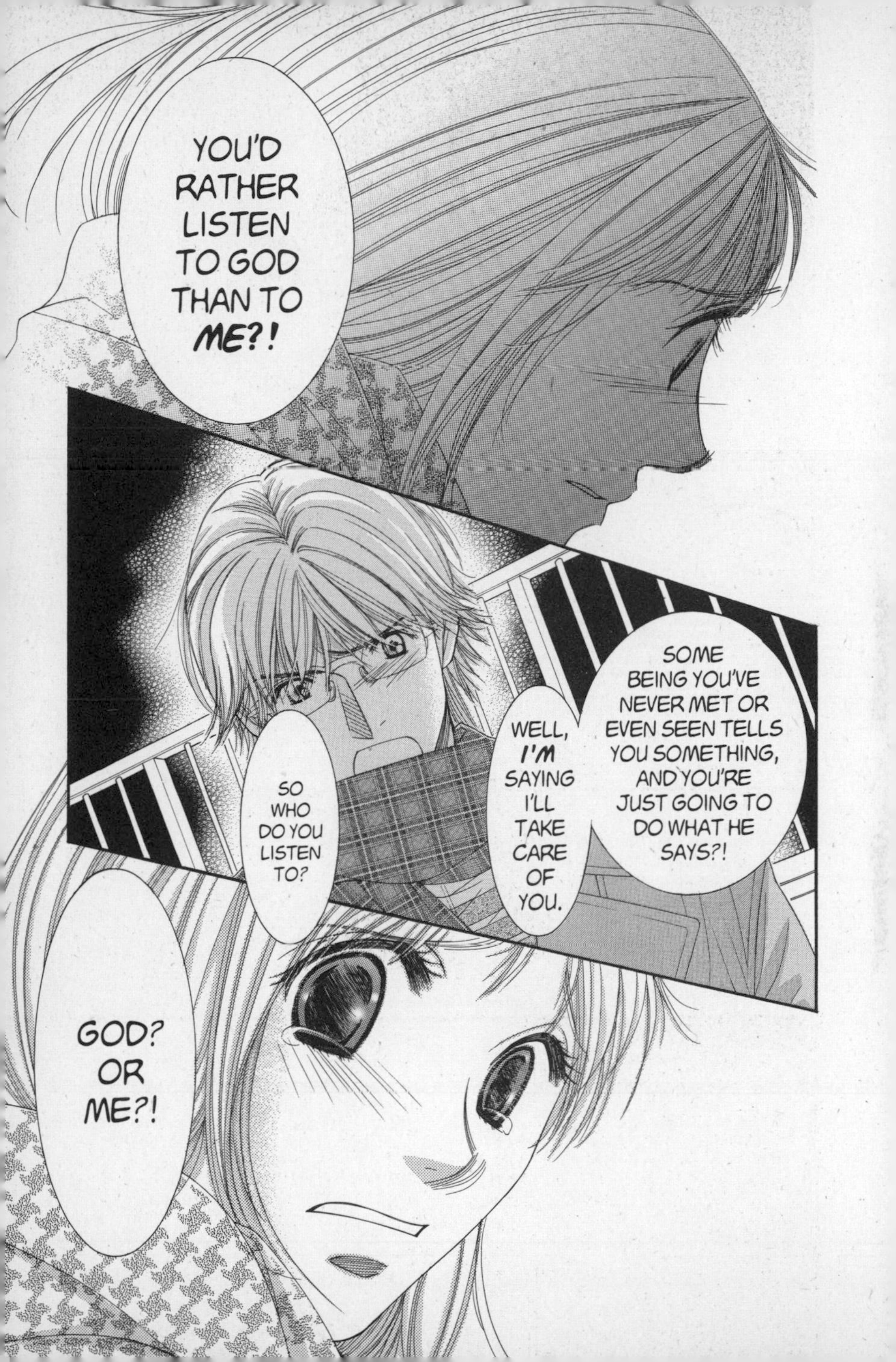
YOU'D RATHER LISTEN TO GOD THAN TO *ME*?!
SOME BEING YOU'VE NEVER MET OR EVEN SEEN TELLS YOU SOMETHING, AND YOU'RE JUST GOING TO DO WHAT HE SAYS?!
WELL, *I'M* SAYING I'LL TAKE CARE OF YOU.
SO WHO DO YOU LISTEN TO?
GOD? OR ME?!

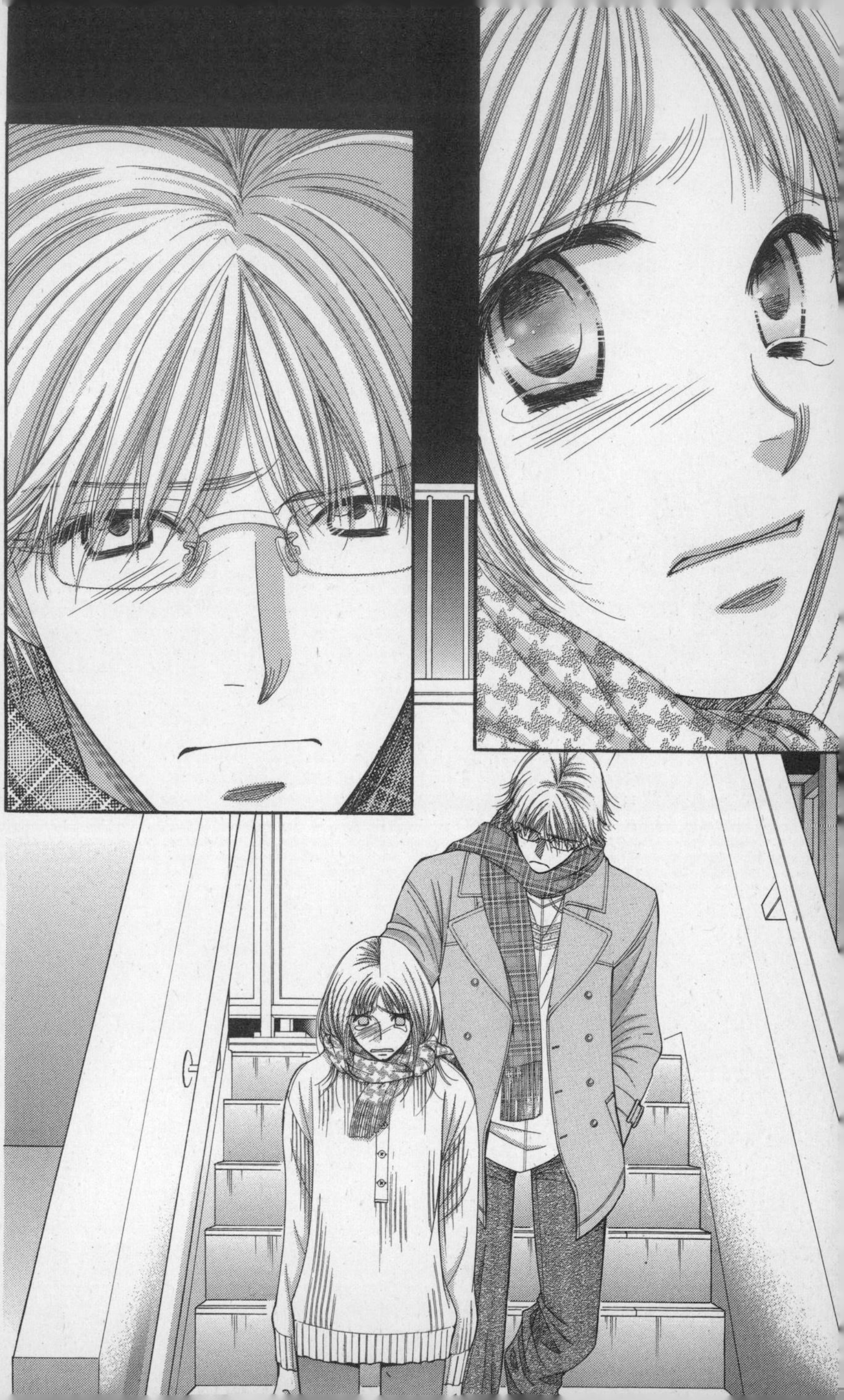

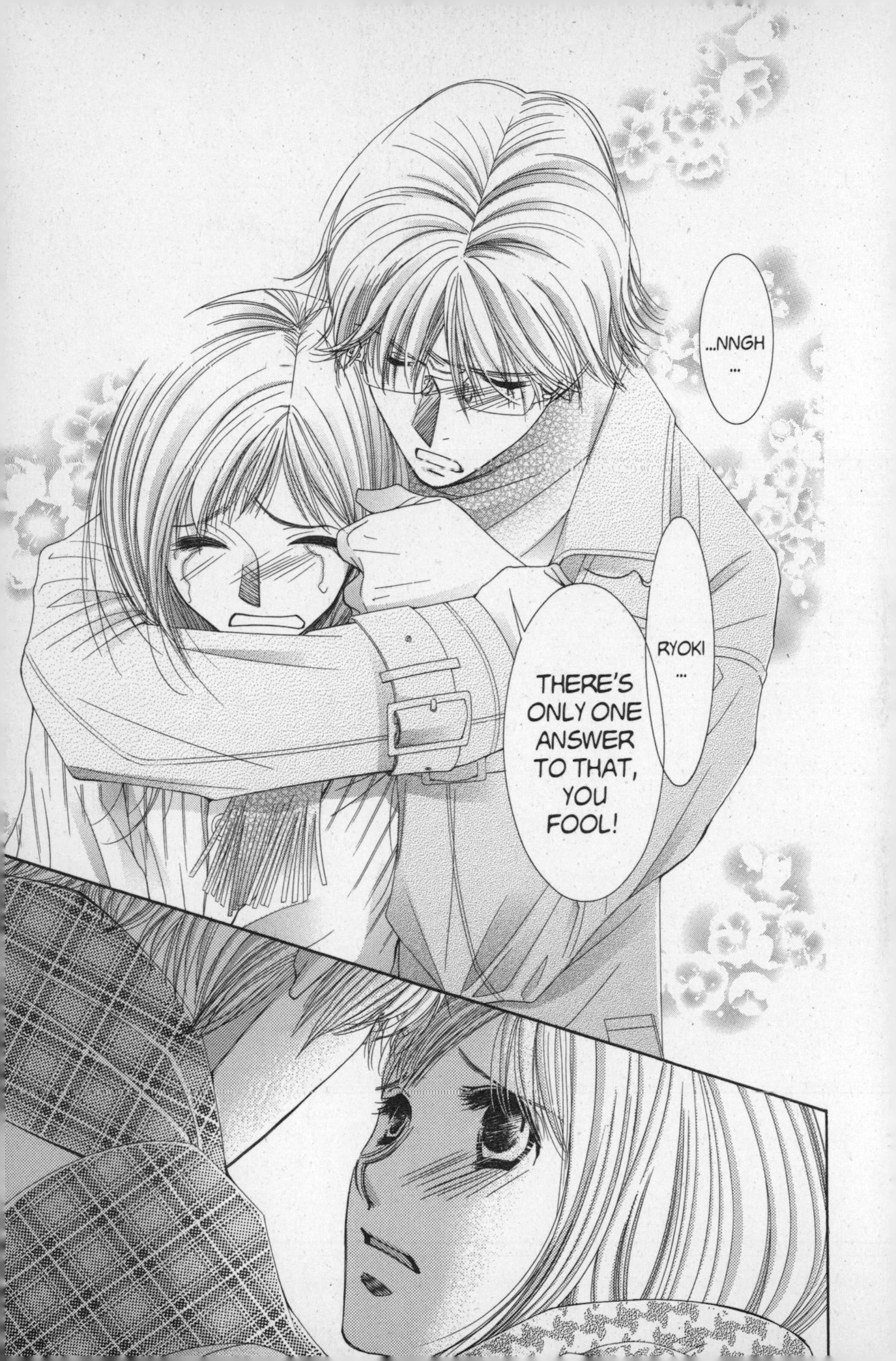
...NNGH
...
RYOKI
...
THERE'S ONLY ONE ANSWER TO THAT, YOU FOOL!

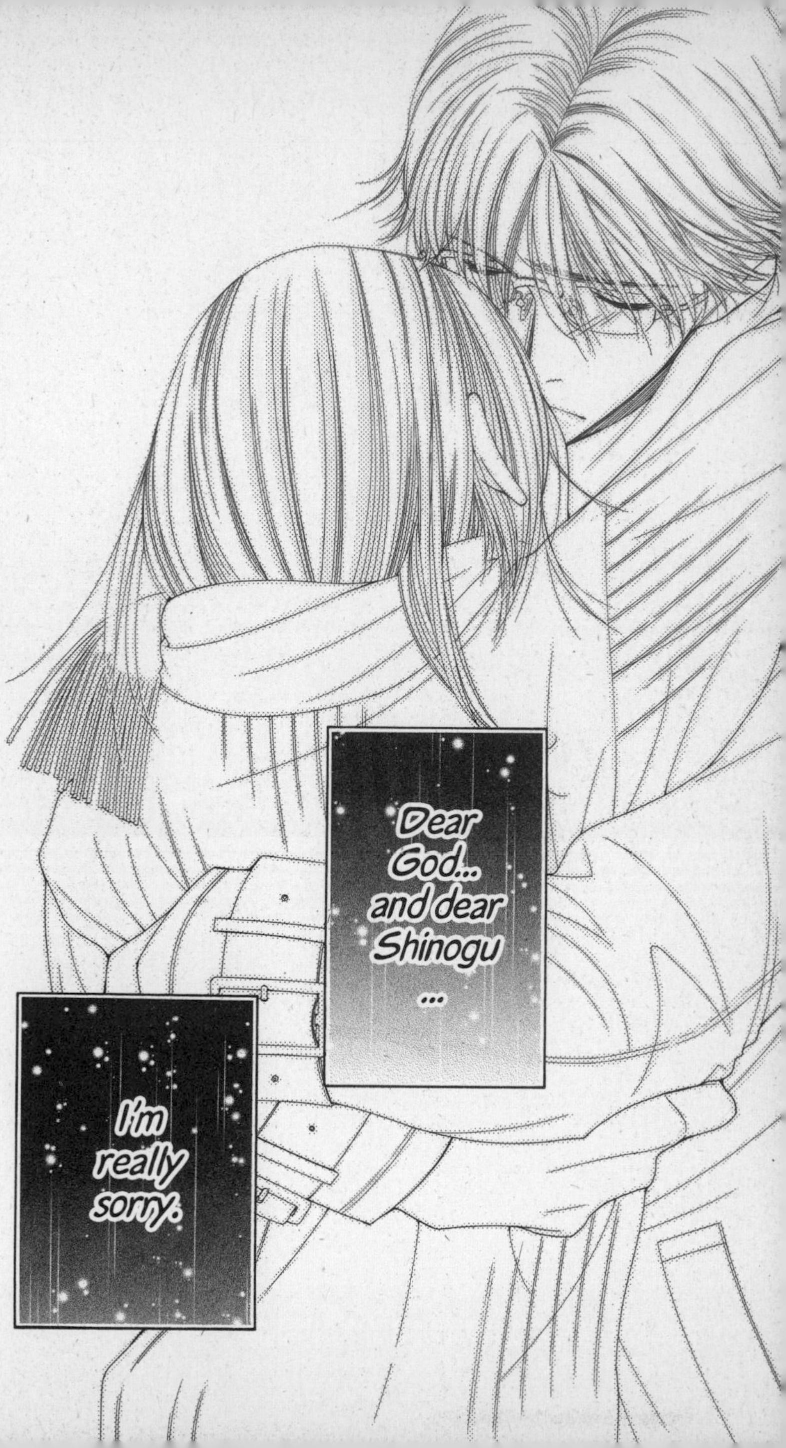
Dear God... and dear Shinogu ...
I'm really sorry.

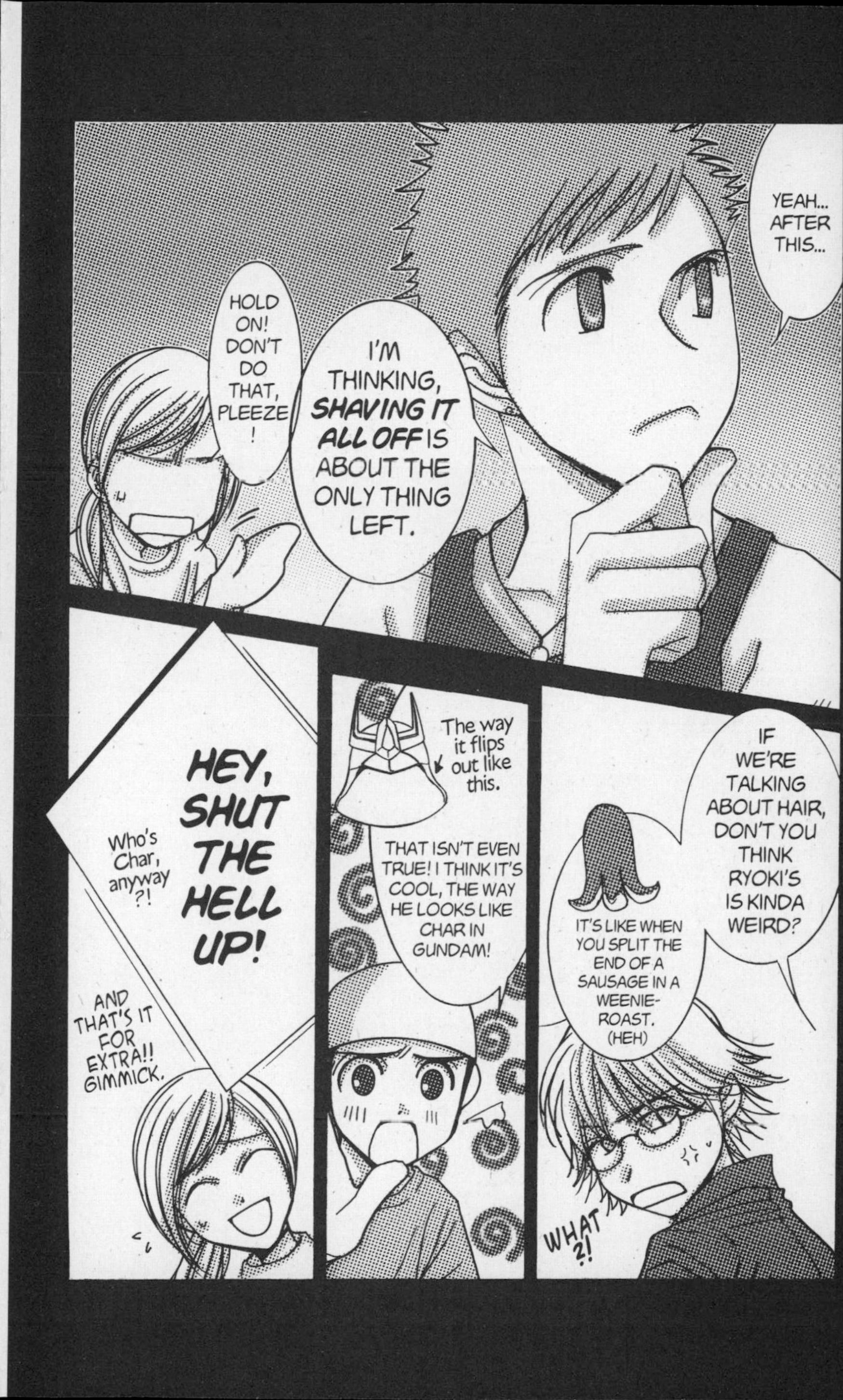
YEAH... AFTER THIS...
I'M THINKING, SHAVING IT ALL OFF IS ABOUT THE ONLY THING LEFT.
HOLD ON! DON'T DO THAT, PLEEZE!
IF WE'RE TALKING ABOUT HAIR, DON'T YOU THINK RYOKI'S IS KINDA WEIRD?
IT'S LIKE WHEN YOU SPLIT THE END OF A SAUSAGE IN A WEENIE-ROAST. (HEH)
WHAT?!
The way it flips out like this.
THAT ISN'T EVEN TRUE! I THINK IT'S COOL, THE WAY HE LOOKS LIKE CHAR IN GUNDAM!
HEY, SHUT THE HELL UP!
Who's Char, anyway?!
AND THAT'S IT FOR EXTRA!! GIMMICK.

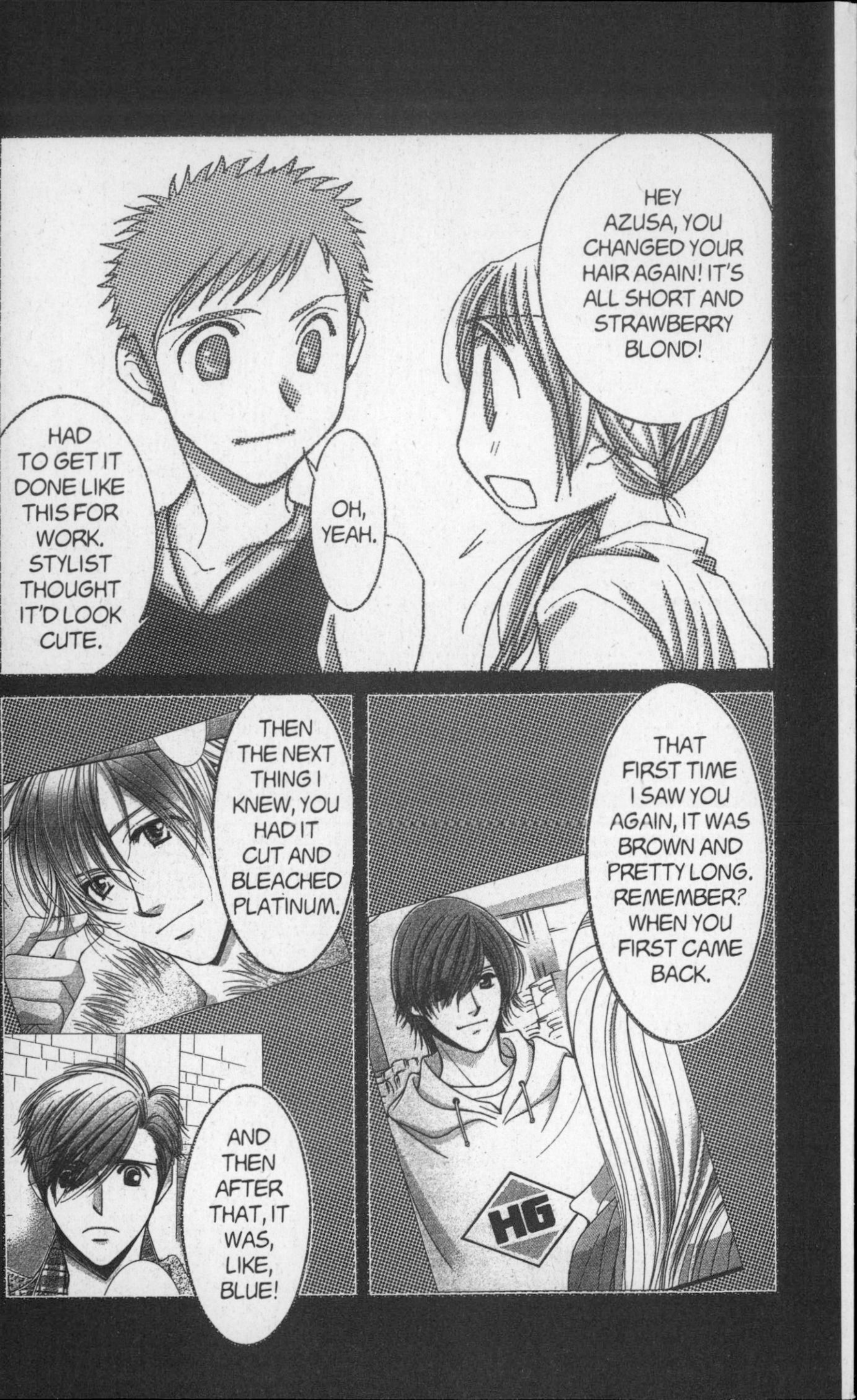
HEY AZUSA, YOU CHANGED YOUR HAIR AGAIN! IT'S ALL SHORT AND STRAWBERRY BLOND!
OH, YEAH.
HAD TO GET IT DONE LIKE THIS FOR WORK. STYLIST THOUGHT IT'D LOOK CUTE.
THAT FIRST TIME I SAW YOU AGAIN, IT WAS BROWN AND PRETTY LONG. REMEMBER? WHEN YOU FIRST CAME BACK.
THEN THE NEXT THING I KNEW, YOU HAD IT CUT AND BLEACHED PLATINUM.
AND THEN AFTER THAT, IT WAS, LIKE, BLUE!
HG

EXTRA!!

GIMMICK

Thank you for buying Hot Gimmick Vol. 11.
My name is Miki Aihara.
Here, just for you manga readers, is
more of that extra information that's so hard
to put into the actual story.
Read on!

To be continued

HOT GIMMICK
Vol. 11

Shôjo Edition

STORY & ART BY MIKI AIHARA

ENGLISH ADAPTATION BY POOKIE ROLF

Touch-up Art & Lettering/Rina Mapa
Cover Design/Izumi Evers
Editor/Kit Fox

Editor in Chief, Books/Alvin Lu
Editor in Chief, Magazines/Marc Weidenbaum
VP of Publishing Licensing/Rika Inouye
VP of Sales/Gonzalo Ferreyra
Sr. VP of Marketing/Liza Coppola
Publisher/Hyoe Narita

Printed in the U.S.A.

Published by VIZ Media, LLC
P.O. Box 77010
San Francisco, CA 94107

10 9 8 7 6 5 4 3 2
First printing, June 2006
Second printing, February 2007

store.viz.com

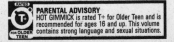

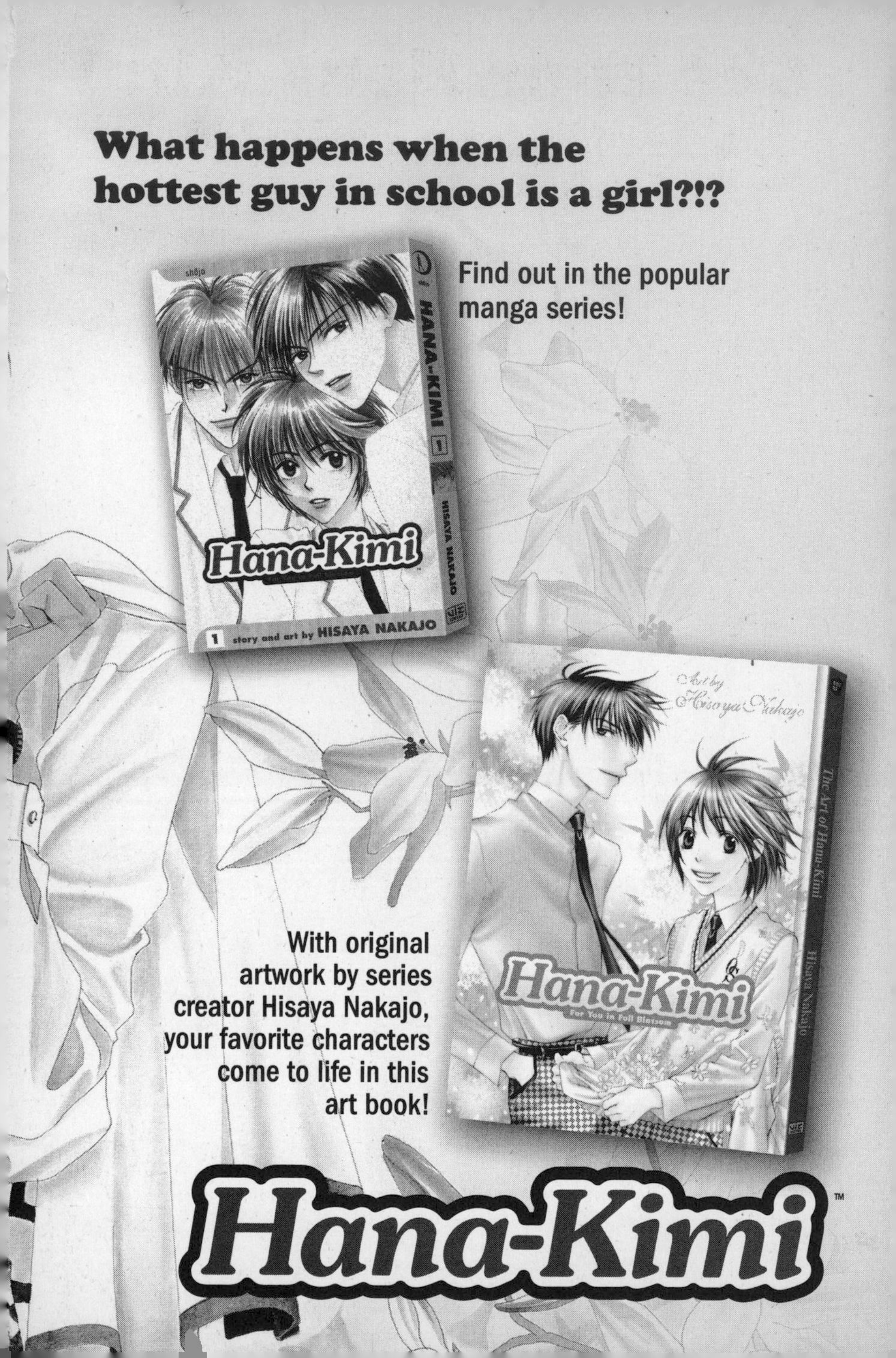
What happens when the hottest guy in school is a girl?!?
Find out in the popular manga series!
shōjo
HANA-KIMI
1
HISAYA NAKAJO
Hana-Kimi
1 story and art by HISAYA NAKAJO
Art by Hisaya Nakajo
The Art of Hana-Kimi
Hisaya Nakajo
Hana-Kimi
With original artwork by series creator Hisaya Nakajo, your favorite characters come to life in this art book!
Hana-Kimi™

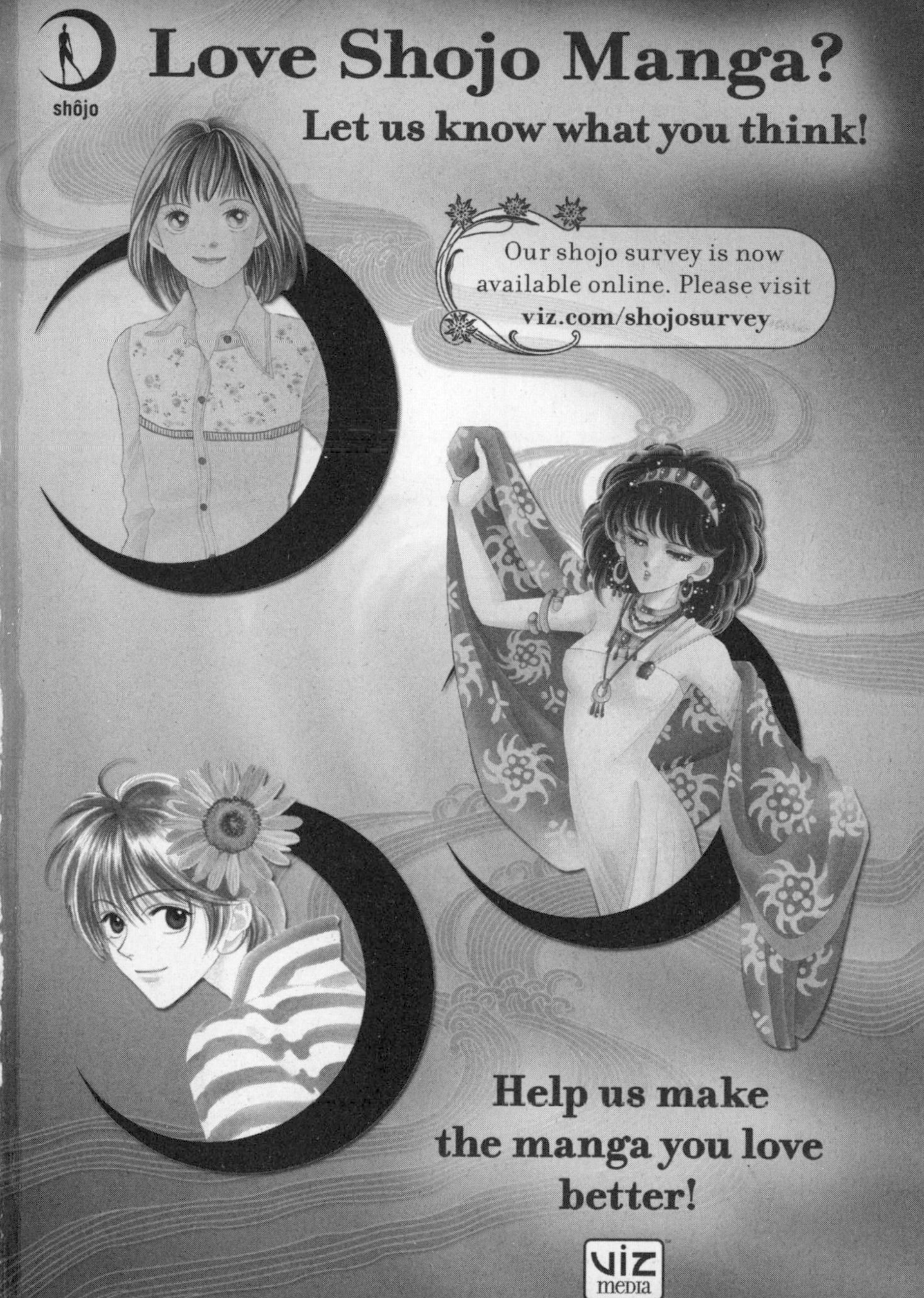
shôjo
Love Shojo Manga?
Let us know what you think!
Our shojo survey is now available online. Please visit viz.com/shojosurvey
Help us make the manga you love better!
viz media